Active Reading

Active Reading

Reading Efficiently in the Arts and Sciences

Shirley Quinn

Wellesley College

Susan Irvings

University of Massachusetts/Boston

HOUGHTON MIFFLIN COMPANY   **Boston**

Dallas   Geneva, Illinois   Lawrenceville, New Jersey   Palo Alto

To Patrick and Mark

Photograph Credits: Elizabeth Crews, pages 60, 146; Susan Lapides, page 14; Ed Hof/The Picture Cube, page 326; Lynne J. Weinstein/Woodfin Camp, page 244; Ulrike Welsch, page 2.

Acknowledgments begin on page 461.

Library of Congress Catalog Card Number: 86-81300

ISBN: 0-395-35783-7

ABCDEFGHIJ-A-89876

Contents

Preface

We wrote *Active Reading* because we discovered a need for a book that would build reading and thinking skills and teach the application of these skills to college texts and related readings. We have successfully taught reading courses based on the methods presented in this text to the wide variety of college students found in both a small liberal arts college and a state university. Although we have written *Active Reading* primarily for first-year college students, students at every level will benefit from its straightforward approach to basic reading skills and the immediate practice it provides in applying this knowledge to college-level reading.

While we were writing this book, we discussed it with our colleagues from different academic disciplines. "My students could use that book—in fact, I could use it too," was a common reaction. Most college students don't realize that it is not too late—in fact, it is never too late—to reacquire basic reading skills and gain control over their reading by learning the importance of reading for ideas; by making associations between what they already know about a topic and the material they are currently reading; by predicting what the author might say about the topic; by making connections and recognizing structure; and by defining purpose and understanding the author's intent.

An active reader, like an active learner, gains knowledge by looking for answers to questions. Questioning leads the reader to an awareness of the author's strategies of exposition and enables the reader to extract the author's essential meanings, whether stated or implied, and to critically evaluate the author's ideas. The art of questioning, with explicit demonstrations of what questions to ask and which answers to look for, is the core of *Active Reading*.

Active Reading has five units. Units I through IV focus on building critical reading skills. Units I and II take a close look at the reading process and stress the foundation skills. Unit III examines the experience of reading from the reader's point of view and teaches strategies for efficient reading that link the activity of reading to the reader's own purpose. Unit IV looks at reading from the author's point of view and teaches the student how to determine the author's purpose, see the organization inherent in the material, and critically examine the author's reasoning. Unit V then demonstrates the application of critical reading skills to academic work in mathematics, the natural sciences, the humanities, history, and the social sciences. These chapters also introduce new material on problem-solving, reading graphics, and using a syllabus.

Just as reading instruction must accompany a writing course, so reading comprehension requires an understanding of writing. We therefore emphasize the student's own writing by including summary- and essay-writing exercises. *Active Reading* further encourages the transfer of reading skills to several important and relevant activities, such as marking up the text, outlining, reviewing, listening, and speaking.

There are seven features that distinguish *Active Reading* as a comprehensive text for college students.

1. Examples and exercises consisting of college-level readings on a wide variety of topics are drawn from textbooks and other academic sources.

2. Many different kinds of individual and group exercises reinforce learning and give students practice in transferring active reading skills to the textbooks they use in other courses.

3. An appendix of seventeen additional readings, accompanied by multiple-choice and essay questions, can be used for extra practice in applying the principles of *Active Reading*, testing reading proficiency, and increasing reading rates. Like the readings in the body of the text, these diverse articles and extracts come mainly from academic texts and journals.

4. The information provided in the rate and comprehension charts provides the opportunity for students to follow their progress in improving their reading rates and comprehension.

5. A glossary defines academic terms used in the college classroom and in *Active Reading*.

6. An Active Reader's Outline on the inside back cover reviews and highlights the fundamental questions an efficient reader asks and the essential information the answers to those questions provide.

7. A comprehensive instructor's resource book, *Active Teaching*, contains commentary, discussion questions, suggested answers to exercises, a three-hour reading workshop for students, notes for a discussion on remembering and forgetting, a workshop for faculty colleagues on the application of reading skills across the curriculum, and a bibliography.

For their help in the preparation of this book we are grateful to the following reviewers for their suggestions about content and organization: Barbara Blaha, Plymouth State College; Suzette Cohen, The Cleveland State University; Valerie Davis, Golden West College; Marilyn G. Eanet, Rhode Island College; Laraine Flemming, University of Pittsburgh; Dennis Gabriel, Cuyahoga Community College; Anne Bradstreet Grinols, Parkland College; Char Hawks, Augustana

College; Mary Leslie, Northeastern University; Sally Lipsky, Indiana University of Pennsylvania; Adrienne Perry, Seminole Community College; and Karen B. Quinn, The University of Illinois.

We would also like to thank the staff of Houghton Mifflin, for their confidence in the project and what they have taught us about the editorial process; our colleagues, for scrutinizing portions of this book and for their useful insights into reading in different academic fields; our students, for their enthusiastic response to our experiments; and particularly our families and friends, for their unwavering encouragement and patience.

Shirley Quinn
Susan Irvings

Active Reading

UNIT

1 *Introduction* to Active Reading

Reading furnishes our minds only with materials of knowledge; it is thinking makes what we read ours.

–John Locke

The introduction to a book tells you about the book: why it might be important to you, how it is put together, what topics it will cover, and what the authors expect you to gain from reading it. The introduction creates a context for your reading by alerting you to what is to come.

The introduction to *Active Reading* consists of two chapters. The first looks at some of your reasons for taking the course, tells you what you can expect to learn from the course, and explains the organization of the text. The second helps you to have a better understanding of what reading is. Together, the chapters prepare you for the task of becoming an active reader.

1 What Is Active Reading?

Each of you has enrolled in this course for a number of special, personal reasons. At the same time, you all have one particular objective: You want to improve your reading. Perhaps you want to understand what you read better, to remember what you read longer, or to read what you read faster. You know that being a good reader will not only help you get the most from your courses now but will continue to benefit you all your life. No matter what your future career, the ability to understand and apply someone else's thoughts through reading will make you a better educated and a more competent person. Although *Active Reading* emphasizes how to improve your reading, we believe that learning to read efficiently will help you to organize, develop, and present your own thoughts more effectively when writing and speaking.

From our experience of teaching this kind of course over the last ten years, we can assure you that you will indeed achieve your goal: You will finish this course a better, more thoughtful, and faster reader than you are now.

A Look at Active Reading

Active Reading teaches you skills that are hard to acquire on your own. The text is based primarily on reading nonfiction, such as textbooks, journal articles, and critical writing—the kind of prose you usually find in your academic work. The only materials you need are this book, paper and pencil, and some of your own textbooks.

This textbook contains a table of contents, which provides an outline of the book and shows how it moves from why and how you read for ideas, to how those ideas are arranged by the authors into recognizable patterns, and finally to how these new strategies can be applied to your academic reading. Each chapter consists of a discussion explaining the concepts that will be covered in the lesson, examples illustrating the concepts, and reading selections to provide practice. The reading selections have been carefully chosen from textbooks, collections of standard readings from different academic disciplines, professional journals, and, occasionally, newspapers and magazines. We have made an effort to include not only entertaining material but also material from which you can learn more about language, reading, and different academic fields.

The Appendix, which starts on p. 326, contains a variety of readings. On occasion you may be assigned one or more of these selections for additional practice or for timed reading. Answering the comprehension questions that follow each reading selection will help you to measure how well you have understood and retained the readings. Although the improvement of reading speed is not the primary objective of this course, active reading inevitably leads to faster reading because it is more efficient than passive reading. We hope you will be excited by your improvement in comprehension and reading rate as you enter them on the progress chart found on pp. 450–451.

Of added benefit is the Active Reader's Glossary of academic terms also found at the back of the book. We think the definition of such academic language as "critical thinking" and "figurative language" and the explanation of the differences between "denotation" and "connotation" will help to clarify academic language for you.

The Aims of Active Reading

Through careful step-by-step instruction you can gain a new understanding of the reading process, particularly as it applies to nonfiction. First, the text encourages you to think carefully about what reading is. You probably have never stopped to consider what is involved when you read. What, for example, is the function of the words? What do authors want to accomplish when they write an article or a book? Do they have a purpose? What do they expect your reaction to be? What are you doing when you read an article or a book? What do you want to get out of it? By questioning your texts, you will discover the author's purpose in writing what you are reading; by questioning yourself, you can understand better why you are reading a particular book, chapter, article, or paragraph.

Next, we shall discuss reading for ideas. You will see how words are arranged to allow you to grasp what you are reading and how ideas are arranged in patterns to guide you from one set of ideas to the next. Posing questions and finding answers in the text will help you to feel as if you were having a conversation with the authors in which you are seeking to understand what they are saying. Understanding and thinking about your reading result in remembering.

Reading Skills

Active Reading also teaches you how to discriminate among your various reading tasks. You can learn what kind of material lends itself to reading quickly and what kind must be read slowly. Breaking down large amounts of information into manageable and connecting units will help you to distinguish the author's key ideas from the subordinate details, to link an author's principal arguments, and to recognize supporting opinions. To comprehension and discrimination you will add flexibility and judgment. Through a variety of exercises, you can apply the principles learned in this course to other areas of your academic and daily work, such as note taking, writing, listening, and speaking.

One particularly valuable exercise is marking up the text. In *Active Reading* you will be asked quite often to show where a new principle applies by marking a passage in an exercise. The direct application of the new principle will increase your understanding of how and why it works. Although it is not always possible to mark up your academic texts, we urge you to do so in this text not only when you are asked to do so in specific exercises, but whenever you feel like it.

An awareness of the reading process and the ability to question what you read result in greater comprehension and retention. Another important benefit is an increase in your reading rate. If you carefully follow the principles of *Active Reading*, you will find that by the end of the course you will probably double your starting reading rate. And this increase in speed will come about not at the expense of comprehension, but because of its improvement.

Questioning Skills

You may have noticed that the table of contents of *Active Reading* emphasizes questions and that we have highlighted preview and reading questions throughout the text. When you ask a question, you are looking for an answer; by looking for an answer, you become actively involved in your reading material—your mind, not just your eyes, is working on it. Looking for answers gives you a purpose in reading that motivates you to continue with an assignment. Maintaining your interest and continuity of effort helps you to concentrate and will ultimately help you to remember. Questioning also leads to improved comprehension through improved analytical and evaluative skills.

Questioning works to establish order in our lives and in our reading. It helps us to see things more clearly and to make decisions based on a rational consideration of a problem. When people act without sufficient questioning, they often feel vague about their purposes. The lack of a well-thought-out objective can influence their motivation for the job at hand. Think for a moment of the big decisions in your own life. Going to college is one. Do you know why you are attending college? Do you know why you chose the college you did? What do you hope to get out of your education? The answers to questions like these may influence how you think about your college experience. If you haven't thought them through, you probably do not have a clear notion of why you are at college or what you hope to get out of it. The resulting feelings of purposelessness will not produce your best performance. On the other hand, a clear notion of why you chose the college you did and what you want to get from your education will help you to set your purpose and to establish priorities.

Asking questions helps you to sort out information, to be precise about what you need to know, to make decisions about where to find additional information, and to discriminate what is important to you from what is not. Asking questions sets your mind to looking actively for answers and prevents you from adopting a passive approach to your reading and learning. Just as you can't learn how to ride a bicycle by sitting by the side of the road and watching someone else struggle, you can't learn how to read efficiently without the active participation of your mind, which is required when you ask and answer questions.

Basic Reading and Preview Questions

At the end of several chapters in *Active Reading* some questions have been highlighted. These are the basic reading and preview questions that we consider central to the reading task. Previewing and questioning are important reading techniques.

The **basic reading questions** are those questions that you can apply to any nonfiction reading you have to do. They are the questions you ask to help you find the author's ideas and then to see how those ideas are organized. The basic reading questions are equally useful whether you ask them of an article or a book, of a part of a book—such as a chapter, a section, or a paragraph—or of a sentence.

You ask **preview questions** before you start reading to orient yourself to the text and get an idea of what it contains, why it was written, and how it is presented. Good previewing sets the stage for learning by helping you to relate what you are about to read with what you already know; to establish a connection with the author and to have a sense of the author's point of view; to define precisely what you want to get out of your reading; and to recognize the ways that authors organize their thoughts so that you will have an idea of what is coming and how it will be presented.

Asking preview questions before you begin to read helps you to start thinking about your reading; asking reading questions as you read helps you to maintain your concentration and to understand better what the author is saying.

2 *Thinking About Reading*

The purpose of this chapter is to help you to define why you are taking this course and to examine the art of reading. What has prompted you at this moment to become an active reader? Why do you read? What do you read? How do you read?

We hope that the motivation and positive attitude that result from clarifying your purpose in improving your reading will lead you to the success you seek. The questions in this chapter will help you

- to establish your purpose for improving your reading.
- to learn about the reading process.
- to analyze your reading habits.

What Is Reading?

Too often people make certain assumptions about the process of reading. Probably you were taught to read in grammar school and have heard little since then about the process or skill of reading. You may feel that some people possess secrets you don't have or that there is a mysterious knack that makes some people good readers though others have to struggle. In the past you may have been told to read carefully, to ask questions of the material, or to look up words you don't know without any reference to the larger and more basic questions associated with the reading process. What kind of interaction should there be between writer and reader? What is careful reading? What is efficient reading?

By analyzing your own reading habits—such as where, when, and how you read—you will see how you can read better, more attentively, and with greater comprehension, over longer periods of time.

Reading and You

The following questions will help you to start thinking about the reading process. Although the answers to some of them may seem obvious, the discussion they provoke may encourage you to think more about reading and your role as a reader.

Because there is more than one right answer to most of these questions, circle the answer or answers that seem closest to what you think or feel.

1. Why am I taking this course?
   a. I want to read faster.
   b. I don't seem to be able to concentrate on my reading.
   c. I want to read with greater understanding.
   d. I wish I could remember better what I read.
   e. I want to find out how to get through all the reading I have to do.

2. What is reading?
   a. looking at words
   b. sounding out letters
   c. translating written words into thoughts or ideas
   d. the opposite of writing

3. What do authors want to communicate?
   a. messages

     b. ideas
     c. words
     d. descriptions
     e. information
     f. thoughts

4. What are words?
     a. a means of transmitting ideas
     b. symbols
     c. ideas

5. Why do I read?
     a. for enjoyment
     b. to complete a reading assignment
     c. to be informed by the author
     d. to be persuaded by the author's ideas
     e. to stimulate my own thinking

6. What do I read mostly?
     a. textbooks
     b. novels
     c. academic journals
     d. newspapers and magazines
     e. readings assigned for courses

7. How do I read?
     a. I read word by word.
     b. I start at the beginning and read right through to the end.
     c. I read everything the same way and at the same speed.
     d. I look for the author's ideas.
     e. I lose my concentration and have to reread.

8. Where do I read?
     a. in a comfortable chair
     b. at my desk
     c. in the library
     d. always in the same place
     e. in a noisy room

9. When do I read?
     a. in the morning when I'm most alert
     b. in the afternoon when I'm most alert
     c. late at night
     d. when I can't think of anything else to do

10. How long should I read at a time?
    a. fifteen minutes
    b. two hours
    c. four hours
    d. It depends on the material.

In responding to these questions, you have been thinking about the kind of reading you do and why you do it. You probably found that you checked almost all the answers to question 1. Concentration is linked to greater understanding, which in turn leads to better retention of the material. In the same way, reading faster and getting through all the reading you have to do in college are connected to how well you understand and retain your reading. Through your answers you may have concluded that the prose on a printed page is a means of communicating ideas from the author to the reader and that these ideas are conveyed in words. These important concepts will be taken up in later chapters of *Active Reading*.

You probably also discovered that how and what you read are determined by why you read. You can relax in an easy chair and read a novel for enjoyment, but you need to study attentively the information found in your physics assignment. When and where do you concentrate best and learn most? The evidence and your own experience suggest that there is a "better" time and a "better" place to read when concentration is your goal. Humans are diurnal animals; that is, we operate best in the daylight hours. The mind, like the rest of our bodies, works best when it is fresh. Therefore, the best time for most people to take in and understand new ideas is in the morning, when the mind is ready for exercise. You can help your concentration by finding a quiet place, like a particular spot in the library, to which you can go to read and study. Soon you will start associating that place with thinking, and you will find your concentration increases as distractions and interruptions decrease.

How long you read at a time depends again on what and when you read. However, we suggest you start by reading in fifteen-minute blocks or for as long as you can concentrate. If you start losing your concentration, move to another task or assignment. Most people cannot really concentrate on academic reading for much longer than an hour at a time without a brief break. After several hours, you can take a longer break to relax a bit before resuming your studying.

This is the beginning of your new reading life. Now is the time to take on new, good habits, like finding a reading place where there is no distraction and resolving to do more of your reading at the time of day when you are most alert. These are first steps in gaining control over your reading.

As you proceed in this course, we shall ask you to experiment with different approaches to reading, thinking, and learning. We are confident that you will be excited by the progress you make as you take charge of your own learning and commit yourself to becoming an efficient and active reader.

II Reading for Ideas

[Language is] a system of arbitrary vocal symbols
by which thought is conveyed from one human
being to another.

      –John P. Hughes, *The Science of Language*

Unit I introduced you to the notion that in most non-fiction reading in college the importance of words rests in their capacity to communicate the author's ideas. You may now be asking an obvious question: How do you read for ideas? How can you extract ideas from a sentence, a paragraph, a chapter, or a book?

Unit II is the core of *Active Reading*. It examines the relationship of words and ideas, discusses vocabulary building, and then provides questions that will help you to find the topic, the key idea, the supporting ideas, and supporting details of readings. These questions are the basic tools for becoming an efficient reader; they lead you to an author's ideas and help you to discriminate among more and less important thoughts and information.

The questions you will learn in this unit can be applied to your writing, listening, speaking, and note taking. Every aspect of your academic life involves finding the ideas contained in someone else's words.

3 How Do Words and Ideas Relate to Each Other?

What is a word? What is an idea? To grasp the relationship of words to ideas, you need to have some understanding of both concepts. Mixing up the two can produce some confusing results. Consider the boy who was asked why pigs were called pigs. He answered, "I call 'em pigs because they're dirty and they smell bad." This statement is amusing to us because the relationship of words to ideas is topsy-turvy.

Words and Ideas

A word is a mere sound or a few black marks. Taken by itself, it has no meaning at all. A word derives its meaning from the reader's previous experience with it. When you first learned the word *pig*, for example, you saw or someone described for you a four-legged, pink animal with a broad snout, a curly tail, and a reputation for making its living quarters muddy and smelly. Later, all these details automatically flashed through your mind whenever you saw the word *pig*, and from them you knew what the word *pig* meant. You could even go on and use the word to illustrate how some other animal is like a pig, even though it is not a pig.

Words are used to express meanings of all kinds. There are words that name things or ideas (nouns), words of being and action (verbs), words of place and words of time (adverbs and prepositions), words that connect (conjunctions), and words that describe or modify (adjectives and adverbs). An author uses a word, such as *slow*, to convey a meaning he or she has in mind. The author can then add other words to convey more complicated and more detailed thoughts: for instance, *very slow, too slow, slow as molasses*, or *not so slow*.

Key Words

Words have meaning only if everyone agrees on what they stand for or say. Readers must have a sense of the part that words play in order to be able to distinguish the important words, or **key words,** which convey most of the author's meaning, from the words that connect thoughts or modify, explain, and develop them. The key words are the strong words in the sentence, usually the nouns and the verbs. Recognizing the words that carry most of the meaning will help you to grasp more quickly what the author is saying, and the first step in identifying the key words is to break down, or analyze, a sentence. Then you can see how the words in the sentence are arranged into phrases that support one or more of the key words by connecting thoughts or by modifying, explaining, or developing the author's ideas.

Example

If you were to time yourself as you read the following selections, how much faster could you read the second one?

pot stove copper black honor place old in the the the mysteriously newly glowing wood polished appeared and of on

The old copper pot mysteriously appeared, newly polished and glowing, in the place of honor on the black wood stove.

The first selection is a list of separate words. It takes a long time to read because each word prompts a disconnected thought. In the second selection the words are reorganized; instead of conveying twenty different thoughts, they work together to elaborate one thought—essentially, "the pot appeared on the stove." When you analyze the second group of words, you can see how they work together to provide information about the main thought. Asking questions helps you to find that information.

What kind of pot? The old copper pot. *Old* and *copper* modify the noun *pot.*

Appeared how? It appeared mysteriously, newly polished and glowing. *Mysteriously* is an adverb modifying the verb *appeared,* and *newly polished* and *glowing* modify the noun *pot.*

Appeared where? In the place of honor on the stove. These are prepositional phrases that have to do with place.

What kind of stove? The, *black,* and *wood* further describe the noun *stove.*

You could even think about what the author has not said but is implying by using the word *mysteriously.* From this you might assume that the pot had not been on the stove for some time and so it comes as a surprise that it is there and has been polished.

Key Ideas

When you read a sentence, you look for key words to understand the author's thought. Similarly, when you read a paragraph, you try to put together the ideas you have found in the sentences in order to find the author's **key idea.** Ideas in paragraphs, like words in sentences, work together to convey the author's key idea. Each paragraph usually has one central thought that is supported by the other ideas in the paragraph. The **supporting ideas** connect, modify, explain, or develop the author's key idea. Chapter 5 provides a detailed treatment of how to find the key idea and Chapter 6 deals with supporting ideas. We mention them here to illustrate the relationship of words and ideas in sentences and paragraphs.

Example

You can start reading for the author's thought by answering some questions about the following paragraph.

Polar bears in the zoo are sad. Subject to the taunts of little girls and boys, these magnificent, large animals are reduced to lumbering around a small enclosure. In the summer the bears have only a small pool of dirty water to keep them cool. They pant in whatever shade they can find, too hot even to be embarrassed by the yellowing grayness of their white fur.

What is the key idea of this paragraph? Polar bears in the zoo are sad.

What is the function of the other sixty-three words? They elaborate on the statement that polar bears are sad by telling the reader why they are sad. They give some of the details of the polar bears' lives by telling you what is happening, where the bears are, how they feel and why. Thus, the words fit together to communicate the author's thought or idea to you, the reader.

Vocabulary

It is generally true that in the academic world ideas, rather than words, are valued. But this does not mean that words are not important, for in order to understand ideas, it is necessary to understand the words that convey them. Sometimes words are used in specialized ways in different academic disciplines, and one must be aware of this. The word *cell*, for instance, has a different meaning in biology, physics, and criminology. One should also be aware of words used not to inform and explain, but to persuade by arousing feeling, such as *mean, outstanding, legendary.* This emotive use of vocabulary does not often occur in writing about the sciences and social sciences. Such use is more frequent in, and indeed characteristic of, specifically literary writing—poetry, drama, fiction—in which the purpose is to bring about an emotional rather than an intellectual response. Remembering that words communicate both thoughts and feelings helps you to read from idea to idea instead of from word to word.

A good reader needs to have a good vocabulary. If you believe you need to develop your vocabulary, and most of us do, we urge you to take a vocabulary course or work on your own with one of the many books on vocabulary building that are available at your local bookstore.

There are steps you can take now to improve your vocabulary. An active reader can often figure out the meaning of an unfamiliar word by noticing the context in which that word is used. That is, you can look at the other words in the sentence or paragraph to try to find clues to the meaning of the unknown word. This is an immediate and practical approach that will often serve you well.

The following illustrate different ways in which contextual clues can be used to clarify the meaning of the italicized words.

Definition   Sometimes a direct definition of the unknown words or a synonym, a word with a similar meaning, is provided in the sentence.

Justice Holmes was known as a man of great *erudition,* or knowledge. (Here, *erudition* means knowledge.)

Explanation   Sometimes the other words in the sentence or paragraph provide an explanation of the unknown word.

An active reader can often figure out the meaning of an unfamiliar word by noticing the *context* in which that word is used. That is, you can look at the other words in the sentence or paragraph to try to find clues to the meaning of the unknown word. (Here, it is explained that *context* means the other words in the sentence or paragraph.)

Contrast   There are times when a word is defined by a statement in the text that gives an opposite meaning to the one you are looking for.

Henry X was a *benign* king, very unlike Edward IX, who terrorized the peasants with his merciless behavior. (You can gather that *benign* must mean the opposite of merciless from the clue that Henry was unlike Edward.)

Inference   A sentence sometimes provides examples that enable you to infer, or guess from the evidence, the meaning of the unknown word.

She decided to give up the luxuries of this world and to live as a *penurious* student with not enough money to pay for her rent, meals, and books. (You can infer that *penurious* means poor: Giving up luxuries and not having enough money are both indications of poverty.)

Association   You can sometimes guess the meaning of the unknown word by associating it with a word you already know. If you've studied Latin or know a foreign language related to English, association may be easier for you.

The article was nothing more than an *enumeration* of the steps needed to perform the new laboratory procedures. (*Enumeration* is similar to the word *number*; an enumeration is a numbered list.)

Because the precise meaning of words is particularly important in academic work, you should always make sure your guess is correct by listing or circling the words you were unsure of and later looking them up in your dictionary. (It is important that your dictionary be a college edition.) In this way you can start your own "vocabulary course" by listing the words you did not recognize, with their definitions, and quoting them in sample sentences. Then, remember to put them to actual use in your own writing and conversation.

Exercises

1. Underline the key words in the following sentences.
   a. The hungry boy dashed wildly past the town hall, through the churchyard, and up the front steps, arriving just in time for dinner.
   b. Joad's lips stretched tight over his long teeth for a moment, and he licked his lips, like a dog, two licks, one in each direction from the middle.

   –John Steinbeck

   c. Calico-coated, small-bodied, with delicate legs and pink faces in which their mismatched eyes rolled wild and subdued, they huddled, gaudy, motionless and alert, wild as deer, deadly as rattlesnakes, quiet as doves.

   –William Faulkner

   d. Whatever the assigned function of social institutions, their psychological function is to protect the citizen against the irrational, incalculable forces that hover about the edges of human life like cosmic destruction lurking within an atomic stockpile.

   –Ralph Ellison

2. Underline the words or phrases that make up the key idea in each of the following paragraphs.
   a. When seen from the tower, the city took on a whole new look. Vanished were the individuals madly rushing somewhere by foot or by car; still were the winds tearing around the edges of the buildings; evaporated were the *raucous* noises of screaming brakes and howling sirens. Instead the eye saw only the designs made by the blue rivers, the gray streets, the red rows of brick houses, and the green parks. The city was a work of art, caught in a moment of time.
   b. Uninhabited since old Tom Coffin died in 1960, the house on Fuller Street grew more and more *dilapidated*. Shutters hung at angles, bushes overran the walks, and the stones in the patio

wall fell out one by one. Birds took to nesting in the attic, and rats were probably living in the cellar. With its loose curtains taking on a ghostly aspect, the house soon became a source of fear for neighborhood children.

c. Reading is both a pleasure and a necessity. By enabling us to know and master *relevant* information, information pertinent to us, reading can lead to success in our jobs. At the same time, reading can provide relief from the stresses of daily life by taking us into a variety of worlds and situations.

3. What do you think the italicized words in the passages above mean? On which clue (definition, explanation, contrast, inference, or association) did you base your guess?

With a better idea of the relationship of words to ideas, you are now ready to learn more about both how to read for ideas and how ideas are connected.

4 Finding the Topic

The previous chapter demonstrated our basic proposition that words are a means of communicating ideas from one person to another. To be an active and efficient reader, you need to identify the ideas behind the words and then to recognize which ideas are the most important to the reading. This chapter will help you take the first step in reading for ideas: finding the topic.

What Is This About?

We shall begin with the first question that naturally comes to mind when you start to read something, sometimes before you have even started: What is this about? Have you ever stopped to think why you ask that question? Usually you ask it to help you decide whether or not you want or need to read the article or book you are considering. Also, asking this question and attempting to answer it set your mind to work and begin the process of thinking about the author's ideas.

Think about this book. What is it about? Active reading. How about Unit II? What is it about? Reading for ideas. How about this chapter, Chapter 4? Finding the topic. These questions and answers both seem easy, so easy that most of the time they don't get asked, much less answered. You will see in later readings that answering this question isn't always so easy, but it remains a very necessary first step in reading for ideas.

The answer to *What is this about?* provides the topic, sometimes called the subject, of whatever it is you are reading—a book, unit, chapter, section, or lesson. In each case the *topic* is the person, place, thing, or idea most often mentioned or referred to. The topic may also be the person, place, thing, or idea that starts or is the basis for the action. We use the word *topic* to refer to the subject of the entire reading. However, each part of a reading also has a topic. Therefore, we use the word *subtopic* to refer to the subjects of the various parts that make up the entire reading, including sentences, paragraphs, sections, and chapters. The topic can usually be stated with a word or a short phrase. Thus, the topic of this book is active reading; a subtopic, reading for ideas, is the topic of Unit II; and a subtopic, reading efficiently, is the topic of Unit III.

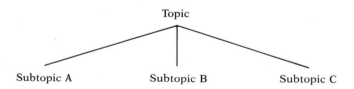

What is this book about? The topic is active reading.

What is this unit about? The topic is a subtopic of active reading, reading for ideas.

What is this chapter about? The topic is a subtopic of reading for ideas, finding the topic.

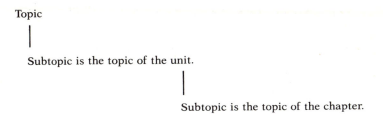

Topic

Subtopic is the topic of the unit.

Subtopic is the topic of the chapter.

Examples

Find the topics of the following examples, some of which we used in Chapter 3. It may help to ask yourself *What is this sentence or paragraph about?* or to refer to the definition of topic found on p. 24.

The old copper pot mysteriously appeared, newly polished and glowing, in the place of honor on the black wood stove.

This sentence is about the pot. It is the pot that is being referred to. The pot *appeared.* The pot was *polished and glowing.* The pot was *in the place of honor.*

The old woman drew the boy to one side and whispered, "You must stop them before they do us all great harm."

This sentence is about the old woman, who is the initiator of the action.

When an American paratrooper first learns to jump, he does more than step out of an airplane. He steps into a new way of life. Furthermore, his training even takes note of this major transition in his life in a formal ceremonial manner. This training period—marked by pomp and circumstance, superstition and ritual—is what anthropologists refer to as a *rite of passage.*

–Melford S. Weiss

It is a little more difficult to find the topic of this passage. Is it about the paratrooper, his training, or a rite of passage? If we look carefully at the paragraph, we can find that the ideas in it support the naming of "his training" as the topic. The training is a "new way of life"; "his training . . . takes note"; and the training period is "a rite of passage." Not only is "training" referred to most often, but it is the basis for the action.

Polar bears in the zoo are sad. Subject to the taunts of little girls and boys, these magnificent, large animals are reduced to lumbering around a small enclosure. In the summer the bears have only a small pool of dirty water to keep them cool. They pant in whatever shade they can find, too hot even to be embarrassed by the yellowing grayness of their white fur.

This example introduces a new thought. Is it talking about all polar bears or just those found in the zoo? The paragraph very definitely is not discussing the plight of all polar bears. Therefore, to be accurate and concise in stating the topic, you would have to specify polar bears in the zoo.

Exercises

1. Circle the topic wherever it appears in the sentences and paragraphs below.
   a. The Fourth of July is our national holiday.
   b. Although the ships sailed out of sight, they did not fall off the edge of the world.
   c. Columbus's theory that the world was round was believed by no one.
   d. Everywhere Joan looked she saw trees—tall trees, short trees, thin trees, thick trees. Although everyone told her how lucky she was to be surrounded by such beauty, she hated the trees because they hid the sky.
   e. In typical hurricane fashion, Agnes began its short but active life in a playful rather than vindictive mood. Then while growing and absorbing moisture from the saturated eastern section of the country, it turned vicious and struck southwest Virginia. In 4 days it loosed on Maryland, the District of Columbia, Pennsylvania, and New York 28.1 trillion gallons of water—enough to fill a lake 2,000' deep by 27 mi. square. Agnes was the most costly disaster in history.

   –David Wallechinsky and Irving Wallace

   f. When a dog bites a man, that's not news. When man bites dog, that is news. This old cliché has been told and retold to every aspiring journalist. What it says is that to be news a story has to be something out of the ordinary.
   g. The still camera, modernized by inventor George Eastman, enabled ordinary people to make their own photographic images; and the phonograph, another of Edison's inventions, made possible musical performances at home. The spread of movies, photography, and phonograph records meant that access to live

performances no longer limited people's exposure to art and entertainment.

—Mary Beth Norton et al.

h. Newspaper reporters and technical writers are trained to reveal almost nothing about themselves in their writings. This makes them freaks in the world of writers, since almost all of the other ink-stained wretches in that world reveal a lot about themselves to readers. We call these revelations, accidental and intentional, elements of style.

   These revelations tell us as readers what sort of person it is with whom we are spending time. Does the writer sound ignorant or informed, stupid or bright, crooked or honest, humorless or playful—? And on and on.

—Kurt Vonnegut

2. State briefly the topic and the subtopics of the following selection. Remember to ask the question *What is this about?* Occasionally you may need to identify the subtopics before you can be sure of the topic.

1   It has finally been established without a doubt that airplanes are not only the fastest, but also the most efficient, the cheapest, and probably the safest way to travel. All of this means that they provide the best way of getting from here to there.

2   Who can deny the hours that are saved by flying across the country or from country to country. In one month alone a person can make numerous trips to Asia; one's stamina is the only limiting factor. And how easy it is to leave Chicago at 8:00 A.M., arrive at your Detroit meeting by 9:30 A.M., and be back in your own office in Chicago for a 3:00 P.M. report to the boss.

3   By now everyone is familiar with the statistics on safety. Air safety comes from years of work devoted to improving the production and maintenance of aircraft and from the scrupulous training and retraining of flight crew with each advance in flight technology. Everything possible is done to ensure that standards are met. In spite of alarming headlines, the result is a form of transportation probably far safer than any other.

4   The cost of air travel is also a good reason to fly. There are many plans that allow substantial savings depending on how early you book your seat, when you fly, and how often. Sometimes flying is even cheaper than any other mode of travel, particularly when you add the cost of time saved or the additional time you can have on your vacation. It is no wonder that airports are busier now than ever before, as more and more people enjoy traveling by air.

3. State briefly the topic and the subtopics of the following selection.

1   Proteins perform a great variety of functions in our bodies. They protect us against disease, help our blood clot, and form the membranes, muscles, and connective tissues that build our bodies.

2   Proteins are very large molecules made up of carbon, oxygen, hydrogen, nitrogen, and sometimes sulfur, iodine, iron, or phosphorus. They are formed when molecules called amino acids link together in special arrangements (peptide linkages). . . .

3   Foods with all the essential amino acids are said to contain complete proteins: these include eggs, meat, milk, and fish. Foods that do not contain all the essential amino acids are said to be incomplete; such foods include nuts and cereals. . . .

4   Proteins are the main constituents of all the cells in the body. Protein molecules are needed to build new cells, to maintain existing cells, and to replace old, worn-out cells. The chemicals that take part in body reactions and those that help control the rates at which body reactions occur (such as enzymes and hormones) are made of protein molecules. In addition, the all-important molecules that carry our genetic information are made of proteins.

–Alan Sherman, Sharon Sherman, and Leonard Russikoff

Using Clues to Find the Topic

The answer to the question *What is this about?* can often be found with very little reading. Usually it is very apparent. However, when it is not obvious, an efficient reader looks for aids provided by the author—a title, a subtitle, a headline, or a picture. Proper attention to these aids can quickly suggest to you the topic of what you are about to read. You may not have thought of looking first for these clues or you may think that there is something dishonest about allowing yourself to do things easily, but it makes sense to use help when it is provided.

When you see an article entitled "Airplanes: Safer Now Than Ever Before," a good prediction is that the article is about airplane safety and that the author takes a positive position. What if the article had the title "Airplanes: Safer Now Than Ever Before?" Again, you would know it was about airplane safety. But because of the question mark, you would probably guess that the author had doubts about airplane safety. How about a book entitled *The Personnel Management Process: Cases in Human Resources Administration*? You can easily decide that this book is about how managers or administrators can most effectively use the people (or human resources) available to them and that much of the book will deal with actual personnel problems in various businesses or industries. A picture of two men playing basketball would certainly tell you that what you were about to read had something to do with sports—more specifically, basketball. All of this may sound too simple to you, but readers often do not take advantage of the clues provided by an author.

You can also use clues to find the subtopics of chapters. For instance, an economics textbook contains a chapter entitled "The Private Sector: Households and Business Firms." The chapter title itself gives us the major topic of the chapter. A quick look at the headings and subheadings within the chapter tells us a good deal more. Under the major heading "Households" we find several subheadings: "Population and Age Groups," "Changes in the Family," "Sources of Income," "Distribution of Income," and "Household Expenditures." Under "Business Firms," the other major heading, are listed "Forms of Business Organization," "Corporations in the United States," "Multinational Corporations," and "Business Accounting." These headings and subheadings have clearly and concisely answered the question *What is this about?* You are well oriented to the content before starting to read a word of text.

If the title of a book or article does not provide you with a clear idea of the topic, then you may have to go further in your search. The topic is normally stated near the beginning of a book or article. If you had to guess at the topic from clues, the first few paragraphs of an article and the introduction or the first chapter of a book will either confirm your guess or give you the correct answer. Your answer will

- tell you, what person, thing, or idea is the subject of the reading,
- help you to decide whether you have an interest in or need to read this material, and
- start you thinking about the topic and your reading task. You will probably start making predictions about what the author will say.

Just as you should first ask *What is this about?* when reading, you can ask the same question when listening. When you go to class, keep these questions in mind: What is this class about? What is the instructor talking about now? At the end of the class, take a few minutes to think about your answers and to underline the topics and subtopics in your class notes. Asking and answering these questions ensure that active listening is part of your active reading and active learning.

Examples

Here are the beginnings of two articles. As you try to establish their topics, note the clues that the authors have provided.

Beer Ads and Gutter Talk

The primary function of language is to communicate ideas. Although proper grammar, spelling, and punctuation do not guarantee accurate communication, they increase the likelihood that the message intended by the sender is the one that will be understood by the receiver.

—Lawrence Casler, President of the Society for the Advancement of Good English

There is not much to go on in this example, but there are some valuable clues. You can guess from the title that the article has something to do with beer ads, and you can infer from the author's position and the first paragraph that it also has something to do with language. Given the term "gutter talk," you might also think that the author doesn't like the language contained in beer ads. Because of your prediction, you will not be surprised to find that the article ends with the following sentences: "We (not us) who value language want to reward companies that share our concern. When the people responsible for the presentation of Miller's corporate image start making fewer (not less) mistakes, we will start taking them seriously."

1   Economic boycotts occupy an important and honored place in the long history of protest movements. They have an advantage over other forms of protest in that they can be conducted in a legal and nonviolent fashion, a fact which no doubt explains their continued popularity in the face of a high rate of failure. Seeking their objectives primarily through a disruption of certain vital services, economic boycotts are usually not allowed to proceed to a point where they can wreak devastation on an economy. At the same time, the inconvenience and hardship that they cause provide strong financial incentives for evasion, among both supporters and opponents. Once substantial evasion occurs, the collapse of the boycott becomes a matter of time. Another reason for the failure of boycotts is that their success can only be guaranteed by a sustained stand by the masses, and this is exceedingly difficult to achieve.

2   The Bugandan trade boycott of 1959 was an attempt to achieve certain political and economic goals through a boycott of alien traders. Its study provides an illuminating lesson on the strength and limitations of the boycott as a medium of protest.

—Dharam P. Ghai

If you consider only the first paragraph, the answer to the question *What is this about?* would seem to be "economic boycotts." That answer easily fits the definition of topic. But is the author discussing *all* economic boycotts? No, he seems to relate the boycott to protest movements. A look at the second paragraph indicates that the first paragraph is an introduction to a more precise statement of the topic, "the Bugandan trade boycott." Thus, we can assume that the article is about the Bugandan trade boycott as part of a protest movement.

Exercises

1. Circle the letter of the choice that best answers the question *What is this about?* Try to answer the question as quickly as possible.

   If you are hiking in the wilderness and become lost you can find the right direction by using the trees for guides. The Indians of North America used this technique when the sun or stars were not visible. Examine several trees—their foliage, the way the tops are leaning, their bark, and the moss growing on them—and they will indicate to you which direction to go.

   –David Wallechinsky and Irving Wallace

   a. trees
   b. Trees have secrets.
   c. Trees can indicate direction.
   d. being lost in the wilderness

2. Circle the letter of the choice that best answers the question *What is this about?*

   It started by mistake in a New Haven laboratory, and turned into a bonanza by sheer chance on New York's Fifth Avenue. There has never been a more accidental toy.
   Maybe it had to be. Who could have sat down and deliberately designed a piece of pink goo that stretches like taffy, shatters when struck sharply with a hammer, picks up newsprint and photos in color, molds like clay, flows like molasses, and—when rolled into a ball—bounces like mad? . . . The prodigy is Silly Putty, still as unique and popular today as it was almost twenty-five years ago, when it was accidentally developed in a General Electric research lab.

   –Marvin Kaye

    a. an accidental toy
    b. an electric toy
    c. a scientific discovery
    d. Silly Putty

3. Circle the letter of the choice that best answers the question *What is this about?*

> When John J. O'Connor was installed as Archbishop of New York (in March) he promised to learn Spanish to communicate better with the 800,000 Spanish-speaking Roman Catholics in the archdiocese. Five months later, before 10,000 people in Haverstraw, N.Y., he proclaimed: "Yo mismo he escrito estas palabras, incluso los errores." ("I have written these words myself, including the errors.")
>
> The Archbishop's effort was hardly a miracle, though one member of the congregation suggested that "the Holy Spirit must have been teaching him." Specialists in foreign languages say there is no reason why most educated adults cannot match this feat. But learning to speak a foreign language fluently requires considerably more than five months, the experts insist.
>
> *–Kenneth B. Noble*

    a. the Archbishop of New York
    b. learning foreign languages
    c. communication
    d. Roman Catholicism

4. The following three paragraphs are the beginnings of three different essays representing three different points of view in a dialogue. What is the topic of the dialogue?

    a. Should revenue sharing be extended to the support of postsecondary education? If more federal dollars become available for postsecondary education, should they be channeled through and administered by state education agencies or be given directly to individual campuses and postsecondary institutions?

    > *–Jerome M. Ziegler*

    b. Social policy is created primarily through the implementation of federal programs funded by federal dollars, and social policy should not be a province of the states in modern society. Three main factors suggest the incompatibility of federal dollars with state control.

    > *–Timothy R. Sanford*

c. Keeping a proper balance between local administrative offices and the federal mechanism in guiding the postsecondary educational enterprise will require continuous attention. Three questions should receive close consideration. First, from what vantage point can educational problems and needs be most readily identified? Second, how can local bodies best be stimulated to meet new needs and societal conditions? Finally, how can the ever-present bureaucratic red tape be kept to a minimum?

—Robert A. Huff

5. Chapter 10 of a book entitled *Broadcasting in America* has the following headings. What do you think is the topic of the chapter?

Why Public Broadcasting?
Rise of Educational Broadcasting
National Organization
Types of Public Stations
The Search for Funding
Programming
Children and Classrooms
The Impact of Public Broadcasting
The Outlook

—Sydney Head and Christopher Sterling

Writing Exercise

In two or three complete sentences, write your answer to these questions.

What is the topic of Chapter 4?
What is one of the subtopics of Chapter 4?
How did you find the topic and the subtopic?

Questioning

What is this about? is your first preview and basic reading question—one you should always ask before you begin to read and continue to ask as you read. Chapters 6 and 7 discuss reading and preview questions in some detail, and more reading and preview questions will be introduced throughout this book. For the present, you should ask *What is this about?* of everything you read.

5 Finding the Key Idea

Thus far you have learned two important aspects of reading. You know that a good reader reads for ideas and that finding the topic is the first step in discovering the author's ideas. This chapter helps you to take the next step—finding the author's key idea.

The Key Idea

An author writes to convey an idea, or a message, to an audience. When you have found the topic, you know what the message is about, but you don't know anything about why the author thinks the topic is important or what direction the author's thoughts will take. For instance, you might not be interested in going to a lecture on careers. But if you questioned further and found that the lecture was called "How to Choose the Right Career for You," you might not only plan to go yourself, but take your friends as well. The key idea tells you more about what the author is going to say about the topic. You can find the key idea by asking, *What is the author's most important idea about the topic?* You could also ask, *What idea does the author develop about the topic?* Or you could simply ask, *What is the author saying about the topic?* Each of these questions will help you to find the key idea.

The **key idea** of a paragraph, chapter, or book is the central thought or principal idea that the author wants to communicate to the reader. The key idea is the most important idea you want to get from your reading or the thought you most want to remember. Another way to think of it is that the key idea is the thought that everything else in the reading supports.

Think again about this book. You know that it is about active reading. What is the authors' most important idea about active reading? The answer is the key idea: Active reading will make you a better reader. How about Chapter 3? The topic is reading for ideas. What is the most important idea the authors tell you about reading for ideas? The answer is that words are used to convey ideas. In Chapter 4 the topic is finding the topic. What is the authors' most important idea about finding the topic? You can find the topic by asking the question *What is this about?*

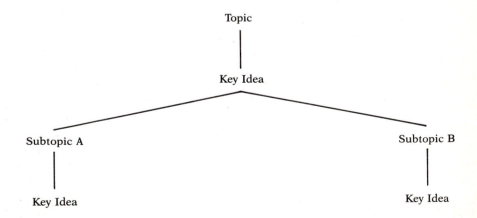

Usually the topic leads directly to the key idea. Sometimes, however, you may find the topic more easily after you have found the key idea. Perhaps you guessed that either this or that is the topic. Finding the key idea will point out which of your guesses is correct.

Sometimes the topic and key idea (or the topic, subtopics, and key idea) are all you need to get from your reading. The ability to find the topic and subtopics and distinguish the key idea, then, is the basis for efficient reading.

Examples

The following examples demonstrate how to find the key idea.

The hungry boy dashed wildly past the town hall, through the churchyard, and up the front steps, arriving just in time for dinner.

This sentence is about the boy. What is the author's most important idea about the boy? It is not how or where the boy dashed but the fact that he arrived in time for dinner.

Reading is both a pleasure and a necessity. By enabling us to know and master relevant information, reading can lead to success in our jobs. At the same time, reading can provide relief from the stresses of daily life by taking us into a variety of worlds and situations.

The topic of this paragraph is reading. What is the author's most important idea about reading? Reading is a necessity and a pleasure. This must be the key idea since sentence two supports the notion of necessity and sentence three supports the notion of pleasure.

May is easily the brightest and most explorable month. But what sets May apart most emphatically—not the apartness of being better, but of being different—is that it is a month of movement.

—*The Washington Post*

This paragraph is clearly about May. The key idea, however, is found not in the beginning statement (that May is the brightest and most explorable month), but in the emphasis given in the concluding statement: "What sets May apart . . . is that it is a month of movement."

[When you say], "I read it only last night, but I forgot most of it. I guess I have a poor memory," you are wrong about forgetting and about having a poor memory. You see, you did read the words in the chapter, and you did understand the words, but you didn't stop to put these words together into ideas. So, instead of isolating the 8 or 10 important ideas in the chapter, you just saw a continuous string of words. It's like pointing a camera at the distant hills and rapidly swinging the camera to get in all the hills while you click the shutter. All you'll get is a blur. And your quick reading of the chapter, without stopping to get a separate mental picture of each idea, will result in a mental blur of the entire chapter. If an idea or fact is to be retained in the memory, it must be impressed on the mind clearly and crisply at least once. A neural trace must be laid down in the brain. You cannot retain something that is not there in the first place.

—Walter Pauk

This paragraph is an example of how sometimes it is easier to find the topic after you have found the key idea. Would you say that this paragraph is primarily about memory or reading? If you can't answer that question immediately, then you might look for the key idea. What is the author's most important idea? What is the central thought of the paragraph? The sentence that everything else seems to support is "If an idea or fact is to be retained in the memory, it must be impressed on the mind clearly and crisply at least once." This thought could be restated as "To improve your memory you must be conscious of each idea as you read it." The key idea, then, leads back to memory as the topic of the paragraph.

Exercises

Preview each of the following paragraphs by asking *What is this about?* Underline the clause or sentence that answers the question *What is the author's most important idea about the topic?*

1. If you see a flash of lightning and start to count seconds, you can estimate how far away from you the lightning is by how long afterward you hear the crash of thunder. In each second, sound travels 330 meters (about ⅕ mile). Of course, the speed of sound varies somewhat depending on the temperature and other physical conditions of the air, but this will give you a good estimate.

   —Joseph F. Weisberg

2. One can speak of film as either a medium (an instrument or means) or an end result (a product—indeed, perhaps an artistic product). If one is speaking of the "art of the film," then presumably the analogy is with, say, written literature (the novel, or poetry, and so on); if one is thinking of film as a medium, then the appropriate analogy is to *print*. It is not a question of one analogy being more legitimate than the other, for film is in fact *both* an art and a medium. As a medium it records and presents the *art* of film

(or at times the art of ballet or opera, if film is being used to record performances in those arts).

—Morris Beja

3. There is one key idea which contains, in itself, the very essence of effective reading, and on which the improvement of reading depends: Reading is reasoning. When you read properly, you are not merely assimilating. You are not automatically transferring into your head what your eyes pick up on the page. What you see on the page sets your mind at work, collating, criticizing, interpreting, questioning, comprehending, comparing. When this process goes on well, you read well. When it goes on ill, you read badly.

—James Mursell

4. Comic performers are very distinctive. They have distinctive faces, mannerisms, or ways of speaking that set them off entirely. More strongly than any other kind of performer, they maintain the ancient concept of the *mask*: the stylized covering which sets dramatic actors aside from reality. The Keystone comics, the Marx brothers, and the Three Stooges have masks only slightly less exaggerated than those of the *commedia dell'arte* [comedy developed in Italy in the sixteenth century]. Chaplin and Keaton kept clownlike masks even in realistic feature films. Later comedians from Eddie Bracken to Jerry Lewis to Woody Allen lost the clown look but exploited funny faces and mannerisms. The same is true of minor comedians, some of whom appear as comic relief in melodramas: they stand apart, thanks to this power of the comic mask.

—George Wead and George Lellis

5. The study of human ecology leaves no doubt that people are the most influential organisms in the biosphere, in that they can raise crops, control infectious diseases, and alter any ecosystem to meet their needs. Yet in a very real sense, people are themselves ecosystems because the existence of all human beings depends on the presence of bacteria that live on or in our bodies. Madison Avenue notwithstanding, human well-being is highly dependent on contact with environmental microbes. Within our guts bacteria recycle metabolic products from the liver and thereby enable us to digest fats. Gut bacteria probably also supply us with at least some of our daily requirements of vitamins, and skin microbes prevent the colonization of our body surfaces by potentially pathogenic [disease-causing] organisms. From the outmost reaches of the biosphere to the very center of our guts, we people are not alone on Earth, nor are our lives isolated from those of other living things.

—Sam Singer

6. For many years there was all this denigration of the wolf. People talked about what a horrible animal it was and how they all ought to be shot. But then the pendulum swung the other way and there have been all these books, lectures, and TV specials about what a nice guy the wolf is. It has gone too far in that direction. All the stuff about the social life of the wolf is obviously interesting information. But there is just not enough talk about the other 50 percent of a wolf, which is equally important. In fact, the animal is a savage, aggressive killer. It walks around in the woods and attacks moose, for example. There are plenty of people up in Alaska who will tell you that a moose is the most dangerous mammal in North America. They will say it is worse than a grizzly bear. Whether they are right or not, it is no sweetheart to mess around with if you have to attack it with your mouth. In a pack a wolf can kill a moose. It is capable not only physically, but emotionally, of doing this sort of thing. This is what a wolf is.

–Gale Cooper

Implied and Unexpressed Key Ideas

In the examples and exercises so far, you have been finding **expressed key ideas**—that is, key ideas that are directly stated somewhere in the passage. As you have discovered, the expressed key idea is not always located in the first sentence; it may be located in the last sentence or somewhere in the middle. At other times the key idea is not explicitly stated in the passage, and occasionally a paragraph may not have a key idea at all.

Implied Key Ideas

When the key idea is not directly expressed, you have to infer the key idea from what the author implies. This is the same as making a generalization from the evidence the author supplies. Sometimes you will need to read through the entire reading before you have enough evidence to infer the key idea. The danger here—and it is a great danger—is that you will substitute your own idea for the author's idea because you have had some experience with or knowledge of what the author is discussing. To do this is to make a false assumption. To avoid making a false assumption, you must always be absolutely sure that you can support your notion of the key idea from the words the author has given you.

When you infer a key idea, you should try to state it in a full sentence and be as concise as possible. This helps you to get a clear notion of what the author is saying.

Examples

I lay rigid in my bed with every muscle from the top of my head to the end of my toes taut and straining. My breathing had stopped. My total being was centered on my ears, which were listening for that creak on the stairs, that slight rustle of clothes, that indrawn breath which would betray the presence of someone.

The key idea in this selection is "I was afraid." Although it is not stated explicitly, the author gives you the evidence of the physical symptoms of fear—rigid muscles, no breathing, listening. From this evidence the reader can deduce the fact that the writer was experiencing fear.

At the center of the world is Ypres and all around the center lie the flats of Flanders. . . . The plain on which Ypres stands stretches like a broken arm through Europe from the Russian Frontier to the border of Spain. This is the one way west into France that does not encounter mountains. (Once, in Napoleon's time, it had been the only way east.) Because of its flatness this alleyway has been the scene of battles since the time of Caesar. All the great armies of modern history have passed this way and through this mud.

—Timothy Findley

In this paragraph the author implies the key idea: that because of their geography the plains of Flanders have been the scene of battles since the time of the Romans. Thus, the topic is the plains of Flanders.

Unexpressed Key Ideas

You will not often come upon a passage without a key idea. However, they can play an important role in a larger work. Sometimes a passage of one or even several paragraphs provides a description; sometimes it is a chronological account with no unifying idea beyond the topic, or a sequence of actions or instructions, or a transition; sometimes it provides background for later action or comment. You can tell that a passage does not have a key idea when you can neither find nor infer an answer to your question *What is the most important idea the author has about the topic?*

Examples

It was a large house overlooking the lake. At the south end there was a glassed-in conservatory, while the opposite side boasted a large portico under which rolled the driveway. A few people could be dimly observed sitting on the terrace, and a group of children were playing on the lawn.

The answer to *What is this about?* would seem to be the house, because that is what is described. If you go on to ask *What is the author's most important idea about the house?* you would have a hard time coming up with an answer. Is it important that the house is large, or that it has a conservatory or a portico, or that there are people on the terrace? Is one of these observations more important than another? Because the paragraph doesn't give you enough information to answer these questions, you would have to conclude that it does not contain a key idea.

Momma made a Sunday breakfast although it was only Friday. After we finished the blessing, I opened my eyes to find the watch on my plate. It was a dream of a day. Everything went smoothly and to my credit. I didn't have to be reminded or scolded for anything. Near evening I was too jittery to attend to chores, so Bailey volunteered to do all before his bath.

–Maya Angelou

The topic of this short paragraph could be a special day, but it is hard to identify a key idea. Instead you have the feeling that something is about to happen. The stage is set.

Exercises

1. For the first three selections take the following steps:

   - Preview for the topic by asking *What is this about?*
   - Find the key idea by asking *What is the author's most important idea about the topic?*
   - Write a brief statement of the key idea in one concise sentence.
   - If there doesn't seem to be a key idea, state whether the paragraph is a description, a chronological account, a sequence of actions, a transition, or whether it simply provides background information.

   a. The first day he went to work for the *Pittsburgh Leader*—long a deservedly dead newspaper—in 1909, George Seldes wrote a story about a street accident. "Stanislas Schmidt, aged 32, of 1811 Center Avenue, driver of a Silver Top Brewing Company delivery wagon, was slightly injured at 2 o'clock this morning at Penn Avenue and Liberty Street when his wagon was struck by a street car." Hours later, in rookie eagerness, he read through the first edition to find his story in print. There it ran: "Stanislas Schmidt, 32 years old, of 1811 Center Ave., driver of a beer delivery wagon . . ." Seldes immediately read the sign language of his newsroom. "Silver Top was not mentioned," he wrote years later. "Silver Top was a large advertiser. My education had begun."

–The Washington Post

b. Further diagnosis, based on angiography, a detailed X-ray study of the circulatory system, showed the tumor to be about two inches in diameter and supplied by many small blood vessels. It rested beneath the brain, just above the pituitary gland, stretching the optic nerves to either side and intimately close to the major blood vessels supplying the brain. Removing it would pose many technical problems. Probably benign and slow-growing, it may have been present for several years. If left alone it would continue to grow and produce blindness and might become impossible to remove completely. Removing it, however, might not improve the patient's vision and could make it worse. A major blood vessel could be damaged, causing a stroke. Damage to the undersurface of the brain could cause impairment of memory and changes in mood and personality. The hypothalamus, a most important structure of the brain, could be injured.

–Roy C. Selby, Jr.

c. When you walk, you don't think about the placement of your legs but of where you wish to go. Flying an airplane or driving an automobile is done in that same way by the skilled performer. When you learned to drive, you concentrated on how to move your arms and legs. Then you worried about the smoothness of your activities. Eventually you reached the point where you simply thought of turning and your actions took care of themselves. But even that phase changed. The skilled driver simply goes somewhere—to the store, home, to the bank. the skilled walker decides to go to the other side of the room. The skilled airplane pilot no longer manipulates controls and watches instruments, but simply flies—not "flies the plane," but "flies." The person is flying or driving or going. The plane or the automobile or the legs are incidental tools to the activity.

–Donald A. Norman

2. These three selections require slightly different steps.

* Preview for the topic.
* Find the subtopic and key idea of each paragraph.
* State the key idea (expressed or implied) of the entire reading.

1   a. The most significant and widespread area of discontent and protest in the post–Civil War period was agrarian in origin and orientation, and the American farmer seemed determined to steer a middle course between "goo-goos" [good government leaders] and radicals. Like the civil service reformer, the farmer avoided long-range considerations of social planning and control, and he had no direct purpose to abandon free enterprise capitalism. Like his radical contemporaries, however, he was fully prepared to attain immediate objectives through State action, and throughout the period his angry cries for governmental intervention to secure economic and political reform seriously threatened and frightened the industrial ruling class.

2   Nor were the farmer's demands for reform without cause. Constantly subjected to the vicissitudes of drought and storm—and market—in many ways the farm population was even more deprived than the propertyless workers who crowded into the city. For as the farmer continued his barren, isolated, and culturally impoverished life, rural areas lagged far behind in the enjoyment of a higher standard of living, and the benefits of the industrial revolution seemed largely confined to the rapidly growing cities. Agriculture suffered a particularly severe depression during the thirty years before 1897, and the farmer's economic situation had grown increasingly more desperate as his costs mounted and prices for farm products tumbled. Cotton that cost 6 or 7 cents per pound to produce sold for 4 or 5 cents, while wheat that had brought $1.45 per bushel at the end of the Civil War brought 49 cents thirty years later, and corn that sold for 75 cents in 1869 fell to 28 cents in 1889. Crushed between minimal farm prices and the intolerable burden of debts assumed in prosperous, expansive years, it was the oppressed and disgruntled farmer who spearheaded America's crusade for reform.

3   Fundamentally, declining farm prices and income were due to a vastly increased competition of farm products on the world market and to the overexpansion of agriculture that had taken place during the Civil War. In assaying his plight, however, the farmer almost invariably attributed hard times to an inadequate money supply and to the immediate, tangible abuses he suffered at the hands of his economic masters, the railroads and the banks. Against the railroads his grievances were real enough. The carriers not only charged the farmer exorbitant rates that frequently took the value of one bushel of wheat or corn to pay the freight on another, but through rebates and other secret agreements they viciously discriminated against him in favor of larger and wealthier shippers. The bankers, too, as money became scarcer, as interest rates on loans and mort-

gages soared, and as foreclosures multiplied, seemed the farmer's mortal enemies. As one Nebraska farm editor lamented, "We have three crops—corn, freight rates, and interest. The farmers farm the land, and the businessmen farm the farmers."

–Richard Heffner

1   b. One of the most vivid of the mythical episodes added to the history of the Celtic captain, Arthur, is that deed by which he was disclosed to be the predestined king. His father, Uther Pendragon, had died, and the powerful lords of the kingdom were all grasping for the crown. By Merlin's advice and counsel it was finally decided that the supernatural powers should be left to determine the troubled issue. Before the greatest church in London a stone had appeared in which a sword was buried; and letters of gold were to be seen on the stone around the sword to the effect that the one who could draw the blade should be recognized as king. Many tried in vain. Then, at last, this unknown youth, Arthur, who had been reared secretly under the guardianship of Merlin, rode up to the church and, ignorant of the magic of his deed, pulled out the sword.

2   This striking symbol of the hero's election and sacred power is derived from the prehistoric period at the close of the Age of Stone. Swords were not made until after the discovery of bronze and iron: before that time there were only spears and arrows and axes. And so, who is the one who frees the metal from the stone? The culture-hero: the magic smith, who released the worlds from the Stone Age and taught mankind the art of smelting bronze and iron from the ore. The hero who can draw the iron sword from the stone is not necessarily a great warrior, but always a powerful magician, lord over spiritual and material things: a seer comparable, in terms of the Iron Age, to the modern inventor, chemist or engineer, who creates new weapons for his people. And just as today we live in awe—and some fear—of the man of science, so it is only natural that the folk of that faraway other day should have thought of the one who freed for them metal from stone as the chosen master of the secrets of existence.

–Heinrich Zimmer

1   c. The frog is a "cold-blooded" vertebrate, as are the fishes and the reptiles. This does not mean that the blood of these animals is always cold. It means that their body temperatures vary with the temperature of the surroundings. Man maintains a constant average body temperature of about 98.6°F through the regulation of the rate of food oxidation and resulting heat release in the tissues as well as of heat loss from the body surface.

The cold-blooded vertebrates carry on much slower oxidation and do not maintain relatively constant body temperatures.

2   With the coming of fall and the seasonal lowering of temperature, the body temperature of the frog drops to the point where the frog can no longer be very active. It buries itself in the mud at the bottom of a pond or finds shelter in some other protected place in the water. Heart action slows down to a point at which blood hardly circulates in the vessels. The greatly reduced amount of oxygen necessary for life is supplied through the moist surface of the skin. The tissues are kept alive by the slow oxidation of food stored in the liver and in the fat bodies attached to the kidneys in most frogs. Nervous activity almost ceases, and the frog lies in a stupor. This is the condition of the frog during hibernation, or winter rest. With the coming of spring the warm days speed up body activity, and the frog gradually resumes the physiological and functional activities of a normal life.

3   The hot summer months bring other problems. Lacking a device for cooling the body, the frog must escape from the extreme heat. It may lie quietly in deep, cool water or bury itself in the mud at the bottom of a pond. This condition of summer inactivity is called estivation. Many smaller ponds dry up during midsummer, and the frogs and other cold-blooded animals only survive by burying themselves in the mud and estivating. With the coming of cooler weather and the return of water to the pond, they come out of estivation and continue normal activity until hibernation.

–James H. Otto and A. Towle

Writing Summaries

In the writing exercise at the end of many chapters you will be asked to write a short paragraph (three to four sentences) summarizing the lesson. We have included summary writing in *Active Reading* because we believe that by thinking about the work you have just done and then writing down your thoughts in full sentences, you can become a more active learner. Consciously and systematically reviewing the main points made in each lesson will imprint those points on your mind. Memory experts tell us that it is through such conscious effort that we put what we have learned into our short-term memory. Later repetition and review will transfer the information to long-term memory. It is like remembering a dream. If you wake to the distracting sound of an alarm, jump out of bed thinking about the tasks of the day ahead, you probably don't remember the dream you know you had. If, however, you have some time to lie there thinking about your dream, you probably can remember it and continue to remember it later when you tell one of your classmates about it.

Writing a summary does not allow you to have hazy, half-formed or semiunderstood ideas about what you have read. Writing in sentences exposes the gaps in your comprehension. You will also find that this immediate review and summary will help you when you review for exams.

In writing a summary, you can focus your thoughts by making use of the questions you have learned to ask.

1. Think about the entire text you have been asked to summarize.
2. Find the topic by asking yourself *What is this about?*
3. Identify the key idea by asking yourself *What is the author's most important idea about the topic?*
4. Look for the subtopics by asking *What is this about?* of each paragraph or section.
5. Find the key ideas of the subtopics by asking *What is the author's most important idea about this subtopic?*
6. Put the topic, subtopics, and key ideas together in sentences, the number of which will depend on the length of the text you are summarizing.

In writing a summary, you should try to be completely objective. That is, you should not include your personal views about good or bad, right or wrong, or other judgments you might want to make about the topic or its treatment. You are to deal only with the author's ideas and words. Your objective is to make the summary shorter than the reading selection without changing the author's ideas or emphasis given them. You can do this by identifying what is important and stating it essentially in your own words. You should not include examples or any other illustrative material unless it is essential to the author's point. You can include some of the author's words in your summary, particularly those terms or phrases that convey the essence of what the author is writing about, but you should usually not quote complete sentences or paragraphs. If you do, you should always put such material in quotation marks.

Examples

A summary of the passage on flying (p. 27), could be worked out like this:

> Topic: flying
> Key idea (found in paragraph 1): Airplanes are the best way to travel.

Subtopic, paragraph 2: flying speed
Key idea: Airplanes are fast.
Subtopic, paragraph 3: safety
Key idea: Airplanes are relatively safe.
Subtopic, paragraph 4: cost
Key idea: Flying is relatively inexpensive.
Summary: Airplanes are the best way to travel because they are fast, relatively safe, and inexpensive.

A summary of the article on the frog, found on p. 44, might read as follows:

In the article on the frog, the author states that frogs are cold-blooded animals; this means that their body temperature reflects the temperature of the world around them. Therefore, the frog has to adapt to changes in temperature. When it gets cold in the wintertime, the frog's bodily functions slow down; it buries itself in the bottom of the pond and hibernates over the winter. In summer it again buries itself as protection against the heat. This is called estivation.

You can apply the technique of summarizing to your other courses. Try it in the very next class you attend. At the end of the class, take a few minutes to write a summary of the topic, subtopics, and key ideas of the class, asking *What was this class about?* and *What were the instructor's most important idea(s) about the topic and subtopics?* You will find that you will improve not only your comprehension but also your writing.

Writing Exercise

Think about the chapter you have just finished working on, Chapter 5, and write a short paragraph summarizing what it is about and what is the most important idea the authors tell you about the topic.

Questioning

What is this about?
What is the author's most important idea about the topic?

Asking *What is the author's most important idea about the topic?* helps you to find the key idea. Like *What is this about?* this is both a preview and a basic reading question to be asked before you start reading and as you read.

6 Finding Supporting Ideas and Supporting Details

Thus far you have learned two basic reading and preview questions: What is this about? and What is the author's most important idea about the topic? The answers to these questions give you the topic and the key idea. Sometimes the topic and the key idea will be all you need to get from your reading. More often you will need to ask many more questions if you are to understand your texts fully. This chapter will help you to ask these questions and to find the answers.

What Are Supporting Ideas and Supporting Details?

Authors support and develop their key ideas by providing supporting ideas and supporting details. Let's start examining these concepts by looking again at this book. You know its topic is active reading; you also know its most important idea is that through active reading you can become a better reader. What would your next questions be? They might be *Why do I want to be a better reader?* or *How can I become a better reader?*

By asking very specific questions—such as *Who? How? What? Where? When? Which? What kind?* and *Why?*—you challenge the authors to provide you with answers. Why is this idea so? On what is it based? How is it being done? The answers to your questions lead you to the secondary ideas that support the key idea. Supporting ideas and supporting details give you a better understanding of what the authors are writing about.

Supporting Ideas

Chapter 4 dealt with the difference between topics and subtopics. The topic is what the entire reading is about. The subtopics are what each section of the entire reading is about. Chapter 3 emphasized that each piece of reading has a key idea. The key ideas of the sections of a reading are called the supporting ideas. **Supporting ideas** elaborate on and develop the key idea by answering the questions *How? Who? What? Where? When? Which? What kind?* and *Why?*

Perhaps the concept can best be explained by analyzing a sentence:

The library committee was pleased to see the newly acquired shelves filled with all the books that had previously been heaped on the floor.

The topic is the committee. The key idea is that the committee was pleased to see the shelves; and the supporting idea—answering the question *Why?*—is that the shelves were filled with books. If we mark up the text by underlining the key idea and bracketing the supporting idea, the sentence would look like this.

The library committee was pleased to see the newly acquired shelves [filled with all the books] that had previously been heaped on the floor.

To take an illustration from biology, the circulatory, respiratory, digestive, and reproductive systems contribute to the total

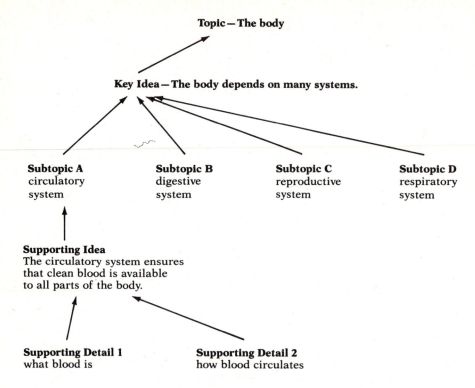

functioning of the body. The key idea is that the body depends on many systems. A supporting idea is that the digestive system maintains the body; another supporting idea would be that the reproductive system permits the body to propagate itself. Both these ideas answer the question *How?* and support the key idea, not each other.

Supporting Details

The key idea may be supported by several supporting ideas. **Supporting details** back up the supporting ideas by also answering the questions *Who? How? Why? Where? When? What? Which?* and *What kind?* Both supporting ideas and supporting details elaborate or amplify, clarify, and explain or modify. They can take the form of illustrations, examples, verifying statistics, reasons, definitions, and descriptions. This notion can be explained by one of our previous illustrations.

By diagramming the text, you can see the relationships between the topic and subtopics, the key idea and supporting ideas, and the supporting ideas and supporting details. When you know the roles of the various parts of a reading, you can discriminate the important from the unimportant and distinguish what you need to know from what you don't need to know. Many instructors have told us that their successful students can see how the ideas presented in a reading relate to each other. Less successful students block themselves by thinking only of the details of what the author is saying. It's the old business of the forest and the trees. If you get too involved in trying to describe each tree, you will not see the shape of the forest or how the forest fits into the landscape. Therefore, it is essential for a reader to know which is the forest and which are the trees—that is, to be able to discriminate the key and supporting ideas from the supporting details.

Examples

Marking up the text as in the following paragraphs helps you to see these fundamental relationships.

> *Key Idea*
>
> The word *reading* can take a variety of meanings depending on the context in which it appears. [Sometimes, for example,
>
> *Supporting Idea*
>
> the verb *to read* clearly implies comprehension;] it would usually be redundant if not rude to say to a friend, "Here's a book
>
> *Supporting Idea*
>
> you might like to read and comprehend." But [at other times the verb does not entail comprehension;] our friend might re-
>
> *Supporting Idea*
>
> ply, "I've read that book already and didn't understand it." [Obviously, there is little to be gained by asking such abstract questions as "Does reading involve comprehension (or thinking, or inferential reasoning) or does it not?"] Everything de-
>
> *Key Idea*
>
> pends on the context in which the words are used. [In its specific detail the act of reading itself depends on the situation in which it is accomplished and the intention of the reader.]
>
> *Supporting Idea*
>
> Consider, for example, the differences between reading a novel, a poem, a social studies text, a mathematical formula, a telephone book, a recipe, an advertisement, and a street sign.
>
> *—Frank Smith*

In reading this paragraph, you probably found that you needed to read the details that explained the key and supporting ideas to be sure that you understood exactly what the author meant by "the word *reading* can take a variety of meanings depending on the context." The supporting ideas answered the questions *How?* and *When?*; the supporting details answered the question *What?* Why do you think the key idea was repeated midway through the paragraph?

If you are having trouble finding the topic or key idea of a paragraph or an article, the supporting ideas and supporting details sometimes can help you. The passage on the frog, which you did as an exercise in Chapter 5, is an example. As you read it, bracket the supporting ideas and note them in the margin.

1   The frog is a "cold-blooded" vertebrate, as are the fishes and the reptiles. This does not mean that the blood of these animals is always cold. It means that their body temperatures vary with the temperature of the surroundings. Man maintains a constant average body temperature of about 98.6° F through the regulation of the rate of food oxidation and resulting heat release in the tissues as well as of heat loss from the body surface. The cold-blooded vertebrates carry on much slower oxidation and do not maintain relatively constant body temperatures.

2   With the coming of fall and the seasonal lowering of temperature, the body temperature of the frog drops to the point where the frog can no longer be very active. It buries itself in the mud at the bottom of a pond or finds shelter in some other protected place in the water. Heart action slows down to a point at which blood hardly circulates in the vessels. The greatly reduced amount of oxygen necessary for life is supplied through the moist surface of the skin. The tissues are kept alive by the slow oxidation of food stored in the liver and in the fat bodies attached above the kidneys in most frogs. Nervous activity almost ceases, and the frog lies in a stupor. This is the condition of the frog during hibernation, or winter rest. With the coming of spring the warm days speed up body activity, and the frog gradually resumes the physiological and functional activities of normal life.

3   The hot summer months bring other problems. Lacking a device for cooling the body, the frog must escape from the extreme heat. It may lie quietly in deep, cool water or bury itself in the mud at the bottom of a pond. This condition of summer inactivity is called estivation. Many smaller ponds dry up during midsummer, and the frogs and other cold-blooded animals only survive by burying themselves in the mud and estivating. With the coming of cooler weather and the return of water to the pond, they come out of estivation and continue normal activity until hibernation.

                                                            –James H. Otto and A. Towle

You may have found earlier that the key idea was not readily apparent. The supporting ideas that emerge from your reading of the individual paragraphs provide you with the information that the frog is a cold-blooded vertebrate that slows down its body functions in winter as a protection against cold and is inactive in the summer to escape the heat. These ideas support the key idea of the entire reading, which is that frogs have to adapt to changes in temperature. Supporting details, such as the definition of cold-blooded, the way in which the frog is kept alive during hibernation, and the way in which it keeps cool in the summer, elaborate on the supporting ideas.

Basic Reading Questions

The questions *Who? What? Where? When? Why? Which? What kind?* and *How?*, which help you to find the supporting ideas and supporting details, bring you to the last of the basic reading questions. As we have mentioned, the basic reading questions form the foundation for all other questions that might come up as you read. In fact, if you have no other questions, the basic reading questions will always serve to disclose what the author's ideas are and how the ideas are organized. These questions are equally useful whether you ask them of a whole essay or book or of a part of a book, such as a chapter, a section, a paragraph, or a sentence. We hope that in time you will ask and answer these questions automatically as you read.

As a brief review, these are the basic reading questions:

What is this about? for the topic.
What is the author's most important idea about the topic? for the key idea.
Who? What? Where? Why? When? How? Which? or *What kind?* for the supporting ideas.
Who? What? Where? Why? When? How? Which? or *What kind?* for the supporting details.

The diagram on page 54 shows how we have applied the basic reading questions to *Active Reading*. We think it gives a very clear idea of how the various levels of ideas relate to and support each other.

Exercises

1. Preview the following passage to find the topic and the key idea. Then read the passage, looking for the supporting ideas and supporting details.

   Like most of the related terms, *junk* is vague in meaning. It is like the non-putrescible fraction of garbage, except that it consists of material too bulky or objects too large to be squeezed into the can. Size, not kind, is of the essence. A small transistor radio goes out as garbage; a large set goes as junk. From that point the size ranges upward to old cars and trucks, and eventually to old locomotives, airplanes, and steamships. So also, paper bags and wrappers, along with scattered newspapers, go into the can, but waste paper in bulk and newspapers in bundles are an important element in junk. Just as junk cannot altogether be distinguished from garbage, so also it is only differentiated from *trash* and *rubbish* in

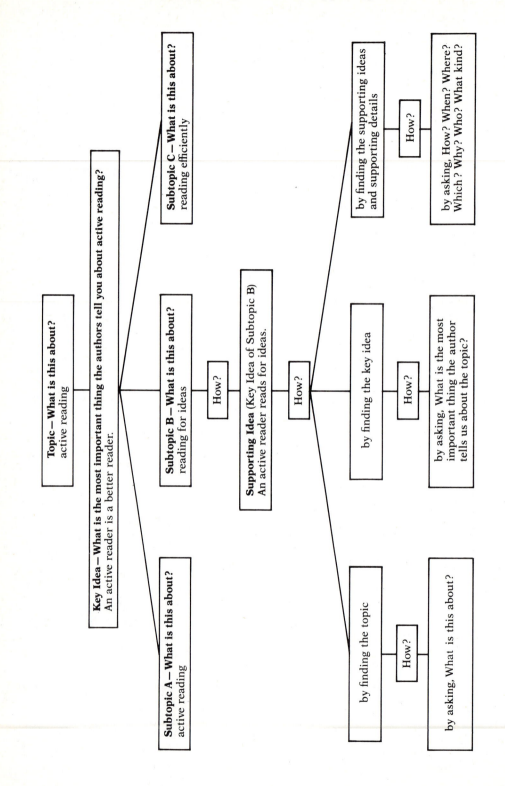

Topic — What is this about?
active reading

Key Idea — What is the most important thing the authors tell you about active reading?
An active reader is a better reader.

Subtopic A — What is this about?
active reading

Subtopic B — What is this about?
reading for ideas

Subtopic C — What is this about?
reading efficiently

How?

Supporting Idea (Key Idea of Subtopic B)
An active reader reads for ideas.

How?

by finding the topic

How?

by asking, What is this about?

by finding the key idea

How?

by asking, What is the most important thing the author tells us about the topic?

by finding the supporting ideas and supporting details

How?

by asking, How? When? Where? Which? Why? Who? What kind?

a vague manner. As opposed to these two, junk implies a possible re-use.

—George R. Stewart

a. What is the topic?
b. What is the key idea?
c. Place the two supporting ideas in brackets. What questions do they answer?
d. Note three supporting details in the margin. To which of the supporting ideas are they related? What question or questions do they answer?

2. Preview the following two paragraphs for the topic and key idea. Read for the supporting idea found in each paragraph.

1   A solitary ant, afield, cannot be considered to have much of anything on his mind; indeed, with only a few neurons strung together by fibers, he can't be imagined to have a mind at all, much less a thought. He is more like a ganglion on legs. Four ants together, or ten, encircling a dead moth on a path, begin to look more like an idea. They fumble and shove, gradually moving the food toward the Hill, but as though by blind chance. It is only when you watch the dense mass of thousands of ants, crowded together around the Hill, blackening the ground, that you begin to see the whole beast, and now you observe it thinking, planning, calculating. It is an intelligence, a kind of live computer, with crawling bits for its wits.

2   At a stage in the construction, twigs of a certain size are needed, and all the members forage obsessively for twigs of just this size. Later, when outer walls are to be finished, thatched, the size must change, and as though given new orders by telephone, all the workers shift the search to the new twigs. If you disturb the arrangement of a part of the Hill, hundreds of ants will set it vibrating, shifting, until it is put right again. Distant sources of food are somehow sensed, and long lines, like tentacles, reach out over the ground, up over the walls, behind boulders, to fetch it in.

—Lewis Thomas

a. What is the key idea of the passage?
b. What are the supporting ideas found in the two paragraphs? How do they support the key idea of the passage?
c. How do the two paragraphs relate to each other?

3. In the following paragraph underline the key idea, bracket the supporting idea or ideas, and note the supporting details in the margin.

True believers among social planners and research and development innovators envision the day when all the many bits and pieces of communications technology now on the market or projected for the near future will coalesce into a single, multipurpose home communications center. In contrast to the earlier trend toward miniaturized, personalized, highly portable units, the home center would be an elaborate and permanent installation. It would probably require setting aside an entire room primarily for the reception, recording, storage, playback, and initiation of communications. There the television screen, like a queen bee glowing in the center of an electronic hive, would be fed by an army of working inputs—disc and tape recorders and players, cable and over-the-air program suppliers, teletext reception capable of making hard-copy printouts as required, direct broadcast satellite relays picked up by rooftop dish antennas, two-way communication circuits, and so on.

—Sydney Head and Christopher Sterling

4. Preview and read the next passage. Then answer the questions that follow it.

1   Beauty, once repressed, reviled and buried beneath baggy clothes, is rebounding to its place of honor in China. In what for years was a sere and somber society, the renaissance and renewed appreciation of beauty can now be seen in a touch of lipstick, the swirl of a skirt, the tending of a flower or the care of a songbird.

2   During the Cultural Revolution, women were reprimanded for their vanity, and some even bound their breasts beneath bland Maoist shrouds. But today beauty, color, individuality, even sexuality are back with a force that will be difficult to stem. Witness the pastel scarves, innocent summer dresses, fitted trousers and even painted nails.

3   Glamorous cover girls now sell everything from cashmere sweaters to heavy machinery. On Sundays women promenade in parks, peeking out from under parasols, striking sexy poses for their shutterbug boyfriends. Some even undergo plastic surgery to widen their eyes.

4   Likewise love, once considered bourgeois and selfish, abounds reassuringly—to the distress of puritanical social planners. Young people stroll frankly arm-in-arm. They crowd benches along Shanghai's Bund [the main avenue] and rustle the bushes at night. In one thronged park, sly, entrepreneurial kids charge lovers one yuan (50 US cents) for space on a crowded bench. Love is the constant theme of songs, books, films and plays. Newspapers give advice to the lovelorn and urge the jilted not to seek revenge, while the Communist Party plays cupid, setting up matchmaking centers all over the country.

5   In China, however, love is for keeps and for marriage, and sex for the unmarried is supposed to be taboo. Marriage itself is forbidden until men are 22 and women are 20. In the official version, married couples are instructed to be chaste, make love rarely, then go straight to sleep and conserve their energy for socialism.

–Liu Heung Shing

a. What is the topic?
b. What is the key idea?
c. What is the first subtopic?
d. What is the second subtopic?
e. List the ideas that support the second subtopic. What questions do they answer?
f. List the details that support the ideas you found in e, above. What questions do they answer?

5. Mark up the following paragraphs by underlining the key idea and bracketing the supporting ideas. Note the topic, key idea, supporting idea(s), and supporting detail(s) in the margin.

1   Two kinds of logic are used [in motorcycle maintenance], inductive and deductive. Inductive inferences start with observations of the machine and arrive at general conclusions. For example, if the cycle goes over a bump and the engine misfires, and then goes over another bump and the engine misfires, and then goes over another bump and the engine misfires, and then goes over a long smooth stretch of road and there is no misfiring, and then goes over a fourth bump and the engine misfires again, one can logically conclude that the misfiring is caused by the bumps. That is induction: reasoning from particular experiences to general truths.

2   Deductive inferences do the reverse. They start with general knowledge and predict a specific observation. For example, if, from reading the hierarchy of facts about the machine, the mechanic knows the horn of the cycle is powered exclusively by electricity from the battery, then he can logically infer that if the battery is dead the horn will not work. That is deduction.

–Robert M. Pirsig

6. The following passage was written by Bertrand Russell, who was one of the leading British philosophers of this century. Preview and read it. Then fill in the blanks in the following diagram.

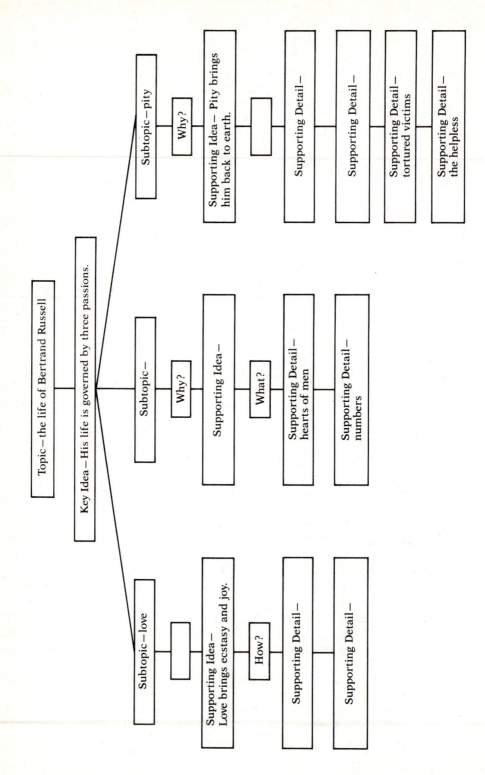

1   Three passions, simple but overwhelmingly strong, have governed my life: the longing for love, the search for knowledge, and unbearable pity for the suffering of mankind. These passions, like great winds, have blown me hither and thither, in a wayward course, over a deep ocean of anguish, reaching to the very verge of despair.

2   I have sought love, first, because it brings ecstasy—ecstasy so great that I would often have sacrificed all the rest of life for a few hours of this joy. I have sought it, next, because it relieves loneliness—that terrible loneliness in which one shivering consciousness looks over the rim of the world into the cold unfathomable lifeless abyss. I have sought it, finally, because in the union of love I have seen, in a mystic miniature, the prefiguring vision of the heaven that saints and poets have imagined. This is what I sought, and though it might seem too good for human life, this is what—at last—I have found.

3   With equal passion I have sought knowledge. I have wished to understand the hearts of men. I have wished to know why the stars shine. And I have tried to apprehend the Pythagorean power by which number holds sway above the flux. A little of this, but not much, I have achieved.

4   Love and knowledge, so far as they were possible, led upward toward the heavens. But always pity brought me back to earth. Echoes of cries of pain reverberate in my heart. Children in famine, victims tortured by oppressors, helpless old people a hated burden to their sons, and the whole world of loneliness, poverty, and pain make a mockery of what human life should be. I long to alleviate the evil, but I cannot, and I too suffer.

—Bertrand Russell

7. Make up a topic with three subtopics, supporting ideas, and supporting details, and diagram it following the pattern used in exercise 6. Your topic might be "My Neighborhood," "My College," or "Sports."

Writing Exercise

Write a summary of this chapter. Make sure you include a discussion of how the topic, the key idea, the supporting ideas, and supporting details are related to each other. To make your point, you will probably need to include a brief example. (Turn to p. 46 if you need more information on writing summaries.)

III Reading Efficiently

There is always a reason that you read, even though you may not be aware of it. This is just as true if you are sitting at breakfast, idly reading the cereal box because you haven't anything else to read; if you sit down to study and learn; or if you turn with pleasure to a recommended novel. Behind each act of reading is a purpose: to pass the time, to learn, to be amused or entertained. The way you read reflects your purpose. The amount of time you give to your reading and the ways you think about what you are reading are prescribed by the use you intend to make of it.

To be an efficient reader, you must consciously link how you read with why you are reading. Why and how you read depend on what you already know about the topic and what you hope or need to get from your reading. Thinking about the topic and what you already know about it associates what you are about to learn with what you have learned. Association produces greater understanding and better retention. Association also is a good basis for predicting what you will find in the reading. Purpose, association, and prediction enable you to be more precise in asking questions of your reading. The more thoughtful your questions, the more efficient your reading.

Efficient readers are also flexible readers—people who read different things in different ways depending on their purposes. The four approaches to reading and the strategies of previewing, skimming, and sectioning will help you to be a flexible reader by adjusting how you read to why and what you are reading.

7 Setting Your Purpose, Associating, and Predicting

With your basic reading questions in place, you can now think about your purpose in reading a particular selection. The next preview question—*Why am I reading this?*—leads you to think about what your reading task is and what you want or expect to get from it. The answer to your question will tell you why you are reading what you are reading and also something about how you will read it.

Closely linked to *Why am I reading this?* is your answer to the preview question *What do I already know about this topic?* What you need or want to get from a reading depends to a great extent on your previous knowledge of the topic. Associating what you already know about a topic with what you are about to read will also help you to understand and remember what you have read and to predict what the author might say about the topic.

Setting Your Purpose

Thinking about why you do anything helps you to define your purpose and forces you to articulate for yourself a reason for doing it. Often this thinking tells you how the current task fits into your larger scheme. For instance, as a possible business major, you read an accounting text both to learn how to do accounting and to pass the course. Your immediate purpose in reading the accounting text is joined to your long-term goal of finishing college and finding a place for yourself in the world.

To learn as much as you can from your accounting course, you need to think about what you hope to get out of the text used in the course. Is the text the basis for the course? Why must you do this particular assignment? How does this assignment relate to the last assignment? Is it something you need to read in depth, or is it something you can look through quickly, noting only the key ideas? What questions will you ask yourself as you read?

You can judge how to read an assignment when you know why you are reading it. If your purpose is to do a chemistry experiment or assemble some apparatus for a physics problem, you will read the instructions about the procedure very carefully, for each step matters. If you are looking for a particular piece of information, you may have to skim through several publications to find it. If you are reading about the drought in Africa for a sociology course, your principal concern will be how the drought affects the people: What are the mortality rates? What is happening to the family or tribal unit? On what basis is aid being distributed? and so on. If you read the same article for an economics course, your questions will have more to do with what caused the drought, and what effect it is having on the economy, the labor force, the balance of payments, and exports and imports. In an election year an independent voter will read the various parties' platforms very carefully so as to be able to come to some decision. People who are already convinced will probably look over the arguments quickly just to see what they are and maybe the ways in which their preconceptions are confirmed. The difference in interest produces a difference in emphasis and influences how each of two people read the same article.

Efficient reading requires you to be very active in defining your purpose, pursuing it, and limiting yourself to achieving it. An efficient reader doesn't take the time to read every word of every reading list. Given the demands on your time, instructors do not expect you to read word by word everything they assign, but they do expect you to read with intelligence and discrimination. Selecting what is relevant to your task and letting the irrelevant go constitute the art of efficient reading.

Example

In a European history course the instructor has been lecturing on the factors that contributed to the strengthening of Germany after World War II. Three articles have been assigned as supplementary reading: "The German Miracle," "Currency Reform and Industrialization in Postwar Germany," and "The Marshall Plan and German Recovery." Why do you think these articles were assigned? An obvious, but vague answer might be: To learn more about what went on in Germany at that time. A more precise definition of why you are reading the assignment will lead to more relevant questions.

If you are reading to amplify your knowledge of the subject that your instructor has been dealing with, you might be seeking answers to these questions:

- What was the currency reform?
- How did it contribute to the strengthening of postwar Germany?
- What was its relationship to industrialization?
- What was the Marshall Plan?
- How did it strengthen postwar Germany?
- What was its relationship to industrialization?

But suppose it is clear that your instructor thinks the Marshall Plan had little to do with German recovery and has assigned the articles to give you a different point of view. You would read the three articles to learn the three authors' views about the Marshall Plan and German recovery. But first you need to ask,

- Why does my instructor think the Marshall Plan had little to do with the postwar strengthening of Germany?

Your instructor might not have had time to explain fully the details of the currency reform, so you will read to learn more, to go beyond what has been covered in class by asking questions like these:

- What was the currency reform?
- How did it work?
- Who was affected?

Or your instructor has asked you to compare the views of author X with author Y. Here you would take notes on the views of the separate authors and then compare them by asking where and why they differed.

In each of these situations you will be asking different questions and looking for different answers. Thinking about your reading in these ways helps you to know why you are reading the material and what you hope to gain from it.

What Do You Already Know About the Topic?

An apocryphal story that is sometimes told about John Stuart Mill and sometimes about Edward Gibbon makes a relevant point. It seems that whenever one of these great minds decided to read a book, he thought about its topic for several days, trying to remember everything he could about the subject matter involved, and formulated questions based on what he knew and what he didn't know about it. The result of this practice was that when he started to read, his mind was totally engaged by the topic, his questions were ready, and a foundation for the new concepts or information he would get from his reading was already in place. It seems our minds are like a reef, which is built by the skeletons of tiny coral, each adding a minute encrustation to the base laid down by previous generations. The reef grows and grows and grows. You, too, can prepare for your reading by asking the next preview question, *What do I already know about this topic?*

Associating

When you think about what you have previously learned about a topic, your mind is **associating** the topic with what you know about it. This process relates your purpose in reading something to what you know about it, because your previous knowledge will define the questions you will ask. For example, in connection with a course on nineteenth-century English literature, you have been asked to read the article in *The Encyclopedia Britannica* on Charles Dickens. You don't know much about Dickens, but you do know that his novels deal with the social problems of his day. Therefore, your questions might explore this topic further. Who exactly was Dickens? What was his social milieu during his youth and later in life? What social or political attitudes did he have? What did he think he was trying to achieve through his writing?

Association also plays a very important part in the learning process. Learning takes place when you add a new idea or piece of information to what you already know. Relating the new to the old and finding the connections between them make the new familiar; once something has become familiar, you can understand it and use it.

As students you are constantly enlarging your foundation of knowledge and ideas. The broader the base, the easier it becomes to make connections and see relationships. Eventually you become sophisticated students, students who can quickly grasp new ideas, recognize the relationships, and move on to discuss or create new relationships that are, in effect, "original" ideas.

It is important for you to learn—to learn facts and to learn from your own and others' experiences. The more you know, the more you have to relate to new information and new ideas. Let's take a concrete example. If you know what a mammal is and someone tells you that a whale is a mammal, you can compare a whale to other mammals and know that this creature breathes air and produces live young, which it nurses. You can go on to contrast a whale with a fish, because you know something about fish. Whales breath air directly through blowholes; fish filter air from water by means of gills. With this knowledge as a base you can ask other questions about the whale: How does it breathe? How did a mammal end up in the ocean? How does the brain of a whale compare to that of other mammals? Thinking about the whale as a mammal, listing its attributes, and understanding the difference between a whale and a fish are far more likely to make this information stick in your mind than if you quickly read it in a book and thought no more about it. The philosopher and psychologist William James said, "The more other facts a fact is associated with in the mind, the better possession of it our memory retains."

When you consciously refer to your knowledge base, you can be prepared to receive new ideas and information and can make associations faster. Your art history course, for example, makes more sense because you can associate it with what you learned in a history survey course; an American literature course is more meaningful when you know something about the setting in which the authors were writing; and the information contained in a personnel manual is greatly enhanced when you know some of the psychology on which it is based. Associating new material to what you already know builds understanding and knowledge. It is a process that never ends.

Understanding

A thorough understanding involves being able to use the new bit of knowledge, whether it is a word, a formula, or a concept. The best way for you to demonstrate to yourself that you have this understanding is to write, or perhaps draw, what you understand. Use the new word in a sentence; write the new concept in your own words; draw a diagram or write an outline of the relationships that emerge from the new formula; or try to explain it to someone else. Be active. Don't cheat yourself by allowing yourself to pretend you understand when you really don't. Such practices build very shaky foundations that will collapse all too easily when put to a test. If you can't use your new learning because you don't understand it, go to a person who does: the instructor, the teaching assistant, a tutor, or a fellow student.

Asking the preview question *What do I already know about this topic?* is an important step toward gaining an understanding. The next questions that arise might be:

- How does what I already know about it relate to what the reading contains?
- How does what I am reading now relate to what I read yesterday by a different author?
- Can I find the key idea?
- Do I understand it?
- Can I diagram this information?
- Can I rephrase it in my own words?

When you have trained yourself to use this approach to your reading, you will see that you can also apply these questions to the experience of learning in class. Take a few minutes before the class starts, perhaps when you are walking to the classroom or driving to the campus, to think about what you have already learned in that course and, in particular, what you learned from the last class. Review the reading you did for this class by going over the key ideas in your head. These techniques will prepare you for the class, and your mind will be ready to integrate the new information or ideas that you will be exposed to. At the end of the class you can check yourself out in the same way by answering these questions:

- What were the two or three main points made in this class?
- Do I understand them?
- Can I relate them to something else?

You will remember what went on in that class because the new ideas and information have been made part of your store of knowledge. Experts agree that no technique works better to establish information securely in your memory than association and active review.

Example

Chapter 13 of a textbook, *The American Communications Industry*, is entitled "Television Advertising." How can asking the preview question *What do I already know about this topic?* help you as you approach Chapter 13?

What do you know about television advertising?

First, from your experience of looking at television, you know there's a lot of advertising. You may also know that certain programs seem to attract a certain kind of advertising: Football games draw beer and truck ads, but soap operas are accompanied by ads for detergents and diapers. Does this say something about what kinds of advertising are considered appropriate for certain kinds of programs?

Second, some of the sections of the previous chapter were about the economics of the television industry and its financial framework. Reviewing this information might be useful in thinking about how advertising brings in revenue.

Finally, perhaps you have a friend who gets odd jobs acting in television commercials. Your friend has told you something about how the commercials are cast.

When you put all this information together, you find that you do, indeed, know quite a lot about television advertising. You are reading now to relate what you are about to learn with what you already know by asking specific questions: How are decisions made about which television ads are shown when? What is the influence of television advertising on programming? What are the connections among television shows, the commercials, and the advertising agencies?

The relating of new information to old will make it meaningful to you so that it can be more quickly added to your knowledge. You will remember it because you understand and know it.

Predicting What the Author Is Going to Say

In a modern morality story, James Black is a smart businessperson who thinks very carefully before he goes into an important meeting. He knows his job may depend on knowing not only what he is talking about, but also what his associates will be talking about. He takes a good look at the agenda for the meeting so as to know what is coming up; then he tries to remember what he knows about that topic so as to be well prepared for the discussion. His previewing may also reveal what he doesn't know about the topic under discussion and what he needs to study up on. James also gives careful thought to the other personalities who will be at the meeting so that he can anticipate what to expect from them. What point of view will Sam Brown have on this subject? Does James agree with him? Why or why not? How about the president of the company? What kind of information is she going to want—budget figures, production figures, sales figures, market forecasts? Where does this kind of thinking put James, as compared to Sam, who rushed into the meeting direct from a late lunch? It is obvious which of the two is more apt to be successful.

Good predicting can give you an edge over the competition, but, even better, such thinking prepares you for what is to come.

Predicting is based on two kinds of questions: questions that develop from the way you have prepared yourself by questioning what your purpose is and what you already know about the topic and the author and questions that arise from the clues, such as chapter and section headings, that you have picked up in your preview. Among the questions you might ask are these:

- Might the author have a point of view or position on the topic?
- Does this author agree with the person whose article I read on the same subject yesterday?
- What particular pieces of information will the author deal with? What kind of supporting information will the author use?

Example

Let's use these questions to predict what we can about the following article.

You start to think about what you already know about it by previewing for the topic. The title tells you that it is about "the desexing of English." But what does that mean? It doesn't say "the English," so it must refer to the English language, not English people. But what is "desexing"?

You continue your preview by finding the author's key idea, which seems to be stated in the first sentence and confirms your guess about the title: The time has come to ask whether the crusade of the women's-rights movement to purge the English language of sexism has been successful.

When you ask yourself what you already know about desexing the English language, you find you know that some people are conscious enough of sexism in the language to try to make some changes, like "Ms." or "s/he." In your college they may even have stopped using the term "freshman," referring instead to "first-year students."

What do you think the author's point of view might be, and how do you think he will deal with this topic? As an editor of *The World Book Dictionary*, he is probably interested mainly in words, not politics, so maybe he will take a fairly objective view. No doubt Sol Steinmetz will use examples to discuss what effect these changes have had on the language and whether or not sexism has been eradicated from the English language.

The Desexing of English

1   After a dozen years of aggressive campaigning by the women's-rights movement to purge the English language of sexism, the time has surely come to ask whether its crusade has been successful. From the start, resistance to the

campaign was surprisingly mild, confined mainly to facetious comments in the press on the proliferation of "person" compounds (chairperson, spokesperson) and the elimination of "man" in occupational titles (camera operator, mail carrier). But despite frequent references to these developments in the popular press, one vainly looks in recent books on language for a serious discussion of the subject. (A book that specifically addresses this subject is "Words and Women" by Casey Miller and Kate Swift, which was published in 1977.)

2   To take one example, in Jim Quinn's "American Tongue and Cheek: A Populist Guide to Our Language" (1981), a provocative book that lays to rest many a myth about English grammar, a full chapter is devoted to "Language Changers," people such as ghetto blacks, teen-agers and influential intellectuals whose speech and writings leave their stamp on the language. Yet in this chapter, and for that matter in the entire book, no mention is made of the influence on language of the antisexist movement. I could list at least six other recent books on language whose authors are guilty of the same omission. The authors, incidentally, are all males and I leave it to the reader to draw his or her own conclusions.

3   Note that I have just used "his or her." My choice of this phrase to avoid using the so-called generic pronoun "his" is directly due to the influence of the antisexist campaign. My study of new usages during the past 10 years has convinced me that a good many similar changes have made their way into the writing and speech of many Americans. The changes have been wide-ranging, affecting not only our stock of common words but such diverse areas of language as forms of address, proper names, phrases and idioms, word endings and grammatical constructions.

4   Writers, editors and educators in particular have become acutely self-conscious about using words and phrases implying sexual bias. Their consciousness, to use a phrase introduced by the feminists, has been raised. In the introduction to a 1979 book on words and their misuse, the writer William Woolfolk laments that there is no appropriate formal salutation in English for a letter addressed to both a man and a woman. He toys with "Dear Gentlepeople" and "Dear Gentlepersons," but cannot get himself to use either. Then he recalls that we also don't have a word for "his or her" or for "brothers and sisters together" (he considers "siblings" inadequate). For him and many others, there are suddenly pitfalls everywhere: Should one use "housewife" or the less natural "homemaker"? Will "actor" do the service of "actress," and "hero" that of "heroine"? Is it all right to use the awkward "humankind" in place of "mankind"?

5   Guidelines issued by various groups to promote nonsexist usage make the going tougher by proposing alternatives like "of human origin" or "synthetic" to replace "man-made," and urging the abolition of certain emotionally loaded words such as "womanish," "effeminate," "manly," and "man-size." For the benefit of people like Mr. Woolfolk, Webster's Secretarial Handbook (1976) lists "Dear People" and "Dear Sir, Madam, or Ms."

as possible nonsexist letter salutations for groups that include men and women.

6   But there is more. The Government's Dictionary of Occupational Titles (1977) has purged itself of all "sex and age-referent language and job titles considered to be potentially discriminatory." You won't find in it such homely old words as "shoeshine boy" (now "shoe shiner"), "bellboy" (now only "bellhop"), "cleaning woman" (now "cleaner"), "washerwoman" or "laundress" (now "laundry worker"), to mention a few. Not to be outdone, the General Accounting Office Thesaurus (1978) has replaced "manned undersea research" with "oceanographic research" and "manpower management" with "personnel management," among others.

7   While in the 1970's cyclones were still designated by female names (Hurricane Edith, Typhoon Hester), by 1980 alternating male and female names became the standard (Hurricane Frederic, Typhoon Judy). And in 1980, in an editorial entitled "Gender Justice," The New York Times congratulated the members of the Supreme Court for dropping the title "Mr. Justice" from their orders and opinions and adopting the unadorned title "Justice So-and-So." Of course, they will no longer be called "the Brethren."

8   Opponents of such deliberate tampering with the language—liberals and conservatives alike—might well argue that by allowing this to happen we are in effect exchanging one set of taboos for another. For even as books, periodicals and dictionaries (not all, to be sure) are liberally opening their pages to obscenities and vulgarisms, they are unliberally leaning over backward to ostracize all usage deemed offensive to the sexes. Some might call this blatant hypocrisy. Others might view it as the expression of a new morality. Yet, strangely, nary a voice is raised anywhere in either protest or praise. And this great silence seems to me to imply that the matter has been settled already in the minds of most people, and that the feminist campaign against sexism has made a triumphant breakthrough in the area of language.

9   If this is so, we are confronting for the first time since the 18th century the success of a small but vocal group of activists bent on reforming the English language. While attempts to reform English go back to the Middle Ages, no previous or subsequent reforms have matched those of the 18th century grammarians and lexicographers, who promulgated most of the rules and prescriptions that have come down to us enshrined as laws in innumerable English grammars and textbooks.

10   After this successful "fixing" of the language, further attempts at reformation met with invariable failure. The public, resentful of extreme innovations in what it now regarded as an immutable language, rejected the simplified spelling systems widely advocated in the 19th century, just as it rejected artificial languages for international use, and even a simplified form of the English language such as Basic English.

11   How to account, then, for the success of the antisexist reforms? Part of the answer is that these reforms have been long in the making and that present social conditions merely helped to bring them to fruition. As long

ago as 1858 the composer Charles Converse coined the word "thon" (a contraction of "that one") as a neuter pronoun to replace the generic "he," and this coinage was actually entered in two unabridged dictionaries: in Funk & Wagnalls in 1913; in Webster's Second Edition, 1934. 🖋

12   There have been many similar proposals since then, the latest being the orthographic "he/she," which is more widely used than is generally realized. It is also not generally known that the recently defeated equal rights amendment was first introduced in Congress in 1923, and that the title "Ms." was in use in the 1940's.

13   But the real answer might simply be that the feminist movement's interest in language is ultimately not linguistic but moral. Its concern is not with changing the language itself, but with modifying that part of it that is discriminatory and morally offensive. The feminists' crusade appeals particularly to those who deplore and wish to eliminate other "wrong" uses of language, such as racial epithets and opprobrious terms.

14   The feminist cause also touches a responsive chord in individuals who believe, along with the American linguists Edward Sapir and Benjamin Lee Whorf, that the structure of a language influences and often shapes a person's view of reality. For them, a language that is structurally biased against one of the sexes can inflict serious psychic damage to members of that sex. This argument is as hard to prove as it is to disprove, but to many people it makes profound psychological sense.

15   Twelve years is a short time. It is too early to predict the future course of the feminist movement and its reforms. Suffice it to recognize that the anti-sexist movement has made remarkable inroads in the language. But even from the worm's-eye view we now possess, it seems fairly clear that the "King's English" will no longer be his exclusive domain.

—Sol Steinmetz, general editor of The World Book Dictionary

Exercises

1. Preview the following article, "Japan's Two Economic Miracles" by answering these questions:

   What is this article about?
   What is the most important idea the author has about the topic?
   Why are you reading it?
   What are three things you already know about the Japanese economy?
   By referring to your answers to the questions and looking for clues in the section headings, what do you predict the authors might say about the Japanese economy?

Japan's
Two Economic Miracles

1   The existing system of international economic relations—the old international economic order—has come under economic attack as an exclusive club run by the industrial countries of North America, Western Europe, and Japan for their own benefit, with its rules rigged to make it almost impossible for outsiders to share its benefits. For example, workers from poor countries cannot immigrate freely into rich countries, and the products of their cheap labor are imported freely into rich countries only if they do not compete with these countries' products.

2   If we examine the historical record, however, there is one country that has risen from the ranks of the underdeveloped to the ranks of the industrial countries without being heavily populated by people of European origin. That country is Japan.

3   Japan has experienced not one but two "economic miracles" during the period since 1853, when Commodore Matthew C. Perry and his American naval squadron forced Japan to open itself to the West against its own will. The first was a miracle of *development* during the Meiji Era (1868–1912, between the end of the American Civil War and the beginning of World War I). The second economic miracle has been a miracle of *reconstruction* following Japan's defeat in World War II and the destruction of some 25 percent of the country's total stock of physical capital, and seven years of American occupation (1945–1952). We shall examine each period in turn, with special attention to the *international economics* of each miracle.

4   These miracles occurred despite the lack of certain aids to growth. Japan had few natural resources in 1853, and many of those that Japan had then are depleted or inadequate today. Nor was the population sparse in relation to the available resources. Japan's population in 1853 was 30 million (in an area slightly smaller than the state of California). Its 1981 population was estimated at 118.5 million, or 52 percent of the American population (including Alaska and Hawaii). In Japan during the Meiji Era, there was no foreign aid at all, and its few loans from abroad were all on a strictly commercial basis.[1] Japan was never a colony, but "unequal treaties" with the Western powers established foreign concessions in various "treaty ports" until 1899, and limited Japan's import tariffs to the 5 percent level.

---

1. One of these financed Japan's first railway, which covered the 25 miles between Tokyo and Yokohama.

The First Miracle

5   How could Japan rise over the 45-year Meiji Era to become an important world economic power? We shall explain Japan's success in terms of the availability of human capital, the opportunity to develop it further, access to world markets to import the materials Japan lacked, a government that desired economic growth and was proud of it for both civilian and military reasons, and a population more willing (or more compelled) than others to sacrifice consumption and to work hard.

6   ***The Pre-Meiji Era.***   In the words of Adam Smith the three requisites of economic growth are "peace, easy taxes, and a tolerable administration of justice." Japan under the Tokugawa family of Grand Marshals (Shoguns) had the great advantage of 250 years of peace before Commodore Perry's arrival. To ensure and preserve this peace, Japan had isolated itself for 200 years of that period,[2] except for Nagasaki Harbor, where a little trade was carried on with the Dutch and Chinese. Of course, any major European power might have forced its way in, but Japan was at "the end of the line" from Europe, much farther than India or China. Also, there was little to attract Europeans there when they were busy fighting each other and colonizing the Americas, the Indies, Siberia, and so on.[3]

7   Japan's cultural tradition was also in its favor. While preserving a fierce national pride in "things Japanese," the Japanese had shown themselves unusually willing and able to learn from foreigners—from the Chinese in earlier times and more recently from the Europeans during the "Christian Century" and from the Dutch in Nagasaki. The assimilation of Western products and processes was therefore easier for the Japanese than for any other Asian country. The Japanese were also relatively literate. During the period of Tokugawa peace, they had developed a wide range of both fine arts and everyday handicrafts, as well as harbors, schools, and even roads.

8   Japan was also fortunate in the early rise of its silk industry, since exports of silk and silk fabrics financed nearly 40 percent of

---

2. This isolation policy followed a "Christian Century" (1540–1640 approximately) of contact with Europeans, especially Spaniards and Portuguese, whom the Tokugawa Shoguns came to suspect of the desire to take over the country.

3. In the twenty years after Perry's visit, Japan was still weak, but the Westerners were busy elsewhere. Examples were the Crimean War, the unifications of Germany and Italy, the Indian Mutiny, the American Civil War, and the French effort to set up a Mexican Empire. It was thus relatively easy to avoid becoming a colony or being divided into spheres of foreign influence.

Japan's imports in the Meiji Era. Had rayon and nylon existed in the late nineteenth century, Japanese economic history would have been decidedly different. The rise of silk as Japan's staple export industry was also aided by the misfortunes of rival silk producers—silkworm disease in France and Italy, and a great civil war, the so-called Taiping Rebellion, in Central China.

9   ***Economic Policies in the Meiji Era.***   We date the Meiji Era from 1868, when Tokugawa rule was overthrown in a near-bloodless revolution, giving the fifteen-year-old Meiji Emperor a new set of advisers. They were the so-called "Meiji statesmen," revered in Japan like the "founding fathers" in the United States. Because these men all feared the fate of India, which became a British dependency, or of China, which had been divided into areas of foreign dominance, they made a number of wise economic decisions.

10   For example, they not only displaced a dominant military caste (the so-called *samurai*) but successfully transformed the members of this class into policemen, teachers, bureaucrats, and business people while opening the higher ranks of the armed services to people of other classes.

11   The Meiji statesmen also devised a system of pilot plants, especially in textiles and shipbuilding. The government established such plants and bore the losses involved in adapting them to Japanese conditions. Then after the "teething troubles" had been overcome, and after skilled Japanese workers had been trained, these plants not only became models for private industry in general but were themselves sold (usually at substantial losses) to favored private companies.

12   These leaders provided Japan with a financial system that kept inflation under reasonable control. During the Meiji Era, the price level approximately doubled, a mild inflation rate by later standards, and the inflation process was itself interrupted by periods of deflation, particularly in the late 1880s.

13   Another of the Meiji policies was a regressive fiscal system, based mainly on taxes levied on agricultural land and improvements. This system has been faulted for falling most heavily on the poor peasants in the countryside. At the same time, however, it provided for public capital formation, estimated at over 40 percent of the total investment of the Meiji Era—or more than half if military capital in the form of arsenals, navy yards, war ships, and the like, is included. This capital went largely into the social and military underpinnings of development. Higher education and technical training played especially important parts as well.

14   While building up more military and naval strength than proved really necessary to repel foreign aggression, the Meiji

statesmen resisted for over 25 years all temptations to engage in costly military adventures overseas. When they did expand to the Asian continent, the expansion was primarily into the Korean peninsula, which the Japanese saw as a possible springboard for invasion of Japan by some Russo-Chinese alliance. (Japanese expansion into China proper came only later.)

15   ***The Open World Economy.***   We have left to the last a neglected aspect of Japanese growth, namely, the openness of the world economy. By building up export industries on a cheap-labor basis, Japan was able to increase exports enough to purchase from abroad the essential food[4] and raw materials needed for the people and the economy. Free trade was not the rule, except in Great Britain, but tariffs were low. Also, "cheap coolie labor" and "unfair competition" arguments against Japanese exports were ineffective. The old international economic order, then, helped Japanese growth rather than slowing it down. But this was the pre-1914 economic order. Had Meiji Japan been faced with our present structure of tariffs, quotas, and administrative protection, it is very doubtful whether its history would have been a success story, let alone an economic miracle.

The Second Miracle

16   Only a generation elapsed between the end of the first miracle of development and the beginning of the second miracle of reconstruction—which eventually went far beyond mere reconstruction!

17   The main source of the second miracle seems also to have been human capital—the volume of inexpensive labor, much of it now highly educated, trained, and skilled, released into the civilian economy from the armed forces, the war industries, and the short-lived Japanese Empire overseas, mainly in Korea and North China.

18   ***The American Contribution.***   Another gain from the restoration of peace was the availability of foreign, particularly American, civilian technology. Japan had fallen far behind during its concentration on military expansion. With human capital available, the catching-up process was much faster than most observers had expected it to be.

19   The Japanese postwar inflation, which raised prices in 1948 to 300 times their levels of 1936, of course had a disruptive effect.

---

4. Japan was self-supporting in rice until about 1890.

But it had one important benefit as well. It permitted Japanese firms in war industries to pay off their debts in inflated yen. Without the inflation, these firms would have been bankrupted when the American occupation forces forbade the Japanese government to pay for materials supplied during the last months of the war.

20   Nor should we forget the role of American aid, partly in outright gifts and partly in low-interest loans. The total amount was $2 billion. This aid warded off large-scale famine during 1945–1947. Later on, it included machinery, which restored Japanese productive capacity in a number of industries, especially textiles.[5]

21   ***After Independence.***   After the end of the American occupation in 1952, and the accompanying end of American aid, there remained some doubt that Japan could balance its international payments without some slowdown in the improvement of its living standard. However, "special procurement" of both civilian and military supplies for United Nations forces in Korea, and later for American efforts in Indochina, helped to ease the transition to complete independence for the Japanese. By the late 1950s, Japan no longer needed such support, and took off on Premier Hayato Ikeda's program for doubling the national income in the decade of the 1960s. In fact, the doubling took only seven years. The planning had been too modest!

22   ***World Trade Effects.***   On the international economic front, postwar Japan faced quite different market situations in North America, in Western Europe, and in the Third World. The North American markets were relatively open for a long time. However, North America, including both Canada and the United States, has tended to restrict Japanese exports as Japanese competition has become stronger, especially in periods of recession, despite the increasing volume of Japan's raw material and agricultural imports. The restrictions have taken the form primarily of "voluntary" agreements by the Japanese to restrict their exports of an increasing range of products. Western Europe, which was racing with Japan to recover from the damage of World War II, has tended toward extreme and discriminatory hostility toward Japanese exports.

---

5. The wartime Allied plan had been to build up China as a replacement for the Japanese "workshop of Asia," and also as a showpiece of capitalism. Much Japanese equipment was to be transferred, primarily to China but also to the Philippines and other Southeast Asian nations that Japan had occupied. These plans were reversed when it became obvious that General Chiang Kai-shek would not win the Chinese Civil War with Mao Zedong's Communists, or restore peace to the Chinese Mainland.

The Third World countries have taken positions somewhere in between. Those with positive trade balances with Japan, due to raw material exports, tend to cooperate with Japanese efforts. So do those desirous of attracting Japanese capital. On the other hand, many LDCs would prefer to build up finished and skilled-labor-intensive products like steel rather than raw materials like iron ore or coal. Also, Japanese investors, especially the large multinational companies, have not been much more popular in their host countries than have American or European ones.

23   It would again appear that the existing international economic order, especially its open-economy aspects, has helped rather than hindered Japanese recovery and growth. If the whole world had adopted the anti-Japanese policies of the European Community, it is doubtful that the recovery could have succeeded at all. After the oil and other shocks of the early 1970s, the failure of Japanese economic growth to resume its "miraculous" pace of the 1960s can be blamed in large part on the increasing protectionism of Japan's other trading partners, including the United States.[6]

24   Of course, there is strong protectionist sentiment in Japan itself. Japan has erected trade barriers, mainly in the form of administrative protection, for the benefit of new industries like automobiles and computers, for old industries like textiles to ease the phasing-out process, and also for agriculture in order to avoid becoming even more dependent on distant foreign countries for basic foodstuffs. However, Japan continues to gain rather than lose on balance from the maintenance of the existing economic order in its present, or a freer, form.

—Martin Bronfenbrenner, Werner Sichel, and Wayland Gardner

2. In this exercise you are to work with a partner. Through your questions try to help each other to be as precise as possible about what your purposes in reading may be, what you already know about the topic, and what you predict the author will say.

   Each of you should think of two pieces of reading you are going to undertake either because they are assigned or simply because you want to.

---

6. There are other reasons as well: Japan had at least caught up with Western technology; shortages of labor were developing; the high cost of energy affected Japan as much as, or more than any other country; investment was being shifted to environmental protection, to residential housing, and to "welfare state" institutions rather than being concentrated, as previously, in the construction of "factories, factories, and factories."

Discuss your purposes in reading by asking and answering these questions:

Why am I reading it?
Why was it assigned? or
Why do I want to read it?
How might it be useful to me?

State three things you already know about the author and the topic.
Predict some of the points the author will make.
Think of five questions relevant to the text you are about to read.

Writing Exercise

Once again you are asked to write a brief summary of a chapter. In this summary you should state your purpose in writing a summary and mention the benefits to be gained by asking the question *What do I already know about the topic?*

Questioning

Chapter 7 has added two preview questions to the two that you already know. The four preview questions you can now use for all your reading are

What is this about?
What is the author's most important idea about the topic?
Why am I reading this?
What do I already know about the topic?

8 Previewing a Textbook, Chapter, or Article

You can orient yourself to your reading by clearly defining the purpose of your reading task, relating what you already know to what you are about to learn, seeking out the organization of your reading material, and getting a sense of the author's point of view. Previewing textbooks and other course materials, such as the course outline (syllabus) and supplementary readings, starts the process of understanding.

Previewing a Textbook

You have been learning to preview all along. In Chapter 4 you learned your first preview question, which helped you to find the topic: *What is this about?* Chapter 5 discussed the second preview question, *What is the author's most important idea about the topic?* In Chapter 7 you learned the utility of defining your own reading purpose, relating what you already know about the topic to what you are about to learn, and predicting what the author will say. Previewing—asking yourself these questions—can help you to see how your textbook or supplementary reading fits into the course and how chapters from a textbook fit into the whole book.

Most textbooks are organized to make previewing an easy task. Much information can be quickly located in parts of the text you may not ordinarily read. For instance, the topic can be found in a quick survey of the title, preface or introduction, and table of contents. The key idea of the book can also be found in the preface or introduction, table of contents, or the first and last chapters of the book. The author's reason for writing the book will usually be stated in the preface or introduction. The supporting ideas can be found by previewing the individual chapters. When previewing, you don't need to read for the supporting details; these should be left for a later reading.

Example

To get a better sense of how to apply the preview questions, let's take a look at the textbook *Meteorology: The Earth and Its Weather* by Joseph S. Weisberg.

What Is This Textbook About?   A glance at the title will provide the obvious answer: It's about meteorology. But the author further defines the topic by including a subtitle, *The Earth and Its Weather*.

What Is the Author's Most Important Idea About the Topic?   Authors usually use the preface as an opportunity to speak directly and personally to the reader. It is here that the author states the thesis and discusses the most important aspects of the book. Therefore, look at the preface first for the answer to this question.

You can see in the preface that "Weather is not constant. Change is inevitable, continuous, and all-pervasive." The author continues, "This text emphasizes the interchange of energy between the various realms of the Earth—gaseous, solid, and liquid—and the effects of these interchanges." From this you can guess that the key idea is that change in weather is caused by interchanges of energy. In the preface

Professor Weisberg states several other things about his book that he thinks are important: specifically, the effects of the ocean on climatic changes, biometeorology (the effects of human beings on weather and climate), and the way in which the various elements of weather—temperature, pressure, wind, moisture, and solar energy—operate and relate to one another.

Like many students, you probably haven't extracted such important information from the preface because you may not have thought it was worth reading. You may have thought that the preface consists of nothing more than acknowledgments thanking all the people who had a part in writing the book. Yet the preface is often one of the most valuable parts of the book, although usually it is not part of the required reading for the course.

Why Did the Author Write the Book?   By reading the title page, you can tell that the author teaches at Jersey City State College; it is a safe assumption that he is an expert in the subject of meteorology. An author's preface or introduction often states the author's objective in writing the book. Here you can expect to find a statement of what the author hoped to achieve by writing the book, why the book is different from other books in the field, what the author emphasizes, and how the book is organized. Let's see what Professor Weisberg says in his preface on page 83.

In the preface Professor Weisberg states that he wants to discuss the applications of meteorology to human affairs and the effect of the ocean on climatic changes. You can conclude that he thinks these topics are important and you should be conscious of them as you read because these topics will probably run as a theme throughout the text.

Why Am I Reading This?   This preview question will be answered somewhat differently by every reader. However, when it is applied to reading a textbook, we can assume that you are reading the text because you are taking the course and that you are taking the course because you want to learn about meteorology. Of course, the reasons go deeper than that. If you are a farmer or like to fly or want to major in broadcasting, you will have very specific reasons for taking meteorology. Even if you can't be so specific, trying to state a reason for taking this course over other courses will help you to set a purpose for your reading.

What Do I Already Know About This Topic?   All of us know at least something about the weather, if only because so much of what we do depends on it. Your experience with the weather gives you a great

Preface

1   This second edition of *Meteorology: The Earth and Its Weather* is designed for introductory-level meteorology courses for nonscience students. It offers a nonmathematical introduction to modern meteorology and features many applications of meteorology to human affairs. In this edition, the coverage of a broad range of basic topics has been updated and expanded. The text now offers 13 chapters instead of 11, with the final two chapters devoted to climate. The second edition, like the first, reflects my feeling that other texts do not deal adequately with the effects of the ocean on climatic changes. This book discusses biometeorology and human beings' inadvertent effects on weather and climate, with special attention to the legal and commercial aspects of weather modification.

2   The re-ordering, revision, and expansion of topics in this edition is based on input from many users—teachers and students—of the first edition. In particular, analysis of weather, effects of the ocean on weather, atmospheric stability, and weather modification receive increased coverage. The text has been entirely rewritten to make it as readable, straightforward, and interesting as possible for the reader who does not have a background in science. At the end of each chapter is a "Weather in the News" story that highlights the role of weather in current or historical events, or provides practical information about lightning, hurricanes, blizzards, and tornadoes. The illustration program has also been expanded and now includes a four-color insert, weather maps and satellite photographs, and weather symbols used, with relevant illustrations.

3   One fact emerges as a universal truth: Weather is not constant. Change is inevitable, continuous, and all-pervasive. This text emphasizes the interchange of energy between the various realms of the Earth—gaseous, solid, and liquid—and the effects of these interchanges.

4   The meteorologist is concerned with a number of factors—those characteristics of air we call the elements of weather: temperature, pressure, wind, moisture, and solar energy. The meteorologist is also concerned with how the various elements operate and relate to one another. The weather forecast, arrived at by using scientific principles, is based on what these relationships imply for a specific place at a future time.

5   Like the first edition, this edition offers a comprehensive set of study aids. Each chapter begins with a chapter outline and concludes with a summary, list of key terms, and review questions. An extensive glossary, an annotated bibliography, and a greatly expanded set of appendices also serve to make the subject accessible to the student. Throughout the text, newly introduced terms are indicated by boldface type. Measurements are given in the English system, followed by their equivalents in the metric system.

6   At the end of each chapter there is a Weather in the News story, to help the reader realize the enormous impact that weather has on all our lives.

7   An instructor's manual accompanies this second edition of *Meteorology*. It contains a bibliography, a list of films, answers to the questions in the book,

suggested objective test items, and—for each chapter—a discussion of the general approach taken.

8   All works of this sort encompass the input of many people and the support of numerous aides and planners. I acknowledge my debt to L.T. Engelhorn, Grossmont College, El Cajon, California, Robert C. King, San Jose City College, and William D. Sellers, University of Arizona, for valuable aid. I especially thank my good friend and colleague, David Letcher, of Trenton State College in Trenton, N.J., for his wisdom and thoughtful suggestions. He reviewed this book throughout the manuscript and proof stages. His sensitivity to beginning students made him particularly helpful in rooting out the inadvertent errors that inevitably occur when a sophisticated science is presented at a basic level. I am also grateful for the assistance of the editorial and art staff at Houghton Mifflin Company. Any flaws that remain in the book—and I trust that they are few—are of course my own responsibility.

—J.S.W.

---

deal of information that you can bring to your reading. For instance, you may have seen a tornado and become curious to know more about how tornadoes form. The fact that you have lived through a tornado will make that part of the book much more interesting to you. All of us have observed clouds, and some of us may have theories about why some clouds look the way they do and what they tell us about the weather. You may be interested in what the chapter on clouds says that will help you predict the weather. Watching the weather report on the television may have made you wonder about what a good forecaster looks for. The more you can apply your previous experience, knowledge, and even guesses to the reading at hand, the more relevant and interesting it will become. The more interesting your reading is, the more meaningful and, thus, the more unforgettable it will be.

How Is the Material Presented?   Your answers to this question are important because they help you to orient yourself to the book by seeing its physical layout and by becoming acquainted with the flow of the author's ideas. There are several places to look for the answers to this question.

First, one may check the preface. In addition to stating the topic and key idea, this preface, like most others, gives information on study aids provided in the text, such as outlines, summaries, key terms, and review questions. The preface also states that the book contains a glossary and various appendices.

Next, consider the table of contents that follows. It also provides

CONTENTS

useful information about the text. You can see that every chapter has a title and is broken down into sections and subsections, each with a title or heading. You know that each chapter will have a topic and a key idea that are supported by the subtopics and supporting ideas taken up in the sections and subsections. You can learn something more about the book if you read the chapter titles. For instance, Where does the book start? How does each chapter relate to the one before and the one after? Do the topics of the chapters build to a conclusion? What do you learn from the fact that of the thirteen chapters in the book, four have the word *atmosphere* in the title?

Take a look at the complete list of chapter titles listed below. These titles can be grouped into sections to get an even better sense of how the topics and subtopics relate to each other.

Chapter titles	Sections
The Atmosphere	
Atmospheric Energy	
Evaporation and Condensation	The relation of the
Atmospheric Stability	atmosphere to weather
The Sea and Energy	
The Dynamic Atmosphere	
Air Masses and Frontal Systems	
Storms	The weather itself
Analyzing the Weather	
Weather and Our Health	
Modifying the Weather	The weather and us
Climate	
Climates of the World	The effects of weather

Third, one may check the text to determine the physical organization of the book.

Just as the author said, each chapter starts with an outline and ends with a summary, key terms, and review questions. You can see that the sections of the text are indicated by headings. The section topics are usually indicated by larger type; subtopics are usually printed in smaller type. In addition, important words and terms are shown by boldface print. These words are defined in the glossary at the back of the book.

You can summarize what you have learned in the short time it has

CHAPTER OUTLINE

AIR STABILITY
Causes of Air Movement
Temperature Inversions
Stable versus Unstable Air
Lapse Rates and Adiabatic Changes
The Adiabatic Chart: Lapse Rates

FORMATION OF CLOUDS
Types of Clouds
Measuring Characteristics of Clouds
Types and Formation of Fog

SUMMARY, KEY TERMS, QUESTIONS

WEATHER IN THE NEWS

As air is heated, the heat energy affects all the individual molecules of air. The air molecules move about and collide with each other. A given parcel of air then rises, and experiences decreasing pressure. These changes are the direct result of (a) the temperature of the air and (b) the attraction gravity has for gases in the atmosphere. Changes in pressure cause air to move, both horizontally and vertically. Vertical movements introduce changes in the physical character of a given air parcel. In turn these changes affect both the degree of heat that is stored in the air and the volume of air that is being affected. In this chapter we shall discuss some of these changes, which are of crucial importance in our daily lives.

Changes in air temperature result from either expansion or contraction of an air parcel as it rises or sinks. Such expansion or contraction affects both (1) the capacity to hold water vapor, and (2) the rate of condensation of water vapor.

The evaporation of water from the Earth's surface plays a vital role in the weather systems that move across the Earth. The daily weather events that make up the overall view we have of local weather from one season to the next are the result of (1) the rate at which condensation or evaporation occurs, and (2) the manner in which changes in temperature of air masses take place. It is these changes in the vertical distribution of air temperature that affect the stability of the air and the vertical movements that result.

AIR STABILITY

The heating and cooling of air and the activity of the jet stream in the upper air levels create vertical air movements. When warm air that is less dense rises, it carries heat upward with it. As it is replaced on the lower levels by cooler, denser air, a convection current is set up. These phenomena are important considerations in the analysis of air movement.

Causes of Air Movement

Stability refers to the manner by which air moves up or down. Changes in temperature within a parcel of air may produce instability within the air parcel. As we have said before, the existence of different temperatures in adjacent parcels of air induces motion.

The dry adiabatic [occurring without gain or loss of heat] lapse rate is what determines whether a given parcel of air will be stable or unstable. If the environmental lapse rate of the air parcel exceeds the dry adiabatic lapse rate, the air is **unstable.** Instability means that the air tends to rise upward because it is warmer and less dense than its surroundings, and displacement causes it to move.

If the environmental lapse rate is less than the adiabatic lapse rate, the air is **stable,** and tends to sink back toward the level from which it was displaced. This air is moved downward because it is colder than its surroundings, and denser.

Neutral air, or neutral stability, is achieved when the air that is being displaced upward, or is moving downward, achieves a temperature similar to that of its surroundings. Its density equals the density of the air surrounding it, motion ceases, and equilibrium is achieved. . . .

SUMMARY

Changes in the temperature of air corresponding to changes in pressure result in differences in density. These changes in density affect the stability of the air. They may lead to air becoming unstable. Air rises when it is less dense than the surrounding air and falls when it is denser than the surrounding air. These movements keep on until the air is neutral, or equal in density to the surrounding air. Normally the temperature of air decreases with height at a rate of 0.65°C/100 m, but as air rises the rate of cooling (in dry air) is 1°C/100 m. In wet air masses, it is 0.5°C/100 m.

Adiabatic changes (mechanical changes) often result in **latent heat** [heat released by a substance undergoing a change of state] being released into rising air parcels. When air masses cool, water vapor or ice may form various types of clouds. These clouds occur at low, middle, and high levels. Clouds may exist from the ground level to more than 8 km (5 mi), in the case of clouds with great vertical development. Clouds forming close to the ground are **fogs.** They occur when (1) radiational cooling reduces the surface temperature, (2) **advection** cools air moving onto cool surfaces, or (3) warm air at frontal surfaces intermingles with cool air.

KEY TERMS

Unstable air
Stable air
Neutral air
Radiational cooling
Stability
Convective motion
Thermals
Adiabatic change
Dry adiabatic lapse rate
Saturation level
Cloud
Lifting condensation level
Latent heat
Wet adiabatic lapse rate
Adiabatic chart
Saturation mixing ratio
Orographic uplift
Cyclone
Genus
Species
Stratus cloud

Cumulus cloud
Nimbus cloud
Scud cloud
Cumulonimbus cloud
Nimbostratus cloud
Altostratus cloud
Cirrus cloud
Cirrostratus cloud
Cirrocumulus cloud
Ceiling
Ceilometer
Cloud cover
Fog
Radiation fog
Ground fog
Advection fog
Sea fog
Upslope fog
Frontal fog
Front
Smog

QUESTIONS

1. What is ceiling? What characteristic does it measure?
2. Describe the manner in which three types of fog form.
3. Describe the major categories of clouds and give two examples of each.
4. Explain the differences between stable, unstable and neutral air. How does a parcel of air behave in each case?
5. How do birds and humans use thermals? How does a thermal form?
6. Define latent heat. How does this affect cooling, moist air?
7. What is the saturation mixing ratio?
8. Why does a dry air mass descending a lee side (opposite side from the wind's origin) of a mountain become warmer than the original moist air at the same height on the windward side of the mountain?
9. Suppose that there is an air parcel located at the surface of the Earth with a temperature of 26°C (79°F), and that the dew point is 11°C (51°F). At what height will condensation occur?
10. What is meant by orographic uplift?

taken us to preview *Meteorology* as follows:

Professor Weisberg of Jersey City State College has written a textbook about how the earth's weather constantly changes because of the effects of interchanges of energy. The author is particularly interested in applications of meteorology to human affairs, the effects of the ocean on climatic change, biometeorology, and the way in which the various elements of weather (temperature, pressure, wind, moisture, and solar energy) interact. Atmosphere seems to play an important role in the phenomenon of weather.

The book begins with a discussion of atmosphere, goes on to the role of the sea, an analysis of storms, people's relationship to weather (health and control), and finally an examination of the climates that weather produces. The book is clearly organized to reveal the main topics and subtopics, and it has useful study aids, particularly chapter summaries and study questions.

This is a lot of information. You have created a context for your reading, and you have some knowledge on which to base your questions. You have a clear sense of what is important and will be able to follow these ideas through the book, relating them to what has come before and anticipating what is to come.

Exercise

This exercise is to be done in pairs. Choose a textbook from one of your courses (or use this textbook). Preview that textbook by answering the following questions. Then discuss your answers with your partner.

> What is the topic of the textbook? Where did you find this information?
>
> What is the key idea of the textbook? Where did you find this information?
>
> Who is the author?
>
> Why did the author write the book?
>
> Does the book have some special features like chapter summaries or a glossary? What are they?
>
> What can you tell from reading the table of contents? Where does the book start? What subtopics are emphasized, and how do they lead up to the conclusion?
>
> Can you group the chapter titles into units? What are they?
>
> What is your answer to *Why am I reading this?*
>
> What do you already know about the topic?

Previewing a Chapter

Just as it is important to preview a book before reading any part of it, so it is necessary to preview a chapter. In this instance, instead of seeing the shape and theme of the whole work, you look to see how one part of a work fits into the larger whole and also how it stands alone.

Most textbook chapters are set up in a way that makes previewing easy. The topic is most often the title of the chapter. But if the topic is not readily apparent from a survey of headings or if there are no headings, look to the introduction (the first four or five paragraphs) and the conclusion or summary. The key idea may also be found in the introduction and the conclusion or summary. Bear in mind that some introductions contain a good preview of the author's topic and key idea, but other introductions serve to provide background material, to create a setting, or simply to spark your interest. Be careful not to assume the key idea too quickly. Check your guess with a glance further on. The concluding paragraph may also provide good clues, but, again, don't depend on it. Check the last four or five paragraphs to verify your guess.

Example

Meteorology: The Earth and Its Weather illustrates how the whole book depends on each chapter and how each chapter is a sequence of sections. The detailed table of contents on page 92 shows not only the title of each chapter, but also the titles of each chapter's sections. Each section of a chapter discusses a particular topic. This organization makes the chapters very easy to preview because you can find all you need in the introduction and the table of contents. For instance, from the table of contents you know the topic of Chapter 1 is the atmosphere. By looking at the section titles, or headings, in the table of contents, you can find four ideas that support the topic and the key idea of the chapter. However, you don't see a direct statement of the key idea. Therefore, you have to make a guess, based on the key idea of the book and the supporting ideas of the chapter. From these clues you can infer that the key idea of Chapter 1 is something like, "The atmosphere is important in the study of meteorology."

Professor Weisberg's organization is also useful when you start your actual reading because it provides you with a way to ask precise questions about the text. The subtopics give you clues to the ideas and details that support each section of the chapter. Because this is a textbook in science, these details probably will take the form of

CONTENTS

definitions, explanations, and facts (more on this in Chapter 15).
What is the primeval atmosphere? How does the atmosphere affect
life? What is the origin of oxygen? What is the origin of organic compounds? What are the Van Allen radiation belts and how do they
work? Where are they? These are your reading questions, which will
be put off until you finish previewing and actually start reading the
chapter.

Previewing an Article

Articles are not very different from chapters except that instead of seeing them in the context of one larger whole, a book, you should consider how they fit into another larger whole, your course. To what does a particular article relate? Why was it assigned?

Because articles stand alone, how they relate to anything else is not made explicit in a table of contents. Therefore, the author often provides more clues to the topic and key idea in the form of illustrations, a subtitle, or an abstract (a brief summary of the contents of the article). Authors are more likely to use the introductory paragraphs to provide background, so these paragraphs are less reliable than those in chapters as clues to the key idea. However, you can almost always find the key idea stated in the first six to eight paragraphs and in the conclusion of the article.

Example

What can you learn by applying the preview questions to the article "For Liberal Arts Students Seeking Business Careers Curriculum Counts"?

For Liberal Arts Students Seeking Business Careers Curriculum Counts

1 For some time now, career planning and placement offices nationwide have been aware of a common problem: Liberal arts graduates seeking entry-level professional positions in business and industry are having difficulty competing with business and technical majors. In recent decades, various journals have noted this trend, often followed by a cry from students, parents, and faculty that career planning and placement offices should do more to help liberal arts graduates find jobs.

2 A major problem typically associated with the employment of liberal arts graduates is the lack of on-campus recruiting for this population. At The Pennsylvania State University, more than half of all on-campus interviewing activity goes to engineers and other technical majors and about a third to business majors, while the remaining 15 percent goes to all other populations combined. Despite many innovative attempts over the years by the placement staff, recruiters have simply not been attracted to campus to interview liberal arts students.

3   Although liberal arts students have difficulty obtaining interviews, many representatives of education as well as corporations have noted that liberal arts graduates can succeed in professional business careers. A number of studies support this notion. For example, a study conducted at Harvard University demonstrated that "students trained in the liberal arts are better able to formulate valid concepts, analyze arguments, define themselves, and orient themselves maturely to their world" (Winter, Stewart, and McClelland). Their leadership motivation also seemed stronger.

4   These findings were substantiated by the results of two AT&T studies that used the management assessment center method of evaluation (Beck). In reviewing the Bell System research, Ritchie noted that liberal arts students are particularly strong in interpersonal skills, very competitive in administrative skills, and motivated for advancement. Regarding actual management progress, they are more likely to be promoted to middle management than are mathematics/science majors or engineers.

5   A number of other corporations have found that liberal arts graduates hold potential for success in business. In 1980, General Motors announced an experimental program to recruit the best liberal arts graduates it could find. At that time, although the company already employed 9,000 liberal arts graduates, who constituted 22 percent of all college graduates employed by the firm, the announcement was considered very newsworthy (Smith).

6   The American Can Company also initiated a small recruiting program for high-achieving liberal arts graduates, to facilitate the development of those graduates who want to work in business but have not determined a specific area of interest (Alexander).

7   Despite the increasing emphasis on the importance of liberal arts skills in business, liberal arts students are not experiencing increased employment upon graduation. A large number of these students remain unemployed for up to one year after graduation, and many must resort to low-paying blue- or pink-collar jobs that require few advanced skills (Lee). Employers often explain that liberal arts graduates are not adequately prepared for jobs in business, noting that these graduates lack clearly defined career goals and knowledge of basic business principles (Johnson).

A Possible Solution

8   That a problem exists for liberal arts students with business aspirations is evident. The liberal arts curriculum teaches the necessary liberal skills but does not provide in-depth information on business operations. Therefore, students who want to major in the liberal arts and work in a business setting lack the knowledge that would enable them to identify specific areas of interest, clarify career goals, and compete more successfully for entry-level positions in business. The need exists for a curriculum to provide students with both the liberal skills and the business knowledge that are necessary for success.

9　　This position is supported by educators and college placement personnel who endorse the addition of more technical or specialized courses to the liberal arts curriculum. For example, the American Council on Education suggests including courses in business-related subjects and computer science. Sagen recommends that liberal arts students take courses in economic and basic business concepts as well as in more specialized areas such as marketing and finance. He believes students should acquire accounting and technical writing skills, which require the application of general abilities to specific occupational tasks.

10　　The University of Maryland is among several institutions that have developed curricular innovations to make liberal arts students more competitive. It has initiated a pilot program for these students that includes courses in speech and the history of business. Chatham College offers students the opportunity to participate in the Essentials of Business Administration Program, which was initially funded by the IBM Corporation (Cordisco and Walker). This program teaches participants the fundamental skills and knowledge for understanding business and how to apply their backgrounds to a business setting. The curriculum includes courses such as financial analysis, accounting, and statistics. However, students receive no credit for their participation.

11　　The Pennsylvania State University has also developed a business curriculum to supplement the major liberal arts program. In 1980, the university began offering a business option to liberal arts students who wanted to add a business dimension to their general preparation. The program eventually evolved into a liberal arts/business minor, requiring a minimum of 27 credits for completion. Students must complete at least nine credits in accounting and economics and at least nine credits in courses such as business law, finance, insurance, management, and marketing. The remaining credits may be selected from a wider variety of subjects, including computer science, journalism, psychology, and speech communications.

Determining the Effects

12　　The notion, then, of integrating business courses with the liberal arts curriculum has been suggested by many and recently implemented by some colleges. However, there is little evidence that such an academic foundation changes employer perceptions as well as their actual hiring practices. To determine the effect of the business minor on liberal arts students' employability, in the fall semester of 1983, the Career Development and Placement Center at Penn State conducted a study of the interview activity of liberal arts students carrying a business minor. The study was designed to determine employers' perceptions of the liberal arts/business minor as it relates to the marketability of liberal arts students seeking entry-level positions within a business setting.

13　　Twenty-two liberal arts/business students (7 men and 15 women) who were registered with the on-campus recruiting system at Penn State's career center during the 1983 fall semester participated in the study. These students were among the first group in the liberal arts/business program to reach their senior year. Their names were taken from the interview request registration forms submitted to the placement office. All were informed of the purpose of the study, and participation was voluntary.

14   The students' majors varied, reflecting most of the liberal arts disciplines: English, foreign language, general arts and sciences, journalism, social sciences, and speech communication. Their overall grade point average was 2.89 on a 4.00 scale. The grade point average for all university liberal arts students during the 1983 fall semester was 2.77.

15   All students were asked to submit a weekly interview request log, which was developed for this study. Each week for 12 weeks, participants listed the companies with which they requested interviews, as well as the companies that granted requests and the dates of the interviews.

16   At the career center on the day of the interview, recruiters received a 12-item questionnaire for each student they interviewed. The questionnaire was divided into two parts. Part I was designed to determine the recruiter's perceptions of the particular student's interview and the role of the business minor in that student's candidacy. This section included questions such as "Was the student able to express clearly his/her career goals?" and "To what extent was the liberal arts student's minor in business a factor in your evaluation of the candidate?"

17   Part II contained questions specific to the recruiter's general perceptions of the liberal arts/business minor concept and was not associated with the evaluation of a particular student. This section included questions such as "Do you believe that the liberal arts/business minor positively affects students' marketability for employment within a business setting?" In cases where a recruiter interviewed more than one student, the recruiter was asked to complete Part II only once, but encouraged to make any additional comments.

18   The study was conducted at the Career Development and Placement Center within the established recruiting system in which students are pre-screened by employers before selection for interviews (Swails and Hess). The recruiters were informed of the confidentiality of their responses on the questionnaire. Students were permitted to discuss general comments with a counselor only after interviewing with more than one firm.

Employers' Perceptions of the Interviews

19   The 22 students who participated in the study requested 352 interviews and received 64. In other words, 18 percent of the requests yielded interviews, for an average of 2.9 interviews per student. By comparison, the average for all liberal arts students during the 1983 fall semester was 0.8 interviews per registrant, while the average for all students in the College of Business Administration was 3.1 interviews. Of the total requests for all 10 colleges of the university, 25 percent were granted.

20   The interview activity of the liberal arts/business students in this study indicates that these students did better than traditional liberal arts students and were competitive with business students who sought interviews with business recruiters during the 1983 fall semester. In addition, the fact that 18 percent of the liberal arts/business students' requests yielded interviews—compared with 25 percent for all majors, including engineering, computer science, accounting, and other specialties—further indicates that the liberal arts/business curriculum enables liberal arts graduates to be more competitive in the recruiting process.

21   It is important to note that these conclusions are not definitive, since the sample was not random and the data were not tested for significant statistical differences. However, there was no known sampling bias.

22   For Part I of the employer questionnaire, of the 64 questionnaires distributed to recruiters, 40 were returned by representatives of 22 companies, for a 63 percent response rate. The companies represented a cross section of business and industrial organizations, including manufacturing, consumer products, utilities, petroleum, retailing, and financial institutions.

23   Employer responses to Part I indicated that 22, or 55 percent, of the students were evaluated positively and recommended for further employment consideration, while 18, or 45 percent, were rejected for employment. By comparison, in a one day recruiting event for liberal arts students that was viewed favorably by employers, 33 percent of the students were selected for second interviews. Also, data compiled over the past several years from a sampling of employers recruiting at Penn State suggest that approximately 30 percent of an initial interview schedule for all disciplines is invited for second interviews. Again, it appears that the liberal arts/business curriculum strengthens the liberal arts major in the employment process.

24   Also in Part I of the questionnaire, employers commented on the attributes of the candidates that affected selection decisions, citing communication and interpersonal skills most often as positive qualities (see Table 1). This finding is consistent with the results of a previous study at Penn State, in which employers noted communication skills as one of the most important selection criteria (Garis, Hess, Shelton, Slick, and Swails).

25   Table 2 summarizes the employers' impressions of the importance of the business minor in evaluating the candidates' interviews. Employers' comments on the effects of the business minor on the students' employability included the following:

1. Helps clarify career goals.
2. Provides a better business perspective.
3. Helps give liberal arts students an edge in the interview selection process.

26   In considering Table 2, it is important to note that the recruiters responded to the question about the importance of the liberal arts/business minor in the candidates' evaluations after the interview selection took place.

TABLE 1 Candidate Attributes Cited by Employers in Making Selection Decisions Based on On-Campus Interviews

Attribute	Number Who Viewed Attribute as Positive*
Communication/interpersonal skills	32
Academic background	12
Confidence	11
Preparation/organization	11
Work experience	9
Motivation/enthusiasm	7
Grades	6
Maturity	6
Analytical ability	3
Enthusiasm	3
Goals	3
Leadership	3
Common sense	2
Activities	1

*n = 40 possible responses

TABLE 2 Employer Ratings of the Importance of the Liberal Arts/Business Minor in Candidate Interview Evaluation

Rating	Number*	Percent
To a very great extent	2	5%
To a considerable extent	13	32
To only some extent	16	40
Not at all a factor	9	23

*n = 40 possible responses

Garis *et al.* reported that some criteria used by employers in *screening students' interview requests* are different from criteria used by on-campus recruiters in *making hiring decisions based on the actual interview.*

27   In the recruiters' evaluations of the candidates, 40 percent indicated that the business minor was a factor in their evaluation only to some extent. When asked if it was a factor in interview selection, one respondent wrote, "The minor does greatly increase the chance of having this interview. Without it, we would not have talked." Another recruiter said, "Yes, a minor would increase the student's chances of being selected for an interview, but once in the interview, the personal characteristics become more important." Still another recruiter responded that the minor confirmed the student's interest in a business career and that had made the difference when prese-

TABLE 3   Employer Ratings of Clarity and Realism of Candidates' Career Goals

Rating	Clear		Realistic	
	Number*	Percent	Number*	Percent
Extremely	9	22%	9	22%
Quite	15	38	17	43
Only fairly	14	35	13	32
Not at all	2	5	1	3

*n = 40 possible responses

lecting candidates. In fact, several recruiters reported that they interviewed the students because the business minor indicated a commitment to a business-related career and showed that the students had knowledge of basic business operations.

28   Table 3 presents the employers' ratings of the clarity and realism of the students' career goals. Approximately 60 percent of the students were rated as extremely or quite clear/realistic in their goals, and about one-third were rated as only fairly or not at all clear. Evidently, most of the students were able to develop and articulate realistic career goals in business, while some needed to improve in this area.

Employers' General Reactions

29   Part II of the questionnaire asked for the employers' general reactions to the liberal arts/business major concept and was not specific to the impressions of a particular student interview. Employers interviewing more than one student participating in the study were asked to complete this section only once. Twenty-nine recruiters returned completed questionnaires for Part II.

30   All employers indicated that the purpose of their recruiting visit was primarily to interview students with majors in business or the liberal arts. Two employers expressed interest in science majors, while one employer indicated interest in agriculture majors.

31   As shown in Table 4, 82 percent of the respondents believed that the business minor positively affects liberal arts students' marketability for employment within a business setting. The employers' positive comments focused on the well-rounded and balanced nature of the liberal arts/business curriculum and on the necessity of a business minor for liberal arts students entering business careers. As one recruiter commented, "It provides a business base along with a broad liberal arts background—which makes for a more well-rounded executive." Another recruiter wrote, "It can add immeasurably to the well-rounded personality versus the tunnel vision we see frequently." Still another recruiter said, "A business combination with the liberal arts degree gives students' career aspirations more focus without the overkill of some business areas."

TABLE 4   Employer Ratings of the Effects of the Liberal Arts/Business Minor on Employment in Business Settings

Rating	Number*	Percent
Affects very much	10	34%
Affects to some extent	14	48
Affects to a slight extent	4	14
Has no effect	1	3

*n = 29 possible responses

32   Weaknesses identified by six employers dealt with the lack of a specific business concentration within the minor. One employer noted that hiring liberal arts/business graduates could increase training costs.

33   Few employers commented on the value of the program in comparison with the technical and business major programs as preparation for entry-level business careers. Seven employers commented favorably on the liberal arts/business curriculum in comparison with other academic backgrounds, while three employers felt that the business minor was weak compared with the business or technical major. However, all 29 recruiters who completed Part II of the questionnaire indicated that in the future they would recommend that their company open its recruiting schedule to seniors in the liberal arts/business minor program.

34   The employers listed a variety of entry-level positions for which they believed the liberal arts/business graduate was qualified:

- Accountant—financial analyst
- Assistant buyer
- Consumer products representative
- Corporate communications trainee
- Customer service trainee
- Executive trainee
- Financial management trainee
- Management trainee
- Marketing—sales representative
- Marketing research trainee
- Personnel management trainee
- Purchasing trainee.

35   Some of the positions they suggested marked a departure from the entry-level jobs in which liberal arts graduates are typically employed, such as personnel. It is important to note that in this study the liberal arts/business graduates appeared to be competing with business majors for the same entry-level marketing and management positions. The employers also rec-

ommended that the students apply for such positions through direct mail inquiries as well as on-campus recruiting.

36   Recommendations for improving the liberal arts/business curriculum included adding human resources management (personnel) courses; providing additional career exposure through internships; and placing more emphasis on the development of communications skills. The latter two suggestions relate directly to the mixed ratings the employers gave on the candidates' abilities to identify career goals. Not all candidates were able to clearly define realistic career goals, and several were judged deficient in communication skills. This suggests a need for increased emphasis on career development programs or courses to help students develop and articulate clear career goals.

A Third Population

37   The results of this study are not intended to infer that a liberal arts/business minor degree is superior to a business or technical degree. Clearly, the merits, the career-related skills, and the employability of business and technical graduates require little debate: With their backgrounds, these graduates will continue to be sought after and indeed required by corporations. However, this study does demonstrate that positions in business do exist that require the mixture of skills that the liberal arts/business curriculum develops. Liberal arts/business graduates may emerge as a third population, in addition to business and technical majors, with an individualized set of skills sought by corporations.

38   Furthermore, this study does not suggest that a business minor is necessary or desirable for all liberal arts students. Students with career goals more traditionally associated with the liberal arts, such as communications or human services, may deem a business minor inappropriate for inclusion in their academic program. For example, a student with a career goal of newspaper reporting may be well advised to focus on writing/communications courses rather than business courses. The decision to minor in business is dependent on the student's educational/career goals.

39   When considered collectively, however, the findings of this study suggest that a business minor is a very desirable curricular component for liberal arts students with business management aspirations.

–Jeff W. Garis, H. Richard Hess, and Deborah J. Marron*

What Is This About?   The title provides a fairly detailed answer: Liberal arts students seeking business careers are the topic of the article. However, the title leaves the reader with another question: How

---

*Jeff W. Garis and H. Richard Hess are with the Career Development and Placement Center at The Pennsylvania State University. Deborah J. Marron is coordinator of career planning at Mount Vernon College.

does curriculum count? From the headings throughout the article you can gather that there is some kind of problem and a suggested solution and that employers have been consulted. However, you still have not found an answer to your question. Check out the graphic material. In Tables 2 and 4 you find references to curriculum: the liberal arts major/business minor. Now you have a better idea of the topic of the article.

Why Did the Authors Write This Article?   The footnote states that the three authors are associated with career development centers; two are at Penn State, whose liberal arts/business minor is discussed at length in the article. Given the fact that the article is directed to career counselors, you might assume that it was written to help them advise students.

Why Am I Reading This Article?   Among a variety of possible reasons, one probably stands out: You are reading the article because you are a liberal arts student who might want to go into business, and you hope you can find some useful advice.

What Do I Already Know About the Topic?   You have heard that liberal arts graduates often have a hard time being placed in business.

What Is the Authors' Most Important Idea About the Topic?   From what you have put together about the topic, you can guess that the key idea must deal with whether or not a liberal arts major/business minor helps liberal arts students who seek business careers. Your guess that the article emphasizes how a liberal arts student's choice of courses may affect a future in business leads to the notion that the authors must think that a business minor is a good idea if a student wants a business career. Here you have done some predicting. A check of the article's last paragraph bears out your prediction.

How Is the Material Presented?   You can see from the article that it is divided into sections and each section has a title. You know that each section will have a subtopic. A further look at the tables indicates that the authors have done some research on the topic involving surveys of employers.

In your preview you have established that on the basis of their research the three authors are suggesting that liberal arts students who want to enter business should add a business minor to their liberal arts programs. You will now be reading for answers to additional questions, such as Why is it a good idea? How do employers react? Is the combination of a liberal arts major with a business minor better than a straight business program? Answers to your questions will come from the subtopics and supporting ideas and supporting details. You now have a context into which to put your reading; you have made many important connections, the material starts to be familiar, and you are anticipating the authors' next steps.

Exercises

1. Preview the preface to *Advertising, Management, and Society: A Business Point of View* and answer the following questions.

   Why was this book written?
   What are some of the points that make it special or different from others in the field?
   How is it organized?
   Who does the author think will be interested in this book?

Preface

1   In both ancient and modern times, many societies have been able to go beyond fulfilling the need for survival. These societies have achieved material *abundance* in different ways, through different customs, laws, institutions, and technologies. Yet they have all utilized the same raw material: the physical, intellectual, and ethical energy inherent in all humans.

2   Along with material abundance comes the gradual increase in *discretion of choice*; consciously or unconsciously, a society and its members are involved in a stream of decisions defining what particular aspects of abundance they are interested in. They are making choices concerning *quality* rather than *quantity*. At this stage of development, the role of intellectual and ethical energy becomes greater relative to that of physical energy. *Affluence* is the opportunity to utilize intellectual and ethical energy in order to shape a future in which individuals are relieved from toil and can work toward achieving aesthetic and ethical goods.

3   At the same time, affluence poses an intellectual and ethical challenge, a challenge so difficult that most societies have failed to grasp its full meaning and potential. When they emerge from the long struggle to harness physical energies and attain material wealth, individuals and societies seem to be culturally unprepared to distinguish between quantity and quality. And failure to change one's own culture—i.e., one's norms, laws, institutions, and technologies—in order to deal with intellectual and ethical matters leads to a loss of historical momentum, to decay, and even to a loss of abundance.

4   *Personal* and *mass communication* have been key factors in shaping the long journey from survival to abundance and, eventually, to affluence and beyond. Modern, affluent societies have become particularly dependent on the existence of a *mass communication* system, for this system carries information about all possible individual and social choices—with regard to work, religion, politics, and so on. Affluent societies are now faced with the problem of managing this system: how can a mass communication system help society and its members make choices concerning the quality of individual and social life?

5   *Advertising* is only a part of a mass communication system, that part that deals with the exchange of economic information. But, as we shall see, this neat abstraction may hide the fact that each ad, as well as the entire advertising institution, is an integral part of a society's mass communication system and, ultimately, a product of its cultural ethos.

6   As a form of mass communication, advertising has been used since ancient times. Its merits and demerits have been debated heatedly and repetitiously but, until recently, few efforts have been devoted to a systematic and detailed examination of what it actually does and why. *Why* do corporation executives use advertising, and how do they evaluate whether or not it works? How do advertising agencies operate? What active roles does the consumer play in the advertising institution? How does the advertising institution work and how does it relate to other social and economic institutions? What value criteria are appropriate for evaluating advertising as an institution? Is our knowledge of this institution sufficient to identify what changes are both desirable and feasible? According to what criteria?

7   Many groups are interested in advertising. We should thus expect to find a *multilogue*—a many-sided dialogue—taking place among them. In fact, however, it is the *critics* of advertising from whom we hear the most. Who has not heard of the views publicized by Packard and Galbraith? And what college student does not remember the negative evaluations of advertising by many (neoclassical) economists?

8   *Consumers* have played a much smaller role in this multilogue. One of the few comprehensive and imaginative studies of consumers' feelings, by Bauer and Greyser, has received curiously little attention. Occasionally we hear from consumers through complaints presented to courts or government agencies, but no foundation or government agency has undertaken any systematic monitoring or analysis of these complaints.

9   The *business community* has also remained relatively silent. As D. M. Kendall, chairman of the board of Pepsico, recently reiterated, "American advertising can sell many goods and services, but it has never found a way to sell itself." Until recently, there have been almost no systematic and comprehensive attempts made to communicate the why, what, and how of advertising from the points of view of business.

10   Nevertheless, an attempt was made to present a business point of view when the Federal Trade Commission held extensive hearings on modern advertising practices in the fall of 1971. Many witnesses submitted written testimonies. The Association of National Advertisers (ANA) and the American Association of Advertising Agencies (4As) organized and coordinated twenty-six written testimonies by corporate executives of member firms. The selection

of practitioners satisfied a previously expressed desire by the Federal Trade Commission for evidence and experience rather than theory. (Exhibit A lists the names, positions, and firms of the witnesses, and Exhibit B gives a brief description of the two associations.)

The Content and Organization of the Book

11 The testimonies of corporate executives at the FTC hearings are the basic material of this book. They provide a new resource for the study of two major facets of advertising: (1) advertising as a managerial function in business firms, and (2) advertising as an entire institution in society and the economy. They provide unique insights into *why* corporate managers consider advertising important at the managerial and the socioeconomic level. The presentations are candid and of immediate interest; more important, they include data that were previously unpublished or not readily available.

12 To make these testimonies accessible to interested audiences, it was necessary to shorten and rearrange them. Furthermore, extensive commentaries were inserted throughout the text for the following purposes: to furnish background information; to outline the main themes and give them continuity; to provide clarification by including additional points that emerged in the discussions between witnesses and commissioners; and to point toward the research necessary to describe and evaluate advertising at both the micromanagerial and macrosocial levels.

13 The commentaries are interpretations of the facts and views submitted by the witnesses. I based these interpretations on the growing number of theories and data in economics and the behavioral sciences that, in my opinion, underlie and explain the testimonies. I also tried to search for some of the still-elusive foundations—conceptual and empirical—that must precede individual and social action.

14 A unique aspect of the book's material is that it covers practically all the fundamental issues and criticisms that have dominated the literature for decades. (It was not an easy task to telescope so much into just one book.) Although comprehensive in its coverage of issues and criticisms, the book discusses advertising from the inside; thus, the resulting picture is one-sided. However unfashionable it may be, this choice of perspective is deliberate. There are two reasons for this: first, since most of the existing literature is *also* one-sided, by presenting the practitioners' responses, the book can contribute another side to the multilogue; and, second, I believe that it is in the interest of all parties to understand why practitioners act and feel the way they do. Understanding the facts, theories, and perspectives presented by the witnesses will help all who are concerned with identifying the parameters of the problems and thus increase their ability to work together toward satisfying individual and social needs. I am told that Oliver Wendell Holmes once said: "Many ideas grow better when transplanted into another mind than in the one where they sprang up." Let us hope that this will eventually be true of our subject.

15 The organization of this book was suggested by two of the most common meanings of the term *advertising*. The first is relatively narrow: it refers to what consumers see—an ad—and, by extension, to the activities that lead to it.

Busy as we are with our daily lives, most of us consumers are unaware of the complexity of these activities, and have only a vague notion of what problems businesses attempt to solve.

16   Part I describes the problems advertisers and advertising agencies face in preparing, executing, and assessing an advertising campaign. It stresses the *why* of advertising management from the overall corporate perspective of one firm. Part I is essentially managerially, micro-oriented; it provides a picture of real-life problems and decision processes.

17   In its second meaning, the term advertising does not refer to a specific ad, to one advertiser or advertising agency, or to one mass medium. It refers to the *entire institution*—the set of all uses by all people and organizations of a society's mass communication system for economic purposes. Although most of the issues and criticisms in the literature ultimately concern advertising as an institution, our basic knowledge of this institution is extremely limited. This should not surprise us, for it is far more difficult to observe an institution than an individual, to study macro rather than micro phenomena. We share this problem with many other disciplines. (Let us recall that, in the 200 years of economic research preceding J. M. Keynes, there was no macroeconomics.)

18   Part 2 has a macro-orientation—that is, it focuses on the institution in its entirety, as a functional whole. It discusses theories and empirical evidence that may help us describe, and eventually explain, the internal structure of the advertising institution, its interactions with other institutions, and its possible roles in socioeconomic change. This macro approach is an attempt to answer a plea expressed a few years ago by Leo Bogart: ". . . the proper study of advertising research is the advertising system, and not of advertisements. . . . Why don't we start with the big picture, with a view of advertising as a tremendous institution which deserves study in its own right . . ." This macro approach is novel and thus naturally far from being conclusive, but it is essential to the comprehension and evaluation of the advertising institution.

19   By approaching Part I first, the reader gains the factual information at the firm level that may help him in considering the broad institutional problems examined in Part 2. Conversely, reading Part 2 first provides the overall perspective for the examination of the operations of advertisers and agencies presented in Part 1. Clearly, the two parts are interdependent, and the choice will depend on the reader's particular interest.

The Audiences of the Book

20   There are several groups of readers who may be interested in the data, viewpoints, and explanations presented in this book. The first group is made up of students and teachers interested in *why* advertising operates as it does. The book may be used in courses on advertising, marketing, and related topics. In view of the growing social concern with advertising, it should be very helpful in courses in Business and Society, Corporate Social Responsibility, and similar topics that are increasingly offered in many departments. The book's material is also relevant for courses in Consumer Behavior and Consumerism, for it provides much information about how consumers actually behave.

21   The second group of readers for whom this book is potentially of interest

are those who work in advertising and other business areas. Many people working in accounting, finance, production, and personnel may seek a better understanding of the advertising function in their own firms. Some may have difficulty in explaining advertising to their friends and neighbors—and perhaps even to themselves. If they are unfamiliar with the advertising business, and given the popularity of the Packard and Galbraith views, they may even be ambivalent about advertising. The facts reported in this book should have a special appeal to this audience.

22   Finally, the information in this book should also be useful to all who are interested in both the daily decisions made by advertisers and advertising agencies and their possible consequences on the economy and society.

–Francisco M. Nicosia

2. Read the table of contents for *Retail Merchandising: Principles and Applications.*

   State what the book is about.
   Guess at the key idea from the information given in the table of contents.
   Section the table of contents into larger units. Then list the topics of the units.

Contents

v

viii CONTENTS

3. This exercise should be done with a partner. Examine a chapter from one of your own textbooks and discuss your answers to the following questions with your partner.

How is the chapter you selected linked to the chapters that follow and precede it?
What is the topic of the chapter?
What is the key idea of the chapter?
How is the material presented? Are there any study aids?
If there are section headings, how can you use them to best advantage?

4. Preview the following article, "What about Negotiation as a Specialty?" and answer the following questions:

What is the topic?
What is the key idea?
Why did the author write this article? Who is the author?
What do you already know about the topic?
From your preview, predict three questions this article might answer.

What About Negotiation as a Specialty?

1   Most legal problems are not settled through legislative or judicial action but by negotiation. All lawyers negotiate, but few of us have either a conceptual understanding of the process or particular skill in it. It is time to recognize negotiation as a field for specialization.

2   Litigation is time consuming and expensive. Cases often drag on because lawyers are not particularly good at settlement, because they have over-convinced themselves of the merits of their client's case, or because taking the initiative toward settlement seems to communicate a lack of confidence in victory.

3   If some lawyers chose to specialize in negotiation, it would improve both our understanding of the negotiation process and the skills of the best negotiators. Specialization also would permit an honest and effective use of a two-track approach—one lawyer, skilled in the process of making deals, would seek to develop a settlement that the client will prefer over the risks and costs of litigation, while a hard-hearted partner prepared singlemindedly for trial.

4   I make this proposal not because of doubts about the adversary process, but because of my belief in it. A judge, in order to maximize the chance of a wise decision, hears opposing points of view from different people. When a client has to decide between settlement and litigation, does he or she deserve any less?

What's Wrong Now?

5   Like warfare, litigation should be avoided. Let's candidly admit that from the client's point of view virtually every litigated case is a mistake. Unless one client or both had made a mistake, the case could have been settled and both would have been better off. They might have been able to craft an outcome reconciling their differing interests far better than a court could later. At the worst, they could have saved and divided between them the impressive legal fees that litigators earn.

6   Not only does every litigated case represent a waste of the money of one or more clients, litigation diverts their time and energies from more creative pursuits. Litigation is worse than a zero-sum game in which the winnings of one client added to the losses of the other equal zero. Litigation is a negative-sum game in which, because of lawyers' fees and other costs, no matter who wins the case, both clients—taken together—have lost.

7   Many law firms do not view mounting legal fees as anything evil, and in fact law firms value litigators because of the large billings they bring in. Today it is a widely held view that law firms will not be interested in any idea that reduces legal bills. But any firm that maintains this attitude is likely to price itself out of the market. Increasingly, law firms will be competing with one another, and corporate clients are becoming fed up with the high costs of litigation. They will shift their business to firms that demonstrate both a desire to settle cases quickly at low cost—and an ability to do so.

8   Expensive litigation also is a burden to society. As taxpayers we subsidize this wasteful process by providing judges, clerks and courthouses—even to litigious millionaires who should have settled. Each unsettled case delays every other case. If only clients had enough foresight and skill, they would promptly settle every dispute and split the savings between them. Why don't they? Why do clients make so many mistakes?

The Diagnosis

9   Like us, clients are human beings. They react. They get angry. They see their own side of a case more clearly than they do that of others, and they lose perspective. So they retain professional counsel. But how good is the advice we give? Perhaps, just perhaps, one reason there is so much litigation is that clients receive less than optimal advice from us lawyers. Like clients, we lawyers sometimes make mistakes by singlemindedly pursuing the litigation option. Let me suggest some reasons for this attitude.

10   Although lawyers negotiate every day—with spouse, landlord, colleagues, neighbors, salesmen and children—they often do so poorly. The more serious the disagreement, the less likely we are to engage in joint problem solving. We usually shoot from the hip. Clients would be better served by our persuading opposing counsel today than by our persuading a judge next year, but we usually prepare far less for a negotiation than we would for a trial. Even in professional negotiations, we often attend meetings with no more purpose in mind than to "see what they say." Because we do not have to agree, we treat negotiation as a preliminary and not a final level of action.

11   In negotiations we are likely to come up with an answer before we fully understand the perceptions and concerns that create the problem. We vacillate between being hard and soft, not knowing which is better. We see no third alternative. We frequently reward the other side's stubbornness by making a concession, forgetting the lessons of Chamberlain and B.F. Skinner that we cannot buy good conduct by yielding to threats. If we respond to outrageous behavior with concessions, we will get more of the behavior we reward.

12   We often conduct negotiations in ways that are inefficient, exacerbate relations among the parties and produce unwise outcomes.

13   Another reason so many cases are litigated is that lawyers tend to overestimate the strength of a client's case. There is no doubt that the longer we work on a problem to advance one point of view, the more merit we see in that point of view. We may not be able to persuade a court that our client should prevail, but we always succeed in persuading ourselves. During the two years of arguing cases in the Supreme Court for the solicitor general, I was never on the wrong side—on the side that should have lost. A majority of the Court was sometimes on the wrong side, but not I.

An Experiment

14   Howard Raiffa of the Harvard Business School conducts an experiment that demonstrates the effect of working on a problem as an advocate. Each student is given an identical set of facts about a business to be sold. Half the students are buyers; half are sellers. The facts encourage each side to make a deal. The only question is price. After studying the facts, each student is asked to write down, privately, his or her estimate of the fair price that would be determined by an impartial appraiser.

15   This experiment has been done many times with hundreds of students. The average price that buyers think fair is always substantially lower than the average price that sellers think fair. Taking an advocate's point of view does distort our judgment. With both lawyers unduly optimistic, the clients are doomed to litigate far more than they should.

16   A third factor contributing to the high cost of litigation is the fear by counsel that the first side to propose settlement weakens its negotiating position. Appearing eager to settle is taken as demonstrating a lack of confidence in one's case. Instead, if only to strengthen their hand for future negotiations, both sides concentrate on discovery, preparing for trial and looking tough. Meanwhile, legal fees continue to mount.

The Prescription: Specialization

17 My suggested answer to all three difficulties is for some lawyers to specialize in negotiation and dispute settlement. The existence of these specialists should improve the quality of the settlement skills offered by the bar and avoid the problems of overoptimism and postponing talks for fear of looking weak.

18 John Dunlop, a former secretary of labor and renowned negotiator, once suggested that lawyers never would take negotiation seriously until it became a recognized specialty. He seems to be right.

19 A generation or more ago every lawyer felt competent to draw wills, give tax advice and try a few cases. Today clients can get better service in each of those areas because specialists are available. By concentrating his or her professional services in one field, a lawyer also concentrates on learning. It is far easier to become good at something than to become good at everything.

20 The time has come for lawyers to recognize that negotiation is a special field in which it is possible to acquire special competence. Of course, as in litigation, a lot depends on personality and other factors that are impossible to teach. But study, theory and concentrated experience can make a big difference. Lawyers can learn to produce wiser outcomes, and to do so more efficiently and amicably.

21 Most lawyers have given comparatively little thought to the negotiation process. Suppose, for example, that a husband and wife, with children, property and conflicting interests have decided on a divorce. Suppose they wish to negotiate an amicable settlement and ask a lawyer for advice on how to do so. How many lawyers would feel confident giving such advice? Suppose only the wife were to ask how best to negotiate with her husband, who seemed angry, tough and interested only in "winning"? As a professional negotiator, what would be your professional advice?

22 Working with colleagues at Harvard and elsewhere, a few of us have developed some hypotheses about how best to answer these questions. Recognizing that particular circumstances need to be taken into account, some generalizations appear possible.

23 Some lawyers love the excitement of litigation, the parry and thrust of cross-examination. But others find challenges elsewhere: putting themselves in the shoes of those with whom we differ; understanding their concerns; converting an adversary into a joint problem solver; developing ingenious solutions that dovetail differing interests; persuading people where their true interests lie; and saving clients the costs and anguish of protracted battle.

The Two-Track Answer

24   Specialization also provides an answer to the twin problems of overestimating the merits of a client's case and of postponing settlement talks for fear of looking weak. Pursue a two-track approach. Have one lawyer try to settle a case, while a different lawyer pursues litigation.

25   As believers in the adversary process, lawyers recognize the potential bias in all of us. There is no way in which one lawyer, try as he may, can be counted on to give a judge a properly balanced assessment of the pros and cons. To maximize the chance of a wise decision, the judge needs to hear the case for A from one lawyer and the case for B from another.

26   For a client, the decision whether to settle or to litigate is of comparable importance. Shouldn't the client also be entitled to the benefits of the adversary process? Isn't a client likely to make a wiser decision if one lawyer presents the case for settlement and a different lawyer the case for litigation?

27   In any major case a wise client should ask one lawyer to explore the possibilities of settlement and a different lawyer to pursue the litigation option. An expert in negotiation, with full authority to negotiate, subject to client approval, would seek to develop a settlement that could be recommended to the client. With that proposed settlement in hand, the client then could weigh the negotiator's arguments for settlement against his trial counsel's arguments for pursuing litigation. The chance of making a mistaken decision to litigate would be reduced greatly.

28   This two-track approach also could eliminate that widespread working assumption that the lawyer who is talking settlement must have a weak case. When settlement is being handled by a specialist who never litigates, a proposal to talk settlement is no sign of weakness. On the contrary, a specialist in settling cases has an easy opening: "This case just came into the office. My partner is dying to litigate it and says he is confident of a spectacular victory. My job is to see if I can produce a fair settlement, one that I can persuade our client is better—all things considered—than litigation. Let's see what we can do."

Better for Everyone

29   Having different lawyers work on settlement and litigation is better for the negotiator, better for the litigator, and better for the client. The hand of the negotiator is strengthened by the activities of the litigator. The hand of the litigator also is strengthened.

30   Freed from any duty to explore settlement, the litigating lawyer can concentrate singlemindedly on preparing and pursuing the

strongest possible case in court. The threat of litigation has not been weakened by exploring settlement.

31   And the client is in good hands, knowing that each option— settlement and litigation—is being pursued by counsel with a special skill in that area.

32   With this basic concept in mind, there are a number of variations. Specialists in negotiation might seek to settle a case before it is turned over to other counsel for litigation. Lawyer reference plans might list separately attorneys who specialize in settlement, who might undertake to try to settle a case promptly to the client's satisfaction and, if unable to do so within a given time, to turn the case over to other counsel for litigation.

33   Some small law firms might choose to specialize in negotiation. They could offer to try to settle cases before litigation counsel had been retained or to seek settlement concurrently with the pursuit of litigation by another firm.

34   Major firms with a litigation department might establish a negotiation department alongside it. They also might establish the policy that in every case one lawyer would have responsibility for litigation and a different lawyer would be responsible for trying to negotiate a settlement. Information could be shared but the roles separated.

35   For corporations that frequently are engaged in litigation there are similar options: outside specialists could be retained to seek to settle cases for which inside counsel routinely would pursue litigation. Or outside firms could be retained to pursue both options, through different lawyers. Alternatively, a deputy general counsel or other house attorney could become specially trained and experienced in settlement. Outside counsel might then be retained exclusively for litigation and for providing that best alternative to a negotiated agreement should none appear sufficiently attractive.

36   Some litigators will assume that they are not ready to talk settlement until full discovery has been completed, the admissibility of evidence has been considered and the availability of witnesses has been determined. But as those who negotiate business deals know, uncertainty often promotes agreement. Different predictions about the future, particularly when combined with risk aversion, often increase the pressure for a quick settlement. It is my belief that the modest increased cost to the client of having a specialist in negotiation explore settlement at the early stages of a case would time after time save the client the enormous costs of full discovery and trial.

37   Professor Raiffa has suggested that experts in negotiation also

could offer a special service: "postsettlement settlement." In any dispute involving multiple issues, a settlement on which the parties agree or that may be ordered by a court is likely to be less than optimal—that is, the parties would have preferred a different settlement, but they were unable to find one. An expert negotiator-mediator might offer to talk with each side privately, to clarify their interests and to see if a settlement could be devised, which each side would prefer over the one they have. The case having been settled, the parties might be more willing to let a mediator, perhaps for a contingent fee, learn about their true interests and see if he could generate a package both sides would rather have than the one they worked out. If the mediator can, fine. If not, the parties still have the settlement they reached.

A Task for Experts

38   Everyone should know something about putting out fires, and presumably everyone does, but there is a compelling need for professional firefighters. Similarly, all lawyers should know something about negotiation. Most of us should know more than we do. It is high time that we lawyers, whose calling is to serve justice at minimum cost to our clients and to society, should have some members who specialize in the amicable settlement of differences.

–Roger Fisher

Writing Exercise

Write a summary of the steps involved in previewing, and state why you think previewing is a good idea.

9 *Reading Flexibly*

Once you have defined your purpose in reading, thought about what you already know about the topic, and asked the preview questions you have learned so far, you can adapt how you read to what you need to get out of it by using four different approaches to reading: previewing, skimming, reading, and close reading. In the process of becoming a flexible reader, you will skim to formulate additional questions and to improve your reading efficiency and reading rate, and section to see how authors develop their ideas.

Four Approaches to Reading

The basis of flexible reading is to know what you want to get from your reading and to have the strategies at hand to enable you to adapt the time and effort that you put into your reading to your task. Not everything you pick up to read is written with the same density. Some texts, like science or philosophy texts, have many ideas or a lot of necessary information compressed into a relatively small space. Others, like some of the social sciences, depend on example and illustration to explain the concepts covered in the text. How you deal with the different kinds of reading you have to do is determined by your purpose and the way the material is presented.

You can better adapt your reading to your purpose if you think of four approaches to, or stages of, reading, one or more of which can be applied to any piece of reading depending on what you need to get from it.

1. Preview to orient yourself to your reading by asking the preview questions. When you preview, you relate what you are about to read with what you already know; establish a connection with the author and get a sense of the author's point of view; define precisely what you want to get out of your reading; and recognize the ways in which authors organize their material.
2. Skim to acquire an overview of your reading. In skimming, you get a sense of what the reading and its parts are about. Skimming, as we define it, is reading for the topic, key idea, and subtopics. After you have previewed your reading, the next step is skimming. An active reader previews and skims everything. There are times when previewing and skimming alone will accomplish your purpose. (Skimming is discussed in greater detail further in this chapter.)
3. Read to have a better grasp of the author's ideas, the kind of support the author uses, and the organization of the material. You do this by reading for the topic, key idea, subtopics, and supporting ideas. You may find that there are many times when you can understand your reading without having to read consciously for the supporting details, such as explanations and illustrations.
4. Close read to study and understand fully your reading by reading for the topic, key idea, subtopics, supporting ideas, and supporting details. This approach is necessary when you learn from your previewing and skimming that you will need every bit of information provided if you are to understand what the author is saying.

These four approaches put you in control of your reading and give you the tools to adapt your reading style to the task. Sometimes previewing and skimming will be sufficient for your purposes. Other times, you may need to follow up on the previewing and skimming with reading or close reading. You are the one who decides what needs time and what doesn't; you know what you are after and when you have accomplished it. The time you save in skimming easy material to find the key idea and subtopics is time you will have to give to the reading that requires time—material that is dense with many ideas per square inch of print, material that is sequential with steps that cannot be omitted, and material that is inherently hard to understand.

The preview and reading questions are the basis for previewing, reading, and close reading. Now, we shall look more closely at several strategies that you can use to add flexibility to your reading.

Skimming

> There is much reading that must be done meticulously, of course, but most people could SKIM through, without loss, a great deal of the material they now read carefully. To do this, one must cut all moorings with past reading habits and recklessly take a chance at merely catching snatches of printed symbols here and there. It is necessary to cultivate an attitude of abandon while engaging in the high-powered skill of skimming.

This statement, by Nila Banton Smith, may slightly exaggerate the process of skimming, but it does emphasize the fact that skimming takes courage. Most people think that you have to read every word, that not to do so is wrong. But the good reader reads for ideas, not words. Skimming is a skill that develops from reading for ideas.

What is skimming? As we define it, **skimming** is reading for ideas that don't need extensive amplification, definition, or exemplification. As you recognize, these are the terms we use to describe the function of supporting ideas and supporting details. Therefore, skimming is reading for the topics and key ideas without attending to the supporting ideas and supporting details. Skimming gives you a general, rather than a specific, understanding and establishes the context in which the details take their subordinate place. As an example, think of a time when you are looking for your car in the parking lot. You might look first for the brand or the color. Next you search for the telling detail that distinguishes your car from others, like a well-known dent in the fender or a ski rack on the roof. By then you know it is your car without having to examine all the details, such as the license number or the color of the upholstery or its contents.

How should you skim? First, you must make up your mind that you are going to move very quickly through the material you are going to read, asking not only *What is this about?* as you look for the topic and subtopics, but also *What is the author's most important idea about the topic?* to elicit the key idea. Because at this stage you are not reading for the supporting ideas and supporting details, if you see that what you are reading is illustrating, explaining, describing, or defining something you already know or understand, skip it.

Successful skimming starts with a glance at the beginnings and the ends of chapters, sections, and paragraphs to find what each part of your reading is about. You will probably find the topic and subtopics there. If not, you will have to take more time to read further into the text. You will also find it useful to look for the key words, those strong nouns and verbs that so often answer the question *What is this about?* In addition to the key words, you can look for key phrases, like "the problem is," "the answer to," "we discovered that," and so on, that lead to the topic (and usually the key idea) of that portion of the reading. You may be surprised to find that the material you are looking for seems to stand out on the page.

In the right situation skimming is very good reading. Efficient students skim to get at the essence of their readings. By following the topics, key ideas, and subtopics of the readings, they get a general impression of what the readings are about and a sense of how the authors make their points. In this way active readers are able to see the relationships inherent in the material and to discriminate what is important to them from what is not.

Skimming gives you the overview and context necessary to understand the authors' ideas. Whether your purpose is simply to discern the main points of a relatively uncomplicated reading or, instead, to read difficult material with greater understanding, previewing and skimming must be your first steps. In the first case, it may be all you need to do. In the second case, previewing and skimming will provide you with a sense of the total reading, which will greatly assist you as you try to piece the structure together, placing the elements in their proper niches. Instead of getting bogged down in details that seem to lead nowhere, you will first recognize the forest, next see its place in the landscape, and then identify the separate trees.

Whether skimming is sufficient for your purpose is a matter only you can decide. And that decision may depend on what you discover when you preview. You may find you are already adequately informed about the subject so that you don't need to read the examples and illustrations. Skimming is therefore enough. Or you may find that you cannot understand the material without returning to it after the initial skimming to examine its details very carefully. Just as you cannot skim a recipe, you cannot skim a mathematics text, where every step leads to the next, or a philosophy text, in which virtually every word is important to the discussion. But close reading can be effective only within the context of the overall comprehension that you gain from skimming.

- You skim through a lot of material to get to the part you want.
- You skim looking only for topic, key idea, and subtopics if you know that is all you need to know.
- You skim over supporting examples and definitions if you already know them or can understand the author's thesis without them.
- You skim to gain an understanding of the complete text.
- You skim a text before you go to class to be prepared for the discussion.

Example

Let's turn back and skim the article entitled "The Desexing of English," p. 69, which was used as an example for predicting. As a result of previewing and predicting, you discovered that the article is about English words based on gender and that the author's key idea is the answer to whether the women's-rights movement has been successful in its campaign to desex the language. Then we predicted that the author would deal with examples of changes in the language and talk about the effects of these changes in trying to judge whether the campaign had been successful or not. You've already done a lot. Now you'll see what you can accomplish by skimming the article.

In order to skim, you read for the topic, key idea, and subtopics. The preview gave you the first two, so you are now looking for the subtopics. Remember, your question for subtopics is the same as that for the topic, *What is this about?* You might change it a bit to ask *What is the author talking about now?* or *What is the topic of this portion of the article?*

The first seven paragraphs of the article deal with examples of changes. Beginning with paragraph 8, you have to look more carefully for the answers to your questions. When you look at the beginning and end of paragraph 9, you pick up the subtopic, the success of the campaign. Paragraph 11 gives you the clue that the next portion will deal with why the campaign was successful, and paragraph 13 tells you that it is based on a moral attitude.

This quick run-through does not mean you have read the article. However, you have answered your questions, and now you know exactly what the author is dealing with and how he has developed his material. If you need to, you can now read further to find the supporting ideas and supporting details that answer the questions *How? Why? When?* and possibly *Who?*

Increasing Reading Speed

Flexible readers know that some material can be read quickly and other material cannot. But these terms are relative. Most of you probably hope that by learning to read more efficiently, you will also increase your general reading rate. Increasing your reading rate is directly related to good previewing, predicting, and skimming. The more you know about your reading before you begin, the more precise your questions and the faster you can find the ideas. The foreknowledge you gain from previewing and skimming also results in better concentration and recall, and that means you will not have to give so much time to relearning material you have been previously exposed to. Active reading leads to time saving because you are reading more efficiently. However, here are some steps you can take now that will help you to improve your general reading rate.

1. Make up your mind that you *will* read faster.
2. Preview and skim to orient yourself to your reading.
3. Try, as you read, to be conscious of always moving ahead. Questioning is the way to look for what is coming next.
4. Don't allow yourself to go back over previous reading unless you know you have not read it nor taken it in.
5. Don't read for too long at a time. When you start losing your concentration, turn to another task or take a break.
6. Trust the fact that often you take in many more of the supporting ideas and details than you think you do. Test yourself occasionally by jotting down notes on everything you can remember from a particular reading. Cue yourself to your reading by asking the basic reading questions. (p. 53)

You can read some material much faster when you recognize that you understand the ideas conveyed in the key and supporting ideas and therefore do not need to read the examples or details or when you determine that the material doesn't contain many ideas. Reading speed is not a matter of words per minute, but rather depends on how quickly you can understand the author's ideas.

Sectioning

A strategy closely associated with the third approach to reading— when you read for the topic, key idea, subtopics, and supporting ideas—is that of dividing the material into its component sections to see how authors develop and support their ideas. You were introduced to this strategy in earlier chapters when you looked for the subtopics of your readings and in Chapter 8 when you grouped chapter titles.

A **section** is a unit of one or several paragraphs that are grouped together because they have the same subtopic. As you read, you give each section a different and appropriate title derived from your answer to the question *What is this about?*

Most authors aim to set out information in a way that you, the reader, will easily comprehend. Their ideas are not thrown at you randomly, but are arranged coherently. For instance, if you tell someone about a book you've read, you set the details out in some kind of order. Tony may start at the beginning and go right through, chapter by chapter, until the end. Diane may prefer a different arrangement, dealing first with why she chose the book, then a brief summary of the high points, the characters in it, and finally her opinion of it. These are quite different structures. But in each case the information is sectioned into subtopics under the general topic of "A Book I Have Read." In the first case the organizing principle is chronological sequence; the other moves from subtopic to subtopic as if dealing with a list. In both cases the material is organized into coherent units that you can follow.

Authors aren't there, in person, for you to question as you read. Therefore, it is their task as good writers to put like things together so that you can recognize their organization and follow their thinking as it moves from subtopic to subtopic. As the reader who wants to get as much as possible from your reading, you have to deduce what the author's system is. You discover the system existing in a particular reading by questioning and sectioning it.

Sometimes a textbook chapter or an article is already sectioned. That is, the author provides a series of headings throughout the chapter or article, indicating what the subtopics are. This enables you to follow the author's discussion without much effort. When you have to section your reading yourself, the effort you put into tying the ideas together and finding the threads that join topic with subtopics and key idea with supporting ideas is of great benefit. It helps you to become familiar with the ideas contained in the material and provides you with an easily remembered package, rather than an unrelated scattering of thoughts.

When you section, you follow these steps:

- note where one subtopic ends and another starts, either by marking the text or by making notes,
- write a title for the section, based on its subtopic, in the margin or in your notes,
- write out the key idea of the section, remembering that it is also a supporting idea for the key idea of the entire reading.

As you gain experience in sectioning, you will probably break the material down into larger and larger units as you see the connections between subtopics. The fewer subtopics you have, the easier they will be to remember as you try to reconstruct the reading.

Examples

We have marked up the following two articles to illustrate sectioning and to demonstrate how it works. The first example is sectioned by subtopic.

Piano Manufacturing

Topic —
Piano Manu-
facturing

The piano manufacturing business has seen dramatic changes in the twentieth century, particularly over the last twenty years. In 1900, there were 7000 piano manufacturers in America, including families who made pianos in their homes. One out of every six people in America was involved in some aspect of the piano business, including the production of raw or man-made materials used in constructing a piano. Today, however, there are only about ten independent piano manufacturers and just six major piano companies. A far cry from the mom-and-pop piano makers of the past, these are Steinway, Baldwin, Sohmer, Kimball, Wurlitzer, and Aeolian. Despite the transition from family to corporate ownership, the hand craftsmanship and pride in the product seem to have prevailed. Combined with the most modern business and manufacturing techniques, the piano industry in the 1980s is unique—and healthy, if somewhat pared down.

changes

Subtopic—
changes in
piano industry

According to the National Piano Manufacturers Association and industry estimates, piano manufacturing is a half-billion-dollar-a-year industry. In 1982, 203,000 American-made pianos were sold in the United States, a slight decrease over the past two to three years, but an overall increase over a ten-year period.

Subtopics —
Sales of new
pianos

The sales figures of new American instruments tell only part of the story. Piano manufacturers say that the secondhand piano business is doing remarkably well, and they estimate that nearly 1 million used pianos are sold in America yearly.

sales

sales of
used pianos

In the past decade the American piano industry has been faced with intense competition from the Koreans and the Japanese, the latter having already cornered twenty percent of the American market with Yamaha and

foreign competition

Subtopics— grand pianos and how they are built

upright pianos and how they are built

Building Pianos

rebuilding pianos

Museum

Subtopic— piano museum

Kawai pianos. In fact, in Hamamatsu, Japan, where the Yamaha is manufactured, more pianos are made per year than in any other part of the world. But United States piano manufacturers have risen quickly to the challenge. Piano companies are rapidly increasing their know-how in engineering as well as in marketing and manufacturing. These firms are developing more efficient, profitable methods, and new products that the public can more easily afford, such as the practical spinet, a much smaller and cheaper piano than a grand.

The two basic types of pianos are grands and uprights. Grand pianos are constructed on a horizontal plane, which means that the strings are stretched horizontally across the plate and framework, and come in three sizes; a baby grand is four and a half feet to six feet long; a medium grand, six to eight feet long; and a concert grand, eight to nine feet long and sometimes longer. While only five percent of the pianos manufactured today are grand pianos, they are played and featured most often because they tend to be far more responsive and powerful than uprights.

Upright pianos, also called vertical pianos, have strings that are stretched vertically across the plate and framework. Uprights vary in height: a full-size is forty-eight inches or more; the studio model is forty-four inches; the console is thirty-nine to forty-two inches; and a spinet, popular because of its small size, is thirty-six to thirty-eight inches. Upright pianos have two major types of actions: direct blow action and drop action. Direct blow action makes for a better piano because the action is mounted above the ends of the keys, allowing direct movement of the parts, a strong hammer blow, and maximum tonal response. Drop action, mounted behind and below the keys, sacrifices sound and is harder to fix because the space is so cramped.

Today, there is a slowly developing renaissance in piano making. With the high cost of new pianos, many people are buying used pianos and having them rebuilt or refinished. At least a dozen companies in New York City alone are now starting to rebuild old pianos, which are being sent from all over the country. Trained piano makers are also in considerable demand.

With his own shop in New York's piano district (between 55th and 58th streets on the West Side), Kalman Detrich, a gifted piano rebuilder-technician, will open the Museum of the American Piano in 1983 to represent the evolution of piano making in America. This museum is a testimony to the reawakening of interest in the secrets of piano making and to the unique properties and qualities of the modern piano, a profound cultural achievement.

–Judith Oringer

In this article we were able to connect the subtopics of each paragraph into larger units. Now we have an article with four sections, each with a title, and have followed the author as she has shifted subtopics under the general topic of piano manufacturing. You may find it difficult initially to make the move from a subtopic for each paragraph to the larger sections. However, in time you will find it happens more easily. Test yourself by reconstructing the article using only the four subtopics as cues.

The second article is taken from a chemistry textbook and has the general title "The Origins of Chemistry." Our object here is to break it down into sections, which may consist of more than one paragraph, asking *What is this about?* to follow the change in subtopics. We completed the exercise by also asking *What is the most important idea the author has about the subtopic?* to discover the supporting idea contained in each section.

Topic —
origins of
chemistry

Key Idea —
Three steps lead
to modern
Chemistry

The earliest attempts to explain natural phenomena led to fanciful inventions—to myths and fantasies—but not to understanding. Around 600 B.C., a group of Greek philosophers became dissatisfied with these myths, which explained little. Stimulated by social and cultural change as well as curiosity, they began to ask questions about the world around them. They answered these questions by constructing lists of logical possibilities. Thus Greek philosophy was an attempt to discover the basic truths of nature by thinking things through, rather than by running laboratory experiments. The Greek philosophers did this so thoroughly and so brilliantly that the years between 600 and 400 B.C. are called the "golden age of philosophy."

Subtopic A —
Greek
philosophers

Some of the Greek philosophers (scientists, really) believed they could find a single substance that everything else was made of. A philosopher named Thales believed that this substance was water, but another named Anaximenes thought it was air. A third, Empedocles, said that the world was composed of four elements: earth, air, fire, and water.

Supporting Idea — *Greek philosophers attempted to discover the basic truths of nature by thinking things through.*

During this period, the Greek philosophers laid the foundation for one of our main ideas about the universe. Leucippus (about 440 B.C.) and Democritus (about 420 B.C.) were trying to determine whether there was such a thing as a smallest particle of matter. In doing so, they established the idea of the atom, a particle so tiny that it could not be seen. At that time there was no way to test whether atoms really existed, and more than 2,000 years passed before scientists proved that they do exist.

Subtopic B — *the Alchemists*

Supporting Idea — *the alchemists practiced the art of chemistry instead of thinking about it.*

While the Greeks were studying philosophy and mathematics, the Egyptians were practicing the art of chemistry. They were mining and purifying the metals gold, silver, and copper. They were making embalming fluids and dyes. They called this art *khemia,* and it flourished until the seventh century A.D., when it was taken over by the Arabs. The Egyptian word *khemia* became the Arabic word *alkhemia* and then the English word *alchemy.* Today our version of the word is used to mean everything that happened in chemistry between A.D. 300 and A.D. 1600.

A major goal of the alchemists was to transmute (convert) "base metals" into gold. That is, they wanted to transform less desirable elements such as lead and iron into the element gold. The ancient Arabic emperors employed many alchemists for this purpose, which, of course, was never accomplished.

The alchemists also tried to find the "philosopher's stone" (a supposed cure for all diseases) and the "elixir of life" (which would prolong life indefinitely). Unfortunately they failed in both attempts, but they did have some lucky accidents. In the course of their work, they discovered acetic acid, nitric acid, and ethyl alcohol, as well as many other substances used by chemists today.

Subtopic C — *Boyle*

Supporting Idea — *Boyle realized that every theory had to be proved by experiment.*

The modern age of chemistry dawned in 1661 with the publication of the book *The Sceptical Chymist,* written by Robert Boyle, an English chemist, physicist, and theologian. Boyle was "skeptical" because he was not willing to take the word of the ancient Greeks and alchemists as truth, especially about the elements that make up the world. Instead Boyle believed that scientists must start from basic principles, and he realized that every theory had to be proved by experiment. His new and innovative scientific approach was to change the whole course of chemistry.

—Alan Sherman, Sharon Sherman, and Leonard Russikoff

Our preview and initial skimming provided the topic and key idea. We found the subtopics fairly easily and the supporting ideas of sections A and C were directly stated in the text. However, we had to infer the supporting idea found in section B: What distinguished the alchemists from the Greek philosophers was that they practiced the art of chemistry instead of thinking about it.

Exercises

1. Preview the following selection for the topic and skim it to find the key idea. What does the rest of the paragraph consist of? Which question, or questions, does it answer?

   Suppose a sociologist fills a paragraph with phrases such as "behavioral conformity," "reference groups," and "collective values and norms," without one concrete detail or brief example. The paragraph lies inert and bloodless. Examples add vividness and interest, and they make abstractions easier to grasp and remember. One of the most successful exemplifications in textbook literature occurred in a famous economist's discussion of the choice which every economy has to make between consumer goods and capital goods. He put it in terms of the choice between guns and butter in Nazi Germany—a vivid and homely dramatization of an abstract dilemma which made the problem immediate and real to hundreds of thousands of students who not only could understand it readily but would remember it the rest of their lives. At about the same time another textbook author spoke of "maximizing one's want satisfaction through allocation of one's scarce resources." You can guess which book caught on.

   —A Guide for Authors

2. Skim the following article entitled, "The Go-Between," to find the meaning of the term *go-between* and to find the author's key idea.

The Go-Between

1 Sara sat frozen as her doctor phoned the hospital. Her blood pressure was so high, he had said, that she needed immediate attention and hospitalization. At first Sara had protested. "Can't I go in in a week or so?" she'd pleaded. "I'm too busy at work right now."

2 "In a day or so you could have a stroke," her doctor replied. Sara slumped back in her chair.

3 Once in the hospital, Sara was put on a regimen of antihypertensive drugs. To her relief, a few days later her blood pressure

had dropped and she was no longer in immediate danger. Things seemed to be looking up.

4   But suddenly, everything changed. For no apparent reason, Sara became uncharacteristically moody—brooding and glum one moment, ringing incessantly for a nurse the next. Worse, her blood pressure began to climb again. Sara's doctor tried giving her various combinations of medicines, but nothing worked. Then he took a different approach—he decided to look for an *emotional* cause for her rising blood pressure.

5   And, indeed, he found one. A long talk with Sara revealed that she considered blood pressure an "old lady's disease." She had never even known anyone under age 50 who had it. Sara's feelings were further confirmed when her well-meaning visitors said things like, "Hypertension at your age?" and "Since when are you the nervous type?" In short, Sara—barely 32 and single—was feeling very much the uptight, middle-aged spinster. Because she resented her condition so much, she didn't always take her medicine, she admitted—which certainly didn't help her blood pressure.

6   The doctor set Sara straight immediately: Anyone, no matter how young or even-tempered, can get hypertension, he explained. Knowing the truth about her illness helped Sara. The following day she put on makeup and combed her hair, read the magazine articles on blood pressure that a hospital volunteer brought her, religiously took her medicine, and told her well-meaning visitors what hypertension was really about. Twelve days later she left the hospital with her blood pressure even lower than her doctor had expected.

7   What prompted Sara's doctor to look for an emotional key to her setback? He was tipped off by a staff psychiatrist who had heard Sara joking repeatedly about having an "old lady's disease."

8   The psychiatrist who saw through Sara's jokes is not a traditional consulting specialist—a professional who interviews and evaluates patients only at another doctor's request. Instead, he's a regular part of the hospital's treatment team. He often makes rounds, reviews charts and teaches staff members how to recognize and deal with *non-psychiatric* patients' emotional needs and demands, as in Sara's case. His title: consultation/liaison psychiatrist.

9   The theory behind consultation/liaison psychiatry is that illness can cause emotional distress in a hospital patient, and this distress can make the illness worse, according to Milton Viederman, MD, director of consultation/liaison psychiatry at the New York Hospital-Cornell Medical Center in New York. Consultation/liaison psychiatry short-circuits this destructive cycle and, in doing

so, speeds recovery and reduces medical costs. The mind/body link is, of course, not new. The idea evolved from studies in psychosomatic medicine conducted as early as the 1920's. By the 1930's scientists had begun to acknowledge that emotional factors could play a part in some disorders—ulcerative colitis, hypertension and hyperthyroidism, to name a few. Today most liaison programs are found at large teaching hospitals, where they were originally funded by training grants established in the early 70's by the National Institute of Mental Health (NIMH).

10   Though consultation/liaison psychiatrists sometimes interview patients at a doctor's request (the "consultation" half of the title), their main function is to help the other staff members recognize trouble signs and work out solutions. Among the problems liaison psychiatrists tackle: patients with physical symptoms but no organic illness; patients with psychological disturbances that turn out to be caused by a disease; patients on psychiatric medicines, and patients with serious illnesses such as burns, strokes or chronic diseases.

–Gloria Blum Byron

3. Skim the article on dowsing to answer the following questions.

What is dowsing?
What are the main explanations for the phenomenon?
Where in the article do you find examples of dowsing? (Mark the examples you find.)

Dowsing and Dowsers

1   When a person walks across a field with just a stick in his hand, and by the movements of that stick detects minerals buried far below, he is dowsing. There are few virtuosos at this ancient art, but many people can achieve occasional success. Usually a forked stick is used, one fork held in either hand, but sometimes a single straight twig is preferred. If the stick turns in the hand, this indicates the presence of minerals below. Hazel and peach twigs are the traditional favorites, though other fruit or nut woods have their advocates. In today's society, however, 2 L-shaped lengths of coat hanger or copper wire are often easier to come by than a peach tree, and these seem to do the job just as well.

2   In England and America dowsers have searched mainly for water (hence the expression "water witching") but early European miners dowsed to detect metals. A few people were even able to track down criminals with the rod, but this led to widespread abuses, so the Inquisition condemned this form of dowsing, while approving it for finding water. The subject has always been con-

troversial: Some sects believed the rod was moved by the devil, and Martin Luther stated that dowsing violated the 1st commandment. Not many agree with this today, but we still have no certain explanation of the dowser's successes.

3   For instance, what can we make of John Mullins, a famous English dowser? Wealthy Sir Henry Harben had spent over £1,000 (in the last century, and pre-inflation) on professional geological advice and on well-drilling based on that advice. His estate remained short of water. Finally, Sir Henry sent for Mullins, who promptly indicated locations for 5 wells, giving the depths at which water would be found. In all cases he was correct. Many similar tales are told of him and of his contemporary, William S. Lawrence, both of whom "outguessed" experienced geologists on a number of occasions.

4   The same thing happened in Saratoga Springs, where fortunes were made and lost by men trying to find mineral water. The large companies involved in the search often used several dowsers independently to confirm one another's findings before expensive well-digging was begun.

5   The popular image of a dowser has him striding across the countryside, rod in hand, but this is not always the case. Two of the best-known dowsers have worked successfully while sitting comfortably at a table, dowsing with a pendulum suspended over a map of the area concerned. Henry Gross of Maine, probably America's best-publicized dowser, frequently used this method, as did Britain's Evelyn Penrose. Miss Penrose perhaps brought dowsing full circle in that she dowsed as much for metals as for water. She found metals, oil, and water for the Government of British Columbia, and worked for tough-minded businessmen located in the U.S., England, and Australia. An interesting point about her dowsing was that she described different physical sensations according to which metal she was seeking. Silver, she said, itched, while tin gave her a feeling of exhilaration.

6   While dowsing has brought fertility to previously arid farmland and financial success to miners, it is also credited with saving lives. In Vietnam, American forces made good use of the L-shaped coat-hanger dowsing rod to detect mines and other booby traps. Most of the men did not profess to know how or why the rods turned to give them warning—they were just glad that they did!

7   Perhaps prompted by the news reports from Vietnam, the U.S. Dept. of the Interior and Utah State University conducted a dowsing research project in which over 150 people were asked to place wooden blocks wherever they got a dowsing reaction along a certain course. Each subject walked separately, not knowing where his predecessors had placed their blocks, yet there was a strong

tendency for the blocks to be grouped in specific locations. These locations also tended to be where the earth's magnetic field changed abruptly. Such changes may be caused by water below the ground, so in this sense the experiment's results may help explain dowsing. However, magnetic-field changes are not necessarily due to water, and Professor Duane Chadwick, who conducted the experiment, emphasizes that since no wells were dug, there is no proof that any of the places chosen by several subjects would actually yield water.

8   One explanation put forward is that the dowsing rod may serve as a sort of "amplifier" of ESP impulses. This is supported by the fact that Dutch psychic M. B. Dykshoorn often uses a divining rod to supplement his clairvoyance. Perhaps the dowser receives information by ESP, and, though he is unaware of it, his muscles react just enough to move the rod. Some believe the dowser perceives the water itself; others say he senses the change in the magnetic field. Since the 5 senses do not perceive magnetism, the latter would still be a form of ESP, but with a rather more physical tie-in.

9   Another theory is that different substances give off specific vibrations to which a dowser is physically sensitive, making his muscles twitch so that, unconsciously, he turns the rod. The study of the effects of different substances and their vibration is termed radiesthesia, and its proponents consider it a science that can be used in medical diagnosis.

10 .   Yet another theory maintains that the rod itself is affected by the substances being dowsed. Most dowsers sincerely try to hold the rod still, yet it moves anyway. Unwilling to accept the unconscious muscle-movement theory, some are convinced that the rod moves of its own volition. In 1530 Georgius Agricola commented that if this were the case the rod would move for everyone, which it does not with any degree of accuracy. Nearly everyone can get *some* dowsing reaction, whether right or wrong (of Chadwick's more than 150 subjects, only one got no reaction at all), but few can approach Evelyn Penrose's purported 80% success rate. An even higher rate of 93% "hits" was reported for American John Shelley, former president of the American Society of Dowsers, based in Schenectady, N.Y.

11   Skeptics dismiss the whole subject as a sham. They say that a dowser's successes are due to an understanding of geology, a surveying of the lie of the land, vegetation, and so on. The record of the many dowsers who have repeatedly succeeded where geologists have failed suggests that this is not the whole story.

—David Wallechinsky and Irving Wallace

4. Preview the following article to establish what the topic is, what
your purpose in reading it is, and what you already know about
it. Skim it to find the key idea, if possible, and to get a sense of
how the author deals with his topic. Section the article by indicating where you think one subtopic stops and another starts, and
title the sections.

Space Technology

1   A hallmark of the twentieth century is mankind's entrance into
space. The convenient boundaries of 1900 and 2000 can serve for
a journey from the theory of space travel to a plateau of space
technology that will set much of the twenty-first century's economic agenda. The importance of the twentieth century will become increasingly clear as we observe space technology develop
in the 1980s and 1990s.

2   The first serious scientific work to examine the possibility of
space travel was undertaken by a self-taught Russian genius, Kon-
stantin Tsiolkovsky. Stimulated by Isaac Newton's mathematical
theories on gravitation and action/reaction and by Jules Verne's
science fiction, Tsiolkovsky at the turn of the century wrote a series of papers outlining the machinery needed for space travel. His
work was followed by that of the American rocket pioneer, Robert
Goddard, who built and flew the world's first liquid fuel rocket in
1926, and by Herman Oberth in Germany, who wrote popular
books on the technical aspects of space travel in the 1920s and
stimulated rocket clubs for its realization. The German army in
the 1930s, used the work of these three pioneers to develop the
world's first large-scale rocket program. The program's leader,
Wernher von Braun, was a former Oberth club member and future
leader of the U.S. Apollo program. The Germans culminated their
program in 1944 with the infamous V-2 rocket, which, besides
reigning terror on London, was a critical stepping stone in the
technology of space travel.

3   Soon after World War II, the Soviet Union decided to develop
the intercontinental ballistic missle (ICBM) to counter the U.S.
strategic bomber force, and in 1958 the Soviet program brought
forth a rocket with the capacity to lift a satellite into orbit—Sputnik I.

4   Shocked by the Sputnik launch, the United States responded
with a space program that placed men on the moon in 1969. It
also launched in the 1960s, weather and communication satellites,
the latter being the first commercial use of space. Both the U.S.
and Soviet military services found satellites useful for reconnaissance and communications.

5   The 1970s were highlighted by eye-opening probes to Mercury, Venus, Mars, and Jupiter; by the establishment of a small but long-term Soviet space station; by the launch of satellites to study the universe through X rays and other new methods and to provide commercially useful information about the earth's agriculture, forest, oceans, and mineral resources; and by the beginnings of the European, Japanese, and Chinese space programs. The 1980s began with striking photographs of Saturn and the launch from America of the first reusable space vehicle, the Shuttle. What might we expect during the rest of the century?

6   In scientific exploration, the Voyager II Probe, which previously photographed Jupiter and Saturn close up, will pass near the planet Uranus in 1986, and if all goes well, near Neptune in 1989. A satellite will orbit Venus in 1988 to prepare detailed maps of that planet's surface. Much exciting exploration will also occur beyond our solar system. A telescope with a ninety-six-inch mirror will be launched in 1986 to study the universe with unprecedented penetration and clarity. Other satellites in the 1980s will study gamma rays and infrared light in space to learn more about neutron stars, blackholes, quasars, and other phenomena so as to increase our understanding of the universe's history, structure, and processes.

7   We will also continue our search for life in the universe. The quest for intelligent life will be through an ongoing program that computer-analyzes cosmic radio waves reaching earth to determine if any are the product of conscious thought rather than random universal emissions. In the 1990s, the search for primitive unintelligent life in the solar system may result in probes to a comet, to Saturn's moon, Titan, and a return to Mars. These are the most promising celestial bodies for finding the basic chemical building blocks of life in earth's neighborhood.

8   The commercial development of space will most likely follow three tracks: the expansion of services provided by communication satellites; the wider integration of earth-sensing technology into economic development; and finally, the evolution of small factories in space to produce specialized high-value products.

9   Communication satellites up to now have provided television, voice, and computer data transmission through centralized systems. That is, signals are fed into a central point and relayed by satellite to another central point, which receives and re-transmits them through ground-based airwaves or telephone lines. Starting in the mid-1980s, satellites will transmit television programming directly to the home without intermediary ground stations. Rural areas poorly served by ground-based transmitters will be able to receive clear, high-quality television pictures. In the late 1980s, if

current programs are successful, satellites will relay voice and data transmission directly from small mobile units carried by vehicles or individuals. In one case, an individual could use a small hand-held communicator to send telegraph-like messages to anyone else having a similar communicator without resorting to any telephone lines. People could keep in touch with each other at any time, no matter if they were driving, sailing, flying, backpacking, or whatever.

10   Earth-sensing satellites provide pictures of our planet utilizing visible light, infrared, and other techniques that have commercial applications. These include prediction of crops, probable location of fish, promising sites for oil drilling, likely directions of forest blights, and other applications that can mean millions of dollars in savings through better planning. Earthsensing satellite technology has been an experimental government program. In the future, it will be developed by private enterprise, which will tailor the technology to specific market needs.

11   The most interesting commercial development of the 1990s will be the establishment of small manned and unmanned factories in space to produce pharmaceuticals, alloy metals, electronic crystals, and other valuable, low-volume products. Space offers special conditions that are advantageous to certain engineering and production processes; near zero gravity, near vacuum, and the natural availability of cryogenic temperatures. Space Shuttle missions in the 1990s, especially those including Space Lab, will provide experimental information necessary to determine which products can be most effectively manufactured in space. Actual manufacturing may be in independent, free-flying units placed in orbit by the Shuttle and later retrieved after automated equipment has processed materials utilizing the unique characteristics of space. Other production will require humans in space. NASA is suggesting that the United States establish a space station in the early 1990s as a multipurpose facility with modules for manufacturing purposes. The speed that space production develops in the 1990s will depend upon governmental development of a space station and the profitability of space-manufactured products.

12   The military will be increasingly involved in space unless Soviet/American agreements dictate otherwise. Both the United States and the Soviet Union are researching and developing a variety of space weapons. The most immediate are anti-satellite weapons designed to explode near or to crash into existing military reconnaissance and communication satellites. Attacking an enemy's satellites is an effective first step in any strategic war. Given the current pace of development, anti-satellite systems will be operational in the 1980s. There is also intensified research into

laser and particle-beam weapons, which fire concentrated energy at targets in pinpoint fashion and at the speed of light. In the openness of space, their capabilities are global and instantaneous, and are especially adaptable to stopping intercontinental ballistic missiles, if properly targeted. If efforts to develop the energy sources and the precise targeting devices needed for these weapons continue at the current pace, some form of laser and/or particle-beam weaponry can be operational in the 1990s. The impact of this on the international balance of power and the future development of space is a topic of intense debate.

13   If space weapons have not thwarted the civilian development of space, interesting new possibilities will emerge around the year 2000. By the late 1990s, some profitable activities will have probably developed in space manufacturing. For instance, the moon is rich in silicon, magnesium, titanium, and other commercially useful minerals. There is a possibility that we will return to the moon in the first part of the twenty-first century to set up mining operations. Lunar ores could be catapulted into space by electromagnetic devices taking advantage of the moon's low gravity and absence of atmosphere. The ores would be caught and collected by large cones in stable orbits around the moon. They then would be transported by space tug to a factory that would process them into metals, later to be used in the construction of gigantic satellites. Some of these satellites could contain mini-space towns and others could provide electrical energy for earth. The latter would collect and convert solar energy into electricity, twenty-four hours a day, using silicon cells. The electricity would be transmitted to the earth's power grid through microwaves or lasers. In a sense we would be developing raw material acquisition and production centers in space analogous to the rise of the Mesabi iron ore range and the Pittsburgh steel works in the nineteenth century. Industrial production would be developing in a new physical region.

14   In exploration, the year 2000 may see the re-emergence of the age-old dream of a manned trip to Mars. Again, the space station and experience of crews being in space for long stays will be useful in making this dream possible. Its realization, however, will be determined by the nation's fiscal priorities at that time. Overall, our space activities in the twenty-first century will be similar to the opening of North America in the eighteenth and nineteenth centuries. First exploration, and then economic development—this will set the stage for a new round of exploration.

–T. Stephen Cheston

5. Preview the following excerpts from a chapter of the book *Overcoming Math Anxiety* by Sheila Tobias. Skim to locate as many of

the subtopics as possible, and mark them with a check. Predict some of the supporting ideas. Section and title the reading.

The Primacy of Mathematics, or If I Could Do Math I Would . . .

1 One day soon after we began working with people who avoid mathematics, a visiting Soviet mathematician stopped in at the Math Clinic. It took a while to explain to him what the clinic had been designed to do, how people who have long ago given up on their ability to learn math need to be recaptured and motivated to try again. Finally he seemed to understand. Then he began to laugh and with a big, generous smile he commented: "You Americans are all the same. You think everybody has to know everything."

2 In a way this is true, although he needn't have been quite so smug.* The United States graduates more young people from high school than most other nations, and we have a larger proportion of people enrolled in some sort of post-secondary schooling than any other nation in the world. On paper at least we are committed to the belief that everyone should receive a general education and that specialized training should be postponed until later. Still, not everyone learns everything. Many of us elect to stay within a fairly narrow comfort zone of knowledge. If we do well at reading long, nonfiction books and writing essays about them, we take more courses in history. If we excel at learning one foreign language, we take another one or two. If we learn best by handling things, we opt for lab courses. And so on.

3 By the time we are adults we are pretty smart in our special fields but feel rather dumb when we move outside our comfort zone. What began as a set of preferences becomes in time a mental prison that makes us feel conflicted and even anxious about stepping outside. It is difficult enough for a young person to be a beginner, dependent on other people to show the way. To be a beginner as an adult takes a special kind of courage and enthusiasm for the subject. That is why I believe that a slight discomfort with mathematics acquired in elementary or secondary school can develop into a full-fledged syndrome of anxiety and avoidance by the time one has graduated from school and gone to work.

---

*Soviet children seem to have just as much trouble learning elementary arithmetic as American children. A collection of essays on teaching arithmetic in the Soviet Union reports one child's strategy for getting the right answer as follows: "I add, subtract, multiply, and then divide until I get the answer that is in the back of the book."

4   How do these preferences and antagonisms develop? Are they inevitable? Do we hate math, as so many say they do, because one elementary school teacher made us afraid of it? Did we simply get off on the wrong foot and get stuck there? Or have we accepted someone's assumption about our kind of mind and what we thought was the nature of mathematics? Were we too young, from a neurological point of view, when we were first exposed to numbers? Or was too much going on during our adolescent years when we should have been concentrating on algebra? Does the fault lie in the curriculum, in the subject, in ourselves, or in the society at large?

5   There are no easy answers to such questions. But some interesting insights have come from people who have avoided mathematics all their lives. In dozens of "math autobiographies," the nature of math anxiety, its causes, and its consequences begin to emerge.

6   "If I could do math I would . . ."*

7   Ask anyone who "hates math" to complete this sentence and the first response will be incredulity. "What, me do math? Impossible." If prodded, however, people reveal all kinds of unexplored needs. "If I could do math I would . . . fix my own car." "If I could do math I would . . . fly an airplane." "If I could do math I would work the F stops on my camera." "If I could do math . . ."

8   People who don't know what math is don't know what math isn't. Therefore, fear of math may lead them to avoid all manner of data and to feel uncomfortable working with things. Any mathematician will tell you that you don't need mathematics to work the F stops on the camera, or to fix the car, or even to start your own business.** But fearing math makes us wary of activities that *may* involve ratios (F stops), or neat rows of numbers (bookkeeping), or mechanics. What could we do if we could do math? It depends, of course, on how much math we know and how confident we are of our knowledge. But it is safe to say that if we were comfortable with numbers we could do something we are not doing now.

9   Most people leave school as failures at math, or at least feeling like failures. Some students are not even given a chance to fail. Identified early as noncollege material, they are steered away from pre-college mathematics and tracked into business or "general math." But high school students who are not going on to col-

---

*"If I could do math I would" is a phrase used by Bonnie Donady of the Wesleyan Math Clinic in her counseling.

**F stops are a measure of the lens opening: The higher the number, the smaller the opening.

lege need algebra and geometry just as much as the college-bound. Algebra and geometry are not just pre-college courses. There is evidence that knowing these two subjects alone will make the difference between a low score and a high score on most standardized entry-level tests for civil service, federal service, and many industrial occupations, not to mention the armed services. Lucy Sells, who has been studying the link between mathematics and vocational opportunities, believes that knowledge of algebra and geometry divides the unskilled and clerical jobs from the better-paying, upwardly mobile positions available to high school graduates. She estimates that mastery of high school algebra alone will enable a high school graduate to do so much better on a civil service or industrial entrance exam that he or she could immediately start working at a higher level and be earmarked for on-the-job training as well. Just one more year of high school math could make the difference between a starting salary of $8,000 and one of $11,000. . . .

10   It comes as no surprise that fields like engineering, computer programming, accounting, geology, and other technical work all require some mathematics. It is not widely known, however, that mathematics, disguised as "quantitative analysis" or "handling data" or "planning," will be used even in nontechnical work areas. It can be very painful to discover in mid-career that we cannot get facts from our figures or that an occupation that looked comfortably free of mathematics at the lower levels will require familiarity with quantitative methods for advancement. Yet those who supervise, plan, and manage in fields such as social work, librarianship, retail sales, school administration, and even publishing now need to be familiar with or at least willing to learn more math. . . .

11   Since fear of math spills over into fear of "data" and "things," one way to measure the effect of math avoidance on our lives is to ask ourselves how we feel about "data" and "things." The Dictionary of Occupational Titles, published regularly by the U.S. Department of Labor, uses "data," "people," and "things" as one way to categorize occupations. A quick glance at any page in that volume indicates that if we cross "data" and "things" off our lists of possibilities, our occupational choices will be very limited indeed. Another measure of math avoidance can be inferred from vocational interest tests. Typically these group an individual's personal traits into categories which in turn can be translated into jobs. One of the tests, the Self-Directed Search Inventory, lists as "interest-types" *realistic, investigative, artistic, enterprising, social,* and *conventional.* John Holland, designer of this inventory, also

publishes an *Occupation Finder* in which occupations are coded according to the same categories. Engineering, for example, is defined as "realistic-investigative," management as "realistic-enterprising-social," and so on. In fact, far more occupations require realistic, enterprising, and investigative skills than require primarily "social" attributes.

12   Of course, the characteristics of each occupation are derived from people currently at work. Thus, there is a tautology: if engineering is dominated by "realistic-investigative" types, people in the field will of course report that this configuration of skills and temperament is highly valued in engineering and essential to it. Also, these opinions may contain hidden biases against women and "feminine" traits. John Holland is himself very mindful of this and tries to factor out such bias. But when an entire society associates math, science, things, and data with male pursuits, it is difficult to eliminate this bias altogether. And nothing changes the fact that math avoidance is extremely limiting for people at all levels of work. Competence in math is, as Sells put it, truly a vocational filter.

13   Not everyone who avoided mathematics in school remains incompetent, however. In two years of interviewing adults who are math anxious and those who are not, I have found that some people learn to cope with numbers in interesting and sometimes extraordinary ways. They know they have gaps in their knowledge, but they are sufficiently confident and familiar with the way their own minds work to reconstruct problems and solve them.

14   In a session for a mixed group of adults, Knowles Dougherty, a specialist in teaching the math disabled, demonstrated this phenomenon. He began by asking the group to do a simple subtraction problem in their heads:

A woman is 38 years old. It is now 1976. In what year was she born?

15   "Don't tell me the answer," he said. "But as I go around the room, do tell me how you worked out the solution." The methods were astonishingly varied. One adult male said, "I had that certain feeling I had to get to the nearest ten. So I added two to 38 to get 40 and then subtracted 40 from 76 and then added two to the answer." Another person reported that she had adjusted the problem to her own age. Starting with her own year of birth, she added and subtracted until she got 1938 (the correct answer).

16   Each adult was a little ashamed of his system. Everyone assumed that just as there was only one right answer to math problems, there was probably only one right way to subtract. But Dougherty reassured them the systems they were using were le-

gitimate algorithms (an algorithm being just a system for getting an answer). If you have to get to the nearest ten, then get there. If you have to use some personal reference point, use it. The fact that most people had not used the method they had been taught in school indicated that they had probably learned a fair amount of mathematics on their own since second grade.

17   Many adults know all this intuitively and develop ways to work out number problems that make sense to them. In Washington, D.C. a professional woman receives bimonthly account records from her bookkeeper. She can make no sense at all of what they show until she goes off by herself and reorganizes the data. She turns columns into rows and rows into boxes, adjusting the numerical information to fit her thinking style. Then she returns to the discussion with her bookkeeper, facts in hand. Some people need to draw pictures. Some have to speak the numbers or the problem out loud.

18   These people share a willingness to restructure a problem so that it makes sense to them. The executive who could not get the facts from her figures had not yet learned how to do that.

19   Why can't everyone make such a healthy accommodation? Why can't we just go out and learn the math we need when we need it? . . . Apart from the psychological blocks that may grow up over time, some of the issues are these: Math is difficult because it is rigorous and complex. As we advance in math, the notation becomes abstract and general. This adds to its mysteriousness. Besides, there are conflicts between the common everyday use of words and the use of these words in math. Moreover, unless we are concurrently studying science or engineering, math is not as integrated into the rest of the curriculum as are reading, writing, and spelling. Hence we do not immediately apply the math we learn.

20   Math typically is not learned as part of a group effort. Since we work by ourselves, the process by which we either get or do not get an insight is very obscure. And since we do not learn how our own minds work, we never understand why one idea is difficult for us and the next one not.

21   Finally, people remember math as being taught in an atmosphere of tension created by the emphasis on right answers and especially by the demands of timed tests. Their math teachers, who may well have been patient and sincere to begin with, became frustrated by the challenge of getting students to understand "simple" ideas; even if they did not start out this way, many of them eventually became cantankerous, short of patience, and contemptuous of error. Math anxious adults can recall with appalling

accuracy the exact wording of a trick question or the day they had to stand at the blackboard alone, even if these events took place thirty years before.

22   It will surprise no one that millions do not learn mathematics successfully, however well or poorly it is taught. . . .

23   Why should adults want to relearn arithmetic? Why should those of us who have successfully avoided mathematics all these years bother about it at all? Mathematicians have usually been admired for their intelligence but also somewhat scorned for their otherworldliness. Why is their subject suddenly so central to modern life?

24   To some extent mathematics has always played a role, particularly at the higher occupational levels. The news is that math is increasingly pervasive and also that these occupational levels are beginning to be reached by different people. No longer are academically bright males from advantaged homes the only ones who are expected to go as far in math as they can. In the last twenty years, females and males from less advantaged backgrounds have been encouraged to take school seriously and to expect advancement on the job. These groups have traditionally had little success with higher math and have "mercifully" been allowed to drop it. Much to their surprise and dismay, as their careers advance, math returns to haunt them.

25   The primacy of mathematics in today's world, then, exhibits the traditional themes of American history: ever-increasing dependence on technology and ever-increasing democratization of jobs.

—Sheila Tobias

Writing Exercises

Choose one of the following exercises. As you write, be conscious of where your subtopics start and end. Could someone else section your writing easily?

1. Write a summary of one of the following topics:

   Flexibility
   Skimming and Sectioning
   Close Reading

2. Just as there are different ways of reading, there are different ways of looking at a painting: from far away, from mid-distance, and

from close up. By referring to the four approaches to reading on
p. 120, describe what the artist looks for from each point.

3. Write a short paragraph outlining when you would try to read fast
and how you would go about it.

IV How and Why Did the Author Write It?

That there is more order in the world than
appears at first sight is not discovered until the
order is looked for.

    –N. R. Hanson, *Math in a Changing World*

In this unit your attention is directed to the authors. We shall examine the various techniques authors use to present their material, and we shall discuss why it is important to know the author's purpose in writing. Recognizing the principal patterns of organization will give you a firm grasp of the techniques or strategies an author uses to make a point and will provide you with another method of predicting the direction of the author's thinking. You will continue to preview, skim, and section your reading so as to recognize these patterns and gain a clear notion of the flow of the author's ideas.

    We have already discussed why it is important for you to know why you read something. It is equally important—perhaps more so—for you to understand why the author has written it. Authors have two main purposes for writing nonfiction: to inform and to persuade. This unit includes an examination of these two types of writing and a discussion of how you can become a critical reader by applying certain criteria in evaluating the work of the author. The unit ends with a chapter that demonstrates how active reading leads to active learning, enabling you to apply questioning and other reading skills to studying and reviewing as well as to writing, listening, and speaking.

10 *Recognizing Basic Structure*

Letters make up words, words form sentences, and paragraphs develop topics. Letters must appear in a specific order for you to understand the word. Words in sentences must also have some kind of order. Sentences must have an appropriate beginning, middle, and end in order to be clearly understood. In the same way, reading selections are structured with a beginning, middle, and end: an introduction, development, and conclusion.

Authors use the basic structure of introduction, development, and conclusion to connect their ideas. Seeing how the topic, key idea, subtopics, supporting ideas, and supporting details are presented and connected through this interdependent structure will help you understand and remember what you read.

The Introduction

Although the introduction is not always labeled and may vary in length from only the first paragraph to the first several paragraphs of a passage, it is easy to recognize. It is always located at the beginning of each book, chapter, article, or section. What other common traits do introductions have? It usually provides you with a sense of the key idea that will be explained further in the development of the reading. Frequently, the introduction also contains the subtopics, in the order in which the author will present them, as a preview of the major points that will be discussed in the development of the passage. The introduction gives clues to help you predict what the article will include.

In addition to, or instead of, being a plan of the reading, the introduction may serve two other purposes: It may provide background information about the topic or give a context for the reading selection. Or it may explain the importance or the relevance of the key idea by stating how the key idea applies to you or why you should know about it. This involvement helps you to focus on why you are reading a particular selection. Regardless of the specific function of the introduction, it must attract your attention and convince you that the passage is worth reading. Occasionally, to arouse your interest the author may begin a selection by describing a situation that is contrary to the key idea and that will be refuted in the article or by asking provocative questions that will be answered in the development of the article.

Example

Read the first paragraph, or introduction, of the reading selection entitled "Photographing Emotions." What is the function of this introduction? It tells you the topic, photographs, and introduces the key idea that the author will explain in the selection: "Photographs that appeal to basic human emotions have a special kind of impact." What else does the author include in this introduction? The author states that "some of the subjects that appeal to basic human emotions are related to conflict, sex, ambition, and escape." Ways of appealing to each of these four different basic human emotions are the subtopics. Now you know what the topic, key idea, and subtopics of this selection are, and you can predict the author's major points and the probable order in which he will discuss them.

Photographing Emotions

1
Key
Idea   Photographs that appeal to basic human emotions have
a special kind of impact. The viewer does not simply
observe the subject, but reacts emotionally to it. The
viewer may laugh, feel sad, or simply empathize with
sub- the emotions of the subjects. Some of the subjects that
topics appeal to basic human emotions are related to conflict,
sex, ambition, and escape.

}*Introduction*

2   Conflict exists when people compete against others
or against the forces of nature or society. It may be seen
in photographs of firefighters battling a blaze, residents
sandbagging to fight a flood, ordinary people struggling
against disaster. The human competitive spirit is seen
also in sports, in elections, in business, and in a grimmer
way, in war. Accidents are another context in which we
can observe basic human conflict against the forces of
nature and society.

3   Sex appeal has become a standard phrase in our language and it describes another appeal to basic human
emotions. Photographs of attractive men and women,
singly, in couples, and in groups, usually appeal to human beings of both sexes: they attract the eye and trigger
emotional responses. Sex appeal may be observed in action in newspaper and magazine advertisements and in
human interest stories and articles.

}*Development*

4   The appeal to ambition can be seen in pictures of
people who have achieved success in any area of business, science, athletics, cultural activities, industry, or
in other human pursuits. People are interested in others
who have achieved success, who have overcome odds,
or who by the workings of chance have attained a measure of fame or a notable position.

5   Finally, photos of people in recreational activities
possess escape appeal. Escape is represented when the
subjects portrayed are shown attempting to escape the
monotony of everyday life by having fun, in the pursuit
of pleasure and adventure. The person with an interesting hobby, the surfer, or the mountain climber, appeals
to the viewer's desire for escape. For a moment the
viewer can empathize with the subject and escape the
routine of life.

6   Seeing picture possibilities that appeal to basic human emotions is a skill that can be developed. Look at

your photographic subjects. Ask yourself what feeling or
emotion the subject generates in you. Then consider
how best to convey that same feeling or emotion to your ⎫ *Conclusion*
viewer. Ask yourself not only what the idea of your photograph is to be, but also what the emotion of the photograph is to be. Your own emotional sensitivity to the
scenes you perceive can be developed.

–Marvin Rosen

The Development of the Topic

After you have read the introduction and have answered the questions *What is this about?* and *What is the author's most important idea
about the topic?* you are ready to move on to the development of the
selection. The development elaborates on the ideas that were mentioned in the introduction. It constitutes the bulk of the selection because it restates the key idea, includes the supporting ideas and the
supporting details, and answers these questions for the key idea, supporting ideas, and supporting details: What is the most important
thing the author is saying about the topic? Who? What? Why? How?
When? Where? Which? What kind?

   In the development part of the reading the author may connect the
supporting ideas by listing the information, by putting the information in a specific order, by comparing and contrasting two or more
ideas, or by discussing the causes or effects of the key idea. (These
ways in which the author may organize information are discussed in
detail in Chapter 11.)

Example

Let's return to the reading selection, "Photographing Emotions," and
see how the development of this passage builds upon its introduction.
You learned from the introduction that the topic is photographing
emotions, the key idea is the importance of appealing to basic human
emotions when taking photographs, and the subtopics are the ways
of appealing to each of the four basic human emotions: conflict, sex,
ambition, and escape. Read the next four paragraphs of "Photographing Emotions," looking for the ways by which the author connects
the subtopics presented in the introduction to the ideas he presents
in the development of the selection. Each of the subtopics introduced
in the introduction is expanded upon or supported in the develop-

ment of the passage. The author explains each of the appeals to human emotions and gives examples of pictures that may arouse these emotions. Your predictions from reading the introduction help you to understand and retain the material you will encounter in this part of the passage.

The Conclusion

The final part of a reading selection is the conclusion, which pulls together the ideas presented in the introduction and development. You can find the conclusion in the last paragraph or paragraphs of a reading or as a separate section or chapter. The conclusion may be a summary of or a commentary on the selection. If it is a summary, it will review the most important ideas of the passage, usually in the order presented in the reading, as the introduction frequently does. Like the introduction, the conclusion will answer the questions *What is this about?* and *What is the author's most important idea about the topic?* It may also repeat the subtopics and the supporting ideas. If it is a commentary, the conclusion will tell you what the author believes to be the implications of the material. The author may derive a generalization from the passage or use the conclusion to recommend an action or thought. Sometimes the conclusion consists of both a summary and a commentary.

Example

Let's return again to "Photographing Emotions," remembering the connection of the ideas from the introduction to the development. Now read the final paragraph, or conclusion, of the passage. Is it a summary of or a commentary on the ideas that the author presented in the development of the selection? Or is it both? Does it review the key idea or does it make recommendations based on the key idea? This conclusion does not restate the ideas in the selection, but rather offers suggestions to the reader based on these ideas. It tells the reader how to develop the skill of taking pictures that appeal to basic human emotions. How is this idea related to the introduction and development of the selection? The introduction and the development of the passage tell the reader *why* it is important to appeal to basic human emotions when taking photographs; the conclusion tells the reader *how* to appeal to basic human emotions. Even though it is not a summary of the reading, it builds on the introduction and the development of the selection and extends the key idea of the selection.

Signal Words

Understanding the basic structure of a reading helps you to comprehend and retain the author's ideas. You can identify the structure of a reading more easily by recognizing special words called **signal words.** Authors use signal words to connect ideas and to help readers follow the directions of the authors' thoughts. Signal words tell you, the reader, what to expect. They help you predict what you will read.

Signal words can indicate that a key idea, supporting idea, or supporting details are about to appear. These signal words can be divided into two groups: those that signal that the thought is continuing in the same direction and those that signal a change in course or the introduction of a new thought. You can think about signal words as road signs: Some tell you to continue in the same direction as you were proceeding, but others indicate that you should turn in another direction.

Words that indicate a continuing thought

also	first
besides	next
furthermore	then
in addition (to)	one reason
likewise	another reason
similarly	for example
moreover	for instance

Words that indicate a shift in direction

although	on the contrary
but	on the other hand
despite	otherwise
however	rather
in spite of	whereas
nevertheless	yet
notwithstanding	

Signal words also indicate the introduction and the conclusion of a reading selection. Many textbook chapters begin with the words "We shall study." You have probably read these words many times, but you may not have thought of them as introducing the introduction and predicting the key idea. The following phrases indicate the introduction and may help you predict the key idea.

The main point is . . .
There are three major ideas shown here . . .
This chapter deals with . . .
In the following chapter . . .

Some words mark the beginning of a summary or the consequence of ideas previously presented. These words indicate that you are about to read a conclusion.

accordingly
as a result
consequently
finally
in conclusion
in summary
therefore
thus
to sum up

You do not need to memorize these signal words, but you should recognize them and think about them when you read and write. They enable ideas to flow smoothly, and they help you to follow those ideas. By using signal words to cue you to shifts in the author's thoughts, you can anticipate the meaning of what you will read.

Exercises

1. Preview "The Feminization of Academe." Then read the selection. Identify the introduction, development, and conclusion by labeling them in the text. Describe the function of the introduction and the conclusion. Next, identify the key ideas, subtopics, and supporting ideas by marking them in the text. Finally, circle the signal words and explain the purpose of each signal word. (For instance, to indicate a continuation of the same thought, to introduce a new thought, or to introduce the introduction or the conclusion.)

The Feminization of Academe

1   American colleges once devoted themselves almost exclusively to the preparation of young men for the ministry and teaching. By the middle of the nineteenth century this practice appeared to be placing colleges in ever greater financial trouble. As commercial growth agitated a country in the midst of rapid industrial expansion, the country's young men sought business success and shunned both the ministry and teaching. With declining enrollments, colleges faced three alternatives: They could go bankrupt, they could open their doors to women, or they could revise their curricula to cater to the needs of youth determined to exploit the possibilities of an industrial society.

2   Turning to women seemed natural enough to many, though

there was little precedent for it. As men focused their attention on commercial success, women came increasingly to be seen as the guardians of culture. Because colleges had long been the repositories of culture in America, women and colleges seemed ideally suited to one another. When schools opened their doors, women flocked to them, some seeking training for careers as teachers, a very few hoping to break the barrier of such traditionally male domains as the ministry or medicine, and many more searching for literary and artistic fulfillment. It seemed a happy marriage.

3   But at the same time that the colleges were encouraging the enrollment of young women, they were revamping their curricula in the hope of recapturing their male audience. Through courses in political science, economics, sociology, engineering, medicine, law, and business administration, college administrators sought to convince the public of the colleges' utilitarian character. Many colleges, emulating the example of European institutions, transformed themselves into universities with graduate departments and professional schools and began to argue that science could speed economic and social development. At the turn of the century these schools were often available to women; because of overexpansion, some had little choice. But it was assumed from the beginning that they would appeal primarily to men.

4   These curricular and institutional innovations proved tremendously successful, but the success was tinged with irony. By welcoming young women at the same time that they were altering their curricula to appeal to young men, universities found themselves with a growing female student body dedicated to an educational ideal that the university was trying to abandon. The danger, as many saw it, was that women would overrun the university and jeopardize the reform effort.

5   In 1902 fear gripped many at the University of Chicago, who foresaw the imminent feminization of their school. One professor, economist J. Lawrence Laughlin, sought to reassure his colleagues. He was aware that in the ten years since the university's opening the female enrollment had increased from 25 percent to 50 percent of the student body, but he predicted that once the university's scientific programs and professional schools became firmly established the trend would be reversed.

6   The congestion of numbers [of women students] is now due largely to the fact that the undergraduate courses are practically used by women as an advanced normal school to prepare for teaching, the one profession easiest to enter by them. At present, this part of the university is the main part. The best men are going less and less into teaching. Just so soon as proper support and endowments are given to the work which offers training for careers in engineering, railways, banking,

trade and industry, law, medicine, etc. the disproportion of men will doubtless remedy itself.*

7   On one level the concern over female enrollment at Chicago, as well as Laughlin's reassurances, reflected the new university's parochial desire for status; but on another level it reflected the pervasive fear of feminization that plagued American society in the early twentieth century. As the economic change of a rapidly industrializing society brought social dislocation, Americans clung ever more tenaciously to their most basic assumptions about sexual identity and fought any changes in accepted sex-role divisions.

8   Education played a singularly important role in this drama, because the special circumstances of the development of the university placed American higher education at the fulcrum of social change. No sooner had higher education been opened to women as a relatively unnecessary pursuit in a commercial, industrializing society, than it became clear to many that education could make a significant contribution to that industrialization. But by the time education's potential value was perceived, women had flooded the schools, filling 50 percent of the student body at many schools by 1900. Society was faced with two alternatives. It could acquiesce in the surrender of education to women and thereby protect the separation of sexual spheres, but suffer the loss of a valuable institution for male training, or it could continue trying to make higher education more attractive to men and risk the danger to sex-role divisions posed by sexual integration. Apprehensively, society chose the latter alternative and accepted coeducation.

–Carol Ruth Berkin and Mary Beth Norton

2. Preview the following selection. Then read it. Identify the introduction, development, and conclusion by labeling them in the text. Describe the function of the introduction and the conclusion. Finally, circle the signal words and explain the purpose of each signal word. What type of signal words are most frequently used in this reading selection: signal words that indicate a continuing thought or signal words that indicate a shift in direction?

1   The radical *behaviorists* led first by John B. Watson (1913) and later by B. F. Skinner (1938) argued that science must investigate public, observable events. The behaviorists concluded that since

---

*J. Lawrence Laughlin to A. K. Parker, July 25, 1902, the President's Papers, University of Chicago Archives.

mental events such as thoughts and images and consciousness cannot be observed directly, they have no place in the science of psychology.

2   The behaviorists' arguments had tremendous impact on American psychology and, indeed, on American society. From the early 1920's through the late 1950's almost all experimental psychologists abandoned the investigation of mental events and substituted the study of behavior, the latter being more readily observable and, thus, more amenable to study by scientific methods. As a consequence of this choice of subject matter, these decades led to many statements about the effects of reinforcement on the behavior of people and laboratory animals, but they provided little insight into the mysteries of memory, language, and thought. Since the late 1950's, however, a revolution has occurred. Experimental psychologists have turned their talents increasingly to the investigation of the mind, and there has been a rebirth of interest in what is now called the cognitive approach to psychology.

The Cognitive Approach

3   The essence of the cognitive approach can be summarized by considering three of the major characteristics that distinguish it from behaviorism. First, it emphasizes knowing, rather than responding. Cognitive psychologists are concerned with finding scientific means for studying the mental processes involved in the acquisition and application of knowledge. This means that their major emphasis is not upon stimulus-response bonds, but on mental events. This stress on mind as opposed to behavior is consistent with intuition; we define ourselves at least as much by our thoughts as by our actions. Descartes said *"Cogito ergo sum"* ("I think; therefore I am"). His words would not have rung so true had he proclaimed, "I behave; therefore I am."

4   Of course, the cognitive approach does not ignore behavior, but rather than being the object of study, responses are used as indicators that enable inferences regarding mental events. Perhaps the best way to state the distinction is to paraphrase Noam Chomsky, the great linguist, who wrote that calling psychology "behavioral science" is like designating natural science "the science of meter readings" (Chomsky, 1968, p. 58). Chomsky eloquently expresses the cognitive viewpoint: to call psychology the *science of behavior* is to confuse the evidence studied (behavior) with the goal of the study (an understanding of the mind). Indeed, in attempting to banish unobservables from the realm of psychology, the behaviorists were striving to impose a restriction on psychological theorizing that is not imposed in any of the other sciences. No one has

ever observed directly either gravity or a quark, yet physicists are not deemed unscientific for including these concepts in their theories.

5   A second characteristic of the cognitive approach is that it emphasizes *mental structure* or *organization*. It is argued that an individual's knowledge is organized and that new stimuli are interpreted in light of this knowledge. This stress on organization is particularly apparent in the theory of Jean Piaget, the Swiss scholar who has contributed so much to our understanding of human development. Piaget has argued that all living creatures are born with an invariant tendency—to organize experience—and that this tendency provides an important impetus for cognitive development.

6   The third characteristic of the cognitive approach is that the individual is viewed as being active, constructive, and planful, rather than as being the passive recipient of environmental stimulation. The analogies frequently used by the behaviorist reveal a passive view of the organism. Humans are described as blank slates upon which the environment writes, wax upon which the environment impresses itself, and mirrors that reflect the environment. On the other hand, the cognitive theorist views the individual as an active participant in the process of acquiring and using knowledge. The individual is thought of as actively constructing a view of reality, selectively choosing some aspects of experience for further attention, and attempting to commit some information to memory. The cognitive theorist assumes that any complete theory of human cognition must include an analysis of the plans or strategies people use for thinking, remembering, and understanding and producing language.

7   A good way to highlight the distinctions between the behaviorist and the cognitive views of human nature is to examine how proponents of each approach have attempted to study morality, a topic outside the realm of this book. Behaviorists have focused on certain moral (or immoral) behaviors, such as cheating, helping others, and disobeying authority (reflecting characteristic 1). They have assumed that moral development involves nothing more than the learning of additional moral behaviors (characteristic 2), and have viewed such moral development as the result of reinforcement and punishment to which the individual has been subjected (characteristic 3). Cognitive theorists, on the other hand, have focused on the thought processes by which people decide between right and wrong (characteristic 1). They have argued that moral development brings with it increasingly complex and organized rules for making moral decisions (characteristic 2), and that such development is dependent upon the active construction

of the individual (characteristic 3). It is hard to imagine two more radically different approaches to the same topic!

–Darlene Howard

Writing Exercise

Write a summary of this chapter. Your summary should include an introduction, development, and conclusion. Signal words should indicate how the ideas are related.

11 Recognizing Patterns of Organization

Recognizing how authors structure reading selections helps the reader to understand and to remember the information. This chapter examines the more specific methods, or patterns of organization, that authors use to present their ideas and considers the ways in which authors use these patterns of organization to clarify the topics and subtopics, to help the reader to understand the key ideas, and to show the relationship between the supporting ideas and supporting details.

Patterns of Organization

Authors typically use standard patterns of organization to present their material. The most common patterns of organization are the list pattern, the order pattern, the compare/contrast pattern, and the cause-and-effect pattern. Although authors frequently use more than one pattern of organization in their writing, most reading selections will have a dominant pattern. Recognizing that dominant pattern is another way to help you to predict what the author is going to say.

An exercise will help you to see different patterns of organization and the relationships they signify. Eleven people and events are listed below. Organize them in as many groups or categories as you can with a topic for each category. A category does not need to include all the listed items, but must include at least two of them. For example, George Washington, John F. Kennedy, Martin Luther King, Jr., and Abraham Lincoln could all be classified under a topic, men. Washington, Kennedy, and Lincoln could form a subgroup, American presidents.

George Washington
Indira Gandhi
Civil War
John F. Kennedy
United Nations
Revolutionary War
Martin Luther King, Jr.
Margaret Thatcher
desegregation
World War II
Abraham Lincoln

After you have grouped the items, think about the different ways the items might be connected. Relating these items will show you different patterns of organization. For instance, you could connect the group of men simply by a list. The topic is men; the subtopics are Washington, King, Lincoln, and Kennedy. So you have a list of men. Another possibility is order. You could read or write about the men in chronological order, the order in which they lived. A third option would be to compare and contrast different characteristics of these men: their leadership styles, their beliefs, and so forth. The final relationship among these men may be cause and effect. The men from further back in time may have had an effect on the men who lived more recently. The same topic and subtopics appear in each of these examples; however, the key ideas are different, so the connection among the supporting ideas will be unique for each method of organization.

List

The **list pattern** is simply a series (or list) of ideas, facts, or details about the key idea. The order in which the ideas or details are listed is not important and can be switched without changing the meaning. This is the least structured of the patterns of organization, and it shows the simplest relationship of ideas. Authors typically use this pattern when they want to present straightforward information with a list of examples, clarifications, or attributes. Statistical information is also often presented in the list pattern.

Signal Words

The following words may signal that the author is using the list pattern.

many
much
a few
a number of
several
most
another
besides
also
furthermore
too
in addition
one, two, three, etc.

Example

The following paragraph is an example of information organized in the list pattern. The topic of the paragraph is legitimate authority. You learn from the first sentence of the paragraph that the key idea is that there are three types of legitimate authority: traditional, legal, and charismatic. In addition to telling you the key idea and the sub-topics, the author is indicating that this paragraph is organized in the list pattern by using the signal words "three types." With this knowledge, you can predict that the author will tell you about the three types of authority without showing another relationship among them and that the author could explain these subtopics in any order without changing the meaning of the paragraph.

Max Weber distinguishes three types of legitimate authority: traditional, legal, and charismatic. Traditional authority gets its legitimacy from its history. Such authority is right and legitimate because that is the way it has "always" been, because "God made it that way when He created the world," whether the monarch was called king, pharaoh, Inca, sultan, shah, khan, patriarch, or Papa (pope). Legal authority, however, is based on "rational" claims. Those who hold office do so because of rules and procedures arrived at by reasoning and approved by general agreement such as the vote, the electorate, the plebiscite. Charismatic authority rests on a very special quality of leadership to which Weber gave the name charisma. Its original meaning was "grace," but he added to that a heroic, sacred, or magical quality in the individual that makes the leader close to superhuman. He becomes the symbolic embodiment of a cause, a nation, or an idea, and attracts loyalty from his followers.

—Jane Dabaghian

Order

The **order pattern** also presents readers with a list, but the list must be in a certain order. There are many variations of the order pattern. The ideas, facts, or details that support the key idea can be ordered chronologically, or according to a time sequence; according to a process, or a sequence of steps; according to size or place; or according to order of importance. In each variation of the order pattern, the author arranges the material in a logical order, with each step related to the steps preceding or following it. Once you have established that an author is using the order pattern, you can ask these more specific adaptations of the basic reading questions:

What is happening or what happened? This will give you the key idea.

How does it happen or how did it happen? This will give you the supporting ideas.

In what order did it happen, or what is the order of the steps or stages? This will give you the supporting details.

Chronological Order

When authors organize material in **chronological order,** they list the steps or events in the order in which they occur (or occurred). Each step or event relates to the steps or events that follow or precede it. Chronological order is often used to tell stories and is frequently found in history texts.

The following is an example of events occurring in a chronological order.

The Cinderella "tragedies" usually had happy endings. They starred Joan Crawford, Barbara Stanwyck, and, later, Lana Turner. First, Cinderella falls in love with the rich boy. Then she realizes that the barriers between them are too great and nobly sacrifices herself so that she will not cause him (and his family) to suffer. Although he marries one of his own station, he never forgets her, and, after several reels of poignant misery, they are reunited, this time with the blessings of the family.

Key idea	*What happened?* The Cinderella tragedies usually had a happy ending.
Supporting idea	*How did it happen?* Cinderella's experience consists of several stages.
Supporting details	*In what order did the stages happen?* (1) She falls in love; (2) she realizes that the barriers are too great; (3) the lovers do not forget each other; (4) they are reunited.

Process

When authors explain a **process**—the steps necessary to do or to make something—they are also using a version of the order pattern. When explaining a process, it is important that each step closely follows the one preceding and that no step is left out. Examples of a process, or sequence of steps, are often found in chemistry textbooks; you must follow laboratory procedures carefully in order to get the desired results. They are also found in cookbooks.

To make ice cream you must first gather rock salt and ice and put them in an ice cream freezer. Second, put cream, sugar, and flavorings in the ice cream container. Third, start turning the handle or press the button. Continue turning the handle for ten to twenty minutes, or until the ice cream is done.

Size and Place

Arranging material according to size or place is also a variation of the order pattern. A group of items can be presented from the largest to the smallest, or vice versa. Sometimes a paragraph shows how the details of a particular place (for example, a room, a field, or a city street) are arranged. The paragraph might describe the details from right to left (or left to right), from top to bottom (or bottom to top), from near to far (or far to near), and so forth. The important thing to remember is that the details are logically arranged according to where they are located. This type of order pattern is usually found in descriptions, which occur in all academic disciplines and especially in literature.

The city itself, I knew, could not be far away. The houses became more splendid, and with this splendor was a haunted look, like the ghostly houses in Borges's stories. They were built in the French style and had Gothic grille-work and balconies and bolted shutters. They were the color of a cobweb and just as fragile-seeming and half hidden by trees. The next open space was a park in a burst of sunlight, then a boulevard, and a glimpse of Europe and the hurry and fine clothes of people on a busy sidewalk. It was as if I had been traveling in a tunnel for months and had just popped out the other end, at the far side of the earth, in a place that was maddeningly familiar, as venerable as Boston but much bigger.

–Paul Theroux

Order of Importance

Authors use a version of the order pattern when they arrange ideas or details from most to least important or from least to most important. This kind of order pattern can be very useful; once you have determined how the author has arranged the ideas or details, you can quickly zero in on what he or she considers the most important. Try it with the following example.

The federal court system is organized on both a geographic and hierarchical basis. The lowest level of the system is the district court. There are over ninety districts, at least one in every state and territory of the United States. There may be as many as thirty judges in a single district. The district court is the general trial court, where most federal civil and criminal actions begin. The large number and geographic distribution of the district courts are necessary to ensure convenient and timely adjudication of disputes involving parties subject to the federal jurisdiction. The next level of federal courts is the court of appeal. There are eleven such courts, one for the District of Columbia and ten others for numbered "circuits," which each include up to ten states and territories. The courts of appeal primarily hear appeals taken from decisions at the district court level. The purpose is to ensure that the district courts do not make serious errors of judgment and that laws are interpreted and applied uniformly in all the district courts in the circuit. The ultimate level in the federal court system is the Supreme Court. The Supreme Court reviews those relatively few cases appealed from the courts of appeal that raise substantial and important questions of federal law. With its national focus the Supreme Court is designed to resolve conflicts in interpretation that might exist among different circuits.

When you recognize the order pattern in a reading selection, you can look for the specific variation of the pattern and predict the order in which the author has arranged the ideas.

Signal Words

The following words may signal that the author is using the order pattern.

first, second, etc.	at last
next	ultimately
then	begins
soon	ends
later	more, most
after	less, least
finally	worse, worst
subsequently	better, best

Compare/Contrast

To **compare** is to explain the similarities between two or more ideas, people, places, events, things, and so forth. To **contrast** is to explain the differences. People compare and contrast all the time. In fact, comparing and contrasting can be seen as the foundation for understanding and learning. Whenever you encounter something new, you ask, How is it similar to something I already know? How is it different?

Whenever you make a choice, you compare and contrast two or more things to come to your decision. For example, if you are trying to decide what to have for lunch, you may think about whether a hamburger or a tuna fish sandwich appeals more to you. They are both lunch food, so they have that in common. They have a basis for comparison. In evaluating the nutritional value of lunch foods, you could not compare or contrast a hamburger and a toy; they do not have a basis for comparison. You make your choice by thinking about how a hamburger and a tuna fish sandwich are alike and how they are different. This is a very simple example, but more complicated ideas or items can be compared and contrasted as well.

An author may use compare/contrast to inform the reader, to emphasize or evaluate particular qualities, or to persuade the reader that one thing is better than another. One of the most frequent uses of compare/contrast is to explain the unfamiliar in terms of the familiar. By comparing and/or contrasting new information to familiar material, the author is building on prior knowledge. The preview question *What do I already know about this topic?* helps you to understand new material by comparing and contrasting it with what you already know.

Once you identify the pattern of organization, you can see how the ideas are related. In the case of the compare/contrast, the key idea usually states that there are similarities and differences between items that make up the topic. As you are looking for what is being compared, you can ask yourself the question *What is the basis for comparison?* In our previous example the basis for comparison is that a hamburger and tuna fish sandwich are both foods one might eat for lunch. Lunch food is the topic; there are similarities and differences between types of lunch food is the key idea. After you have determined the key idea, you can find the subtopics by asking, What types of lunch foods are you comparing and contrasting? Hamburgers and tuna fish sandwiches are the subtopics. You can then move on to determine the supporting ideas by selecting the similar and dissimilar aspects of the subtopics that you want to compare and contrast. The supporting ideas answer the question *What aspects of the subtopics are being compared and contrasted?* For example, you might think about the following aspects of a hamburger and a tuna fish sandwich: the nutritional value of each, the availability of the ingredients for each, the time needed to prepare each, and the cookware required for each. As you think about the specific characteristics of each of the supporting ideas, you see the supporting details. You might compare and contrast the time spent preparing a hamburger and a tuna fish sandwich by determining that a hamburger takes fifteen minutes to cook, whereas a tuna fish sandwich can be made in five minutes.

The following chart is useful for recognizing and understanding the relationships among these components.

	Nutritional Value	Availability of Ingredients	Time for Preparation	Cookware Needed
Hamburger on a roll	protein fat carbohydrates	meat roll	15 minutes	stove pan spatula
Tuna fish sandwich	protein fat carbohydrates	tuna fish mayonnaise bread	5 minutes	fork spoon

There are two ways that authors may organize the information they are comparing and contrasting. They can present all the supporting ideas and supporting details about one subtopic and then compare and contrast all the supporting ideas and supporting details about another subtopic. Or they can compare and contrast one supporting idea and supporting details for both (or all) the subtopics, followed by another supporting idea and its supporting details about the subtopics, and so forth. Sometimes authors may combine the two methods. They may begin with one way of comparing and contrasting and then move on to the other.

Applying the first method to our lunch food example, you would first provide all the supporting ideas and details about hamburgers: nutritional value, availability of ingredients, time for preparation, and cookware needed. Then you would compare and contrast those with all the supporting ideas and details about tuna fish sandwiches. If you used the second method, you would compare and contrast the nutritional value of a hamburger to the nutritional value of a tuna fish sandwich. Then you would compare and contrast the availability of ingredients for a hamburger to the availability of ingredients for a tuna fish sandwich. You would continue to do this with all the supporting ideas and supporting details.

The following two paragraphs show how you would organize the supporting ideas and supporting details using each method.

What do I want to eat for lunch today? Maybe I'll have a hamburger. Its nutritional value includes protein, fat, and if I have it on a roll, my lunch will also contain carbohydrates. Having a hamburger for lunch is also an easy, convenient meal. I have all the necessary ingredients (meat and roll) and cookware (stove, pan, and spatula), and it will take me about fifteen minutes to prepare. On the other hand, I could eat a tuna fish sandwich for lunch. It contains protein, fat, and carbohydrates. I have the ingredients—tuna fish, mayonnaise, and bread. All I need to use to make it are a fork and spoon. It will take me five minutes to prepare.

Hamburger
☐ *nutrition*

☐ *ingredients and cookware*
☐ *time to prepare*
Tuna fish sandwich
☐ *nutrition*
☐ *ingredients and cookware*
☐ *time to prepare*

What do I want to eat for lunch today? I'll have either a hamburger on a roll or a tuna fish sandwich. Both of them contain protein, fat, and carbohydrates. Which is easier to prepare? I have all the ingredients for both of them at home: meat, roll, tuna fish, mayonnaise, and bread. To make the hamburger, I'll need to use the stove, a pan, and a spatula. However, the only things I'll need for the tuna fish sandwich are a fork and spoon. It will take about fifteen minutes to make the hamburger, but just five minutes for the tuna fish sandwich.

Hamburger/Tuna fish sandwich
☐ *nutrition*
Hamburger/Tuna fish sandwich
☐ *ingredients and cookware*

Hamburger/Tuna fish sandwich
☐ *time to prepare*

Signal Words

Some signal words tell you that two or more ideas are being compared. Words indicating comparison signal that the author is telling you how this thought is the same as another; words indicating contrast signal that the idea following the signal word is different from the previous concept.

Words that indicate similarities

like
as
again
still
likewise
same
similarly
in comparison

Words that indicate differences

but
on the other hand
on the contrary
however
rather
in comparison
different
in contrast
instead

Example

The reading selection entitled "Dispute Resolution" is an example of material organized in the compare/contrast pattern of organization. The key idea of the passage is that there are similarities and differences between types of dispute resolution. The subtopics are arbitration and mediation; the author is comparing and contrasting them. Specifically, the author is comparing and contrasting three aspects of these two types of dispute resolution: characteristics of persons, power, and purpose. These are the supporting ideas.

Dispute Resolution

Often newspaper reporters writing about labor or international disputes use the terms *mediation* and *arbitration* interchangeably. Many people, therefore, believe that the terms are synonymous. Although mediators and arbitrators share some common attributes, they in fact have fundamental distinctions. Both mediators and arbitrators are neutral or disinterested persons who intercede between or among two or more parties for the purpose of resolving the parties' dispute. They may be private citizens or members of some governmental agency. There the similarities end. A mediator is armed only with the power of persuasion. He or she first listens to the respective positions and demands of the various parties and then tries to bring the divergent positions together to some mutually beneficial settlement point. This is done by helping parties see the strengths and weaknesses of their own and their adversary's positions; prioritize their demands; and explore different avenues for meeting the essential needs of all disputants. If the parties cannot be made to see that settlement is in their mutual interest, that the costs of confrontation are greater than the costs of compromise, then the mediator's job is done. A mediator has no power to impose a settlement on recalcitrant parties. In contrast, an arbitrator is more like a judge, chosen by the parties to make a binding decision. After listening to the parties' presentations and considering relevant agreements or laws, an arbitrator issues an award, or a ruling. With rare exception, the parties have no choice but to comply with the award. If one or more parties feel the arbitrator's award was deficient in some way, their only real remedy is not to use that arbitrator in the future.

The subtopics and supporting ideas in this selection are shown in the following chart. Fill in the supporting details.

	Characteristics of Persons	Power	Purpose
Arbitration			
Mediation			

Cause and Effect

When one event happens as a direct result of a previous occurrence, the two events are linked by a **causal** relationship. Our lives are made up of cause and effect. For example: I was late for class because I overslept. Why was I late for class? I was late for class because I overslept. What happened as a result of oversleeping? I was late for class. Several effects may sometimes be cited for one cause, or several causes may explain one effect. For instance, I may have been late to class because I overslept, the bus was late, and I stopped to speak with friends.

When you recognize the pattern, you can more easily find the key idea and can state the key idea in terms of effects or causes. The question *What is the author saying about the topic?* might become more specific: *How is the topic affected or caused?* or *What does the topic affect or cause?* If an author states that the failure of the government to enforce pollution controls has resulted in many problems, you can find the key idea by asking, *What does the lack of enforcement cause?* After determining that the key idea is that unenforced pollution controls cause many problems, you can find the supporting ideas by identifying the problems or effects. They may include health problems, dead fish, and a decrease in tourism. A diagram of the key idea and supporting ideas would look like this:

Key Idea (Cause) ⟶ Unenforced pollution controls cause many problems.

↑

Supporting Idea (Effects) ⟶ Health problems, dead fish, decrease in tourism.

Sometimes the connection between the cause and effect is not immediately apparent. When the author writes about a series of events chronologically without stating that something happened because of another event, it may be difficult to see the cause-and-effect relationship. For example, the unenforced pollution controls themselves did not cause the decrease in tourism. Rather, the health problems and dead fish caused by the unenforced pollution controls caused the decrease in tourism. In situations like this, you need to read critically to see if any other events occurred in between.

Supporting ideas may also be introduced by statements such as these:

The list of causes or effects of the key idea are . . .
The reasons for the key idea are . . .
The results of the key idea are . . .
Why did the key idea happen?
What are the reasons?
What are the causes?
This happened [the effect] because of that [the cause].

Signal Words

The simple "because" statement is not difficult to understand (I was late for school because I overslept). But more obscure cause-and-effect situations may not be so easily recognized. Signal words help the reader to connect ideas and to find the causal relationship between two or more ideas.

because	results
since	resulted in
therefore	as a result (of)
consequently	for this reason
so	leads to
brought about	thus
is the outcome of	effects
determines	affects
if, then	either, or

Example

The following selection about stretching is an example of information presented in the cause-and-effect pattern. The key idea of the passage is that stretching too far causes your muscles to contract (stretch reflex).

1   Your muscles are protected by a mechanism called the stretch reflex. Any time you stretch the muscle fibers too far (either by bouncing or overstretching), a nerve reflex responds by sending a signal to the muscles to contract; this keeps the muscles from being injured. *Therefore,* when you stretch too far, you tighten the very muscles you are trying to stretch!

2   Holding a stretch as far as you can go or bouncing up and down strains the muscles and activates the stretch reflex. These harmful methods *cause* pain, as well as physical damage due to the microscopic tearing of muscle fibers. This tearing *leads to* the formation of scar tissue in the muscles, with a gradual loss of elasticity. The muscles *become* tight and sore.

–Bob Anderson

The italicized signal words indicate the primary cause-and-effect relationship, as well as secondary relationships that introduce supporting details.

Exercises

1. Read the following paragraph and identify the pattern of organization.

Shortly after World War II, decades of investigation into the internal workings of the solids yielded a new piece of electronic hardware called a transistor. Transistors, a family of devices, alter and control the flow of electricity in circuits. . . . They are solid. They have no cogs and wheels, no separate pieces to be soldered together; it is as if they are stones performing some useful work. They are durable, take almost no time to start working, and don't consume much power. Moreover, as physicists and engineers discovered, they could be produced cheaply in large quantities.

–*Tracy Kidder*

2. Read the following paragraph and identify the pattern of organization.

Every new administration at Washington begins in an atmosphere of expectant good will, but in this case the airs which lapped the capital were particularly bland. The smile of the new President was as warming as a spring thaw after a winter of discontent. For four long years the gates of the White House had been locked and guarded with sentries. Harding's first official act was to throw them open, to permit a horde of sightseers to roam the grounds and flatten their noses against the executive window-panes and photograph one another under the great north portico; to permit flivvers and trucks to detour from Pennsylvania Avenue up the driveway and chortle right past the presidential front door. The act seemed to symbolize the return of the government to the people. Wilson had been denounced as an autocrat, had proudly kept his own counsel; Harding modestly said he would rely on the "best minds" to advise him. . . . Wilson had seemed to be everlastingly prying into the affairs of business and had distrusted most business men; Harding meant to give them as free a hand as possible "to resume their normal onward way." And finally, whereas Wilson had been an austere academic theorist, Harding was "just folk": he radiated an unaffected good nature, met reporters and White House visitors with a warm handclasp and a genial word, and touched the sentimental heart of America by establishing in the White House a dog named Laddie Boy.

–*Frederick Lewis Allen*

3. Read the following paragraph and identify the pattern of organization. Circle the signal words.

In order to keep his other livestock functioning, Joe had to supplement their diets with hay bales bought locally or from outside or with hard-to-come-by grazing permits which allowed him to fatten them up on government grass, or by playing a frustrating, frantic, and never-ending game of musical pastures: that is, by switching his livestock from one small field to another small field to another small field in town, renting these fields from neighbors or borrowing them from friends. This was the most common way for animals to survive in Milagro, though also one of the most tedious, since almost everyone else also owned animals of one sort or another that they were simultaneously and continually switching around, too. Thus, just about every small pasture was overgrazed and had been overgrazed ever since the government and the Ladd Devine Company appropriated most of the rest of the county some one hundred years ago.

–John Nichols

4. Read the following paragraphs and identify the pattern of organization. Circle the signal words.

1   From the burial vault and the cemetery Frankenstein gets the raw materials of his creation, the fragments of death he sutures together to create a "being"; from death he creates a life, a triumph. But this being of a new species becomes lonely and embittered and learns to curse his creator. The only one of his kind, obsessed with the need for companionship, the being, now a "monster," demands that Frankenstein give him a mate, an Eve to the being's Adam. Frankenstein the creator has become Frankenstein the victim. If he creates a female being, a whole new species may be spawned upon the earth, to destroy or enslave mankind; if he refuses, all those whom Frankenstein loves will be killed.

2   Frankenstein submits to his creation's demands and creates a mate, but Frankenstein rebels, and the being's mate is destroyed, beginning a total war between the creator and his creation. The monster kills Frankenstein's loved ones, his best friend first, then his bride, Elizabeth. The monster flees to the polar wastes with Frankenstein in hot pursuit; each one is determined to kill the other, and, ultimately, both succeed.

–Jane Dabaghian

5. Read "Eye and Camera" and then make a chart showing the subtopics, supporting ideas, and supporting details that the author is comparing and contrasting.

Eye and Camera

1   The human eye provides a good starting point for learning how a camera works. The lens of the eye is like the *lens* of the camera. In both instruments the lens focuses an image of the surroundings on a *light sensitive surface*—the *retina* of the eye and the *film* in the camera. In both, the light-sensitive material is protected within a light-tight container—the eyeball of the eye and the *body* of the camera. Both eye and camera have a mechanism for shutting off light passing through the lens to the interior of the container—the lid of the eye and the *shutter* of the camera. In both, the size of the lens opening, or *aperture*, is regulated by an *iris diaphragm*.

2   The eye adjusts automatically to high and low light conditions. In a darkened room the iris of the eye opens wide to allow as much light as possible to enter. In bright light the iris of the eye closes down to prevent too much light from entering. Observe the pupil of your own eye in a mirror as you switch a bright light on and off and you will see the iris adjust the size of your pupil for each condition.

3   Most adjustable cameras do *not* adjust automatically for high and low light conditions. In most cases you must adjust your camera manually to regulate the amount of light that enters it. To help you with this manual adjustment, many cameras have built-in features that inform you of changing light conditions. Nevertheless, some cameras, even as the eye, do adjust themselves automatically for varying light conditions.

4   The eye also adjusts automatically to focus on the objects of interest to you. Small muscles attached to the lens of the eye alter its shape to focus now on nearby objects and then on distant objects. Most adjustable cameras do *not* adjust focus automatically: in most cases you must adjust your camera manually to focus on the objects of interest to you. To help you with this adjustment, most cameras provide built-in features that let you know which objects are in and out of focus on the film: some cameras even adjust focus automatically. Thus in many ways the camera functions much as the human eye.

5   One important difference between eye and camera is that the eye *sees selectively:* the camera *sees indiscriminately.* In other words, human beings tend to observe only those details that are important to them. Their minds have the ability to filter out all details except those to which they are paying attention. The camera, on the other hand, tends to see all the details in view and to record them on the film. It has no mind of its own to help it pay attention to some details and not to others. Those who have taken

pictures have had the experience of finding in some finished print a strange object which they did not notice when they snapped the picture because they had been concentrating on the subject at the time. In other words, they saw selectively only those details to which they were attending, but the camera saw indiscriminately all the details in its field of view. As a photographer you must train yourself to see what the camera sees.

–Marvin J. Rosen

6. Read the excerpt from *Life in a Mexican Village: Tepoztlán Restudied* and identify the dominant pattern of organization. Then section the passage.

Life in a Mexican Village: *Tepoztlán Restudied*

Collective Labor

1   Collective labor, known as the *cuatequitl,* is in all probability an ancient tradition in Tepoztlán. At present it takes a number of forms, the village *cuatequitl,* the barrio *cuatequitl,* the *cuatequitl* of neighbors, and, on rare occasions, an inter-village *cuatequitl.* The village *cuatequitl* is a compulsory form of collective labor organized by the village authorities for public works such as improving the roads, constructing public buildings, or doing other work which, in theory, will benefit the village as a whole. Each able-bodied man between ages twenty-one and fifty can be called upon for service to the community. Failure to respond to such a call is punishable by a fine or jail sentence. However, a man can pay the daily wage of a substitute if desired. When the task is a relatively small one and more men are called up than are needed for the actual work, some are asked to contribute food or drink instead of labor.

2   The better-to-do families generally do not participate in the village *cuatequitl,* since they consider such work beneath their dignity and prefer to pay for substitutes. The main source of labor for the village *cuatequitl* are the poor who cannot afford substitutes or fines. The men from the smaller and poorer barrios have the reputation of being the most industrious and reliable workers for the *cuatequitl.* This is related to the fact that they have little political influence and have greater fear of the authorities.

3   The village *cuatequitl* is organized in terms of the eight *demarcaciones* or wards into which the village is divided. The *ayudante* or representative of each *demarcación* is ordered to announce a *cuatequitl* in his ward, and specific men are designated to appear at a given time and place. The attendance of the men is checked by the *ayudante* from his list.[1] Sometimes, when men are needed at short notice, more direct means are used to assure successful recruitment.

4   In a recent boundary dispute with the municipio of Tejalpa, the authorities posted aides at all the roads and paths leading out of the village to intercept the men as they went to their fields early in the morning. In this way 600 men were recruited in one day, and they were set to work to cut through the forest overgrowth which covered the disputed boundary line. In this case, since it was a municipio boundary, men from the other villages were also recruited. Other instances of inter-village *cuatequitl* have occurred in the repair of bridges which are used in common.

5   In recent years there have been very few village *cuatequitls* of major importance. In 1934 some work was done to improve the market place. The last important village *cuatequitl* was organized in 1926–27 while Redfield was in the village.[2] At this time, under the initiative of the local political faction known as the Bolsheviki, communal washbasins were constructed. During the twenties, political feelings ran so high and cleavages were so marked that members of the opposition group refused to work in *cuatequitls* organized by those in power. Fines were out of the question at the time because authority could not be enforced.

6   During the early thirties, when political schisms were still strong, there occurred an unusual type of voluntary village *cuatequitl* for the construction of the road to Cuernavaca. Led by two enterprising non-Tepoztecan schoolteachers and with the backing of the colony of Tepoztecans in Mexico City, the villagers decided to build a road to Cuernavaca. The two political factions, the Bolsheviki and the Fraternales, refused to work side by side, and each organized separate shifts, one beginning at Tepoztlán and working toward Cuernavaca, the other working from Cuernavaca toward Tepoztlán.

7   Although the village *cuatequitl* is intended as a means of aiding the village as a whole, there are many obstacles to its successful operation, and it is gradually declining. Perhaps the fundamental difficulty is the inherent individualism of Tepoztecans, the suspiciousness and critical attitude toward the local government, and the paucity of local funds. The village *cuatequitl* has been traditionally associated in the minds of the villagers as a coercive

---

[1]Some men will work until the check-off and then slip away.
[2]Before the Revolution, when there was more money in the local treasury and when the local government was in the hands of *caciques* whose tenure was quite stable, there were many more *cuatequitls* than now.

rather than a voluntary institution. This may be the result of having lived under an authoritarian system in which the local government had been imposed for years. Since the local government, generally the *síndico* or the president, has the power to designate the citizens who are to work in the *cuatequitl*, there is ample opportunity for favoritism and vengeance against political opponents or personal enemies.

8   It may be significant in this connection that children in their games will often say, "Unless you do this I will give you your *cuatequitl*," suggesting that the *cuatequitl* is viewed as a punishment. It should also be noted that historically the existence of a native institution for collective labor was a distinct aid to the Spanish conquerors in their organization and control of the labor supply.

9   The second type of *cuatequitl* is the barrio *cuatequitl*. This is the collective working of the lands of the barrio saints. Barrio members are expected to cooperate in the preparation of the land, planting, cultivating, and harvesting of the crops from the saints' field. The sale of the produce goes for the upkeep of the local chapel. In contrast to the village *cuatequitl*, participation in the barrio *cuatequitl* is entirely voluntary. The barrio *mayordomo* goes through the barrio announcing at each house the time of the *cuatequitl*. While there are no fines or penalties for nonparticipation, there is strong social pressure as well as fear that the saint may be offended by failure to work for his upkeep. Still, in recent years there has been increasing difficulty in obtaining barrio cooperation. Now three of the seven barrios rent out the land and use the rental for the expenses of the chapel.

10   The barrio *cuatequitl* cleans the churchyard and repairs the chapel. Barrio differences in this connection are interesting. Although the smaller barrios of San Pedro, San Sebastián, and Los Reyes are the most reliable workers on the village *cuatequitl*, they appear to be the most neglectful in the upkeep of their respective chapels, indicating perhaps that Catholicism has less of a hold in these barrios. Indeed, it was in the barrio of San Sebastián that a Protestant sect won over about fifteen families. The barrio of Santa Cruz, also very poor, is known for its superior care and great devotion to its chapel. The larger barrios, too, keep their chapels in repair.

11   The third occasion for the *cuatequitl* is that of a group of neighbors within the barrio who may agree among themselves to repair the street or to build a water tank or some other local improvement. This *cuatequitl* generally involves fewer people and still occurs quite frequently. During our visit to the village four new water founts were built in this way. The *cuatequitl* of the barrio and of neighbors would seem to be a natural mechanism for a

great deal of cooperative endeavor on a purely voluntary basis. But the poor quality of human relations in the village, and the fear to take the initiative in any venture, keep cooperative undertakings at a minimum. Yet the fact that there exists a tradition of cooperative forms of labor has occasionally led to truly heroic and dramatic undertakings. The most recent example of this was the construction of the road to Cuernavaca.

–Oscar Lewis

7. Read "Dyslexia—My 'Invisible Handicap'" and identify the dominant pattern of organization. Mark the text for key idea, supporting ideas, and basic structure.

Dyslexia—My "Invisible Handicap"

1   "DYSLEXIA—Oh no, I've got it! Doctor, is there something I can take for it?" Unfortunately, there is no instant cure, only understanding and support from parents and teachers, and the willingness of the individual to compensate for his deficiencies.

2   I have only recently been introduced to dyslexia. Not long ago, it would have been impossible for me to either spell or define dyslexia even though I have, unknowingly, been a dyslexic for over thirty years. I will leave the technical discussion of dyslexia to the professionals; however, what I will do is discuss my experiences, both past and present, with what I consider to be my life-long "invisible handicap."

3   Recent literature contains many articles which describe the total spectrum of success and failure experienced by children and adults who suffer from dyslexia. The accounts range from the totally tragic . . . to those of great success. . . . But what happens, when at age 32, a successful professional is identified as a dyslexic? It is this question which provides the motivation for this article. I would like to make it clear from the outset that I have been, am, and always will be a dyslexic. I can't change the way I am, but what I have done is learned to live with dyslexia even though at times it is not easy for me or the people close to me.

4   I was introduced to dyslexia one summer when my wife became involved with the Slingerland approach to teaching dyslexic children. As she learned more and more about dyslexia during the teacher training course, I became the subject of close examination and evaluation. Many serious and some humorous discussions took place, and it was not long before it became apparent that there was a dyslexic in the house who had no problem at all checking off nearly all the general characteristics listed. . . . More importantly, I finally found out why I can't spell, why I have poor

handwriting, and why I have trouble with oral language. No wonder academics have always been very difficult.

5   The whole evaluation process at first seemed to be contradictory. How could I have achieved my academic and professional success and at the same time have so many learning problems? If one were to read my resume, he would find the following: Bachelors (Valedictorian), Masters, and Ph.D. in Engineering; honor societies; awards; and a career in research. What is not immediately obvious is the cause for the ten year delay in the beginning of my career which, I now know, was due to the failures brought about by my dyslexia. On the other hand, my success was achieved in part by sheer brute force and perseverance and in part by the fact that dyslexics have average or above average intelligence.

6   After realizing I was a dyslexic, it would have been easy for me to say "now I have an excuse for my deficiencies" and just blame everything on dyslexia. However, I chose an alternate path. I became involved with this thing called dyslexia and began a search through my past in an attempt to understand why I am the way I am. I think what bothered me the most was that the problem was not identified when I was a child and, therefore, I was not given any help. The lack of identification and help has its foundation in several areas. First, I grew up in a small town which probably had trouble keeping teachers, and I don't think they were trained in the area of learning disabilities. Secondly, my parents, who were well educated and financially well off, had very strong egos which would not allow them even to consider that something could be wrong with their son. I have since found out that many parents have trouble admitting that their child has dyslexia.

7   The strongest argument against the idea that I have a learning problem of any type is my childhood academic success. At age 4, I was given a series of intelligence tests, and the results indicated that I was in the top 2% of the gifted population. It was on the basis of these tests that I was admitted to kindergarten at the age of four and a half. This was a mistake that haunted me for twenty years. Also, my academic success was recorded on my report cards which, for the first through eight grades, showed that I was an A and B student.

8   However, while looking through some childhood souvenirs, I found letters which I wrote that are strongly contradictory to my report card performance. . . . Samples of my writing in the third and fourth grades are . . . not examples of the quality of work that a gifted child would produce; however, no one, parents or teachers, was cognizant of the severe language problems indicated by this type of work. Let me assure you that these are not isolated examples.

9   The first indication of a possible reading problem occurred at

the end of the fifth grade. The principal required me to read three books of my choice over the summer vacation. I can remember arguing with my parents all summer about reading the books, and I won. I did not read a page. I felt punishment was the better alternative. In the spring of the sixth grade, a report was sent home giving the results of the January testing program. . . . I was above grade level in everything but spelling; however, it also shows a tendency toward weakness in the language area. An example of my sixth grade writing . . . shows improvement, but it is still not without problems.

10   As indicated before, my grades during the 7th and 8th grades were good (88–90 average), but I do remember rebelling against certain assignments. For example, in English class we had to memorize the Gettysburg Address and then recite it in front of the whole class. I decided that an F was more acceptable than embarrassment.

11   At the beginning of the 8th grade, my parents found out that the public school was considering double sessions to combat overcrowding. My parents reacted with "we can't have this for our son" and decided that I would attend a private, boarding school. The admission procedure required an entire day of testing. . . . The first point of interest is that my gifted IQ, measured at age 4, had dropped to an average level at age 13. This would indicate that I was falling behind academically. The second point of interest centers around a comparison of the test scores based on public and private school standards. According to the counselor's comments, the tests were designed to "measure . . . . . academic aptitude and . . . . achievement in certain important school subjects" with normal performance indicated by a public school grade equivalent of 8.7 and a private school percentile rating grade equivalent of 50. By public school standards, I was doing well, but, by private school standards, I was average or below in all subjects. The counselor's evaluation of the test results point out that " . . . . there seems to be evidence of considerable weakness in such fundamentals of English as grammar, punctuation, and spelling and also in reading comprehension." One could say that the public school did not prepare me properly; however, I tend not to blame the public school because many of its students went on to successful academic and professional careers. What is true is that I was not prepared academically. At least the counselor identified my weaknesses, but there was no mention of a learning problem. My parents reacted with summer school for me and with "you would improve if you only applied yourself."

12   I spent four years in the private school doing the minimum amount of work I could get away with, going to summer school, and excelling in sports. During my high school years, friction

between my parents and me increased. There were ugly scenes at grade time, and I was constantly told by teachers, administrators, and my parents that my grades would improve if I would stop being so lazy and begin to apply myself. I graduated with a C minus average (a gift) and was mysteriously accepted by a college. I did not want to go to college, and I certainly did not have the academic background or the maturity. However, my parents insisted that I attend college; there was no other choice. My college experience lasted one semester—I flunked out.

13   Due to the high level of stress in the relationship between my parents and me, I felt that I had to get away from home. I did so by joining the Air Force. Even though I did not like military life, it was probably the best thing I ever did. While in the Air Force, at age 20, I read my first book. I consider this a major milestone and turning point in my life. Also, while in the Air Force and without my parents' knowledge, I applied to and was accepted by Northrop University. I started college (age 22) on probation but managed to succeed due to the tremendous support I received from my professors. I felt that for the first time someone really cared and knew that I could learn. I graduated as Valedictorian of my class, and of course my parents were proud of me, but at the same time they said, "We never thought you would make it." I had failed for so long that everyone expected me to fail again.

14   One of the most important lessons I learned from my undergraduate work was that I could succeed. However, life was not without problems and frustrations. Graduate school was very difficult. I do not react well to change. In any case, I did receive my Masters degree at age 31 and completed my Ph.D. at age 38. I was working full time at my current position during my Ph.D. studies, and I am sure that no one associated with me in my work or school environments had any idea that I had learning problems. I do know that I am proud of what I have accomplished, and I would not have been able to accomplish any of it without perseverance and a great deal of support and understanding from my wife.

15   Education and outward success do not eliminate dyslexia. To illustrate this I will again use samples of my writing. . . . The quality is not bad, but it does show the breakdown associated with transferring information from one place to another. Also, the writing is intermingled with printing and cursive. More typical results of my writing show . . . the results of having to think (i.e. compose) and write at the same time. Not only is my writing very difficult to read, it contains numerous spelling errors and afterthoughts about spelling (i.e. cop(e)ing).

16   More importantly, education and success have not eliminated the strong emotional reactions of frustration, embarrassment, and

anger that are a result of my life with dyslexia. Frustration and embarrassment are due to my poor spelling, poor communication skills, slow reading, trouble remembering what is read or heard, poor handwriting, and reversals of letters and numbers. For example, when making a purchase in a store, I would rather use cash or a credit card than have the pressure of trying to spell everything correctly on a check. Another example is my redoing all telephone messages so that they can be read and so that all the spelling is correct. It is very frustrating to me that I have to spend so much extra time reading, and if I do not read a selection several times, I cannot remember what I read. Also, I have to make marginal notes immediately if I want to remember my thoughts on the subject. I have learned to deal with these kinds of problems although it seems like such a waste of time to have to do so many things more than once.

17   The anger I have comes not from the fact that I have dyslexia but from the knowledge that neither parents nor educators were able to recognize the problem, for whatever reason, or to give me the help I needed. It is a shame that my parents reacted to my poor academic performance with lectures, restriction, and summer school. This along with being constantly told, "You are lazy. . . . you don't apply yourself. . . . if you would only try harder" creates long term damaging results. It is very difficult to try hard or apply yourself when you believe you cannot do the work because nothing will "sink in." If you are told these things often enough, eventually you will believe what you hear and give up. The only possible result is failure. This was true for me, and it took a long time before I pulled myself out of the failure mode and into the success mode.

18   It is not easy to be a dyslexic, but one can, as I have, learn to live with it. I firmly believe that, in addition to the support and understanding from parents and educators, the key to survival and success is compensation. I have learned to compensate for my deficiencies and, consciously or unconsciously, I have developed techniques to cover up my inadequacies. If you cannot spell, use a dictionary. I am sure that everyone has heard the comment, "What good is a dictionary if you can't spell the word?" The answer is *The Bad Speller's Dictionary.* Poor handwriting can be compensated for by printing, typing, or using a word processor with a spelling checker. A dyslexic should proofread everything several times and have someone else read the work whenever possible. Taking the required time is the only answer to slow reading. If you cannot remember things, take notes and keep them in one place. Finally, a dyslexic needs to get organized by establishing a system and sticking to it.

19   There are times that I wonder if it has been such a good thing that I found out I am a dyslexic. The level of awareness of my deficiencies is very high and that in itself creates a certain amount of self-inflicted paranoia about not making errors. There are good days and bad days, but all in all I feel that my ability to perform has increased now that I know and understand what my "invisible handicap" is all about. Recently, when talking to a ninth grade class of dyslexics and hearing their concern of "what is going to happen to me," I could not help recalling my past which contained all the same frustrations and failures that these young adults are experiencing. Experiences like this and expressions of frustration and concern by parents further illustrate that we need to continue to inform both educators and parents that dyslexia is real and that there is no instant cure. We all need to work together to recognize, not cover up, dyslexia.

20   I know I have come a long way from the failures of childhood. Today, I am filled with energy and motivation, but at the same time I cannot forget what could have been gained instead of lost due to this thing called dyslexia. I feel fortunate to have prevailed over my "invisible handicap." For all dyslexics, I think Robert Louis Stevenson said it best:

> To be what we are,
> And to become what we
> Are capable of becoming,
> Is the only end of life.

–Thomas S. Mautner

8. Pick a textbook you are now using in one of your classes. Find an example of each of the patterns of organization: list, order, compare/contrast, cause and effect.

Writing Exercise

Briefly explain the patterns of organization. Which pattern or patterns of organization did you use for this summary?

12 Reading Critically: Determining the Author's Purpose

Most nonfiction is written to inform the reader about something or to persuade the reader to believe or to do something. Is the author writing to tell you about something, to transfer information from his or her head to yours? Does the author want to convince you of something or to persuade you to take certain actions or to think along certain lines? Is the author recounting an experience or telling a story? Knowing the author's purpose helps you to determine what your task as a reader is and how to accomplish it.

Distinguishing Informational and Persuasive Writing

When you read informational writing, you can assume that the data is straightforward and objective. The author presents facts and explains the material. There is a straight transmission of knowledge taking place with no argument involved. The author is not trying to convince you of anything, but is simply giving you the facts as he or she knows them. However, when the author's purpose is to persuade you of something, he or she wants you to accept an argument, to take action, or to change your behavior or attitude. The author states a position and tries to support it by citing facts and authorities and by reasoning from evidence. Persuasive writing needs to be read especially critically. Determining the author's purpose will help you to decide how critically you need to read.

The first step in determining the author's purpose is to ask the preview question *Why did the author write this?* Sometimes you can learn the author's purpose simply by reading the title or by knowing something about the author's background. The title may also help you predict what the author wants you to believe. For example, the title "What the Human Mind Can Do That the Computer Can't" tells you that the author will try to persuade you that computers cannot do everything that the mind can do.

In the following two examples, do you think the author is trying to inform or to persuade?

- "The Special Theory of Relativity" by James Q. Coleman. Mr. Coleman is a distinguished physicist who has done theoretical research on guided missiles at Johns Hopkins University.
- *The Civil War: A Northern Perspective* by Ulysses S. Grant, General of the Union Armies.

If the author's purpose is not clear from the title, you need to look further. As you read the selection, you continue to ask the question *Why did the author write this?*

Example

In the following paragraph the author is writing to inform you about a specific aspect of Japanese painting.

The floating silk thread line of Japanese painting was introduced by the Tosa school of artists eight hundred years ago and has been in favor ever since. It is the purest or standard line and is reserved for the robes of elevated personages. The brush is held firmly and the lines, made to resemble silk threads drawn from the cocoon, are executed with a free and uninterrupted movement of the arm.

—Henry P. Bowie

In contrast, the author of the following reading selection is writing to persuade you. He wants to convince you of the constitutional right of self-determination, particularly as it pertains to terminating life-sustaining treatment.

Every competent adult is considered to be the master of his own body. He may treat it wisely or foolishly. He may even refuse life-saving treatment, and it's nobody else's business. Certainly not the state's. That is the law of the land.

Cold comfort for Peter Cinque of Lynbrook, L.I., who, locked in like an uncharged prisoner, was kept joined to a life-sustaining device—from which he had begged to be released—until reduced to a comatose, vegetative state. His last few days were shorn of dignity, his family was humiliated and his death became a media event.

—Willard Gaylin

Exercises

1. Skim the following introduction to an article and then state the author's purpose.

   "You want to help sick people?" asks my friend rhetorically. "You want to care for people in pain? Become a nurse." We are both medical students. We are both in the middle of a clinical clerkship on the medical wards of the hospital. What she means is, the nurses spend time with the patients. They get to know them, they meet their families, they tend to their immediate and sometimes desperate needs. They offer comfort, encouragement, explanations. The doctors, with the medical students in tow, show up briefly on morning rounds, returning only if the patient is seriously ill, or in need of some procedure or other. When patients leave the hospital, it is the nurses to whom they send thank-you notes, or chocolates, or flowers.

2. Turn to "Photographing Emotions" on page 150. What is the author's purpose? Is the author trying to inform you or to persuade you?

Informational Writing

Articles in which the author wants to tell you about something, like taking a picture or performing an experiment; a journal article outlining a research program in the social, natural, and physical sciences; a geology textbook; a newspaper report—all are examples of informational writing. Knowing the author's purpose helps you define your task as a reader. If you determine that the author's purpose is to inform, then you know that she or he will try to present the material as clearly as possible so that you can easily understand. The author will try to make the meaning clear by using the patterns of organization you learned in Chapter 11. The pattern might be the listing of various detailed applications to illustrate a new concept; or it might be the ordering of information according to some scheme like time, importance, or place; or it might use comparing or contrasting to make an explanation more vivid; or it might present the causes of an event. In each case the author develops the basic topic and key idea by providing generalizations or informational statements supported by details and illustrations that explain, clarify, emphasize, and develop. Your task, then, is to use the basic reading and preview questions to determine what the author is saying and how all the information is related.

Example

The following passage is an example of informational writing. The author's key idea is that the United States is a nation of immigrants, which has produced problems. The supporting ideas include a listing of some of the problems and a comparison of different groups' solutions.

The United States is a nation of immigrants. Between 1820 and 1920 more than 33 million immigrants, fleeing from poverty and oppression, arrived in this country from parts of Europe, China, and Japan. Today millions of additional immigrants, escaping similar conditions, are entering the United States, both legally and illegally, from Latin America and the Far East.

Problems develop when immigrants arrive unschooled and unskilled and bring with them different ways of thinking and living. We have always found it easier to accept those who assimilate more readily into mainstream culture, such as white northern Europeans. In addition, unskilled workers may have greater difficulty in finding employment today than they did at the turn of the century, a time of booming factories and unmechanized farms.

Immigration affects a variety of groups in this country—farmers, business, labor unions, ethnic and religious organizations—who lobby either for or against the admission of aliens based on the way immigration will improve or weaken their own interests. On one side of the controversy are the advocates of a liberal immigration policy; they argue not only that our humanity should encourage us to open our doors to refugees but that immigrants contribute to the social and economic enrichment of the country. On the other side are advocates of a tighter immigration policy, who argue that new waves of immigrants are straining our resources and straining the cultural character of our country.

Various bills have been introduced into Congress that may or may not satisfy the opposing constituencies: bills that punish employers who hire illegal aliens, that grant amnesty to illegal aliens arriving before 1982, that tighten immigration controls, and that change quota systems presently in force.

—Annette T. Rottenberg

You, too, write informationally. When you write an account of a trip, you are giving information; if you tell someone how to do an experiment, you are transmitting knowledge; when you describe the actions of the opposing sides in the French and Indian Wars, you are imparting the relevant facts to the extent you know them. In none of these cases are you trying to convince the reader to think in a certain way or to take a specific action.

Persuasive Writing

Writing to persuade the reader builds upon writing to inform the reader. The interaction between the reader and the author becomes more direct when the author's purpose is to persuade than when it is just to inform. With informational writing the reader has the task of gathering and digesting information, but with persuasive writing the reader must also understand what the author wants the reader to do with this knowledge. You have to read critically to evaluate the author's ideas and to judge whether and how the author has supported his or her convictions.

You can also ask more specific questions to find the key idea of persuasive writing than those you ask when you are looking for the key idea of informational writing. Rather than asking the question *What is the most important thing the author is saying about the topic?* you can find the key idea of persuasive writing by asking *What is the author trying to persuade me of?* or *What is the author trying to prove?* The answer to this question is often called an assertion, a proposition, an opinion, a claim, or a thesis. If the key idea of a reading selection is that frustrated children tend to become aggressive, this is the author's assertion and it answers the question *What is the author trying to prove?* The author wants to convince you that this is the way frustrated children behave. What does the author want to persuade you of if the assertion is that decent housing for all people is desirable?

After you have determined what the author wants to prove, you can see how the author tries to persuade you. It is the assertion or key idea that the author will try to support with evidence and conclusions drawn from reasoned arguments. A critical reader makes judgments about the evidence and reasoning on which the writer's conclusions are based. You can read critically by asking questions: What are the author's credentials? Is the evidence sound? Is the reasoning logical? How is the author trying to persuade me? What supporting information is the author providing?

Author's Credibility

The first thing to consider when evaluating persuasive writing is the author's credibility. Although you may not have sufficient background knowledge of a discipline to do a thorough evaluation, you can learn some information about the author by some simple investigation. Is the author an expert in the field? A chemist analyzing the latest sociological trends is usually less well qualified than a sociologist writing about the same information. Therefore, it is important to find out about the author's credentials. Usually you can learn this background information on the title page and preface of a book or on the bottom of a page of an article. If the book or article does not offer you this information before you begin reading, you may find something about the author as you read the selection.

Assessing the author's bias is also important. Does the author have a special interest in persuading you of something? Was the author paid to advocate a position? Does the author gain or lose anything if he or she succeeds in convincing you or fails to convince you? The answers to these questions will help you determine the author's bias. If you read that drinking three beers a day is good for you, the fact that a spokesperson for the beer industry is making that statement will influence your perception of the legitimacy of that statement. The author's bias is clear.

You will find that informational writing is often contained in writing that is written mainly to persuade, appearing there as part of the argument, although not an argument in itself. Unfortunately, the reverse is also true. Some writing that purports to be informational is also subtly persuasive, depending on the bias of the author.

Fact and Opinion

Once you have ascertained the author's credibility, you can continue to evaluate the supporting ideas and supporting details by asking more questions.

How is the author trying to persuade me?
What kind of evidence does the author offer?
On what is the evidence based?
Is the evidence fact or opinion?

Facts can be proved. They can be tested by experimentation, research, or observation. Opinions cannot be proved. Opinions are beliefs, feelings, or judgments. Although opinions may be based on facts or they may be interpretations of facts, they cannot be objectively verified. Facts are objective, but they often support a subjective point of view. You can find examples of assertions supported by facts in scholarly, scientific, and legal writing. These facts may be in the form of examples, statistics, or observations. (Observations can be objective/a fact: There are three people here. Or they can be subjective/an opinion: He looked sad.) Examples of opinions are often found in literary criticism, newspaper editorials, book and movie reviews, and advertisements. The difference between facts and opinions is the difference between "I know" and "I think." "I know something is true and I can prove it" versus "I think something is true because. . . ."

Although all facts are verifiable, not all facts can support all assertions. You can evaluate facts by determining if they are current (if this is significant), sufficient, relevant and/or representative. The following examples show questions you can ask in evaluating facts.

Are ten-year-old data on the effects of acid rain valid?
Is it sufficient for an author to say that 90 percent of the seniors from Getaway High School went on to college because they had a terrific English teacher? Were there any other factors that might have caused this?
If an author is trying to convince you that imported Swiss cheese tastes better than the domestic one, is it relevant that the imported one costs more?

It is also important to note whether the author cites specific sources or only makes general statements. Referring to specific data or to a specific authority in a field to support an assertion is certainly more credible than stating, "Scientists say . . ." or "Studies prove. . . ." If the author has included footnotes, you can check the author's assertions, rather than merely relying on the author's statements.

Exercise

The following ten statements will give you practice in distinguishing between fact and opinion. Determine whether each statement is fact or opinion, and explain why you have made your choice.

1. Mary is taller than John.
2. History is the most difficult class.
3. *A Streetcar Named Desire* was Tennessee Williams's last great play.
4. Some parents assume an active role in the education of their children.
5. Studies have shown that the effective reader reads widely and frequently.
6. John F. Kennedy was a good president.
7. The results of the survey showed that 75 percent of the students were satisfied with the course.
8. *Gone with the Wind* is the best book ever written.
9. In his research Van Gilder found that the differences in the skills required in various fields lie not so much in the materials themselves as in the type of thinking required.
10. College students enjoy reading more than high school students do.

Reasoning

In addition to being aware of the credibility of the author and the reliability of the evidence, you must also understand the reasoning of the author, or how the author moves from an assertion to a conclusion. Asking these questions will help you understand the author's reasoning:

How does the author interpret the evidence?
Are other interpretations possible?
How does the author arrive at the conclusion?
What is the connection between the assertion and the evidence?
Is the reasoning sound?

There are two basic types of reasoning: inductive and deductive reasoning. Knowing the two types and the errors commonly found in each will help you to evaluate persuasive writing.

Deductive Reasoning   Deductive reasoning moves from a general statement, or premise, to a specific statement, or *conclusion*. For example, college students should be required to study a foreign language. Elsa is a college student. Therefore, Elsa should be required to study a foreign language. The first two statements—that college students should be required to study a foreign language and that Elsa is a college student—are the premises. The last statement—that Elsa should be required to study a foreign language—is the conclusion. To determine if there are errors in deductive reasoning, you have to see if the premises are true. If the premises are accepted, then the conclusion must be accepted as well. Is it true that college students should be required to study a foreign language? Is Elsa a college student? If you accept these premises as true, then Elsa should study a foreign language.

Inductive Reasoning   Inductive reasoning moves from one or more specific instances to a general conclusion. For example, yesterday was Thursday. The bookstore was very crowded. Therefore, the bookstore must always be very crowded on Thursdays. To evaluate inductive reasoning, you should ask the questions we discussed earlier in the chapter: Do I have enough information to draw a conclusion? Is it relevant information? Do I have adequate information to know if it is true that the bookstore is always crowded on Thursdays? The experience during one visit is not sufficient to make a general statement. A large number of specific instances must be observed before a conclusion can be drawn.

You probably have come across this type of reasoning frequently and are familiar with gathering data and drawing conclusions, particularly in the natural and social sciences, where the results of research and investigations are analyzed by this form of reasoning in order to establish that the findings are correct.

Errors in Reasoning

Defects in either the structure or the content of arguments are referred to by the general term **fallacy.** Two common errors in reasoning are related to two of the patterns of organization: the *questionable analogy* (found in compare and contrast) and the *faulty causal connection* (found in cause and effect).

Questionable Analogy   An analogy is a specific type of comparison. It is a likeness between two things that are otherwise dissimilar. Analogies, or analogical arguments, are frequently used to persuade. Whenever the author uses an analogy in persuasive writing, the things being compared must have enough characteristics in common to provide a basis for comparison; otherwise the author's reasoning is faulty. For example, an author may make the analogy that a family is like a business. It can function only if the members obey the boss. This analogy argues for an authoritarian view of parenting. But is it sound? Is a family enough like a business that there is a basis for comparison? If the analogy is questionable, then the reasoning derived from the analogy is not sound. Historians and political scientists frequently make analogies and draw conclusions from the resemblance between a historical event and a current one. During the Vietnam War some political scientists tried to persuade people that this war was the same as the Korean War. There were similarities, such as their location and the fact that both were civil wars; however, the analogy was questionable. Simply because they were alike in some respects did not necessarily mean they were alike in other respects. For instance, the Korean War involved the United Nations organization and the Vietnam conflict did not.

Faulty Causal Connection   Phrases like "the facts indicate . . ." or "these are signs of . . ." suggest a causal connection between the author's assertion and the conclusion. Attempts at explanation usually involve causal reasoning. A critical reader must determine whether a causal connection does in fact exist. An extreme example of a faulty causal connection is the case of the student who blames poor exam performance on the color of the exam booklet. The fact that one event follows another does not guarantee a causal relationship. You can recognize faulty causal connection by using the same criteria for evaluating the author's support of assertions we discussed earlier in this chapter: Is the information sufficient, necessary, and/or relevant? Is there more than one cause of an effect? Is the color of the exam book sufficient reason for failing an exam?

Awareness of faulty causal connection is particularly important when you read the natural sciences and the social sciences. A social scientist who surveys two thousand people may state that you will probably graduate from college if you are a first-born child, because more of the first-born respondents than the later-born respondents in the survey graduated from college. This is faulty causal reasoning, for the social scientist does not have sufficient information to make that causal connection. These particular people may have graduated from college for other reasons that have nothing to do with their being first-born children. It may not be relevant or sufficient that they are first-borns. Another example of possible faulty causal reasoning is when two scientists or social scientists try to persuade you of different interpretations of the same data because they see different causal connections.

You also need to be aware of what you, the reader, bring to your reading. Your thoughts and the way you reach them are shaped by your experiences, your biases, and your expectations. Examining your prior assumptions about a topic and an assertion is particularly important if you have some previous knowledge about the topic of your reading. Without this awareness of your own preconceptions and reasoning strategies, you may find it difficult to understand what the author is saying, or you may easily misunderstand the author's message.

Emotional Appeal

Persuasive writing frequently includes emotional appeal as well as reasoned argument. The degree to which authors employ these two strategies is determined by their purpose in writing the selection and the audience to which they are writing. Advertising usually relies heavily on emotional appeal, and most ads are designed to evoke an emotional response. Further, people often find it difficult to separate reason and emotion. Authors know this and sometimes try to appeal to your emotions in order to convince you. The effective use of emotive language makes the reader more likely to accept a proposition. It is, therefore, important to be able to recognize when and to what extent authors are writing to arouse an emotional response and to be able to evaluate the tools of language they may use for that purpose.

Connotative and figurative language are the two most popular types of emotive language that an author may use to express and arouse emotion. They influence your perception of reality by using words that may cause you to react in a certain way because they appeal to your emotions or biases. Connotative language implies more than the words actually say. Describing a person as "thrifty" provides a different image than describing that same person as "cheap." If an author wants to elicit a negative response about the character of somebody, the author would choose the word "cheap" rather than "thrifty."

Figurative language represents one concept in terms of another. Two types of figurative language are frequently used to evoke emotional reaction: the metaphor, when one thing is used to represent something else ("the evening of life"); and the simile, when two essentially unlike things are compared ("She is as strong as a bull."). Consider the following example.

We know through painful experience that freedom is never voluntarily given by the oppressor; it must be demanded by the oppressed. Frankly I have never yet engaged in a direct action movement that was "well timed," according to the timetable of those who have not suffered unduly from the disease of segregation. For years now I have heard the word "Wait!" It rings in the ear of every Negro with a piercing familiarity. This "wait" has almost always meant "never." It has been a tranquilizing thalidomide [a drug withdrawn from the market because it caused birth defects], relieving the emotional stress for a moment, only to give birth to an ill-formed infant of frustration. We must come to see with the distinguished jurist of yesterday that "justice too long delayed is justice denied." We have waited for more than 340 years for our constitutional and God-given rights. The nations of Asia and Africa are moving with jetlike speed toward the goal of political independence and we still creep at horse and buggy pace toward the gaining of a cup of coffee at a lunch counter.

–Martin Luther King, Jr.

Note the use of figurative language to evoke an emotional response to this selection? There are six metaphors in this passage. How many can you find?

Exercises

1. Read "Excerpt from Arbitration Decision" and answer the following questions.
   a. What is the author's purpose?
   b. What is the author trying to persuade you of?
   c. How is the author trying to persuade you?
   d. What kind of evidence does the author offer?
   e. On what does the author base his evidence?
   f. Is the reasoning sound?

Excerpt from Arbitration Decision

1   The Company discharged Naden on the grounds that the employee had used, and therefore had also been in the possession of, marijuana at work. Because Company supervisors had reason to believe Naden had been smoking marijuana after he reported for work at 7 A.M. on April 15, 1982, they took a blood sample from the employee. That sample was subsequently sent for a gas chromatography/mass spectrometry (GC/MS) assay, which resulted in a finding of approximately 5 nanograms [unit of weight equal to one-billionth of a gram] per milliliter of THC in Naden's blood. The Company asserts that the test result proves the charges against Naden. There are a number of reasons, however, why the test result in this particular case cannot be accepted as conclusive evidence of use and possession of marijuana after 7 A.M. on April 15, 1982.

2   Dr. Reed, the director of the forensic laboratory which performed the GC/MS test, testified that accurate calibration of the highly sensitive test equipment was essential. He did not perform the assay in this case and he therefore could not testify as to the exact procedures followed. The evidence shows that the GC/MS

equipment was calibrated by 9:47 A.M., a technician having run through blank and sample serums. The blood sample taken from Naden was not processed until 11:32 A.M. No explanation was given as to what occurred in the intervening two hours and whether activity during the hiatus could or could not have affected the calibration.

3   The scientific literature introduced in this case included a range of findings regarding THC levels in the blood one or more hours after smoking marijuana and rates of dissipation. It is apparent that THC levels do not alone provide sufficient data for precisely gauging time of ingestion. This fact can be more accurately determined if a test for 9-carboxy-THC is done contemporaneously with the one for delta 9-THC. The requisite test for 9-carboxy-THC had not been validated in April, 1982 and hence, was not available to the Company.

4   The lack of an exact correlation between delta 9-THC levels and time of ingestion tends to diminish the persuasiveness of conclusions based solely on GC/MS findings. Reed testified with "reasonable certainty" that Gordon and Miller, two other employees, had smoked within one hour of their blood being drawn. The GC/MS assays had shown fourteen nanograms of THC in both their blood samples. The Company's evidence showed that Gordon and Miller smoked one and one-quarter to one and three-quarter hours before their blood sample was taken. Reed's "reasonably certain" conclusion was off by as much as 50%. Further, according to the Company's evidence, Naden and the other two were all smoking at the same time. Yet Reed testified with equal certainty that Naden had smoked within two hours of his blood being drawn, a difference in time of ingestion of up to one hour.

5   The Company's plant doctor hypothesized that the difference in the THC levels in the three men's blood could have resulted from Naden inhaling less deeply or smoking for a lesser period of time. While these explanations are apparently plausible, they were not embraced by the expert Reed nor do they establish that GC/MS results alone can be used to correctly establish time of ingestion. Rather, the explanations point up the fact that additional data, such as the manner and duration of marijuana ingestion, must be known before conclusions regarding time of ingestion can be conclusively drawn.

6   Further complicating the issue of the implication of the GC/MS results is the Union's claim that as a chronic user of marijuana, Naden may have a steady state level of THC in his blood. The literature introduced by the Union, reporting the results of reputable scientists in the field of cannabinoid detection, did indicate some marijuana users may have a steady state THC level. In "Quarterly

Progress Report for the Period March 1 to May 31, 1982," Service Laboratory for Drug Quantification (Rodger L. Foltz, et al.), for example, delta 9-THC levels as high as 4.8 nanograms were found in test subjects at least eight hours after any marijuana ingestion.

7   Reed contended that reports of elevated basal levels refer to chronic users only, people who attempt to stay high all their waking hours. He stated Naden, who claimed he smoked two or three marijuana cigarettes at night after work and a few more on weekends, did not fit into this high usage category. While Reed may well be right, based on the record in this case the Union's argument about Naden's possible steady state level cannot be summarily dismissed. None of the articles concerning findings of steady state levels define "chronic users." Hence, there is no factual basis for concluding the authors of the studies shared Reed's understanding of the term. In "Developments of Cannabinoid Analysis of Body Fluids: Implications on Forensic Applications," Dr. Richard Hawks of the National Institute for Drug Abuse alternately referred to findings of steady state levels in "some heavy chronic smokers" and "some regular users." Since Reed agreed Naden was a regular, if not a chronic user, the problem of relying on undefined terms is evident.

8   It is apparent from the studies introduced by the Union that a steady state level of 5 nanograms would be highly unusual. Based on the GC/MS data, the exact calculation of Naden's THC level was 4.49 nanograms. If there was an error in calibration of the equipment of one or more nanograms, the steady state would fall into the somewhat less unusual range. For all these reasons, the GC/MS results do not conclusively prove Naden smoked marijuana at work.

–Mark Irvings

2. Read "What the Human Mind Can Do That the Computer Can't" and answer the following questions.
   a. What is the author's purpose?
   b. What is the author trying to persuade you of?
   c. How is the author trying to persuade you?
   d. What kind of evidence does the author offer?
   e. On what does the author base his evidence?
   f. Is the reasoning sound?

What the Human Mind Can Do That the Computer Can't

1   Like creative acts, there are a number of important mental phenomena that have not yet been simulated by any computer pro-

gram and, many cognitive scientists believe, probably never will be. Surprisingly, most of these are everyday aspects of our mental lives that we take for granted and that seem as natural and uncomplicated to us as eating and sleeping.

2   The first is that obvious, seemingly simple, but largely ineluctable phenomenon, consciousness. To philosophers through the centuries, and to psychologists of recent decades, this concept has proven as elusive as a drop of mercury under one's finger, but the only question we need ask ourselves here is: Can a machine be conscious? Let's say the current is on, the machine has a program stored in it, you address it from a terminal and, in response, it goes through various steps of solving a problem in very much the way a human being would. Now ask yourself: Was it conscious of its cognitive processes as you were of yours? The question answers itself: There is no reason to suppose so. Nothing built into any existing program that I have heard of is meant to, or does, as far as one can tell, yield a state corresponding to consciousness.

3   Much of our own thinking, to be sure, takes place outside of consciousness, but the results of these processes become conscious, and each of us *experiences* those conscious thoughts: we know them to be taking place in our own minds. We not only think, but perceive ourselves thinking. Artificial intelligence [AI] has no analog to this. As Donald Norman put it—and he was only one of many cognitive scientists who made similar remarks to me—"We don't have any programs today that are self-aware or that even begin to approach consciousness such as human beings have. I see this as a critical difference between human intelligence and artificial intelligence. The human mind is aware of itself as an identity, it can introspect, it can examine its own ideas and react to them—not just with thoughts about them but with emotions. We can't begin to simulate consciousness on a computer, and perhaps never will."

4   Not everyone would agree that consciousness may forever remain impossible to simulate, but what is clear is that it cannot be simulated at present—and for one very good reason: it remains the least understood and most puzzling of psychological phenomena. I am aware of my own thoughts, to be sure, but what is this "I?" How do I distinguish the "I" from the identity of other people or the rest of the world? Surely it is not a matter of the borders of my physical being, for in the dark, or blindfolded and bound, or even cut off by spinal anesthesia from all feeling, I would know myself: the borders are those of thought, not body. Actually, the question "What is this 'I'?" rarely concerns us, for we experience our own identity as a self-evident reality. But that ineluctable

sense of I-ness does not exist in any computer: there is no evidence that any computer program has ever realized that it is itself, running in a particular machine, and not a similar program, running on another machine somewhere else.

5   Cognitive science does offer at least a rudimentary explanation of consciousness: it is thought to be the product of our internalizing the real world in our minds in symbolic form. We perceive not only the real world but also our own mental representation of it; the experience of the difference between the two results in self-awareness. We recognize that there is not only a real world but a simulacrum [an image] of it within us; therefore there must be an *us: cogito ergo sum* [I think; therefore, I am], yet again. The thought that we have thoughts is the crucial one that becomes consciousness; it is what Douglas Hofstadter, in *Gödel, Escher, Bach*, calls a "strange loop" of the mind, an interaction between different levels, a self-reinforcing resonance. "The self," he says, "comes into being at the moment it has the power to reflect itself." We contemplate our thoughts, but the awareness of doing so is itself a thought, and the foundation of consciousness.

6   Perhaps the key factor is that consciousness develops in us as a result of our cognitive history. As we have seen, the infant gradually becomes capable of thinking about external objects by means of mental images and symbols stored in memory. The newborn does not seem to be aware of the boundaries between itself and the rest of the world, but it perceives them more and more distinctly as its internal image of the world builds up. Consciousness emerges as a product of the child's mental development. The computer, in contrast, though it may acquire an ever-larger store of information, has no such sense or experience of its own history. Nor does it recognize that what is in its memory is a representation of something outside. To the computer, what is in its system is what *is*: it does not contemplate its thoughts as thoughts, but as the only reality. How could it, then, be aware of itself as an individual?

7   Some AI enthusiasts do, however, argue that if a program examines its own problem-solving behavior and modifies it to improve it, as HACKER does, this is the equivalent of consciousness; so says Pamela McCorduck in *Machines Who Think*. John McCarthy of Stanford University, one of America's leading computer scientists, goes even further: he says it is possible to ascribe beliefs, free will, consciousness, and wants to a machine. In his view, even as simple a machine as a thermostat can be said to have beliefs (presumably the thermostat "believes" that the optimum temperature is the one it is set for). But such talk is either metaphorical or, more likely, anthropomorphic; it reads into the ma-

chine what the human observer feels, much as primitive people attribute rage to the volcano and prudence to the ant. There is no reason to suppose HACKER or a thermostat experience anything like awareness of the self; they merely respond to certain incoming stimuli with mechanical reactions. HACKER, to be sure, does register corrections in its program for future use, but so does a vine, growing around an obstruction. It seems most unlikely that anywhere within HACKER some small voice says, "I made an error, but I'm correcting it and I'll do better next time."

8 What difference does it make? If a machine can respond to its own errors and correct them, what does it matter that it isn't aware of doing so?

9 It matters a lot. Awareness of self is the essence of what being alive means to us. If, through some accident, you remained able to talk and reason but could not realize that you were doing so, would you not be as dead, from your own viewpoint, as if your brain had been destroyed?

10 More than that, with awareness of self we become conscious of the alternatives in our thoughts; we become conscious of our choices, and of our ability to will the things we choose to do. Choice and will are difficult to account for within a scientific psychology, since it views existence as a continuum in which no phenomenon occurs uncaused. If no event is, itself, a first cause, but is the product of antecedent forces, then the experience of choice and of will must be illusory; the acts of choosing and of willing, though they seem to be within our power, must be products of all that has happened to us in the past and is happening at the moment.

11 And yet when we are conscious of our own alternatives, that self-awareness is another level of causality—a set of influences in addition to those of the past and present. We are not automata, weighing all the pros and cons of any matter and inevitably acting in accord with our calculations. In mathematical decision theory, the totally rational human being does just that and always selects the most advantageous option; so does a well-designed computer program. But in reality we are aware of our own decision making, and that awareness in itself brings other forces to bear upon the decision—emotional responses to the situation, loyalties, moral values, a sense of our own identity—and these resonances, these loops of thought, affect the outcome.

12 A simple example: you are annoyed by something a friend has said or done, you fume about it, you imagine a conversation in which the two of you argue about it, you prepare your crushing remarks—and suddenly perceive all this as from a distance; in perspective, you see yourself as an outsider might see you, question

your own thoughts and feelings, alter them, and, as a result, accept the friend's behavior and dismiss your anger, or, perhaps, call the friend and talk the matter over amicably.

13   Another example: like every writer I know, when I am writing a first draft I rattle away at the typewriter, setting down words; but once I see them I think, That isn't quite right—that's not exactly what I mean, and tinker and revise and rewrite until the words are right. But it wasn't that the first words didn't say what I meant; rather, in seeing my thoughts, I had thoughts about them; the strange loop yielded something like freedom—the freedom to make a different choice among my thoughts. If the experiences of choice and will are not what they seem to be, they nonetheless reflect real processes that produce results different from those that would come about without them.

14   In any case, there is no doubt that we do not experience our thought processes as automatic but as within our control . . .

15   But what does "want" mean? Can a machine want? In a sense; if its program calls for it to assign different weights to various subgoals and goals, it will proceed to choose that option which its program reckons to have the greatest numerical value. All very neat and simple. Human beings are far less neat and far more complicated. We often desire things but lack the motivation to pursue them; conversely, we are sometimes so strongly motivated by beliefs, values, and emotions that we pursue a particular goal with a devotion far beyond what any realistic evaluation would warrant.

16   Of all the components in human motivation, the one least likely ever to be simulated by a computer is our capacity to find things interesting. It is a mystifying phenomenon. Why do we find any matter interesting? What makes us want to know about, or understand, something—especially something that has no practical value for us, such as the age of the universe or when human beings first appeared on earth? Why do we want to know if there is life elsewhere in the cosmos, if its replies to our messages could not arrive back here for centuries? Why did Pythagoras feel so powerfully impelled to prove his celebrated theorem?

17   This tendency in us, some cognitive scientists believe, is an intrinsic characteristic of our nervous system. We are driven to think certain thoughts, and to pursue certain goals, by an inherent neurological restlessness, a need to do something with the thoughts in our minds and with the world they represent. The computer, in contrast, is a passive system: its goals and the strength of its drive to reach them are those given it by its designer. Left to itself, it will sit inert, awaiting further orders. We will not; we look for new

goals, and, to reach them, are forced to solve problems we did not have before; we do not let well enough alone.

18   Why don't we? Call it restlessness, call it curiosity, or perhaps, like the historian Huizinga, call it playfulness. Other animals play, but with us playfulness becomes cognitive: we play with our ideas, and afterward with the real-world counterparts of those ideas. How would you simulate that on a machine? Allen Newell and a few other AI researchers say there is no reason why a program could not be designed to be curious and to create new goals for itself, but they are a small minority; most cognitive scientists think otherwise. Yet even if a machine could be programmed to cast about in some way for new goals and new problems, it would do so because it had been programmed to; it wouldn't do so because it wanted to. It wouldn't give a damn.

19   And that would be bound to affect the kinds of new problems it chose to tackle and the strength of its motivation to solve them. Maybe the biggest difference between artificial and human intelligence is just that simple: we care about the things we choose to do. Solving a new problem, discovering some new fact, visiting a new place, reading a new book, all make us feel good; that's why we do them. But how would one make a computer feel good? Some AI people have built rewards into their programs: if the machine makes right decisions, its program is automatically altered to strengthen that kind of response, and so it learns. Theoretically, a program could be rewarded if it did something new and different, so that its tendency would be not to maintain itself, unchanged, but to keep changing. But would it *want* to do so or *like* doing so? And lacking that, would there be any meaning to its changes? Perhaps computer-written music and poetry have been unimpressive because the computer itself was neither pleased nor displeased by its own product, as every creative artist is. Without that test, it wasn't able to tell whether it had created a work of genius or a piece of trash. And it didn't care.

20   We, on the other hand, care—and care most of all about those thoughts which express moral values. Each of us is not just an information processor but the product of a particular culture and its belief system. We perceive the world through the special focus of the values we have learned from parents, schools, books, and peers. Those values become a part of our decision-making processes; in making many of our choices, we weigh the alternatives in accordance with our moral, religious, and political beliefs.

21   This aspect of human thinking can be, and has been, simulated on the machine, as we saw earlier, in the form of the simulations

of political decision making created by Jaime Carbonell and his colleagues when he was at Yale (he is now at Carnegie-Mellon). POLITICS has simulated the reasoning of either a conservative or a liberal considering what the United States should do if, for instance, Russia were to build nuclear submarines. Both as conservative and as liberal, POLITICS flawlessly came to conclusions consonant with the assumptions it was programmed to draw upon. Carbonell's purpose was to test his theoretical model of the way in which ideology affects the decision-making process; he did not suggest that POLITICS could be developed into a machine that could do our political thinking for us. But his work does have two important implications for this discussion of what the human mind can do that the computer can't do.

22   First, even though POLITICS can simulate archetypal conservative or liberal political reasoning, it does so in a wholly predictable way; it produces decisions Carbonell could foresee because they are based entirely on the terms and conditions he had put into it. But that is not the way human beings think. Within any party or ideological group, there is a wide range of variations in how individuals interpret the tenets of that ideology. There are always mavericks, dissenters, and innovators, without whom every party, every church, and every culture would atrophy and die.

23   Second, within any given ideological group, some people have the emotional maturity, the richness of human experience, and the soundness of judgment to use its tenets wisely; others do not, and use them foolishly. This is not to say that wise persons will reach the same conclusions everywhere; I would not want the wisest judge in Russia, India, or Iran to hear a civil liberties case in which I was accused of slandering the state. But if it is true that within any culture, its ethical system has internal validity, some of its people will interpret those beliefs wisely, others foolishly, and the majority somewhere in between. Moral wisdom is not so much the product of a special method of reasoning as of an ability to harmonize moral beliefs with fundamental individual and societal needs. I do not see how artificial intelligence can simulate that.

24   Will artificial intelligence, then, ever outstrip human intelligence? Yes, astronomically—in certain ways; and clearly it is already doing so. But in other ways it does not now match our powers, much less exceed them, and seems unlikely to do so soon. And in still other ways it seems incapable of simulating human intellectual functioning at all.

25   For until it acquires perceptual systems as sophisticated as our own, it will not be able to learn directly from the environment. But the development of such systems is bound to prove more difficult, by many orders of magnitude, than the creation of a living cell—a feat not now imaginable—and lacking such perceptual systems, the machine will remain dependent on the human being for its information.

26   But that is the least of it. Until artificial intelligence can duplicate human mental development from birth onward; until it can absorb the intricacies and subtleties of cultural values; until it can acquire consciousness of self; until it becomes capable of playfulness and curiosity; until it can create new goals for itself, unplanned and uninstigated by any human programmer; until it is motivated not by goals alone but by some restless compulsion to be doing and exploring; until it can care about, and be pleased or annoyed by, its own thoughts; until it can make wise moral judgments—until all these conditions exist, the computer, it seems to me, will not match or even palely imitate the most valuable aspects of human thinking.

27   There is no doubt that the computer has already transformed our lives, and will continue to do so. But its chief influence will continue to be its utility as a tool. Supercalculators have radically changed, and will continue to change, all human institutions that require reckoning. Artificial intelligence will reconstruct many areas of problem solving—everything from the practice of medicine to literary and historical research and the investigation of the cosmos—and in so doing will change our ways of thinking as profoundly as did the invention of writing. Tools have powerful effects on the thinking of those who use them (the plow radically altered humankind's view of itself and of the world around it), but tools of the mind have the most powerful effects of all. Still, they are our tools, we their users.

28   But is it not possible that the computer will take over, outthink us, make our decisions for us, become our ruler? Not unless we assign it the power to make our decisions. Joseph Weizenbaum, in *Computer Power and Human Reason*, passionately argues that the computer represents a major danger to humanity not because it can forcibly take over but because we are heedlessly allowing it to make decisions for us in areas where we alone ought to make them. He sees the problem as a moral one rather than a struggle between human and machine: we ought not let the computer function as a psychotherapist, ought not rely on it to tell us whether to bomb civilian enemy targets or only military ones, ought not have it function as a judge in court.

29   Of course we ought not, but is there any real danger that we will? I hope not; I think not. The computer does not set its own goals: we do, and we human beings are jealous of our own powers. We have often delegated them to some leader—a human being, like ourselves, but one we took to be a greater person than we. Or we have asked some god (who often looks like us, enlarged) to make our decisions for us. But would we ever delegate our intellectual responsibilities to a machine that we ourselves created? I doubt it. Though human beings have often enough been fools, I find it hard to believe that we would ever be foolish enough to think our machines wiser than we; at least, not as long as we are aware of, and proud of, the human difference.

–Morton Hunt

3. Evaluate the authors' reasoning in the following two articles about malpractice. Which of the two articles is the more persuasive? Why?

Malpractice Costs Hurt All

1   The cost of malpractice insurance is soaring out of control in Massachusetts, and what, at first, seems only a problem for physicians quickly becomes everybody's problem.

2   Why does the price a physician has to pay for his insurance make any difference to his patients? There are four easily identifiable reasons, and they demonstrate why a financial problem is on its way to becoming a public health crisis.

3   First is the obvious impact on the public: the cost of insurance contributes to the rising cost of health care generally.

4   Second, more and more physicians are avoiding the kinds of medical specialization and treatment procedures that are most vulnerable to claims of malpractice—and those specialties range from general surgery and anesthesia to obstetrics, neurosurgery and emergency medicine, all vital to the continued good health of the public.

5   Third, experienced doctors, faced with almost crippling costs for insurance they may never need, are choosing early retirement rather than risk the financial and emotional costs that even a frivolous suit might produce. Massachusetts is losing its most experienced physicians. Of equal concern is the potential for talented and capable young physicians finding medical practice less and less attractive.

6   Fourth, and perhaps the worst effect of all, is that the situation is turning professional physicians into amateur lawyers. Because

of the mess that malpractice insurance is in, a physician must always be aware that every patient is a potential opponent in some future lawsuit. The corrosive effect on the doctor-patient relationship is obvious.

7   To put it simply, when a doctor is sued, the public gets hurt, and the time has come to repair a system that is breaking down, that is serving nobody well, and that is a threat to the quality of health care in this state.

8   The Massachusetts Medical Society has proposed a legislative package designed to remedy some of the most obvious ills in our medical malpractice insurance system.

9   Medical malpractice insurance is everybody's business now, and, at State House hearings, we have proposed reforms aimed at providing greater benefits to victims of malpractice while cost-controlling a system that actually shortchanges them today.

10   In addition, we have proposed to guarantee that malpractice victims are paid medical costs, loss of income, and rehabilitation expenses and to limit other intangible losses to a quarter-million dollars. Sometimes called "pain and suffering" costs, this unlimited category invites frivolous claims by those unscrupulous enough to turn our system into a game of chance.

11   Under the provisions of our proposed legislation, the majority of malpractice victims would be able to keep more of the money that they are awarded by limiting the amount they must pay a lawyer. That can cost them up to 50 cents of every dollar they deserve.

12   Responsible members of the trial bar agree that a system that turns over as much as one-third to one-half of a victim's money to a lawyer may encourage that small minority of lawyers to file suits not on their merits but in the hope of walking away with up to half of a victim's award. In some such suits, the claim is settled without a court hearing, leaving the patient to still pay all other expenses out of the portion of the award that remains.

13   Other proposed reforms include elimination of duplicate insurance company payments, tighter standards for expert medical witnesses, better reporting of malpractice claims to the state's Board of Registration in Medicine and better funding for the board to perform its duties, and tighter controls on the filing of malpractice claims in order to weed out the frivolous or malicious.

14   The quality and availability of the kind of medical care that has made Massachusetts the envy of the world are threatened by a malpractice-insurance system that has no cost control, that discourages physicians from performing vital work, and that damages the patient-physician relationship.

15   The Legislature this year has an opportunity to correct a problem that only grows worse with time.

—*Frederick J. Duncan Jr. and Barbara A. Rockett*

Blame Negligent Doctors, Not Insurance

1   Doctors claim a crisis in malpractice insurance and are pushing
the Legislature to adopt a package of bills to immunize the medical profession from responsibility for damage done by their negligence at the expense of innocent victims.

2   There is no crisis in malpractice insurance. It is readily available at reasonable prices. The average doctor pays a small percentage of his gross income for malpractice insurance—national
statistics put the figure at less than 3 percent. The average Massachusetts doctor pays a smaller percentage of his gross income
for professional liability insurance than does a Boston independent cab driver. It ill behooves members of one of the highest paid
professions to seek preferential treatment, afforded no other
group, because they refuse to bear the cost of their mistakes.

3   Doctors blame malpractice suits on greedy lawyers, but medical negligence is the real cause of litigation and incidents of medical negligence are far greater than the amount of malpractice
claims. An independent study by the Rand Corp. concluded that
"at most, one in 10 incidents of malpractice results in a claim."

4   If a crisis exists, it is a crisis of medical incompetence, not of
medical insurance. Most doctors are competent, but some are repeatedly negligent and have substantial impact on losses paid. A
Florida study disclosed one physician accounted for 31 paid
claims, yet he was never disciplined and is still practicing.

5   Rather than admit the problem and police themselves, doctors
propose self-interest legislation that should be dubbed "the medical incompetence protection plan." Although the bills differ
widely, they share the common and ignoble goal of preventing,
discouraging and minimizing legitimate claims against doctors.
They seek to carve out a sanctified niche for doctors while the rest
of us remain responsible for our carelessness.

6   One bill would place a limit on recovery for pain and suffering
for the most seriously injured victims of malpractice, not because
the loss wasn't real, but simply to give preferential treatment to
doctors.

7   Victims of drunk drivers and victims of defective products
would still recover without limit for the wrongful destruction of
the quality of their lives. But in malpractice cases, we would have
to ignore human tragedy and pretend that the loss in excess of the

limit really didn't happen, even in catastrophic cases of death, brain damage or paralysis.

8   Another bill would reduce lawyers' contingent fees drastically. The contingent fee system is the citizen's key to the courthouse by giving those with legitimate claims access to the best legal talent. Lawyers have great incentive to eliminate illegitimate cases, for if they lose they receive nothing. Lawyers cannot afford to accept questionable cases and invest hundreds of hours and thousands of dollars with little prospect of being paid.

9   It might appear that while other bills limit the victim's recovery, this one is designed to compensate by giving the victim a bigger piece of the reduced pie. But the real purpose is to make legitimate malpractice cases so financially unappealing that lawyers will not handle them and thus allow doctors to again escape responsibility. It is designed to prevent victims from pursuing their legitimate claims.

10   Doctors contend that malpractice cases force doctors to practice defensive medicine and increase costs. If this means more monitoring, referrals and second opinions before major procedures are undertaken, then I believe defensive medicine is good medicine. The American public deserves nothing less.

11   Most doctors are highly qualified and regularly perform work that can only be viewed as miraculous by the rest of us. They are most deserving of our admiration and gratitude. But in this instance they demean themselves by clinging to a misplaced sense of loyalty to an old-buddy fraternal system and by continuing to participate in the conspiracy of silence.

12   As the New York Times recently stated: "So long as doctors remain reluctant or unable to police their ranks, the threat of litigation is the best deterrent against malpractice."

–David J. Sargent

4. Read the advertisement on page 210. What emotional response does the author want to invoke?

Writing Exercise

Summarize the differences between informational and persuasive writing.

Courtesy Ms.

13 *Active Studying: Applying Active Reading Skills*

Throughout this text we have stressed the importance of asking questions of your reading. Asking good questions helps you to establish a purpose, to discriminate the important from the unimportant, to be an active instead of a passive reader, and to remember the author's ideas. Similarly, asking good questions can help you to study better and more efficiently. Chapter 13 continues to emphasize this technique. It gives suggestions for marking up your texts and taking notes to help you review more effectively. This chapter also shows how to apply active reading strategies to your writing, listening, and speaking.

Active Learning

The basic reading and preview questions you have learned provide the basis for your reading strategies of skimming and sectioning. They enable you to determine how authors organize ideas and how to read critically. The essence of active reading is the use of questions to make connections. Good reading and good thinking and studying depend on seeing the connections among

- the author's ideas
- your ideas and the author's ideas
- how ideas are stated and how they are applied
- the points the author is making and the way in which she or he presents them
- the general and the specific
- what you want from your reading and how you read
- what you know and what you want to know

The reading and preview questions you have learned to use connect everything in this text. We shall now deal with some of the ways the same questions can be applied to your studying.

Marking the Text

We have stressed marking your text in this book because it is another excellent way of analyzing your readings and taking an active part in the reading process. Some students mark their texts only with brief checks in the margin to indicate something important. Others go to the opposite extreme and underline or highlight almost every sentence. Neither of these methods is very efficient. The first does not give enough information, and the second does not discriminate the truly important from the less important. Further, both these methods are mentally passive and provide a false sense of security. It is as if the information went directly from the page, through the hand, and back to the page, leaving no trace on the mind.

The following example is a markup based on the basic reading questions. The key ideas, supporting ideas, and supporting details have been noted, as well as the patterns of organization. In doing your own text marking, you may find it easier to use a code of underlining and bracketing, as we did in Chapter 6; or you may want to write marginal notes, as done here; or you may wish to use a combination. You may also want to circle words you don't understand and need to look up in the dictionary later. Or you may choose to mark passages that are particularly difficult and to which you'll want to return later. It is important only that your marking be consistent and not too complicated; otherwise, you won't use it.

Example

The Partnership

Topic

1   A partnership can be defined as the association of two or more persons as co-owners for the purpose of carrying on a business for a profit. Its major advantage over a proprietorship is that the partners may pool their financial resources and professional specializations to enable the firm to grow. While a proprietor must be a jack-of-all-trades, a partnership may have persons who are experts in different areas of running the business. Partnerships are most often found in service industries, such as medicine and law, and in the finance, insurance, and real estate industries. It is quite common to find public accounting and law firms with partners numbering in the hundreds.

Key Idea

Supporting Idea

Compare and contrast

— Introduction

Supporting Idea

Supporting Detail

2   A partnership presents a situation requiring a tremendous degree of trust and confidence among the partners. Under the law, each partner has the right to be a manager as well as an owner of the business. Any one partner can commit the entire partnership to a *legal contract,* that is, a binding relationship to another party, in the course of the partnership business. This last point is very important. Let us consider an example.

Subtopic

Supporting Idea

— Body

3   Suppose, in the course of usual business, one partner unwisely borrows a huge sum of money from the bank in order to increase the company's production. However, the demand for the company's product falls off sharply, and the company cannot repay its bank loan. What happens? The bank sues *each one* of the partners in order to seek repayment of the loan. Obviously, each person should choose the partner or partners very carefully. The importance of this is re-

Supporting Detail

Cause and Effect

cognized in Section 18(g) of the Uniform
Partnership Act: "No person can become a   Key Idea ⎤ ˌConclusion
member of a partnership without the consent
of all the partners." ⎦

—*F. T. Haner, Stephen K. Keiser,
and Donald J. Puglisi*

Note Taking

Although marking the text is a useful technique for analyzing your
reading, if you want to have a record of what you have read or a basis
for recalling what you have read, then you need to take notes. Translating the author's thoughts into your own words ensures better understanding and longer retention. However, as in marking up, there
is a fine balance between taking so many notes that in effect you duplicate the text and taking notes that are informative enough to ensure your understanding of the concepts when you review them.

Again, you can base your note taking on the reading questions. The
example that follows illustrates what we consider the best method of
taking notes. Draw a line down the page about a third of the way
from the left margin (some college bookstores carry paper ruled this
way). Write the topics and subtopics to the left of the line, and write
the key idea and supporting material—the supporting ideas and details—to the right side of the line. You may also want to include a
note indicating the patterns of organization as a reminder of how the
author developed the material, or you might want to note how to use
the reading later. For instance, you may want to indicate that you
will be tested on the material or will need to compare the reading
with another author's viewpoint. In addition to helping you distinguish the author's ideas, this method of note taking is an ideal arrangement for review. Most students quiz themselves by covering the
right-hand side of the page to see if they can recite the key and supporting ideas. Others reverse the process, testing to see if they can
abstract the subtopic from the key and supporting ideas.

Example

Topics and Subtopics	Key Idea, Supporting Ideas, Supporting Details
The partnership (Topic)	A partnership is when two or more people own a business (Key Idea) Better than proprietorship (Supporting Idea)

Can pool money and abilities
(Supporting Detail)
Most often found in service
industries (Supporting Idea)
Medicine, law, finance, real
estate (Supporting Detail)

(Compare/Contrast)

Need for trust
(Subtopic)

Any partner can make a legal
contract (Supporting Idea)
Example of bank loan
(Supporting Detail)

(Cause and Effect)

Should choose partners with care
(Supporting Idea)
Reflected in law (Supporting
Detail)

(Mostly informative, but also
persuasive—use of "should")

Reviewing

Reviewing reinforces your understanding of the material and enables you to integrate a reading with other material you are learning. When you review you connect your reading notes with your class notes to see how what you learned today fits with what you learned yesterday. Reviewing also prepares you for tests by enabling you to associate one aspect of a course with another, to predict what questions might be asked, and to expose what you don't know or understand. Because you have been asking questions as you read, you have done much of the work that ensures understanding and remembering.

Ideally, you should review constantly instead of waiting for a text or exam. Good reviewing is based on good reading notes, a thorough understanding of the material, and an ability to summarize what you have been learning. If your notes are not well organized, you can start your review by recasting them so that topic, subtopics, key idea, and supporting ideas stand out clearly. Asking and answering the preview and basic reading questions will help to organize your notes and expose gaps in your information.

Because it is important that you see your notes in the larger context of the course, it is helpful to write a short summary of the key and supporting ideas that connect one set of notes with another. For instance, in reviewing Edmund Burkes's philosophy of representative government for a political science course, you may find it useful to compare and contrast his ideas with those of J. S. Mill. Also, by connecting the key and supporting ideas that run through a course, you will be able to see what ideas have been emphasized and how they relate. You can be fairly certain that your test or exam questions will deal with several of those ideas in one way or another. Applying the strategies of active reading to your review will guarantee that you are ready for the exam.

Although this is a book on efficient reading, we have often mentioned, and in some cases expressly indicated, how the knowledge you have gained in active reading can also apply to you as writer, speaker, and listener.

Writing

The exercise of writing summaries has given you a lot of practice in using the principles of this book as you have thought about and reviewed the particular points in each chapter. You have realized how closely reading and writing are linked and how knowing the techniques and strategies of the writer can help you in your reading and your own writing. You have learned that it is the responsibility of the writer to present material in an orderly way and to provide explicit support for ideas and generalizations. You have seen the value to the reader of clarity in putting forth and developing ideas.

A very useful technique for revising your writing is to apply the reading strategies you have learned to what you have written, either by marking it up or by making an outline. This will help you to see whether the supporting ideas clearly relate to the key idea and whether you have supplied the right kind of supporting evidence. You can ask the same questions of your writing as you ask of your reading: Is there sufficient detail to explain your point fully? Is it clear what has caused a certain effect? Have you taken up each point you have listed? Turning the reading questions to you own writing can teach you a lot about how to present your ideas in a clear and comprehensive way.

Listening

For most of you, hearing is a function of being alive. Probably you have given very little thought to the way in which this basic ability is distinguished from listening. What is the difference? The difference is a matter of intent and degree. You change "hearing" to "listening" when you consciously want to hear. You can have music playing in the background and have very little awareness of it; suddenly a new song by a group you know comes on and penetrates your consciousness. You become alert, stop whatever else you are doing, and "listen." When you listen well, you are attentive. Questioning as you listen can help you to focus on the topic under discussion and to maintain your interest in it, just as it does when you read.

Listening is an important part of your life as a student. Classes are the focus of your education because in the classroom is your instructor, who serves as guide, interpreter, and explainer. Therefore, how you listen to what goes on in class may have a powerful effect on what you get out of the course.

Just as you preview a text, you can preview a class by asking yourself what you want or expect to get from it. Then, associate what you are about to learn with what you already know by mentally reviewing your last class and thinking of the topic and subtopics of the class and the three or four most important ideas that came out of it.

Hold your basic reading questions in your mind as you listen in class. In this way you will be listening for the topic, key idea, and subtopics, and you will be ready to fill in with the supporting ideas and, finally, with the supporting details. Just as you use your questions in reading to distinguish the ideas of the author, so you can use them in listening to gauge the relative importance that the instructor attaches to each topic and subtopic. You will find, too, that an awareness of how your instructors use the patterns of organization to make their points will help you to categorize, associate, and learn.

Speaking

When you speak formally, remember the principles of active reading. Be conscious of how you state your key idea and how you develop your supporting ideas. It is as important here as it is in writing to back up your statements with good examples, definitions, and illustrations. Is there a pattern of organization you can use that will help clarify your meaning? Think of your listeners as note takers and summary writers. Are you making it possible for them to follow every step of your thinking? What questions will they have? Can they make the connections?

Good reading, thinking, writing, speaking, and listening are all connected because in each case topics, key ideas, and supporting ideas are arranged in some rational order. As a writer and speaker, you must connect and support your ideas for the reader and listener. As a thinker, reader, and listener, you are constantly seeking the connections you assume are there. This is the foundation of both learning and communication. Mastery of the strategies emphasized in *Active Reading* can give you some control over your reading and other aspects of your intellectual life. These techniques, when constantly and consciously practiced, should become an unconscious habit.

Exercises

1. Preview, skim, section, and mark up the following article.

Political Science: The Study of How Politics Works and of How It Could Be Made to Work Better

1 Political science as the serious and orderly study of politics is about 2400 years old. Yet to this day there is controversy about whether it is a science in the proper sense of the term.

2 *Is it a science? And what is a science anyway?* The term "political science" comes from the German term *Staatswissenschaft—* the science of, or learning about, the state—of the eighteenth and nineteenth centuries. In German, "science"—*Wissenschaft—* means generally any kind of ordered and organized knowledge. At German universities, law and history are considered to this day sciences, sometimes called "cultural" or "intellectual" sciences. In English-speaking countries, a narrower definition of science has been more popular. Here the term usually refers to the "natural sciences," as if human beings and their activities are somehow outside nature, and as if a zoologist watching monkeys is engaged in science in a sense in which a social scientist observing people is not. By the same rule, a veterinarian, whose patients cannot talk, would seem to be more of a "scientist," that is, closer to the natural sciences, than a physician, whose patients can talk back to him.

3 The main points of the argument about how narrowly science should be defined are three:

4 1. Science ought to be based on repeated observation and experiment under controlled conditions. People can be observed, but usually they cannot be experimented with, certainly not under extreme conditions and in large numbers. Neither the French Revolution, nor the Chinese Civil War, nor World War I or II could be repeated for experimental purposes. Even when people have experimented with new laws, constitutions, or other policies, they did so under conditions that were neither completely controlled

nor fully repeatable. But the same difficulty applies to many of the "natural" sciences. Meterologists cannot experiment with hurricanes, nor can a seismologist experiment with earthquakes, or astrophysicists with supernovas. All these scientists can do is compare different examples of such phenomena within their fields and learn as best they can from such comparisons. Just this, however, is what political scientists also do.

5   2. "Natural" sciences are supposed to be more accurate in their measurements and predictions. But the currently accepted *error margins* of meteorology, seismology, or the geological dating of fossils are much larger than the error margins of election forecasts—although these too are fallible indeed.

6   3. "Natural" sciences are not supposed to interfere with the events and objects they observe, but political and social scientists may interfere, by the very act of observation, with the processes they are trying to study. This is a serious problem but it has also bedeviled physicists ever since they learned that anything they do to an electron in order to observe it will greatly interfere with the electron, making it impossible to state its position, direction, or velocity at any one time. This embarrassing fact, discovered by the physicist Werner Heisenberg, has been called the *uncertainty principle,* but it has not led many people to deny that physics is a science.

7   Certainly political science suffers from the same special difficulties as other sciences of human culture and behavior: rarity of controlled observations and experiments, considerable margins of error, and occasional interference between observer and observed. But this should be no reason to give up our efforts to understand political processes and institutions as clearly and accurately, and with as much reproducible evidence, as we can. So long as we are trying to do this and are making some modest progress at it, we are still part of the great and common enterprise of science.

8   Not all human knowledge is scientific, nor will it ever be. The poets and the prophets always will range into ideas that scientists can neither confirm nor deny. Their minds, like those of the great theorists of science, show us the reach of human awareness, which always exceeds the grasp of even provisionally tested scientific knowledge.

9   Science is but one form of knowledge, and a limited one at that. Its limitations exclude the utterly individual, the unique. But out of these limitations it also derives a certain strength, the strength of shared and tested thinking. This holds true for all sciences, "natural" and "human," and it applies to the study of politics as well.

–Karl W. Deutsch, Jorge I. Dominguez, and Hugh Heclo

2. A page of notes on the following article has been partially made. Finish the notes, keeping to the established pattern.

International Style

1   The work of Frank Lloyd Wright had attracted much attention in Europe by 1914. Among the first to recognize its importance were some young Dutch architects who, a few years later, joined forces with Mondrian in the De Stijl movement. The Schröder House in Utrecht, designed in 1924 by Gerrit Rietveld (1888–1964), has a number of Wrightian features—the slablike, overhanging roof and the juxtaposition of closed and open blocks of space—combined with a façade that looks like a painting by Mondrian transposed into three dimensions. At the end of the First World War, the De Stijl group represented the most advanced ideas in European architecture. Its austerely geometric designs, based on Mondrian's principle of an equilibrium achieved through the balance of unequal but equivalent oppositions, had a decisive influence on so many architects abroad that the movement soon became international. The largest and most complex example of this "International Style of the 1920s" is the group of buildings created in 1925–26 by Walter Gropius (1883–1969) for the Bauhaus transferred to Dessau, the famous art school of which he was the director. (Its curriculum embraced all the visual arts, linked by the root concept of "structure," *Bau.*) The plant consists of three major blocks for classrooms, shops, and studios, the first two linked by a bridge of ferroconcrete containing offices. The most dramatic is the shop block, a four-story box with walls that are a continuous surface of glass. This radical step had been possible ever since the introduction of the structural steel skeleton several decades before, which relieved the wall of any bearing function; Sullivan had approached it in the Carson Pirie Scott & Co. store, but he could not yet free himself from the traditional notion of the window as a "hole in the wall." Gropius frankly acknowledges, at last, that in modern architecture the wall is no more than a curtain or climate barrier, which may consist entirely of glass if maximum daylight is desirable. A quarter-century later, the same principle was used on a much larger scale for the two main faces of the great slab that houses the Secretariat of the United Nations. The effect is rather surprising: since such walls reflect as well as transmit light, their appearance depends on the interplay of these two effects. They respond, as it were, to any change of conditions without and within, and thus introduce a strange quality of life into the structure. (The mirror-like finish of Brancusi's sculpture serves a similar purpose.)

2   In France, the most distinguished representative of the "International Style" during the 1920s was the Swiss-born architect Le Corbusier (Charles Edouard Jeanneret, 1886–1965). At that time he built only private houses—from necessity, not choice—but these are as important as Wright's "Prairie Houses." Le Corbusier called them *machines à habiter* (machines to be lived in), a term intended to suggest his admiration for the clean, precise shapes of machinery, not a desire for "mechanized living." (The paintings of his friend Fernand Léger during those years reflect the same attitude.) Perhaps he also wanted to imply that his houses were so different from conventional homes as to constitute a new species. Such is indeed our impression as we approach the most famous of them, the Savoye House at Poissy-sur-Seine: it resembles a low, square box resting on stilts—pillars of reinforced concrete that form part of the structural skeleton and reappear to divide the "ribbon-windows" running along each side of the box. The flat, smooth surfaces, denying all sense of weight, stress Le Corbusier's preoccupation with abstract "space blocks." In order to find out how the box is subdivided, we must enter it: we then realize that this simple "package" contains living spaces that are open as well as closed, separated by glass walls. Within the house, we are still in communication with the outdoors (views of the sky and the surrounding terrain are everywhere to be seen). Yet we enjoy complete privacy, since an observer on the ground cannot see us unless we stand next to a window. The functionalism of the Savoye House thus is governed by a "design for living," not by mechanical efficiency.

3   America, despite its early position of leadership, did not share the exciting growth that took place in European architecture during the 1920s. The impact of the "International Style" did not begin to be felt on this side of the Atlantic until the very end of the decade. A pioneer example is the Philadelphia Savings Fund Society Building of 1931–32, by George Howe (1886–1954) and William E. Lescaze (born 1896), a skyscraper in the tradition of Sullivan that incorporates in its design many features evolved in Europe since the end of the First World War. During the following years, the best German architects, whose work Hitler condemned as "un-German," came to this country and greatly stimulated the development of American architecture. Gropius, who was appointed chairman of the architecture department at Harvard University, had an important educational influence; Ludwig Mies van der Rohe (1887–1969), his former colleague at Dessau, settled in Chicago as a practicing architect. The Lake Shore Drive apartment houses, two severely elegant slabs placed at right angles to each other, exemplify Mies van der Rohe's dictum that "less is

more." He is the great spiritual heir of Mondrian among contemporary designers, possessed of the same "absolute pitch" in determining proportions and spatial relationships.

—H. W. Janson

Topic and Subtopics	Key Idea, Supporting Ideas, Supporting Details
International Style	International Style is a style of architecture influenced by Wright and developed in Europe during the 1920s.
In Holland, the De Stijl movement	The De Stijl movement, started by Mondrian, was the most advanced of Europe Based on austerely geometric designs The Bauhaus, designed by Gropius, largest and most complex example
	Patterns of organization: compare/contrast, chronological
In France, LeCorbusier	LeCorbusier built *machines à habiter*

3. Preview the following article by Michele Wallace. Skim to find and mark the introduction, development, and conclusion, noting the subtopics where possible. Section the reading and write the titles of the subtopics in the margin. List the organizational patterns found in the reading.

Black Macho and the Myth of the Superwoman

1   As the function of the Southern white woman changed, the life of the black woman continued just as if the country were in its first stages of growth. She labored in the fields beside her husband, developed muscles in her arms, bore the lash and the wrath of her master. Her labor and trials became inextricably associated with her skin color, even though not so long before, the colonial woman had not been much better off.

2   Whether slavery would continue seemed in doubt during the Revolutionary War and immediately afterward. The truth is that the Revolutionary forces had enlistment problems. When the Brit-

ish offered blacks freedom if they fought with them, the Revolutionaries had no choice but to enlist blacks too. Five thousand blacks, in integrated and all-black regiments, fought in the Revolutionary War. They did so because they believed it would win them their freedom. The Rights of Man, they had reason to assume, would be extended to them. After the war, when many masters did not make good their promises, many blacks escaped to Canada and to other territories. Others sued for their freedom in the American courts and won. The new government seriously considered the abolition of slavery, but because of cotton and tobacco it was not to be.

3 Gradually a network of lies developed to justify the continuance of the master/slave relationship, the selling of children away from their mothers, the separation of wives and husbands, the breeding of slaves like animals. After the constitutional ban on slave importation, which took effect in 1808, the market required that a brutal emphasis be placed upon the stud capabilities of the black man and upon the black woman's fertility. The theory of the inferiority of blacks began to be elaborated upon and to take hold. It was at this point that the black woman gained her reputation for invulnerability. She was the key to the labor supply. No one wished to admit that she felt as any woman would about the loss of her children, or that she had any particularly deep attachment to her husband, since he might also have to be sold. Her first duty had to be to the master of the house.

4 She was believed to be not only emotionally callous but physically invulnerable—stronger than white women and the physical equal of any man of her race. She was stronger than white women in order to justify her performing a kind of labor most white women were now presumed to be incapable of. She had to be considered at least the physical equal of the black man so that he would not feel justified in attempting to protect her.

5 She was labeled sexually promiscuous because it was imperative that her womb supply the labor force. The father might be her master, a neighboring white man, the overseer, a slave assigned to her by her master; her marriage was not recognized by law.

6 Every tenet of the mythology about her was used to reinforce the notion of the spinelessness and unreliability of the black man, as well as the notion of the frivolity and vulnerability of white women. The business of sexual and racial definition, hideously intertwined, had become a matter of balancing extremes. That white was powerful meant that black had to be powerless. That white men were omnipotent meant that white women had to be impotent. But slavery produced further complications: black women had to be strong in ways that white women were not

allowed to be, black men had to be weak in ways that white men were not allowed to be.

7   It has become a national belief that because the black woman's master was the slaveowner, and not her husband, she became abusive to her husband, overly aggressive, bossy, domineering. But those who trace such characteristics in the contemporary black woman back to her slave ancestry will have to find some other basis for their arguments. So far as circumstances would permit, she was a loyal, faithful and dutiful wife and mother. In partnership with her slave husband, the black woman slave fought to preserve her family, and everything that she did can be seen in that light. Her family structure was simply different from that of whites; it had no fewer rules and allowed women no greater measure of equality.

8   If circumstances permitted, a slave woman often lived with a single man most of her life. If her husband was to be sold, he might assign a friend to look after his wife and children. Or after a time, the woman might take another husband. She would act just as if her previous husband were dead.

9   In choosing a husband, a woman might live with a succession of men, but once she had settled upon a mate, she would be faithful to him. Adultery was vigorously frowned upon by the slave community. Often she was pregnant before she settled down. Her behavior did not indicate what the slaveowners claimed was a unique immorality or moral devastation; it was a carryover from her African home, where it was fairly common behavior, just as it was in many agrarian societies. If the black woman could not get along with her husband, she was allowed to separate from him. These practices were all acceptable under the code the slaves devised for themselves and necessary to their survival. It is easy to see how slaveowners used them to support their contentions that slaves were amoral and socially chaotic.

10   The work of historian Herbert Gutman has revealed that the threat slavery posed to the black family did not prompt the slave to give up all hopes of family life but rather to value it above all else. For the black man and woman family life was their only daily refuge. It offered them companionship, some modicum of comfort, a positive and reinforcing view of themselves and a future. Gutman describes the slaves as having been considerably preoccupied not only with their husbands and wives and children but with their cousins, nieces and nephews, aunts and uncles and grandparents. Whenever it was possible, they maintained family ties across generations.

11   Eugene Genovese suggests that the reputation the slave woman had for beating her children might have resulted from her at-

tempts to teach them to obey quickly that they might later avoid death at a white man's hand. Plantation owners had a habit of spoiling black children, allowing them to play and roam freely with white children until the age of twelve or thirteen. Then abruptly everything would change. The white children would go off to school and the black children would be sent to the fields. The black children would become subject to the whippings and plantation discipline administered to adults. Slave mothers evidently tried to minimize that transition. No precedent for harsh parental discipline existed in African society, where mothers traditionally indulge their younger offspring. It is also known that some black women slaves in America traveled much of the night in order to see their children on another plantation and arrive back home before dawn.

12   In many ways the black woman's plight in slavery was worse than the black man's, not because she fought against a traditional woman's role but because she willingly assumed it. In addition to her labors in the fields or in the big house, she also did the same work expected of early colonial women, and all poor women, in her own house. Certain rituals in which she participated, like the annual corn-shucking parties which Genovese cites in *Roll, Jordan, Roll*, indicated that she believed in the notion of the male slave as provider: The men shucked the corn, competed for prizes, while the women looked on and prepared the food.

13   In this and various other ways, the slaves showed that they had not forgotten what constitutes a desirable relationship between male and female. And no matter what the white master might whisper in the black woman's ear, she usually showed herself to have a mind of her own in matters that concerned her own people. For instance, although their mistresses encouraged them to shun the attentions of the field hands, black female house servants quite commonly married field hands. Whites had little success in effecting a division between house and field slaves like the one that developed in the West Indies.

14   Assimilation was simply not a possibility, much less a problem for the slave woman. Although she often lived in close proximity to whites, the emotional reality of her world remained distant from direct white influence. She was never able to relate freely to whites—the consciousness of the barrier was always there, even in bed with the master—and thus she was unable to absorb the intricate rationalizations for their racism and to adapt them to her image of herself. She had to depend upon her own people for her self-image.

—Michele Wallace

4. "The Language of Pictures" is a long article containing some ideas about how language and art are related. Preview and skim it. Mark up the first half, which ends with paragraph 15, and take notes on the second half, following the method introduced in this chapter.

The Language of Pictures

1   Man has been communicating by pictures longer than he has been using words. With the development of photography in this century we are using pictures as a means of communication to such an extent that in some areas they overshadow verbal language. The science of semantics has studied the conveyance of meaning by language in considerable detail. Yet very little is known as to how pictures convey meaning and what their place is in the life of man.

2   Perhaps this neglect may be due to the poor repute pictures have in our society as a means of communication. For example, in the field of education, pictures, as a part of the group of audio-visual materials available to teachers, are still considered supplementary rather than complementary to other teaching materials such as textbooks or other purely verbal materials. The term audio-visual "aids" persists, although a number of educators have tried for a decade to persuade their colleagues to discontinue its use on the basis of its connotation of (1) something used by poor teachers who cannot teach without gadgets, (2) a luxury to be trimmed off the budget in hard times, and (3) a mental crutch for backward pupils.

3   Pictures are of course surrogates for experience. As such they may be said to be closer to extensional meaning than to intensional meaning. At least their position lies in between these two. They are not always close to the actual experience even though the school of "you press the button and we do the rest" implies that merely pointing the camera at Aunt Minnie results in a good likeness to cherish when she is not around. Neither are pictures symbols as words are symbols, since even Aunt Minnie's nephew, age four, can recognize her snapshot though he cannot read.

4   Pictures are a language in themselves. They are not merely limited representations of reality operating within narrow limits of expression. On the contrary photography is a very flexible medium with a wide range whose limits have not yet been sighted. The range extends from absorbing realism to a fairly high level of abstraction. Let us consider the realistic end of the scale.

5   The tendency today is to say that the heyday of the movies is over. Television is gnawing at the vitals of Hollywood. But the powerfully realistic effect of the film remains. The other day the writer showed to one of his classes a film, *The Cinematographer,* which purports to show the work of the director of photography in a large studio. Excerpts from several dramatic films were shown to illustrate the different types of sciences a cinematographer encounters. None of these excerpts was longer than one minute. After the film ended some members of the class complained that the excerpts were so realistic and exciting that they "lost" themselves in the content of the episodes and completely forgot that the purpose of the film showing was to study cinematography. Each episode in turn caught these students up in a rich representation of reality. The excerpts were very dissimilar in content so that it was a wrench to change from one scene to another. Nevertheless the students were deeply involved in each excerpt in turn, and only when the lights came on in the classroom did they remember where they were.

6   Motion pictures are a powerful medium of persuasion. Hitler's films of the bombing of Warsaw were such terribly realistic records that they could be used as a tool of conquest. At times a motion picture may seem even more realistic than the real experience.

7   At the other end of the scale from realism to abstraction, pictures have many qualities of language. Like words every picture has a content of meaning partly intensional, partly extensional. Whether this meaning is more or less extensionally clear or abstractly difficult to understand depends of course on many factors inherent in the viewer, such as his past experience. But it also is dependent on factors in the picture itself which we might call the grammar of photography.

8   Composition is all important. In chirographic, or handmade pictures, composition is achieved sometimes by selection of the point of view but more often by manipulation of space relationships of objects perceived or imagined. The still photographer, unless he is using techniques which are essentially chirographic, such as retouching, montage, or collage, is bound by the objects of reality as the eye of his camera sees them. He achieves composition by painstaking selection of the camera angle, by using a variety of lenses, by choice of filters and emulsions, and by controlling lighting on the subject or scene. Choosing a camera angle may take a professional photographer days of continuous effort, even though television camera operators may be forced to do it in seconds. The angle and the lens used for the shot determine the basic composition. The lighting, however, gives the photographer an enormous range of control over the representation of reality. High key photography in which all the values are crowded toward the

whites and light grays, gives the impressions of light, of lightness, or happiness, or innocent pleasures. Low key photography with many shadows and low values is appropriate for mystery, danger, depression. Every textbook in photography contains the series of portraits of a model taken with different lighting effects, showing how one face can be made to look like many strange people. Pictures have affective connotations.

9   These constitute the grammar of photographs. The analogy holds even down to details such as synizesis [contraction of two syllables into one by joining in pronunciation two adjacent vowels]. Two crucial objects in a picture, like two syllables, can be blended and not discriminated from each other, thereby changing the meaning entirely. Even though the photographer uses lighting and other techniques to separate the two objects, the viewer may still misread the picture because of lack of experience or poor viewing conditions. Always it is important to remember that pictures, like words, are merely surrogates for reality, not reality itself.

10   In motion pictures we find the syntax of photography. Motion pictures present a flowing discourse in picture surrogates. Like a paragraph, a motion picture sequence is a highly structured time-space analysis and synthesis of reality. Using individual "shots" like words, the sequence inflects the static frame of film by motion. One scene with motion by actors or by the camera resembles a sentence. Short dynamic scenes have the same effect as blunt statements. Longer scenes with complicated changes in composition created by camera movement have somewhat the effect of compound sentences.

11   Pictures, like words, must make a logical continuity, according to accepted rules. For example, a motion picture showing two people conversing must first show them more or less side-to, to establish their relative positions. Then as each speaks he is shown over the other's shoulder. This is the familiar "reverse-angle" shot. That this is a culturally based convention of film syntax is shown by the experience of representatives of the U.S. Office of Information who have found that natives of foreign countries who have not seen motion pictures cannot "understand" the reverse-angle shot. They cannot adjust to our stereotyped representations of reality. They don't understand our language of pictures. Similarly, most of the action in a motion picture must be "matched." That is, if an actor is shown walking up to a door in a distant shot, the following close-up should show him approximately in the same position as he was in the last frame of the long shot. "Matching the action" is a convention in cinematography, part of the film language. It is not always used. When the tempo of the film is fast it is common

practice for the editor to elude some of the action, as an author does when he wants the same effect. And of course films *can* compress time dramatically.

12   Paragraphing is accomplished by the traditional fade-out and fade-in, or by the dissolve or optical effect as soft or hard "wipes." The pace of the narrative is determined more by the film editor than by the script. The editor of words clarifies the presentation of content by eliminating words, sentences, paragraphs, and even chapters. The film editor clips out frames, scenes, sequences, and even large parts of a film (resulting sometimes in "the face on the cutting room floor"). The book editor may achieve lucidity by rearranging the author's text, moving paragraphs and chapters. The film editor boldly changes the order of film sequences. Both the book editor and the film editor can have a decisive influence on the style of the finished work. Both can call for rewriting or new photography. Both can affect the pace of the manuscript or the "rough cut." Both are experts in grammar, syntax, and style.

13   More important than the mechanical analogy to words are the semantic dimensions of pictures. Every photograph is an abstraction of an object or an event. Even the amateur, ignorant of the plasticity of the medium, makes an abstraction of Aunt Minnie when he presses the button. Only a few of Aunt Minnie's characteristics are recorded on the film.

14   The professional photographer in control of his medium knows he is abstracting. If he is competent he abstracts to a purpose. Knowing he cannot possibly record the whole event, he sees to it that the abstracting preserves those features he wants to present to the picture-reader. By manipulation of the variables at his command, he lets us "see" the event as he thinks it should be "seen." If he is a news photographer he probably wants to present a "realistic" event, full of details, although often he is working under such handicaps of haste that the picture as we see it in the newspaper has become simplified and perhaps indistinct. Then it lacks background or environment, it lacks the richness and crispness which a realistic picture must have. Some news pictures are so simplified that they look like symbolizations. They fit the definition of a symbol as "that which suggests something else by convention."

15   The fashion photographer, however, preparing for an advertisement in *The New Yorker*, controls the photographic medium to produce a simple, stylized figure, often against a blank background. This picture is realistic only to a limited extent and approaches the characteristics of a symbol. Carried even further a photograph can be almost purely symbolic, devoid of the very characteristics that are usually associated with photography. Take as an example

the famous combat photo of the planting of the American flag by Marines on the summit of Mount Suribachi. There is nothing in the frame but the men struggling to raise the flag and a few rocks of the mountain top. This picture has been accepted as a symbol. It has even been reproduced in bronze in Washington, D.C., as a memorial to the Marines. We accept a statue as a symbol. But here is a case where the statue was copied directly *with little change* from a press shot. . . .

16   A picture is a map, since there is not a one-to-one correspondence between elements of the picture and elements of the event. We might say, as J. J. Gibson says about the retinal image, that a picture is a good correlate *but not a copy* of the scene photographed. A picture definitely has structure. It is a configuration of symbols which make it possible for us to interpret the picture, provided that we have enough experience with these symbols to read the picture.

17   Pictures can be manipulated like words so as to seem to change their referents. The motion picture editor can lengthen and shorten individual scenes and place them in such a juxtaposition in a carefully planned tempo as to create an impression foreign to the events photographed. It would be possible to assemble a number of pictures of active American businessmen and cut them together to give the impression of frantic competition for money when this did not exist in the actual situations.

18   Once we have established the fact that photographs of events are *not* the events, that they show by intent or accident only a few characteristics of events, we have the perspective to question some reactions of people to pictures. . . .

19   General semanticists know it is hard to make the average person realize that he brings meaning to the word, that the word does *not* contain any meaning. A word is just a series of hen tracks which we are told authoritatively stands for a certain concept.

20   It is still harder to convince anyone that we also bring meaning to a picture. If the picture is well within our previous experience it means something. What it means depends on the kind of our experience. The picture of any political figure is interpreted in radically different manner by opposing parties. City children react differently to a picture of a cow than do farm children. Thus pictures can reinforce stereotypes because the characteristics of people or events which the photographer presents through the medium are not strong enough to overcome the "embedded canalizations" in the reader.

21   When the picture is not within the range of our experience we react to it almost as little as to an unknown word. Scenes of mass calisthenics performed by ten thousand Russians mean to us little

more than "mass conformity," whereas they may originally have been meant to express "ideals." Strange animals are to us just configurations of light and shade on paper. If they moved on the screen we can apply more of our experience to understanding what we see. Professional photographers, like teachers, have their readers carefully estimated. Like teachers, they see to it that their pictures contain plenty of the familiar (to their particular reader) and some of the unusual. We are able to reach out a short distance into the unknown from the solid base of our own experience. The difference here between words and pictures is that the distinction between the known and the unknown is sharpened by pictures. If we read that an emu is like an ostrich, only larger, we have a vague idea about it. If we see a picture of an emu we remember more clearly the features similar to an ostrich and perhaps notice how the emu is different and new.

22   Pictures are multiordinal. They are interpreted on different levels of abstraction. . . . Our Aunt Minnie is just another aunt to strangers; they think she looks like the Genus Aunt. The fact that pictures are interpreted on different levels is the basis for some items in some common intelligence scales. The lowest level is that in which the child merely enumerates objects and people: "I see a woman and a girl and a stove," etc. This is analogous to the descriptive level of words. A higher level of reaction would be description and interpretation such as, "The woman is probably the girl's mother and she is cooking her supper."

23   A picture causing a semantic disturbance is familiar to everyone. "Oh, that doesn't look like me at all. What a terrible picture!" Or the vacationers who have rented a lake cottage on the basis of glamorous pictures in an advertising folder get a shock when they find that the lake is much smaller than they thought, that the trees are scrubby, and that the cottage is in disrepair. Visitors to California complain that the "blue Pacific" is not always blue, as the postcards invariably show it. Or they say, "Is *that* Velma Blank, the great movie star?" It is in situations like these that we can best realize that pictures, although somewhat better than words, are only maps of the territory they represent.

24   Pictures can be self-reflexive. A photograph of a photograph is a standard method of reproduction, for example, in the making of filmstrips. It is by such reproduction that it is possible to present to congressional committees photographs which seem to show members of the cabinet or senators in conversation with persons with whom they never exchanged more than a word.

25   Pictures, then, have many of the characteristics of language, not in the figurative sense of "the language of flowers" but in the very real characteristics of structure (syntax, grammar, style) and of semantics. The most crucial characteristic is that pictures are

abstractions of reality. A picture can present only a few of the aspects of the event. It may, under the strict control of the photographer, become as abstract as a symbol.

26   It is most urgent that there should be more awareness of the abstracting power of photography, that pictures *do lie*. Instead we find great naïveté. People believe what they see in pictures. "One picture is worth a thousand words" not only because it is more graphic but because it is believed to be the gospel truth, an incontrovertible fact. A teacher may present her pupils in a big city with a side view of a cow. They should then know what a cow is! Little do they dream that to a farm boy a cow is a complex of associations which even four hours of movies could not present. We find pictures used as "illustrations." They are inserted in textbooks as a last resort to relieve the copy. One picture of Iowa in the geography text must suffice for Iowa. The author says, "This is Iowa." The general semanticists would recognize this as the error of "allness," ascribing to a word all the characteristics of the thing abstracted from. The danger of "allness" is so much more lively in the case of pictures than in the case of words because everyone assumes pictures *are* reality.

27   Of course pictures provide us with more cues from reality itself (cues for eliciting the meaning we bring to the picture) than the arbitrary hen tracks we call "words." But the basic error is to fail to realize that the meanings of pictures are not in the pictures, but rather in what we bring to them.

–Paul R. Wendt

5. Listed below, at random, are the key words and phrases produced from a review of *Active Reading*. Look them over and arrange them in an order that makes sense to you. Think carefully about how these ideas are connected. Section your arrangement and put the terms into an outline.

supporting details	main idea
author's purpose	close reading
to inform	conclusion
to persuade	order
cause and effect	development
patterns of organization	topic
supporting idea	introduction
list	basic structure
previewing	skimming
compare/contrast	reading
reader's purpose	review
subtopic	

6. Skim and section the following article on memory. Next, develop six multiple-choice or fill-in-the-blank comprehension questions based on the article. The answers should provide the key idea, a subtopic, a supporting idea, a supporting detail, a pattern of organization, and the conclusion. The following represents a sample question that calls for an answer stating the topic.

This article is about ——————— .

a. three memory systems
b. the organization of memory
c. memory
d. remembering and forgetting

The Mysteries of Memory

1   We ask you to begin this section by taking a memory test. Below is an imaginary telephone number. Read it a few times and try to remember it.

368–0691

2   Now cover the number with a slip of paper and read the following paragraph.

3   This section of our chapter is called "The Mysteries of Memory" because there is much about the topic that is unexplained. For instance, it is not clear just what part, or parts, of the brain are used to store information, or how much information the brain can store. Estimates range from 200 million units of information in a lifetime to several billion. We do know that the memory takes in about ten "frames" of visual data a second during every waking hour. Once data have been accepted by the memory system, they jump around like kangaroos trying to find a place to settle down. We know a great deal more about how memory works than what memory is. Some psychologists have theorized that memory is a simple storage-and-retrieval system. Others believe that memory doesn't so much *reproduce* as *recreate* past events. Because we can't see memory at work, we have to infer its operations from people's performances on memory tasks. In fact, you are performing a memory task right now.

4   Can you remember the telephone number you memorized a few moments ago? Chances are you've forgotten it already! But can you recall your telephone number at home? Almost certainly you can. What about the street address of the house you lived in when you were twelve? Now try to remember as many of your "old" phone numbers as you can. Try to remember other addresses or zip codes. Why can you remember so many "old" numbers when

you have already forgotten the new number given at the beginning of this section? . . .

5   Why, for example, is it easier to recognize a person's face than to remember what the person looks like from a verbal description? Why are we less likely to forget a motor skill, such as riding a bicycle or typing, then something we read or hear about? Why does one particular event make a lasting impression while others fade quickly? Why do we tend to forget the names of people we don't like?

Three Memory Systems

6   Psychologists separate the memory system into three parts: *sensory*, *short-term*, and *long-term*. Sensory memory performs a screening function. Incoming information reaches it first and is preserved just long enough to be used in perceiving, comparing, judging, and so on. It lasts for only a very brief time while the brain decides whether or not it needs this information for present or future use. If it seems useful, it is passed on to the short-term memory. If not, it is discarded. Sensory memory employs a "file or forget" approach to its job.

7   Short-term memory performs a second screening operation on the retained information. You can think of it as a sort of desk-top memory. Data arriving in the "in" box is looked over, sorted out, and acted on. Everything is there in front of you. Like most desk tops, however, short-term memory often gets cluttered up with many different items, some of which are more important than others. Often, too, a new item in the "in" box interferes with something you are working on. You put the old item aside and can't find it later. Generally speaking, you can deal with no more than seven or eight items at any one time. (There are strategies, however, for expanding the capacity of short-term memory and prolonging its duration.) To make room for more information, you clean off your "desk" every few minutes, throwing the "junk" mail into the wastebasket and sorting your ideas into meaningful groups. What remains will be filed in the "out" box for transmission to long-term memory.

8   Long-term memory is more permanent, and has a theoretically unlimited capacity. It used to be thought of as a kind of "dead storage," made up of information to be retrieved at some future time. Psychologists now think that long-term memory is a dynamic process, continually interacting with short-term memory to provide *operational*, or working, memory. To make decisions, for example, you constantly refer to material that has been filed away. Long-term memories are reactivated, combined with short-term

memories, and then filed away again, along with any new material that seems worth saving.

9   Another function of operational memory is to call for new inputs from the outside. It says, in effect, "There is not enough information here. Long-term memory doesn't have it. Can you supply more?" You then scan your immediate environment for the needed information or look up additional data.

10   **How Is Memory Organized?**   Images, whether visual or auditory, are *encoded* in the long-term memory. (This is also true of sensations such as taste and smell, although these impressions are of relatively little importance in the thinking process.) Encoding means that images are "tagged" or categorized according to the type of image that is represented. A round object will be perceived as such and filed under the general heading "roundness." If it is also red, it will also be remembered for its "redness." The word *mother* may be stored according to its sound similarity to other words (other, brother, etc.) and its membership in the larger category "female" and the still broader concept "human."

11   Memory impressions are grouped into useful mental associations. Locating one memory sometimes reminds us of another. It is a "search and match" operation. Events that occur in close relationship to one another, but are separated by other qualities, are "cross-indexed" in the brain. Although we are not certain how this takes place, it plays a significant role in learning and thinking.

12   Remember that what we store are not actual images or sounds but impressions that somehow leave their mark. These impressions are usually called *engrams* or *memory traces*. There is some evidence that long-term memory involves chemical changes in the brain as memory traces are laid down. One hypothesis is that each bit of information is embedded in the protein molecules that make up the 10 billion neurons in the brain. If this is so, it would seem that no single part of the brain performs the function of memory. All sections of the cortex, the "thinking" part of the brain, play some role in retaining long-term information.

13   **We Know the Information Is There**   Have you ever been asked a question that you *knew* you knew the answer to but couldn't come up with right away? You might say, "Give me a moment to think about it." Or you immediately reply, "No, I wouldn't know that in a million years." In the latter case, your brain has told you right off that it doesn't contain the information you've been asked for. In the first case, your brain goes right to work without further instructions. It "knows" the material is there someplace and starts

looking for it. Apparently, the brain scans its own instant index before going to work. This automatic process of knowing what you know is truly one of the mysteries of memory.

The Act of Remembering

14   We have been discussing memory systems and the process known as *reproductive memory*—recall of the exact information encoded. Learning foreign vocabulary lists, recalling a statistical formula, repeating a telephone number, reciting a poem, listing important dates in American history—all of these actions are based on reproductive memory. There are many kinds of thoughts and memories for which this kind of recall is neither possible nor necessary. As you study for your next test in this course, you will certainly not try to recall exact sentences, word for word, as written in this textbook or as spoken by your instructor. But you will try to remember the most important ideas and the essential vocabulary. When you produce generalized or "processed" information from your memory systems and when you are not merely relying on rote or verbatim reproduction of memory traces, you are engaging in the process called *productive memory*.

15   The productive feature of memory enables you to pick out a few key events, or images, and build your recall on them. What you get is not an exact reproduction, but a working model. You make your own inferences from what you remember and say, "It must have happened this way." In this sense, memory is reinventing or reimagining what you once knew. This ability is important in dealing with complex loads of information, especially if they have been in dead storage for a long time. In fact, if you did memorize a paragraph you would probably be so preoccupied with retaining the words that you might miss its overall meaning.

16   It is often better to recall the meaningful gist of an event rather than its exact details. We get rid of the excess baggage to better remember what is important. Research has shown that people do not have exact rote memory for the words they learn, but that they do remember the general meaning of those words.

17   In one experiment subjects were read a short story containing the sentence, "He sent a letter about it to Galileo, the great Italian scientist." A recognition test was given either immediately following this sentence, or after 80 or 160 additional syllables of story. On the test, a sentence was presented that was either identical to the original one, changed in *form* but not in meaning ("A letter about it was sent to Galileo, the great Italian scientist"), or changed in *meaning* ("Galileo, the great Italian scientist, sent him a letter about it"). . . . . [T]he subjects were very good at detecting changes in *meaning*. They were not so good, however, at recogniz-

ing the same meaning or at detecting changes in *form* when the meaning had been preserved (Sachs, 1967).

18   The active production of memories is not without its problems, however. For many of us, memory becomes so active that we tend to "remember" things that didn't happen, to create our own memories which are not always accurate reproductions of the past.

19   **How Memory Is Distorted**   One of the first persons to study productive memory was the English psychologist F. C. Bartlett. He believed that the *same* event might be recalled differently at different times. If the information was passed on to another person, and he or she passed it on to someone else, the original information would be even further distorted. (In fact, this often happens when people spread gossip.)

20   Bartlett called this technique *successive reproduction.* He showed that a memory event can be altered as it is recalled under different circumstances or is handed down to other people. For example, one person might be shown a picture and asked to remember it. After some time this person would be asked to reproduce the picture from memory. A second subject would be given the first person's drawing as the picture to be memorized and reproduced, and so on. . . . (Bartlett, 1932).

21   Distortions of memory also occur because of the way you are asked to recall events. It is known that police officers who ask victims, "How *tall* was your assailant?" will get a bigger estimate than if they ask, "How *short* was your assailant?"

22   Loftus (1974) reports another example. After watching two cars collide in an accident, witnesses were asked, "About how fast were the cars going when they *smashed* into one another?" They gave estimates averaging around 40 mph. Other witnesses were asked, "About how fast were the cars going when they *contacted* one another?" These witnesses gave estimates around 30 mph.

23   Leading questions like these can alter your memory of the original event. In reconstructing the scene, you have absorbed certain presuppositions or "suggestions" into your memory. People who are unusually suggestible often distort their recall because they are influenced by what they think others *want* them to remember.

24   **Why We Remember Some Things Better Than Others**   Bartlett thought that memory retention was closely related to other forms of behavior. One's *attitude* toward an event, *interest* in it, and even *temperament* affect memory. In school settings, teachers try to create a positive attitude toward the material to be learned and arouse the students' interest. They know that under these conditions the material is more likely to be retained. They also realize

that the students must be willing to *pay attention*. Good learning, which in this case means good remembering, depends upon "how" a thing is learned as well as on "what" is learned.

25   We don't have to be in school to know how this works. If you followed baseball as a youngster, you probably remember all kinds of batting averages and other odd facts about your favorite players. Recalling these facts does not seem difficult even now. People who were not interested in baseball may recall other trivia, like the names of movies in which their favorite stars appeared. Remembering "useless" knowledge is possible because of one's strong interest in the subject at the time it was learned. Things that were exciting and adventurous are recalled more easily and vividly than tedious and boring experiences. This is because they were laid down as strong stimuli. They stand out from the general background of things that are not worth remembering.

Forgetting: The "Where Was I?" Problem

26   If everything we learned was subject to conscious recall, the brain's data bank would be cluttered up with a lot of useless information. The operational memory would also be hard put to keep up with its sorting out function. It can pay attention to only a few things at a time. We have all had the embarrassing experience of being interrupted in the middle of a conversation and not being able to pick up where we left off. We have totally forgotten what we were talking about. Often, the people we were talking with will help out by giving us a cue: "You were saying something about John Smith." Our companions haven't forgotten because they were not interrupted.

27   The "Where Was I?" phenomenon illustrates the role of *interference*. Experimenters study it to learn how new material gets in the way of old material. This type of interference is called *retroactive inhibition* (*retroactive* means "backward-working"). Conversely, if an older memory inhibits the retention of new material, the process is called *proactive* ("forward-working") *inhibition*. When we say, "Where was I?" we are exhibiting retroactive interference. We have been interrupted and the new experience interferes with our memory of the earlier discussion. If, however, we had been so involved in our earlier discussion that we continued to think about it and did not pay much attention to the interruption, we might have forgotten the new information—or never have learned it at all. Such a situation would be an example of proactive interference.

28   ***Why Do We Forget?***   If there is one fact about learning that all of us know, it is that we do not remember everything. In fact, there

are times when it seems we can't remember *anything*. People's names, appointments, material crammed for an exam, telephone numbers—all elude us just when we need them. At the same time, we often remember other things that don't strike us as being very important. Much research has been done on this topic and several alternative theories have been proposed to explain how and why we seem to forget material we have learned.

29   *Decay theory*. One of the earliest attempts to account for forgetting was *decay theory*. The memory traces in the brain that we spoke of earlier were thought to fade away from disuse. Supposedly, decay could be prevented if we repeatedly used or practiced the knowledge and thus maintained the trace. However logical this seems, it has not been supported by recent research. Moreover, all of us have very vivid memories of things we have not thought about for years. The lapse of time in itself would not seem to explain why some memories are retained and others are not.

30   *Interference theory*. As opposed to decay theory, which suggests that time itself is the critical factor in forgetting, *interference theory* argues that it is *what occurs* during that time period that is crucial. If there were nothing to interfere with our knowledge, we would never forget anything. The proactive and retroactive inhibition discussed before are examples. If very little new information interferes with our knowledge, then we should be able to remember it better than if a great deal of unrelated information is added.

31   One of the earliest tests of this hypothesis was done by Jenkins and Dallenbach in 1924. The subjects were given lists of nonsense syllables to memorize and were later tested for recall of these lists at several different time intervals. During these time spans, of course, new, interfering material was acquired by subjects who went about their daily activities. Some subjects slept instead. It was assumed that since there was less interference for them, they should be able to recall more of the memorized material. This is exactly what happened—the sleepers forgot less than subjects who remained awake.

32   What explains the interference process? One theory suggests two explanations. The first explanation is that new material "overpowers" the older learned material and becomes stronger and more dominant in our memory. An alternative idea that has received more experimental support is that the interfering material causes the other knowledge to be *unlearned*—we forget old material so that we may learn new material more readily. This view (also called *displacement theory*) suggests that there is a limit to

memory's storage capacity at any one time. As new information arrives, it pushes out, or displaces, items that are already in readily available or easily retrievable locations. If no additional material comes in, then no forgetting will occur.

33 *Dead storage: forgetting as loss of access.* If you put something in the attic, or in a cabinet that is seldom used, you often forget what you did with it. You know it's in the house, but where? You look in the obvious places without success. You have to think back, to search for clues that associate the object with something you do remember. Then, because one thing leads to another, you discover that the object is not lost after all. You simply had to get on the trail of it.

34 By the same token, some psychologists think that we never forget anything. For one reason or another, the information merely becomes temporarily inaccessible "in the back of our mind." If only we can use the right retrieval cue, it will come to us. These cues are the key to unlocking long-term memory. Three types of cues have been widely studied.

35 One cue involves the *associations* we make between one word and another (or one person and another). If you hear an arbitrary list of unrelated words, the chances are that you would be unable to recall many of them a few minutes later. But if you were given a cue word, *pear,* and asked to recall all the words in the list that rhymed with it, you would probably come up with most of them. Or suppose you meet a man on the street and are unable to remember his name. Suddenly his wife Alice, whom you know very well, appears and the name *Fred* springs to mind. *Alice* is the cue word that retrieves the less frequently remembered name of her husband.

36 Another type of cue is the *context* in which material is learned and remembered. You can see how this works if you try to "re-create" a particular event. A general memory will lead you to increasingly precise details. A third cue may be the person's *internal mood,* or body posture. Rand and Wapner (1967) tested this notion by having subjects either stand erect or lie down while they learned a test word and while they later tried to remember it. Subjects who were in the same position for *both* learning and recall had a better memory for the test than those who changed their posture. This could explain why studying in bed might not be as effective as studying at a desk—unless you can persuade your instructor to let you take the exam lying down!

37 *Wanting to forget: motivational theories.* In all of the theories discussed so far, the memory system has been viewed as more or less

automatic, beyond conscious control. A very different approach was taken by Sigmund Freud, who argued that forgetting may be intentional. Some things are so painful or disturbing that they get pushed into the unconscious mind. Freud called this *repression.* Although the material is "forgotten," it is certainly not gone, for it may persist at an unconscious level and produce emotional conflicts for years to come. Freud also believed that repressed memories that do pop up, often in distorted form (as in dreams), provide an important clue to one's personality.

38   Freud emphasized the negative influence of motivation on memory. But isn't it possible that we also *want* to remember some things more than others? When you cram for a test, you are highly motivated to keep the information intact, at least until the test is over. This works surprisingly well for many people. But then you discover that the learned material is very quickly forgotten afterwards, when there is less motivation to remember it.

39   This experience is very similar to what is called the *Zeigarnik effect,* named after the woman, Bluma Zeigarnik, who studied the effect of task completion on memory. Very simply, this phenomenon means that if you have been working at something—perhaps solving a riddle or doing mental arithmetic problems—you are more likely to recall the details of the task later *if you are interrupted* before the task is completed. By contrast, people who have finished a mental task show poorer recall of its features. The difference in recall ability, however, disappears within twenty-four hours. The Zeigarnik effect is assumed to be a function of *task tensions* a person experiences by not having reached the goal of finishing a task that has been started.

40   The Zeigarnik effect does not occur under stressful conditions. More recent studies have shown that memory is impaired when anxiety-arousing stimulus words are used, where there is a threat of failure associated with the material, or when frustration or other unpleasantness is experienced between learning and recall. This would seem to bear out Freud's theory that material that threatens the individual's self-esteem—frustration in working a test, for instance—is likely to be repressed, or forgotten, rather than well remembered.

41   **Information, Please**   Is a repressed, or "lost," memory gone forever? There is some evidence that this is not the case. Wilder Penfield, a Canadian neurosurgeon, discovered that when he stimulated certain portions of the brain with electrodes, his patient exhibited total recall of past events.

42   People who are hypnotized are also able to recall long-lost

events of their past in exact detail. In everyday life, of course, we neither get stuck with electrodes nor hypnotized when we want to recall something. Most recall is voluntary on our part—we make an effort to remember certain events. We want these memories back so that decisions about incoming information can be made.

43   Often, we can retrieve information simply by asking for it. Telephone numbers come back in this way. Likewise, when you see an automobile, you don't need to search your memory to know what it is. For most common objects, just seeing them brings recognition.

44   But the model and make of the car might present difficulties. This is when your memory starts comparing certain features of the car—size, style of fenders, design elements—with stored images. It may take a few minutes for your memory to scan its holdings, check out the categories for size, fenders, and style, and arrive at a correct match. Certain features of the car have been grouped in your memory to make it easier to recall them. Finally, you say, "This is a 1954 Chevy Bel Aire. I wish I owned it."

—David Dempsey and Philip G. Zimbardo

7. This exercise should be done in pairs. One should be the listener and one should be the speaker. After you've done the exercise once, switch roles.

As the speaker, choose a topic from the following list or make up a topic of your own.

Why I like my job
The best thing about my home town
What I think about parades
Why Gandhi was a great man
Why I'm going to college
How television works

Think about your topic for a few minutes and jot down some notes on the key idea, subtopics, supporting ideas, and supporting details. Then turn to your partner and give a short speech on the topic.

As listener, listen carefully to your partner and jot down what you think are the key idea, subtopics, supporting ideas, and several supporting details. What patterns of organization has your partner used? Finally, compare notes with the speaker.

Writing Exercises

1. Choose one of the readings from the exercises and write a summary of it, paying particular attention to the author's use of the con-

clusion. Is it a restatement of the key idea? Is it a generalization that adds to the key idea? Is it a transition? If none of these, what role do you think the conclusion plays?

2. This is a good time to reflect on what you have learned in the course thus far. Evaluate your learning by stating three ways in which this course has been important to you and naming two areas in which you feel you need more practice.

V Reading in Different Academic Fields

"Critical thinking is actively using one's own intelligence, knowledge, and skills to develop a questioning and reflective attitude which penetrates beneath the surface of what is being presented."

—John Chaffee, *Thinking Critically*

This unit applies everything you have learned so far to the reading you are actually doing for your courses. Using examples of academic writing, you will see how patterns of organization in these fields support, explain, and illustrate topics and key ideas; you will observe how rules of evidence are applied in the social sciences, the natural sciences, mathematics, and the humanities; you will learn more about your responses as a critical reader; you will see that there are some universal rules that you can apply to the task of reading; yet you will also recognize that each field has its own ways of handling the written word.

The preview question *Why am I reading this?* evolves into *What is the role of this piece of reading?* Is the course you are taking based on a textbook so that classwork is a matter of explaining, amplifying, clarifying, illustrating, and reviewing the textbook? Or is the course based instead on lectures, and it is the readings that amplify, give examples, provide case studies, or present another point of view? To judge your approach and the attention you should give your reading, ask yourself these questions: How am I going to use this material? What am I responsible for? The way in which you read and the speed at which you read depend on how dense the material is—not the number of words per paragraph, but the number of ideas per paragraph or section—and on what you need to get out of your reading.

You will look for the similarities that build on introduction, development, and conclusion and will make your guesses as to what can be expected of each part. You will analyze, interpret, and apply your new knowledge, evaluating the author's thoughts and drawing your own conclusions.

One of the major differences between going to high school and studying at college is in the amount and kind of reading you are expected to do. College readings are long, and often the material is complex. Your instructors hold you responsible for the content of your reading assignments. At the same time, authors assume you have the background knowledge applicable to your reading and the specialized vocabulary of the discipline.

For this section we have chosen readings from representative disciplines; we have not tried to cover every field. However, most fields fall into one or another chapter. For example, the concepts found in the chapter on mathematics can apply to accounting and other quantitative fields; some fields, like psychology, computer science, and economics, will span one or two chapters; interdisciplinary fields, like psychobiology, women's studies, and black studies, may combine all the strategies. Because few students are specialists at the undergraduate level, you should learn as much as you can about each area in order to be able to apply the pertinent strategies to all your future academic work.

14 Reading Mathematics

We begin applying the concepts you have learned to specific fields by relating them to the reading of mathematics. At first glance it may appear that this is the area in which you will encounter the most difficulty in using these principles. Remember, however, that mathematics is concerned primarily with making connections and seeing relationships. These two operations are basic in all disciplines and are the foundation of active reading.

Past experiences may affect your ability to function in mathematics. Many students have a fear of mathematics because of childhood episodes of embarrassment or failure in a mathematics class. These unpleasant memories may cause otherwise competent students to underestimate their mathematical capabilities and even to avoid mathematics totally in all its forms. If you freeze or cannot think confidently when you see numbers, it is important for you to realize that early difficulties may have been caused by factors other than your innate ability. Also, as an adult, you are now capable of doing things that you could not do when you were younger. Mathematics is a good example of this. Actively reading mathematics will help you attain the success you seek in this field. By using a systematic approach and your developed analytical powers, you can treat numbers as just another source of information.

It is true that reading mathematics is different from reading other subjects. Close reading is usually necessary in reading mathematics, because mathematical writing is very dense. It is packed with information that you must unpack by dealing with terms and symbols that have precise meanings. You may have to check backwards and forwards from text to formula or diagram, but the overall process for understanding what you read is the same. You read for ideas. Asking questions to determine your purpose and the author's purpose, to connect what you already know with what you want to know, to find what the author is writing about, and to determine what he or she is saying about it helps you to see the reasons behind the mathematical processes. You must thoroughly understand a mathematical concept before you apply it.

Preview Questions

As always, you begin reading actively by asking preview questions. Although you should answer all the preview questions, two of them are particularly important when you read mathematics: Why am I reading this? What do I already know about the topic?

Why am I reading this? Is this material something that I already know and am now reviewing or is it new material that I must master? Mathematics builds upon itself; therefore, you should review material in mathematics frequently to make sure you have a strong foundation before you move on to new material. Determining your purpose will help you know how to read the material. If you are reviewing, you need only skim to find what you may not understand. If you are learning new material, you will have to read closely.

What do I already know about the topic? This is a very important question to answer when you read mathematics, because the study of mathematics is cumulative: New material directly builds upon previous knowledge. The author, therefore, assumes you have learned the necessary preparatory information and can make the requisite connections between previous knowledge and new material. For example, in algebra it would be difficult to understand polynomials if you did not know the properties of exponents and of combining sign numbers.

Vocabulary

The author also assumes you are familiar with mathematical terminology. There are different types of terms: general vocabulary that is used in mathematics, general vocabulary that is used in a specialized mathematical sense, and vocabulary that is unique to mathematics. In general usage "irrational" means unreasonable, but in mathematics referring to numbers as irrational does not mean that they are unreasonable. Irrational numbers are the square roots of numbers that are not perfect squares ($\sqrt{2}$, $\sqrt{6}$, $\sqrt{7}$, and so forth). You have to know the mathematical meaning of the term "irrational" in order to understand the concept.

The meanings of symbols and notations are examples of vocabulary that is unique to mathematical language and that you must know in order to learn new material. In algebra, for example, relationships may be expressed through formulas, equations, and graphs. There are certain rules and formulas that you need to know and understand. These are methods that have been devised to show complicated ideas in simple form. The author represents quantities and their relationships through algebraic language. Explanations and instructions are frequently expressed by using these symbols and notations. Here again, authors frequently do not explain them, because they assume you are familiar with the attributes of the specific symbols. For example, the author will write the symbol rather than the word "add" to show the connection between letters or numbers. You have to know the meaning of the letters and symbols to understand how the ideas they stand for are related. If you are more comfortable with words than with numbers and symbols, you may need to translate mathematical language into a language with which you are more familiar. You may want to picture an algebraic sentence as a sentence with the terms (a, x, and so forth) as the nouns and the symbols ($+$, $-$, and so forth) as the verbs.

The Textbook

Mathematics textbooks are written to inform and to teach the reader; their chapters are usually divided into three sections: explanation, example, and exercises. You become increasingly more involved as you proceed from the explanation to the example to the exercises.

Textbook Explanations

The explanation is the initial presentation of the idea. The author will first state and explain a concept or principle in words. She or he may define terms and discuss strategies and relationships, sometimes illustrated by formulas or diagrams. The following is a typical textbook explanation.

> Objective: To find the mean of a set of numbers
> The *average* or *mean* is the sum of all numbers in a group divided
> by the number of items in the group.

Textbook Examples

The explanation does not stand alone. In fact, if you are not aware of the importance of actively reading the example before you continue, you may find mathematics textbooks ambiguous or difficult to understand. The author provides an example to illustrate the explanation and assumes that you will read both before you move on to the exercises.

Most mathematics instruction occurs in the examples. As the strategies for problem solving are laid out into meaningful ideas, you should ask yourself questions to make sure you see the connection between the ideas that the author presents.

When reading examples in a mathematics textbook, ask yourself questions like these:

> What would I do? Then look and think about why the author answered the problem in the way he or she did.
> Do I understand every step in the author's solution? More specifically, what calculations did the author perform to get to the next line?

The following is a typical example of an example in a mathematics textbook.

A student's test scores for five tests are listed below. Find the mean.

Test 1	Test 2	Test 3	Test 4	Test 5
86	95	94	87	93

$$\frac{\text{Sum of scores}}{\text{Number of tests}} = \frac{86 + 95 + 94 + 87 + 93}{5} = \frac{455}{5} = 91$$

The mean is 91.

Textbook Exercises

After you have read the explanation and the examples, you then move on to the exercises. Too frequently students go right to the exercises and try to do them as quickly as possible without first making certain that they understand the explanation and the examples. Then their reactions to the exercises are "This makes no sense" or "Where did they get this?"

The following is a typical example of an exercise that might follow the previous example.

Three students hiked the following distances. Student A hiked 20 miles, Student B hiked 17 miles, and Student C hiked 25 miles. What is the mean distance the three students hiked?

There is one right answer to a mathematics problem, but not always one right way to get to that answer. All problems are not done the way the example is done. An author may present too much information in one step, so you may have to further break down the procedure in order to understand what is being done. However, if you are reviewing material you understand, one step that includes several procedures may not be a problem. Conversely, sometimes there is a discrepancy between the steps shown in an example and the steps necessary to complete an exercise. The author may show steps in the example that you do not need to use in order to do the exercise. Seeing the connections between the steps will help you determine which of the steps of an example are applicable to a particular problem.

When answering exercises in a mathematics textbook, ask yourself questions like these:

What do I need to know?
What am I asked to find?
What am I told?

What facts are given? (This will determine the information that
   is given.)
What symbols are used? (This will identify the operations used.)
What is the relationship of the information given to what I am
   asked to find?
What mathematical concepts can I apply to this problem?
What process should I use?
What (specific problem) do I need to set up to solve the
   problem?
How can I complete the problem?
What do I think the answer is? (Estimate or predict.)
Then compute. Finally, test or apply knowledge by solving the
   problem.
Does the answer make sense?
Is there a way to check the answer?

Example

If you had to do the following exercise, you would answer the questions listed above like this:

Joan scored 25 times for 39 points in the last basketball game.
Some of her points were for field goals worth 2 points each; the
others were for free throws worth 1 point each. How many of each
type of basket did she get?

Need to know: How to translate words into numbers and
                 symbols
Asked to find: Number of field goals
                 Number of free throws
Told: Total points
        Total number of times scored
        Number of points of each type of basket

Relationship of information given to what you are asked to find:
   Concepts: Use information you have to show relationship of
                known facts to unknown facts
   Process: Let a letter represent one thing you do not know:
               n = number of field goals Joan scored
               Then:
               $2n$ = points Joan scored by field goals
               25 = number of times Joan scored
               $25 - n$ = points Joan scored by free throws
               39 = total number of points Joan scored
Specific problem: $2n + (25 - n) = 39$

Completing the problem:
    Predict: Fewer than 20 field goals because 2 × 20 is more than
            39
    Compute: $2n + (25 - n) = 39$
                $2n + 25 - n = 39$
                    $n + 25 = 39$
                        $n = 14$ field goals
                $25 - 14 = 11$ free throws
    Check answer: Put value of n in the equation
                $(2 \times 14) + (25 - 14) = 39$ points
                    $14 + 11 = 25$ times

Exercises

1. Answer the following questions as they relate to an explanation, an example, and three exercises in a mathematics textbook.

    Why am I reading this?
    What do I already know?
    What do I need to know?
    What facts are given?
    What steps do I need to take to find out what I need to know?
    What do I think the answer is?
    Does the answer make sense?

2. Answer the following problem.

    Bill is seven years older than Linda, and Mark is twice as old as Linda. The combined age of the three people is 23. What is each person's age?

Writing Exercise

Summarize the importance of each part of a mathematics textbook.

15 Reading in the Natural Sciences

The preceding chapters discussed the need for precision in reading mathematics and the need for good judgment in making critical evaluations of all your reading. Most important is the ability to discern relationships among ideas. Active reading in the natural sciences draws on all these techniques.

Scientific Investigation

The natural sciences deal with humankind's investigation of the physical self and the natural phenomena that surround us. The key word in this definition is *investigation*. Here, questions are asked whose answers reveal the physical foundations of our existence. How does it work? What happens? When did this occur? How do they know? How do I know? What is the evidence? How can I make it work? These questions are as valid in chemistry and biology as they are in physics, astronomy, and geology.

Science is a dynamic process based on fact. Scientific knowledge evolves from the continual gathering of data and the testing of hypotheses. Scientists experiment to test and prove a hypothesis or prediction they have formulated about something they don't understand. Building knowledge step by step, experiment by experiment, scientists use the known to discover the unknown. Although they rely on past experiments as the basis for their hypotheses, scientists never accept anything as a final truth because with increased knowledge accepted truths change.

How does an active reader approach scientific texts and reports? Scientists agree that the key to understanding the meaning of science lies in making connections and seeing relationships. Science comprises many details, and it is easy for the uninitiated to think that learning the details is the most important part of the course. But the details are important only because they define, explain, describe, and support the author's ideas. Before mastering the details, you must have a clear view of the major ideas contained in your reading. This understanding helps you to make the larger connections and to know which details you need to learn. For instance, does it make sense to know how the heart works without knowing the function of the heart and how it relates to the rest of the body? Poor readers memorize and try to learn isolated facts; good readers connect ideas.

Science textbooks are the compilation of years of experimenting and searching for answers. They are written to bring the student up-to-date with the knowledge in the field; it is safe to assume they are written to inform. Lab reports are written to give a complete and accurate record of what happened in the testing of a hypothesis. Science articles report the results of investigation and research, provide the evidence on which the conclusion is based, and interpret the meaning of the observations. They connect current research with past research and form the basis for future research. Scientific reports follow very specific rules that give scientific writing a more formal structure than is found in other fields. (The specific rules will be discussed later in this chapter.)

Your task as the reader of science is

- to learn new information by relating it to what you already know,
- to evaluate the supporting evidence by discovering what it is and comparing it to what you know,
- to evaluate the procedures by following the author's steps in an experiment or an investigation,
- to consider how to apply the concepts to work you are doing or are about to do. Sometimes it helps if you can apply a new concept to something with which you are completely familiar.

The Textbook

Previewing the textbook chapter provides you with some precise questions to ask as you define your purpose in reading. Of course, you are reading to learn, but to learn what? You will often find that the chapters are already sectioned and that the key ideas or topics are emphasized within the sections. You can easily turn the headings (for instance, "The Role of Carbon in Dating Rocks") into questions ("What is the role of carbon in dating rocks?") and then proceed to read for the answer. When the author has not provided sections and titles, you may have to formulate your own questions, remembering to make them as exact as possible. For example: "I need to know how the respiratory process of a flower works before I can examine air circulation. How does a flower take in air? What organ does it use? To what use does it put air? How does it exchange oxygen for carbon dioxide?"

Patterns of Organization

As science is based on process, you can expect that much of the material will be arranged in a step-by-step sequence. It may also be organized into lists or categories. To illustrate their points, authors may compare or contrast, or they may demonstrate cause and effect. The following paragraph illustrates the use of cause-and-effect and list patterns.

Fog comes about when (1) moisture is added to a warm air mass or when (2) a moist air mass is cooled to its dew point. In the second case, a mass of air cools either because it comes into contact with cooler ground or water, or because it expands rapidly, or because it receives an invasion of cooled air. The moisture condenses out of the air mass and a thick cloud forms on the ground. . . . There are several types of fog, classified according to formation and point of origin. These classifications are rather descriptive.

For our purposes here, we shall discuss three types of fogs, each formed by a slightly different set of circumstances: radiation fog, advection fog, and frontal fog.

—Joseph Weisberg

Scientific Terms

Because each branch of science has its own vocabulary and terms, you should not depend on gaining the exact definition of terms from context. The words may seem familiar to you, but their actual meanings may be different from those in common usage. For example, you probably know the word *energy* as a synonym for activity, *volume* as something you control on your record player, and *tissue* as a paper cloth with which you blow your nose. Yet these words are given very different and precise meanings in physics, chemistry, and biology. Without understanding their exact meanings, you could become confused. Therefore, it is important to learn the definitions provided in the text, in the glossary, or by your instructor.

Symbols

It is also important to learn as quickly as possible the language of the symbols used in the branch of science you are studying so that you can start using it and thereby build your fluency. Symbols are a shorthand way of naming elements and quantities. You probably are already familiar with many symbols; for instance, % stands for per hundred, MW stands for megawatt, and C stands for carbon. Symbols also indicate operations, such as the familiar $+$ (add) and $\sqrt{}$ (take the square root of). Symbols are combined in formulas, which state a general rule or principle in terms of the relationships of the individual symbols. For example, H_2O, the symbol for water, indicates that two parts of hydrogen are added to one part of oxygen to make water. There is no easy way to learn symbols and formulas. You have to work at learning them, like words that you don't know but whose precise meaning is important to you. This is not a place to guess. When you come across a symbol you don't know, look it up in your textbook or ask what it means. Sometimes it is a good idea to have a page in the back of your notebook on which you list symbols with their meanings. Say what the symbols mean out loud and use them. The more you use them, the quicker they will become familiar to you.

Graphic Aids

When reading your science textbook, do not neglect the aids provided by the authors, such as diagrams, graphs, tables, summaries, study questions, glossaries, and math reviews. Your initial preview of the text should reveal these useful additions. You may also find it useful to construct your own aids as you read the text. Some instructors say students should always read with a pencil in hand. You can make the relationships more vivid by sketching a diagram or a time line. Further, because you have taken some action to understand the material you are learning, you will remember it better. For instance, if your text stated that the earliest traces of life arose 4 billion 600 million years ago, fish and amphibians appeared 345 million years ago, mammals came 225 million years ago, primates came 65 million years ago, and the spread of humankind started 2 million years ago, you would quickly realize the magnitude of time if you put the information into percentages:

- Fish have existed 7 percent of geological time.
- Mammals have existed around 5 percent of geological time.
- Primates have existed for 1 percent of geological time.
- Humankind has existed for little more than .04 percent of geological time.

Or you might find it more dramatic to put the information on a time line.

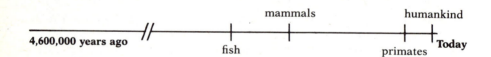

Problem Solving

You should not overlook the importance of problem solving, which is as applicable to work in the sciences as it is to mathematics. In fact, most of the problems you deal with in science are problems in mathematics, even though they may be expressed in words. Here are two examples, one drawn from chemistry and the other from physics.

A chemist working for a drug company synthesized toluene, to be used for the later synthesis of flavorings and perfumes. Toluene is composed of carbon (atomic weight 12.00) and hydrogen (atomic weight 1.01). If the formula of the compound is C_7H_8, what is the percentage by weight of hydrogen?

You are being asked not just the weight of the hydrogen, but the percentage by weight. From the problem you know the elements that make up toluene and their atomic weights and the formula for the compound. You know from your course that you have to find the molecular weight to discover the percentage by weight. Now you need to find or work out the equations that will put these figures together to produce the answer.

The rate of flow of the Gulf Stream is about 2200km³ per day. How many 100 MW(e) [megawatts of energy] power plants could be driven by this warm water, if we make the assumption (admittedly an extreme one) that all the warm water of the Gulf Stream could be similarly used? How significant a contribution would this many power plants make in supplying energy for the United States?

—Robert H. Romer

There are two questions in this problem: How many power plants? and How significant a contribution? The problem provides the rate of flow of the Gulf Stream and the capacity of the power plants. You need to find out how much water is needed to drive a 100 MW(e) power plant and how many 100 MW(e) power plants there are in the United States before you can find out how many power plants can be driven and calculate the benefits of this energy source.

Example

Let's first preview a passage from a chapter called "Respiration" in a biology text and then apply what we have been discussing.

Pressure Changes During Scuba Dives

Topic

1   Under certain circumstances, the human body must cope with gases at greater than normal atmospheric pressure. For example, gas pressures increase rapidly during a dive made with scuba gear. The pressure exerted on the human body increases by 1 atmosphere (the usual pressure at sea level, 760 mm Hg [millimeters of mercury]) for every 10 meters (33 feet) of depth in sea water so that at 30 meters (100 feet) in sea water a diver is exposed to a pressure of about 4 atmospheres. The pressure of the gases being breathed must equal the external pressure applied to the body; otherwise breathing is very difficult. Therefore all of the gases in the air breathed by a scuba diver at 100 feet are present at four times their usual pressure. Nitrogen (N_2, which composes 80 percent of the atmosphere) usually causes a balmy feeling of well-being (euphoria) at this pressure.

Subtopic: Diving

Key Idea: The pressure of what you are breathing must equal external pressure.

At depths of 5 atmospheres or more (40 meters) nitrogen causes symptoms resembling alcohol intoxication that are called *raptures of the deep,* or, more technically, *nitrogen narcosis.* Nitrogen narcosis apparently results from a direct effect on the brain of the large amounts of N_2 dissolved in the blood. Deep dives are less dangerous if helium is substituted for N_2, because under these pressures helium does not exert a similar narcotic effect.

Supporting Idea: The effects of increased pressure of N_2 can be dangerous.

2   As a scuba diver descends, the pressure of N_2 in the alveoli [tiny air sacs] increases. N_2 then diffuses from the alveoli to the blood, and from the blood to the tissues. The reverse occurs when the diver surfaces: the alveolar N_2 pressure falls, and N_2 diffuses from the tissues into the blood, and from the blood into the lungs according to the pressure gradient. If this return to the surface is too rapid, N_2 in the tissues and blood cannot diffuse out rapidly enough, and N_2 bubbles are formed, causing the symptoms of *the bends* (also known as *decompression sickness* and *caisson disease*). Bubbles in the tissues cause severe pains, particularly around the joints, and bubbles in the blood stream, which occur in more severe cases, may even obstruct arteries to the brain, causing paralysis, respiratory failure, and death. Treatment is a prompt reestablishment of high pressure in a pressure chamber, followed by a *slow* return to normal atmospheric pressure.

Subtopic: Surfacing

3   Another complication may result if the breath is held during ascent. During ascent from a depth of 33 feet (about 10 meters), the volume of air in each alveolus will double because the air pressure at the surface is only half of what it was at 33 feet. This change in volume may distend and even rupture the alveolar walls. If air escapes from the ruptured alveoli into the veins of the lung and from there to the rest of the circulation, it may be fatal. This condition, called *air embolism,* has occurred during rapid ascent from depths of less than 15 feet. To avoid this tragic event, a scuba diver must ascend slowly, never at a rate exceeding the rise of exhaled air bubbles, and must exhale during ascent.

Subtopic: Surfacing, continued

Supporting Idea: Diver must ascend slowly to avoid ill effects.

4   During a free dive without scuba gear there is no danger, either from ascending without exhaling or from the bends. The reason is that the air in the lungs has been taken in at the surface, under just 1 atmosphere of pressure. Therefore the volume of air in the lungs is correctly adjusted for life at the surface. Similarly, nitrogen is not

Subtopic: Free diving

Supporting Idea: There is no danger because the pressure equalizes.

taken in under greater than normal pressure and it will not build up in the blood and tissues in excess of its normal concentration during ascent from a free dive.

—Sam Singer and Henry Hilgard

Since the chapter from which this section is taken has the title "Respiration" and since the title of this section is "Pressure Changes During Scuba Dives," you can be sure that the section will deal with the way in which changes in pressure affect respiration in scuba dives. Your preview also indicates that the first sentence is the introduction and repeats the topic. You can assume the author is informing you (and not persuading you) about the relationship of breathing and scuba diving. Perhaps you are interested because you've heard of the bends, but don't know exactly what causes it, or because you learned in your last class that fliers need oxygen for high altitude flying and wonder if diving deep into the ocean is similar. You may develop some specific questions from your preview questions, such as, What is the connection between transfer of gases and pressure changes? or How does scuba diving affect pressure changes?

A first reading reveals the key idea, sections, titles, and supporting ideas, as shown in the example on pp. 259–261.

Although many of you may not understand the details, you have a general comprehension and a sense of the connections between respiration and air pressure as applied to scuba diving. Noting the author's strategies provides you with more useful information. The supporting details are presented through cause and effect; for example, the effect called "raptures of the deep" is caused by the pressure of gases. And the article ends with an implied comparison and contrast. A close reading will tell you precisely why and how "the pressure of the gases being breathed must equal the external pressure applied to the body; otherwise breathing is very difficult."

Scientific Reports

We have all heard reference to the scientific method as a systematic and exact way of analyzing scientific data. Briefly, the scientific method entails

- stating a problem,
- forming a hypothesis,
- gathering evidence,
- testing the hypothesis,
- forming a conclusion or general principle.

Scientific writing that reports on the results of research and investigations follows this basic structure. It is plain, unadorned, objective writing. However, one could also say that reports on research are written to persuade, because the authors want to convince the reader that their points of view or conclusions are correct. They do this by marshalling the strongest evidence possible from their personal observations or experiments to support their positions. As always in persuasive material, the reader asks, What is the author trying to convince me of? What evidence supports the arguments? Other questions might be asked: Does the author present the conclusion first and then demonstrate its validity by going through the experimental process step by step? Or does the author present a hypothesis, then the process, the findings, and finally the conclusion?

Sectioning a scientific report reveals the form followed by all authors when presenting the results of research:

- the title, telling us what it is about;
- an abstract, which is a very brief summary of the report;
- an introduction giving the purpose of the experiment or investigation, the way in which it fits into other research in the field, and, occasionally, the findings;
- a section on methodology and materials;
- the results of the research, which may include a graphic presentation of the observations and data;
- a conclusion or a discussion of the findings.

Perhaps it is simpler to think of the form of a research report by answering these questions:

What is it about?
Why was it done?
How was it done?
What was found?
What does the researcher conclude?

Example

Reports on scientific research that appear in journals are written for those who work in the field. They may therefore be hard to read for those not familiar with a particular discipline because of the terms used and the procedures described. However, as a science student, you may be asked to read journal articles to see how the professionals report on their work. As an example, we shall apply the model of a research report to sectioning the following article from *Science Digest*.

Reinventing the Wheel

1   From a speeding bullet train to the lowly paramecium, nothing moves with more economy than the humble bicycle. At least that's what bicyclists say. But for Larry Brown, retired consultant and MIT graduate, the bicycle is "highly under-engineered." *what is it about ?*

2   Brown has proceeded to replace the heart of the bicycle's drivetrain with a device called the Powercam, which provides more power with fewer revolutions per minute (rpm) of the pedals. Physiological tests show that riders using the device get more miles to the calorie. Purists grumble, but Powercam is winning converts— and races.

3   A bicycle's drivetrain consists of pedals attached to arms, called cranks, that turn the front gear, or chain ring. The turning of the cranks makes the rear wheel go around by means of a chain connecting the front and rear gears. Efficiency is highest at a pedaling rate of about 60 rpm. But a racer trying to ride fast with this relatively slow cadence would have to increase his gearing to knee-busting levels. *Why was it done ?*

4   Racers, therefore, use easier pedaling gears, sacrificing efficiency for speed by "spinning" the pedals at 90 to 120 rpms. They try to distribute force throughout the 360-degree revolution of the crank by pushing down *and* pulling up with toe clips and cleats that unite pedals and feet. Today, spinning is the technique of choice— even among average riders.

5   Biomechanically, the most powerful portion of the rotation lies between the one o'clock and five o'clock positions of the circle. The rest of the arc is a relative dead zone in which the leg does less work. Brown maximized the power portion of the stroke with a drivetrain that replaces spinning with a push-rest-push rhythm. "It's a very natural motion, just like walking up stairs," says Elliot Malach, who set a course record using the Powercam in the 1984 Lone Star Full Triathlon in Texas. *How was it done?*

6   In a conventional drivetrain, the crank and chain ring move in lockstep. In the Powercam, they move at different rates. A cam controls the rate at which the crank moves. From one o'clock to five o'clock, the crank moves faster than the chain ring. From five o'clock to seven, the crank slows and the chain ring catches up. (It speeds up and slows down again on the up stroke to

keep in sync with the other crank.) In practice, the leg surges downward during the power stroke. Then the rider relaxes, letting momentum carry the crank through the dead zone. "You get more of a rest on the portion where no power is being delivered," says Brown.

7   The fast downward surge gives the *feel* of a light gear precisely when the leg is exerting peak power, so the rider can actually use an extremely high gear without *[What was found?]* putting severe stress on his knees. A higher gear means fewer pedal strokes and more economy. Scott Dickson, the first American finisher in the 750-mile Paris-Brest-Paris race, said his Powercam saved him 150,000 pedal strokes. Jim Cerrato used it to spare his legs on a record-breaking 2,009-mile race from Texas to Canada.

8   One study showed that oxygen uptake was lower during workouts with stationary bicycles equipped with Powercams than on those with standard drivetrains. Oxygen consumption is a good measure of energy expenditure, so the Powercam workouts were more efficient.

9   But it is not for everyone. Since the high gearing *[What does the researcher conclude?]* makes sprinting difficult, it is of little use in short races, where competitors dash from the pack in "breakaways." Powercam is better suited for long-distance events, in which endurance is key. But the ultimate market is the cyclist who hops on the bike for that feeling of wind in the face. The hell-bent breakaway is great on *Wide World of Sports* but unthinkable on the weekend ride.

—Dawn Stover

What is it about? The topic is a new invention for the bicycle.
Why was it done? The bicycle is underengineered because the drivetrain is inefficient.
How was it done? The drivetrain was changed to become more efficient.
What was found? Riders benefit from greater efficiency.
What does the researcher conclude? The change is suited only to certain situations.

Critical Reading in the Sciences

Active readers go beyond simply reading a text to evaluating it by making some decisions about how accurate they think it is, how it relates to what they already know, and how they can make use of it or incorporate it into their own thinking. Once you have read to see

what the author is explaining or proving and have a clear understanding of the methodology employed, you need to assess what you
have just read. As a beginner in a field, you can relate what you are
learning only to your own experience and observations. What have I
found out? Does it seem right? Have I ever observed anything like it?
Have the proofs been developed in a systematic way without leaving
out any steps? Has the author accomplished what he set out to do?
Are the conclusions consistent with the observations? Can I use this
knowledge in my current work?

As you proceed in your study, you will find yourself examining
each new concept or principle in relation to what has gone before and
what is to come next. How does it fit in? How can it be used? What
is its likely effect? You will develop many more questions for yourself,
always remembering that the more precise your questions are, the
better. As you gain knowledge and sophistication, your questions will
become sharper and your judgments more accurate, because you will
have better criteria on which to base your evaluations.

Exercises

1. Working in pairs, preview a chapter of a science text. Find the
   topic of the chapter and discuss the organization of the chapter
   with your partner.
   a. Is it sectioned? If so, what questions should you ask as you
      read? If it is not sectioned, what are some reasonable questions
      you can ask?
   b. How does this chapter relate to the ones that follow and pre-
      cede it? (You may need to refer to the table of contents).
   c. Predict some of the points that will be made in the chapter.
   d. Note any words that are unfamiliar to you.
   Now read a section (or at least two pages of the chapter) and identify all the patterns of organization used by the author, such as
   compare and contrast, listing, cause and effect. Finally, write a
   brief summary of the section you have read.

2. Preview and section the following excerpt from a chemistry text,
   noting the topic, the key idea, the subtopics, and the supporting
   ideas as they appear in each section.

1 Water—the most vital substance for human survival—must be
     free of contamination from deadly chemicals and bacteria in order
     to be potable (drinkable). In the United States, which uses more
     than 35 billion gallons (132 million cubic meters) of water every
     day, pure water is becoming scarce. Most of the earth's water is in
     the oceans and is therefore unfit for drinking. Of our sources of

potable water—lakes, rivers, springs, and wells—the last two are rapidly being drained. And we are using more water per person with each year that goes by. For that reason, most big cities and towns are turning to their rivers and lakes as sources of drinking water.

2   To be considered potable, water must meet standards set by the U.S. Public Health Service. But very few of our rivers and lakes can now meet these standards.

3   In the past a nearby river was usually the discharge point for used water. Raw sewage by the millions of gallons is still being dumped into our rivers—in the United States, more than 260 million gallons per day. The pollutants in this sewage come from many sources. Industries release poisonous chemicals containing mercury, arsenic, lead, and other metals. Farms use chemical insecticides that leach down through the soil and pollute the ground water, which in turn pollutes lakes and rivers. For example, in 1969 the commercial salmon fishermen who fished in Lake Michigan had to suspend operations because DDT was found in the canned salmon from the lake. DDT accumulates inside fish, in their tissues, in alarming concentrations, because it isn't excreted. People eat the fish and the DDT begins to accumulate in *their* tissues. Birds eat the insects that are killed by the DDT, and the substance builds up in the birds to such an extent that their eggshells become thin. The thin shells break, and the young birds die before they hatch. So the population of birds begins to dwindle, which in turn means that there aren't enough birds around to eat the insects. The insects then multiply and destroy the crops so that farmers need still more pesticides, which leach down into the water supply, and so on and so on. It is now illegal to use DDT in the United States, but other substances in use now as insecticides could be equally harmful.

4   Farms also are responsible for tremendous amounts of phosphates that have filtered into the Great Lakes, making them anything but "great." These phosphates (from fertilizers) have destroyed the natural balance of life in the Great Lakes, causing huge growths of algae, especially in Lake Erie. The algae consume large amounts of oxygen—so much that fish and other forms of life die for lack of oxygen.

5   Any chemical that gets into the water supply is taken up by these algae, or by bacteria or plankton, all of which are then eaten by other forms of life—including fish, and, finally, people. So that we, as the final link in the chain, become the victims of our own pollution.

6   In better days, lakes and rivers were able to clean themselves. But pollution begets more pollution. Millions of dead and decay-

ing organisms in our rivers and lakes form toxic products that in turn kill more organisms. Once the natural, healthy balance is upset, the normal cleansing action of the river or lake stops. And this is the source that we must now turn to for potable water.

7 If we are going to survive, it will take massive action on the part of all of us to stop pollution. The technology to do so exists today; it is the *cost* that is holding us back. But the cost must be paid if we are to have water to drink.

—Alan Sherman, Sharon Sherman, and Leonard Russikoff

3. The following report of an experiment was written by a student in psychobiology. Preview, section, and title it according to the outline for a research report provided on p. 262.

Can Rats Count?

Abstract

1 A rat was trained to press a bar four times, then push a pole to release a reward of food. The apparatus used was a Skinner-type box with food port, pole to activate food reward, and bar press to demonstrate counting. The subject was a male hooded rat. It was food deprived to 80% of its average daily weight prior to training. Behavior was shaped by successive approximation. The rat spent an hour a day in the experimental apparatus. It was allowed to respond freely. The apparatus was fully automated. Data were collected on a polygraph. Results show the rat learned the task accurately. Data also suggest the rat may have an attention span and may be dependent on sensory information in determining the way it will respond. Although they surely stem from the rat's intact processes, such as motivation, and handling, i.e., training, the reasons for success at the task are unclear. It cannot be concluded that the rat conceptualizes numbers or learns them by associative processes.

Counting

2 The evolution of cognitive processes in animals raises questions about how far different species have come. This experiment asks whether a rat can count to four. Counting is defined as a specific number of repetitions of an arbitrary act.

Experiments

3 It has been shown that birds and squirrels have a prelinguistic number sense (Hassmann, 1952). Prelinguistic number sense is defined as a capacity to recognize as similar, groups of diverse objects which resemble one another solely in being comprised of the

same number of elements. Birds and squirrels are thus able to abstract the concept of numerical identity from groups of up to seven objects, according to Hassmann. There is some evidence that internal counting in the jackdaw is based on memory of a series of previous actions (Koehler, 1951). If all of this is true, then there is a basis for ideation in animals, intention, rather than imitation (Kirkman, 1911).

4   Very few efforts have been made to study counting capacity in rats (Kuroda, 1937; Wesley, 1959; Chen, 1967). Barnett (1975) reports that rats have been trained to press a lever repeatedly 10 times, after which a light comes on. When the light comes on, the rat must stop pressing for five seconds to get a food reward. Chen trained rats to circle a runway a specified number of times before receiving food as a reward. The maze in which the rats ran consisted of two parts: a circular runway and a radial stem. Animals were trained to emerge from the stem, circle the runway for a definite number of turns in one direction, and return to the stem for food. If they made too many or too few turns, they received no food. Some of the rats achieved 80% success. During experimental trials, each time a rat passed the entrance to the stem, it paused or stopped before making the next turn. The rats' behavior was concluded to represent a guiding process used to solve the problem. The author related this behavior to intentional movement or mediational response.

Subject

5   The subject was a male hooded rat, 57 days old at the beginning of the experiment, and averaging 215 gm body weight prior to food deprivation. Rats available for use in this experiment were being kept in individual cages. They were all males. I first observed them when they were 44 days old and selected my subject rat at that time. Barnett (1975) observed that rats bred for laboratory purposes were more willing to approach when compared to wild rats for whom there is greater survival value in avoiding the unfamiliar. The subject rat was chosen because it exhibited even more willingness than the other rats to approach novel stimuli.

Apparatus

6   An automated experimental box designed by Eichenbaum and Paul (1984) was modified to minimize external cues by adding a surrounding enclosure. Observation of the animal during preparation for training showed that its willingness to explore decreased when it was moved from its cage to the plexiglass box set up in a teaching laboratory at Wellesley College. It was decided to exploit the rat's affection for enclosed spaces (Barnett, 1975) by

enclosing the box itself in a larger container much like a small refrigerator, outfitted with a small incandescent lamp, a ventilating fan, and a peephole in the door through which the experimenter could observe the subject. The original box design included a reward light and buzzer, which we disconnected shortly after training began in order to prevent confounding the inherent with conditioned effects (Myers, 1962). Note one advantage of having the pole and bar press on opposite sides of the box is avoidance of competition between the responses required.

7   A bar press is a good response choice for a rat. Schoenfeld, Antonitis, and Bersh (1950) found food-deprived rats pressed a bar more often than water-deprived rats, suggesting paw movements made during eating somehow transfer to paw movements required in bar pressing.

8   The rat was provided visual stimulus in the form of light from the lamp in the enclosure. The rat was also provided auditory stimulus in the form of clicks resulting from electrically automating the bar press, pole, and food release. (Auditory stimulus was removed for one run on the day following the end of my formal experiment. Behavior changed dramatically. A future experiment could be designed to follow up on the changes.)

9   Data were automatically collected on a polygraph. Continuous automated feedback on performance was advantageous to training successions of behaviors, as well as to collection of final data.

Task

10   The rat learned to press a bar four times, then push a pole to get a reward.

Procedures

11   In Thorndikian learning situations, it is especially important to control drive level (Bitterman, 1966). Rat was deprived of food to reduce its weight to 80% of normal. It was weighed every day before the run. Weight was maintained at 72–84% by supplementing food rewards with some food in the cage when necessary.

12   Training was begun by simply handling the animal. Handling included blowing at it, scratching behind its ears, rubbing its abdomen, petting its nose, making a hide-and-seek game out of stereotypical burrowing behavior (Barnett, 1975). Handling also included nestling in the hands of the experimenter, with only nose and paws unsheltered from the warmth of bodily contact, and carrying. One behavioral note is that the movement of carrying appeared important to the animal after its isolation in a stock cage. At first, when the rat checked the food port, it was rewarded. Then, when the rat oriented toward the pole, it was rewarded. Later,

when the rat touched the pole, it was rewarded. Finally, when the rat pushed the pole, it was rewarded. The pole push phase of the desired response was set. Bar pressing and successive bar pressing were similarly shaped.

13   The animal was monitored in the box for an hour each day and permitted to carry out the task at will. If and only if the appropriate response was carried out would the reward be presented. And this happened every time the reward was presented. That is to say, the rat was continuously reinforced or was on a continuous reinforcement schedule.

14   Dinsmoor's (1966) criteria for the conditioning technique therefore have been applied and met. 1) Accidental fluctuations have been minimized to show relationships easily. 2) Unnecessary components have been eliminated to reduce the number of alternative interpretations. 3) Properties chosen for study have been restricted, so that principles may be applied to a wide range of behavior. 4) Delivery of stimulus and recording of response have been automated to overcome the disadvantages of the technique, such as the "Clever Hans" effect.

Results and Discussion

15   Data were collected automatically on a polygraph. In considering the data, we realized the rat's problem was choosing among more than seven alternatives! It could press the bar one time before the pole, two, three, four, five, six, or more than six times. Its span was pretty much limited to this because it had only been trained to four. Therefore, chance of choosing the correct response was less than one in seven or less than 14%. Percent accuracy on the task of counting to four turned out to be more than 40% each daily run for one week of testing. That's three times greater than chance. No other response occurred more often than 14% of the time and other responses, especially at one and greater than six, occurred at very low rates. Results of different days were considered independently and not averaged, because interesting observations can be lost.

16   From our observations, we report the following. The first part of training consisted of just putting the rat in the box for a couple of days, then letting it eat food at the port for a day or so. Teaching the rat to push the pole to release the food into the port was not attempted on any schedule. Once commenced, it took the rat two days to learn the task. It took the rat longest to learn when a second task was involved—four days or more. The rat could now carry out the sequence of one bar press and one push of the pole to release the reward of food. Increasing the number of bar presses was easily done. The rat learned to go from one to two bar presses in a day. At two bar presses, for no systematic reason, we kept it

at that level for three days. When we began reinforcing three bar presses, it took the rat a day to learn that. The next day it learned four. We maintained it at four for twelve days. The rat received 107–130 reinforcements per daily one-hour session. Stricter control and recording of learning data are recommended to future experimenters.

17　　Some behavioral observations during counting to four are included here. They are burdened with the usual anthropomorphism, as well as qualitative judgments. These are the observations of one experimenter on one rat.

18　　1. The rat would press the bar three times, and the pole once, and once again, without checking the food port until the total number of clicks equalled those of four bar presses and one push of the pole. The rat would press the bar twice, and twice again for a total of four, before completing the sequence. While the press-press, press-press occurred in rapid succession, they were distinct. An intriguing question is whether the rat was adding up the clicks.

19　　2. The rat did not seem concerned with getting each one right. It appeared to be able to remember how to release the reward or how to figure out the problem of no reward when it wanted to. Maximum number of successes in a row = 4. Often successes and failures alternated. Time was taken out for investigation.

20　　3. Sometimes, the bar press equipment stuck in the down position. The rat taught itself to reset the bar with its nose and *always* did.

21　　4. The rat appeared to grow accustomed to our increasing the number of bar presses on successive days. On the day it learned to "count" to four, during the first 25 minutes, most errors were fewer than four bar presses. During the last 35 minutes, many errors were five bar presses.

22　　5. An interesting note—Behavior altered when auditory cues, primarily clicks of the automated bar and pole, normally present during trials, were removed. On the day following the experimental period, for about a half hour only, the rat ran continuous free trials without sound cues. In virtually all other sessions, regardless of accuracy, the rat moved from bar to pole or bar to pole to food port. Without the auditory cues, it moved from bar to pole to food port, *to pole, to food port*; to bar to pole to food port, *to pole, to food port*. Although behavior changed dramatically, percent accuracy on the task remained high.

23　　The purpose of this experiment was to determine whether a rat can learn to count. Counting is defined as a specific number of repetitions of an arbitrary act. We trained the rat using a modified Skinner box and recorded responses on polygraph paper. Data from final testing show a food-deprived rat succeeded in learning to press a bar four times before pushing a pole to release a reward of food.

24   There is no doubt the rat learned to count to four by our own definition of counting and by its success at that task. The experiment was well controlled. The rat's successful performance at the task was somehow the result of its intact physiological processes (e.g., spatial perception, motivation, general motor skills, auditory perception) and the way in which it was handled in the laboratory (e.g., trained response, knowledge of procedures).

25   There is also no doubt the rat remembered the task from day to day because it started with a correct response most of the time, as well as achieved a high degree of accuracy within the first few minutes of the run.

26   According to Barnett (1975) if some goal object, such as food, can be reached only by a particular set of movements, the animal will probably develop the habit of performing these movements. The wild squirrels outside my dining room window have become very efficient indeed at raiding the birdfeeder. However, Barnett goes on to link habit formation with progressive loss of ineffectual movements. We observed no such thing in our experiment. As results show, the rat spent considerable time doing something besides counting to four. Given its performance on the first trial(s) of the day was accurate, it is unlikely the rat forgot what to do to get the food. Why didn't it give up the ineffectual movements? Food may be an inappropriate reinforcement for more cognitive behaviors. Perhaps the rat is rewarded just by the opportunity to be out of its cage. Perhaps it enjoys the box with its two manipulanda. Attention span of the rat may be limited. Perhaps someone will invent a clever experiment designed to test learning and attention in rats. Perhaps this is not a habit.

27   If learning is a change in overt behavior (Barnett, 1975) and if the ability to perform a new behavior becomes predictable, then what can we say about learned ability to perform a specific number (four) of bar presses? Does this represent an adaptation to environment, a behavioral change which keeps the animal alive, vs. a more cognitive learning process? If we change our definition slightly to say counting is acquiring a *concept* of a particular number of repetitions of an arbitrary act, then there is still evidence from this experiment to show the rat learned this, too. Numbers of bar presses were upped daily by one during training, because that was the rate at which the rat acquired the new information. On the day it learned to count to four, most of its errors during the first 25 minutes of the one-hour session were below four. Many errors during the last 35 minutes of the session were fives. That is,

the rat may have acquired the concept of a particular number, plus one.

28   Behavioral theories usually shy away from notions of concept. This n = 1 experiment is not strong enough alone to invoke a notion of concept. However, if future experimenters could show a positive transfer of "counting" to four to another mode, then evidence to conclude that performance is based on a concept of number would gain strength. Further studies on a rat's span for numbers and on its ability to discriminate a particular number offered randomly on different days could also be used as evidence for number concept in rats. Perhaps a rat could be taught to add. The dictionary defines number not only as how many, but also as sum total, and defines counting not only as naming numbers in regular order, but also naming numbers in groups to reach a total, such as counting money by $5.00s, possibly clicks or bar presses by twos.

29   This experiment is replicable. It should be done again with other subjects in other laboratories in order to test the assumption that findings apply throughout a random sample of the rat population. The experiment might also be replicated with specific alterations (Sidman, 1960) in an attempt to demonstrate more generally whether a rat can count. I'd be interested to know if increased rewards were given according to the number of bar presses, e.g., one pellet for a bar press, two for two, *n* for *n*, would the rat learn to count faster? Experimentation with this rat might be extended (Dinsmoor, 1966). If training to successively higher numbers of bar presses at some point fails to result in the desired behavior, then that might indicate a limit to the rat's counting. The experiment could be carried out on a different species. If another mammal, such as a ferret, can reach criterion, and if it performs with consistency and accuracy at criterion, then findings may apply across species.

30   It would be interesting to follow up on removing the auditory cues. Audition is an important sense to rats. For example, lactating mothers eject milk at the sound of their young (Barnett, 1975). Drastic change in motor behavior without any significant drop in percent of accurate responses occurred after apparatus was silenced. This suggests to me that sensory input is important to the animal in the way it responds.

31   At this time, I agree with Rashotte (1976). Performance of counting is not the same as learning to count, because the degree to which it is influenced by associative processes, if at all, is unknown.

–Dale S. Helfgott Cohen

16 Reading in the Humanities

Like reading in mathematics and the natural sciences, reading in the humanities involves recognizing the author's purpose and evaluating the author's evidence and reasoning. However, in the humanities the author's purpose and reasoning may be obscure. For this reason, what may seem initially to be an easier reading task may in fact be harder. Reading critically is particularly important because much of the writing in the humanities can be seen as an effort to convince or persuade. It is therefore necessary to evaluate constantly the author's ideas and to make informed judgments about what the author is saying.

The humanities are the branches of learning concerned with human thought and culture as represented in philosophy, literature, and the fine arts. Writing in the humanities can take three forms: informative writing, which is found in every field; persuasive or critical writing, which is found in philosophy and in literary and fine arts criticism; and imaginative writing, or literature. This chapter will include discussions of all three types of writing as applied to the humanities.

Informational Writing

In the humanities, authors write to inform you in many different ways.

Factual Writing

Factual writing can provide background information on an author, composer, or artist or on a piece of music, literature, or art. Examples of factual writing include a biography of an author, which you might read in a literature course, or an article describing a style of music, which you might read in a music appreciation course. This kind of writing provides a context for your study of the humanities.

Descriptive Writing

As its name implies, descriptive writing simply describes a piece of music, art, or literature. For example, descriptive writing might list the colors an artist used in a painting or the instruments a composer included in a musical composition. Descriptive writing in the humanities, particularly in literature, is often mixed with critical writing.

Technical Writing

Technical writing explains a process. It tells the reader how to do something or how something was done: for example, explaining the technique used to shoot a film. This kind of writing is often found in art appreciation courses, where understanding how an artist created a certain effect is important.

Example

The following passage from an art history textbook illustrates informational writing. It is a combination of the first two types: factual and descriptive writing.

Scenes from the world of entertainment—dance halls, cafés, concerts, the theater—were favorite subjects for Impressionist painters. Auguste Renoir (1841–1919), another important member of the group, filled his with the joie de vivre of a singularly happy temperament. The flirting couples in ''Le Moulin de Galette,'' under the dappled pattern of sunlight and shadow, radiate a human warmth that is utterly entrancing, even though the artist permits us no more than a fleeting glance at any of them.

–*H. W. Janson*

The first part of the above passage is an example of factual writing. In the first two sentences the author tells you specific information about the Impressionist painters and places Renoir in that time period. After providing you with this background material, the author moves on to descriptive writing by verbally explaining Renoir's painting "Le Moulin de Galette."

Once you realize that the author's purpose is to inform, you can use the reading questions to find out what the information is and how it relates to what you already know. Is the information useful to you as you assess the piece of work? If so, you would then go on to read the material at the depth that you judge to be necessary.

Persuasive Writing

In the humanities the author's purpose is frequently to persuade or convince the reader. However, persuasive writing in the humanities is more overtly subjective than in the natural and social sciences. Authors offer their own opinions with reasons to support their ideas. The evidence is taken from a text, a piece of art, music, or a film or from the writer's own thinking, as in philosophy. Persuasive writing can be further distinguished as being criticism or argument.

Criticism

When an author is examining the work of someone else, subjecting it to analysis and critical evaluation, the result is critical writing. The author looks carefully at what the author or the artist set out to do, how the author or artist went about it, and how well the artist or author succeeded. The most obvious example of critical writing is found in reviews of books, movies, concerts, and art shows, in which the reviewer presents an account of the product and then gives an opinion of how good it is.

Example

The following review of the movie "Citizen Kane" is an example of the writing of criticism in the humanities. The text has been sectioned so you can see the points that the reviewer addresses. The first two paragraphs provide background information on the making of the film. The author makes a general, positive statement in the next paragraph, describing the film as "probably the most original, exciting, and entertaining picture that has yet been produced in this country." This is his key idea, and he supports this idea throughout the rest of the review by evaluating various aspects of the movie (subtopics of review) that he felt to be particularly successful.

Citizen Kane

1   *Citizen Kane* has probably had more advance publicity of one kind or another than any other picture yet produced. Practically everybody connected with the production has been reported on the verge of a lawsuit. Some have said that all this uproar was nothing but exceptionally well-handled publicity, while others have sworn that William Randolph Hearst was determined to prevent the picture's release. Finally it was announced that the picture would definitely be released in the near future, and the press assembled at last week's preview in a state of great expectancy.

Introduction — Background

2   Many would probably have rejoiced to find producer, director, actor, and part-author Orson Welles's ambitious first effort in Hollywood not an unqualified success: after all, the man had no previous cinema experience, and if reports were true he had walked into the studio and produced on a very low budget a film which was a masterpiece.

3   It must be stated here that no amount of advance publicity or ballyhoo could possibly ruin the effect of this remarkable picture. It is probably the most original, exciting, and entertaining picture that has yet been produced in this country, and although it may lack their subtlety it can certainly be placed in the same bracket as the very best prewar French productions.

Key Idea — This is a remarkable film.

4   The film may not have been inspired by the life of William Randolph Hearst, but the story of Charles Foster Kane, as unfolded in the picture, certainly bears a remarkable resemblance to Hearst's career. The incident concerning the Spanish-American War, the vast collection of useless antiques acquired by Kane, and certain details such as the picnic, with the guests compelled to spend the night under canvas, are familiar parts of the Hearst legend; and the castle of Xanadu, Kane's retreat from the world, with its endless acres and private zoo, is more than reminiscent of San Simeon. If Mr. Hearst

Subtopic — resemblance of Hearst's life to Kane's.

decides, as many others undoubtedly will, that the film is only the most thinly disguised version of his life story, he will perhaps be favorably impressed with the sympathy and understanding with which the subject has been treated, and may even be delighted to have provided material for a drama of almost classical proportions.

5   The film opens with the death of Kane, a very old man, alone in the colossal, ugly monument to his wealth and power—Xanadu. A sort of March of Time dealing with Kane's life is then presented. The producers of this short are dissatisfied, finding it too superficial and impersonal, and are determined to obtain more intimate details of the man's personal history. The remainder of the picture deals with the information on Kane's life and character obtained respectively from his guardian, his chief assistant, a dramatic critic who was once his best friend, his second wife, and his butler. This technique of unfolding the story necessitates five separate flashbacks and creates a certain amount of confusion which is more than compensated for by the powerful effect obtained by the gradual illumination of character, until with the click of the final switch he is fully revealed—empty, lonely, and unhappy, a victim of his own personal power.

6   This excellent cinematic material Welles has embellished with brilliant directorial, pictorial, and dramatic touches. He breaks, with the greatest effect, practically every photographic rule in the business, employing very few close-ups, playing whole scenes with the faces of the performers in shadow, using lighting to enhance the dramatic value of the scene rather than the personal appearance of the actor. He is, in fact, one of the first Hollywood directors really to exploit the screen as a medium, and it is interesting to note that in doing this he has used an entire cast with no previous screen experience.

Subtopic — Welles breaks rules.

7   The acting both of Welles and of the rest of the Mercury Theater cast is excellent. Dorothy Comingore as Kane's second wife, whom he forces to sing in opera to gratify his ego, is particularly effective; so is Joseph Cotten as the dramatic critic. Welles himself gives an amazing performance as Kane, equally convincing in youth, middle age, and senility. The photographer, Gregg Toland, has achieved some wonderful effects, particularly

Subtopic — excellent acting.

the scene in the projection room of the newsreel company.

8   The picture has made a tremendous impression in   *Conclusion* Hollywood. Charlie Chaplin is reported to be prepared to back any venture that Welles may have in mind. Perhaps when the uproar has died down it will be discovered that the film is not quite so good as it is considered now, but nevertheless Hollywood will for a long time be in debt to Mr. Welles.

—Anthony Bower

As a reader you can evaluate this kind of persuasive writing by asking the critical reading questions from Chapter 12. Who is the author? This will help you ascertain the author's credibility. What kind of evidence does the author use? By determining whether the author's evidence is fact or opinion, you can begin to evaluate the evidence. How does the author present the evidence? Is the reasoning sound? Is language used to influence the reader?

Critics often see and understand things differently. You can learn from their different perceptions and illuminations. But in every instance their judgments are personal, based on their own knowledge and experience.

Argument

One of the best illustrations of writing based on argument is found in philosophy. Philosophers attempt to understand and explain the nature of the universe, sometimes even questioning whether there is a universe. Some philosophers are interested in finding out why things are the way they are; others, in why people believe as they do. For example, What is justice? What is truth? Which is the best form of government? Does God exist? These are the kinds of questions philosophers ask as they speculate and challenge existing notions. Philosophers write about their beliefs, building their arguments on a foundation of rational thinking. Very often they derive their hypotheses from their responses to the thinking of other philosophers; subsequently, the new hypothesis becomes subject to challenge, and thus it goes in a never-ending—because never-provable—spiral of higher and higher levels of thinking.

Philosophers examine many different areas of human experience, including forms of government, human knowledge and how it is acquired, and religious and moral belief systems. But regardless of the topic or belief a philosophical work examines, that work always presents an opinion supported by logical reasoning. Once again, it is your task as a critical reader to evaluate whether the reasoning is sound by asking questions: How does the author/philosopher interpret the evidence? How does the author arrive at the conclusion? What is the connection between the assertion and the evidence?

Knowing that philosophy has a specialized vocabulary will help you understand your reading. Philosophical terminology is often taken from common language, but used in a special way. In general usage, "practical" means useful; however, in philosophical writing "practical" means of or pertaining to practice or action, and "practical reason" is when reason is guiding an action. "Idealism" is another example of how the general usage of a word differs from its philosophical meaning. The common definition of this word is that it pertains to the ideal. In philosophy "idealism" refers to the theory that the nature of what we see around us has to do with ideas, or our minds.

A philosophical work often proves to be difficult reading. The writing is dense, with many complex thoughts and few examples. Asking questions, finding the patterns of organization, sectioning the material, and knowing the vocabulary will help you to understand this material.

Example

The author of the reading on philosophic doubt believes that philosophic doubt is a positive characteristic. In the first paragraph he explains why he thinks this is true. The next paragraph is about the limitations of science and mathematics. He further supports his assertion by writing about the limitations of human reasoning. The author claims that human reasoning is only as valid as our perceptions. He offers specific examples of these boundaries as evidence for his opinion.

1   Philosophic doubt is not the pitiable condition of the *advantages of philosophic doubt* soul that timid spirits imagine. It is not pessimism or cynicism, but a healthy and cheerful habit. It gives peace of mind. Men who stop pretending can sleep o' nights. There is a certain scepticism which is in no sense the spirit that denies. It is a frank recognition of the things as they come. It is almost a test of a man's honesty, among those who have stopped to think about the nature and limitations of our knowledge. Certainly cultivated people do not exhibit the same degree of cocksureness as do the ignorant. People think the old saying

about "doubting the intelligence that doubts" is funny. Popular audiences will always laugh at it. But why not? It is a platitude that the more a man learns the more he realizes how little he knows. Existence is filled with inscrutable mystery. To none of the profound questions that we ask of it is there any final answer. We must be satisfied ultimately with surmise, with symbol and poetic fancy. Speculations about the soul, God, the ultimate nature of reality and the course of destiny, and as to whether existence has any meaning or purpose beyond our own, or whether our life itself is worthwhile— all these speculations and many others of similar nature lead to no conclusions in fact, and we return always to the point from which we started. The very terms in which we put such questions are often meaningless when closely examined by the intellect, and the answer to them is determined by our own moods.

2   There is a general belief that science can answer the riddle. But science is only one possible view of things, the one best adapted to the needs of creatures like ourselves. It cannot deal with questions of value. It can tell us how things operate, their relative mass and positions in space and time, but it cannot tell us what they are in themselves, nor why they exist nor anything about their goodness or beauty. The more exact scientific knowledge becomes, the more closely it approaches mathematics. Pure mathematics deals only with abstractions and logical relations and can dismiss the whole world of objects. Science presupposes the data of experience and the validity of its own logical principles. It substitutes its mechanized order of things for things as we experience them.

limitations of science and math

3   Human reasoning is partial in all its processes. We think successfully about things when we ignore all the aspects or qualities of them except those which are relevant to the purpose at hand. The H_2O-ness of water is no more the ultimate nature of water than is its wetness, or its thirst quenching quality. That it is H_2O is only one of the things that may be said about water. Now if we add together bits of onesided and partial scientific knowledge, we do not thereby gain a sum total which is the equivalent of reality as a whole. We have a useful instrument for dealing with our environment, because in thought we have greatly simplified it by ignoring in each instance all that is irrelevant. But what we now have is

limitations of human reasoning

a universe of discourse, a human construction which is what it is because we are always more interested in some aspects of things than in others.

4   All our ideas are views—they have been likened to snapshots. The world of which we are part is in flux. It comes to us as process, and our intellect does not grasp the movement any more than we can restore the movement of a man running by adding together a series of photographs. The movement always takes place between the pictures. Intellect is an instrument, not a mirror. Our world is not reducible to a form of thought, and when men speak of truth, reality, cause, substance, they are really only saying what they mean by certain words. The world, as James said, has its meanings for us because we are interested spectators, and so far as we can see none of these meanings are final. Whitehead and others have shown that some of the basic concepts of physical science which have held sway since the seventeenth century are now subject to revision. Santayana says that knowledge is faith—animal faith. It would be strange if it were otherwise, if hairy little creatures such as we are, whose ancestors lived in trees and made queer guttural noises, should so organize human discourse as to be able to say the last word about reality as a whole. It is well that we should marvel at our achievements of knowledge, for they are man's noblest work; but let us remember that human reason, itself a phase and part of the process of nature, can only view the whole process from its own partial standpoint, and that is enough unless we aspire to infallibility.

—Everett Dean Martin

Imaginative Writing

Imagination and creativity are essential parts of the humanistic tradition. The artist provides you with a different, exciting, and sometimes more meaningful interpretation of human experience. Although artistic interpretation clearly takes place in the masterpieces of art and music, here we shall stick to a brief discussion of the imaginative writing found in literature: novels, short stories, plays, and poetry. The inherent difference between fiction, or imaginative writing, and nonfiction is that in reading fiction you deal not only with *what* the authors say, but also with *how* they say it. In fiction, the medium is more important; in nonfiction, the message is. Imaginative writing may appeal to the reader's imagination, emotions, or feelings. It is evaluated more by its artistic effect than by its logic.

Writers use their creative powers to express feelings or ideas in new images. Through their interpretations and insights they aim to help us to understand ourselves and others.

You read literature for various reasons: to be amused, to be delighted by its beauty, and to learn. Part of the pleasure of reading and discussing fiction comes from the fact that it can be interpreted in different ways. It is much harder here than in nonfiction to discern key ideas, or even sometimes topics, because so much depends on the subjective and emotional response of the reader. As always, what you bring to the material is important. Perhaps you have read other works by the same author or selections from the same time period. Your purpose for reading the selection will determine the way in which you read a work and the extent to which you become involved. However, *What do I already know about the topic?* is answered differently in literature. Your previous experience, more than factual knowledge about the topic, will affect your reaction to the reading selection. If you live on a farm, for instance, you may identify with the plight of the farmers in a novel about the Dust Bowl. If you live in the city and have no personal experience with farm life, you may read the same novel from a historical perspective, without the personal involvement.

Awareness of this subjective dimension is imperative in reading literature. In imaginative writing, unlike most nonfiction, the individual words are of great importance. In poetry, especially, you can assume that every word is chosen with extraordinary care. Authors choose each word not only to convey basic meaning (denotation), but also to suggest, imply, and so arouse feelings (connotation). The author may use language to convey a tone or mood. The tone of a reading selection expresses the author's attitude toward the topic about which he or she is writing. The mood is a state of mind or feeling that makes the reader respond in a certain way. The tone and mood can provide a clue to the author's purpose for writing the selection. As a critical reader, you must be particularly alert to the use of symbolic language and its meaning.

Most colleges offer a variety of courses in reading and interpreting literature. Whole books are devoted to just one aspect of literary interpretation. Although this text cannot go into the same level of detail, you will find that applying the reading skills you have learned in *Active Reading* will help you to arrive at a better understanding of a piece of literature. You can become actively involved in your reading of an imaginative work by asking *What is this about? What are the author's most important ideas? What do I already know about the topic? Why did the author write this?*

You can also be a more intelligent and critical reader by going beyond the plot and asking other questions: Who are these characters? How do they relate to each other? How do they influence the plot? Why is the story set in that place at that time? Why does the author use this particular detail?

While you are reading fiction, as in reading nonfiction, you will find that you must question in order to see and understand the basic relationships. However, serious reading of fiction demands close reading. Often, you cannot understand how one thought or action is connected to another without reading and thinking about the total work.

Exercises

1. Read the following selection and identify the types of informative writing the author uses in this article. Where did you find them?

1   A Cuban mode of great importance (and charm) is the *son*. To what extent the *son* came from black use of Spanish elements, or how much it was a general music with strong black content, is not clear. It sprang from an earlier and simpler form, the estribillo, which had been around since the eighteenth century, accompanied in the early days by the guitar and a small three-stringed guitar called a *tres*. At some time the bass came to be filled in by the *marimbula*, the big descendant of the African marimba hand piano, and the *botija*, a jug blown into to give a booming bass note (also used by many jook, spasm, and skiffle bands in the United States). The presence of these instruments, especially the *marimbula*, suggests a black origin for the *son*, which is not invalidated by the early use of the guitars, for there is evidence that black Cubans took to the guitar much earlier than blacks in North America (hardly surprising, since the guitar is fundamental to Spanish music, and not to white U.S. music). The bongos—the linked twin drums—and other small drums were used in *son* groups, and so from time to time were the *güiro* or the *maraccas*. The estribillo developed from the *décima*, the ten-line Spanish poetic form, but is said to have been adopted by black Cubans quite early.

2   The *son* came to town from the country in the early part of the twentieth century. Arrived in Havana, it developed a format of guitar, *tres, maraccas, claves*, bongo, and *marimbula*. Around that time, a trumpet was often added. The *son* then became a major urban popular form with recognized stars, some of whose records you can still buy today, reissued on LP. Among the best-known groups from the great days of the urban *son* were the Septeto Nacional, led by Ignacio Piñeiro; the Septeto Habanero; and the Quarteto Machin. Their groups played in a style still heavily influenced by Afro-American drumming and also (in some of the trumpet playing) by nineteenth-century Spanish military brass techniques. On the other hand, it was taking in influences from jazz both in the brass-playing and in some guitar work (the favorite jazz model in guitar was the French jazzman Django Reinhardt, whose style would blend with Cuban styles much better than most other jazz guitar). Numbers like the Septeto Nacional's "Echalo Salsita" already point the way forward with a B section in a style still played by groups in the Spanish-speaking Caribbean and by the Afro-Cuban groups in the United States.

3   The *son* form was firmly based on African concepts, though with guitar-playing in a strong Spanish vein. Most *sones* use call-and-response singing, and some show an African attitude by making the response the tune, "Para Que No Pago," for example, by the Quarteto Machin. During the B tune, this often drops the solo vocalist altogether, replacing him with improvised phrases first from the trumpet and then from the guitar. The *son* groups are the link between Cuban country folk music and the urban popular groups of today's Hispanic music world. They bridged the gap both in their instrumentation and in their growing complexity.

–John S. Roberts

2. Read the following selection on self-love and section it. Then evaluate the author's reasoning. What kind of evidence does the author use? How does the author present the evidence? Is the reasoning sound?

1   The most obvious objection to the selfish hypothesis is that as it is contrary to common feeling and our most unprejudiced notions, there is required the highest stretch of philosophy to establish so extraordinary a paradox. To the most careless observer there appear to be such dispositions as benevolence and generosity, such affections as love, friendship, compassion, gratitude. These sentiments have their causes, effects, objects, and operations marked by common language and observation, and plainly distinguished from those of the selfish passions. And as this is the obvious appearance of things, it must be admitted till some hypothesis be discovered which, by penetrating deeper into human nature, may prove the former affections to be nothing but modifications of the latter. All attempts of this kind have hitherto proved fruitless, and seem to have proceeded entirely from that love of *simplicity* which has been the source of much false reasoning in philosophy. I shall not here enter into any detail on the present subject. Many able philosophers have shown the insufficiency of these systems; and I shall take for granted what, I believe, the smallest reflection will make evident to every impartial inquirer.

2   But the nature of the subject furnishes the strongest presumption that no better system will ever, for the future, be invented in order to account for the origin of the benevolent from the selfish affections, and reduce all the various emotions of the human mind to a perfect simplicity. The case is not the same in this species of philosophy as in physics. Many a hypothesis in nature, contrary to first appearances, has been found on more accurate scrutiny solid and satisfactory. Instances of this kind are so frequent that a judicious as well as witty philosopher has ventured to affirm, if there be more than one way in which any phenomenon may be produced, that there is a general presumption for its arising from the causes which are the least obvious and familiar. But the presumption always lies on the other side in all inquiries concerning the origin of our passions and of the internal operations of the human mind. The simplest and most obvious cause which can there be assigned for any phenomenon is probably the true one. When a philosopher, in the explication of his system, is obliged to have recourse to some very intricate and refined reflections, and to suppose them essential to the production of any passion or emotion, we have reason to be extremely on our guard against so fallacious a hypothesis. The affections are not susceptible of any impression from the refinements of reason or imagination; and it is always found that a vigorous exertion of the latter faculties, necessarily from the narrow capacity of the human mind, destroys all activity in the former. Our predominant motive or intention is, indeed, frequently concealed from ourselves when it is mingled and confounded with other motives which the mind, from vanity or self-conceit, is desirous of supposing more prevalent. But there is no instance that a concealment of this nature has ever arisen from the abstruseness and intricacy of the motive. A man that has lost a friend and patron may flatter himself that all his grief arises from generous sentiments, without any mixture of narrow or interested considerations; but a man that grieves for a valuable friend who needed his patronage and protection—how can we suppose that his passionate tenderness arises from some metaphysical regards to a self-interest which has no foundation or reality?

We may as well imagine that minute wheels and springs, like those of a watch, give motion to a loaded wagon, as account for the origin of passion from such abstruse reflections.

3   Animals are found susceptible of kindness, both to their own species and to ours; nor is there, in this case, the least suspicion of disguise or artifice. Shall we account for all *their* sentiments, too, from refined deductions of self-interest? Or if we admit a disinterested benevolence in the inferior species, by what rule of analogy can we refuse it in the superior?

4   Love between the sexes begets a complacency and good will very distinct from the gratification of an appetite. Tenderness to their offspring, in all sensible beings, is commonly able alone to counterbalance the strongest motives of self-love, and has no manner of dependence on that affection. What interest can a fond mother have in view who loses her health by assiduous attendance on her sick child, and afterwards languishes and dies of grief when freed, by its death, from the slavery of that attendance?

5   Is gratitude no affection of the human breast, or is that a word merely without any meaning or reality? Have we no satisfaction in one man's company above another's, and no desire of the welfare of our friend, even though absence or death should prevent us from all participation in it? Or what is it commonly that gives us any participation in it, even while alive and present, but our affection and regard to him?

6   These and a thousand other instances are marks of a general benevolence in human nature, where no *real* interest binds us to the object. And how an *imaginary* interest, known and avowed for such, can be the origin of any passion or emotion seems difficult to explain. No satisfactory hypothesis of this kind has yet been discovered, nor is there the smallest probability that the future industry of men will ever be attended with more favorable success.

7   But further, if we consider rightly of the matter, we shall find that the hypothesis which allows of a disinterested benevolence, distinct from self-love, has really more *simplicity* in it and is more comfortable to the analogy of nature than that which pretends to resolve all friendship and humanity into this latter principle. There are bodily wants or appetites acknowledged by everyone, which necessarily precede all sensual enjoyment and carry us directly to seek possession of the object. Thus hunger and thirst have eating and drinking for their end; and from the gratification of these primary appetites arises a pleasure which may become the object of another species of desire or inclination that is secondary and interested. In the same manner, there are mental passions by which we are impelled immediately to seek particular objects,

such as fame, or power, or vengeance, without any regard to interest; and when these objects are attained, a pleasing enjoyment ensues as the consequence of our indulged affections. Nature must, by the internal frame and constitution of the mind, give an original propensity to fame ere we can reap any pleasure from that acquisition or pursue it from motives of self-love and a desire of happiness. If I have no vanity, I take no delight in praise; if I be void of ambition, power gives me no enjoyment; if I be not angry, the punishment of an adversary is totally indifferent to me. In all these cases there is a passion which points immediately to the object and constitutes it our good or happiness, as there are other secondary passions which afterwards arise and pursue it as a part of our happiness when once it is constituted such by our original affections. Were there no appetite of any kind antecedent to self-love, that propensity could scarcely ever exert itself, because we should, in that case, have felt few and slender pains or pleasures, and have little misery or happiness to avoid or to pursue.

8   Now, where is the difficulty in conceiving that this may likewise be the case with benevolence and friendship, and that, from the original frame of our temper, we may feel a desire of another's happiness or good, which, by means of that affection, becomes our own good and is afterwards pursued from the combined motives of benevolence and self-enjoyment? Who sees not that vengeance, from the force alone of passion, may be so eagerly pursued as to make us knowingly neglect every consideration of ease, interest, or safety, and, like some vindictive animals, infuse our very souls into the wounds we give an enemy? And what a malignant philosophy must it be that will not allow to humanity and friendship the same privileges which are indisputably granted to the darker passions of enmity and resentment? Such a philosophy is more like a satire than a true delineation or description of human nature, and may be a good foundation for paradoxical wit and raillery, but is a very bad one for any serious argument or reasoning.

                                                              –David Hume

3. Read "The Story of an Hour" and answer the following questions.
   a. What effect did the short story have on you?
   b. What techniques did the author use to make the writing effective?
   c. Was language used to influence you? How?

The Story of an Hour

1   Knowing that Mrs. Mallard was afflicted with a heart trouble, great care was taken to break to her as gently as possible the news of her husband's death.

2   It was her sister Josephine who told her, in broken sentences, veiled hints that revealed in half concealing. Her husband's friend Richards was there, too, near her. It was he who had been in the newspaper office when intelligence of the railroad disaster was received, with Brently Mallard's name leading the list of "killed." He had only taken the time to assure himself of its truth by a second telegram, and had hastened to forestall any less careful, less tender friend in bearing the sad message.

3   She did not hear the story as many women have heard the same, with a paralyzed inability to accept its significance. She wept at once, with sudden, wild abandonment, in her sister's arms. When the storm of grief had spent itself she went away to her room alone. She would have no one follow her.

4   There stood, facing the open window, a comfortable, roomy armchair. Into this she sank, pressed down by a physical exhaustion that haunted her body and seemed to reach into her soul.

5   She could see in the open square before her house the tops of trees that were all aquiver with the new spring life. The delicious breath of rain was in the air. In the street below a peddler was crying his wares. The notes of a distant song which some one was singing reached her faintly, and countless sparrows were twittering in the eaves.

6   There were patches of blue sky showing here and there through the clouds that had met and piled above the other in the west facing her window.

7   She sat with her head thrown back upon the cushion of the chair quite motionless, except when a sob came up into her throat and shook her, as a child who has cried itself to sleep continues to sob in its dreams.

8   She was young, with a fair, calm face, whose lines bespoke repression and even a certain strength. But now there was a dull stare in her eyes, whose gaze was fixed away off yonder on one of those patches of blue sky. It was not a glance of reflection, but rather indicated a suspension of intelligent thought.

9   There was something coming to her and she was waiting for it, fearfully. What was it? She did not know; it was too subtle and elusive to name. But she felt it, creeping out of the sky, reaching toward her through the sounds, the scents, the color that filled the air.

10   Now her bosom rose and fell tumultuously. She was beginning to recognize this thing that was approaching to possess her, and she was striving to beat it back with her will—as powerless as her two white slender hands would have been.

11   When she abandoned herself a little whispered word escaped her slightly parted lips. She said it over and over under her breath: "Free, free, free!" The vacant stare and the look of terror that had

followed it went from her eyes. They stayed keen and bright. Her pulses beat fast, and the coursing blood warmed and relaxed every inch of her body.

12   She did not stop to ask if it were not a monstrous joy that held her. A clear and exalted perception enabled her to dismiss the suggestion as trivial.

13   She knew that she would weep again when she saw the kind, tender hands folded in death; the face that had never looked save with love upon her, fixed and gray and dead. But she saw beyond that bitter moment a long procession of years to come that would belong to her absolutely. And she opened and spread her arms out to them in welcome.

14   There would be no one to live for during those coming years; she would live for herself. There would be no powerful will bending her in that blind persistence with which men and women believe they have a right to impose a private will upon a fellow-creature. A kind intention or a cruel intention made the act seem no less a crime as she looked upon it in that brief moment of illumination.

15   And yet she had loved him—sometimes. Often she had not. What did it matter! What could love, the unsolved mystery, count for in face of this possession of self-assertion which she suddenly recognized as the strongest impulse of her being!

16   "Free! Body and soul free!" she kept whispering.

17   Josephine was kneeling before the closed door with her lips to the keyhole, imploring for admission. "Louise, open the door! I beg; open the door—you will make yourself ill. What are you doing, Louise? For heaven's sake open the door."

18   "Go away. I am not making myself ill." No; she was drinking in a very elixir of life through that open window.

19   Her fancy was running riot along those days ahead of her. Spring days, and summer days, and all sorts of days that would be her own. She breathed a quick prayer that life might be long. It was only yesterday she had thought with a shudder that life might be long.

20   She arose at length and opened the door to her sister's importunities. There was a feverish triumph in her eyes, and she carried herself unwittingly like a goddess of Victory. She clasped her sister's waist, and together they descended the stairs. Richards stood waiting for them at the bottom.

21   Some one was opening the front door with a latchkey. It was Brently Mallard who entered, a little travel-stained, composedly carrying his grip-sack and umbrella. He had been far from the scene of accident, and did not even know there had been one. He stood amazed at Josephine's piercing cry; at Richards' quick motion to screen him from the view of his wife.

22   But Richards was too late.

23   When the doctors came they said she had died of heart disease—of joy that kills.

–Kate Chopin

4. By answering the following questions, compare and contrast this review of "Citizen Kane" with the one found on pp. 277–279.

   a. What are the subtopics of the two movie reviews?
   b. How do the authors' perceptions of the movie differ?
   c. What reasons do the reviewers give to support their critical evaluations?

Radio Boy Makes Good
(Citizen Kane)

1   I do not call Orson Welles a radio boy to remind people either of his early terrorism or his later development as a first class producer of radio drama. On two successive days I listened to and looked at the works by which he is today being judged: his production of *Native Son* and his creation of *Citizen Kane*; and all through both, which were miles above anything in the theater or the movies of the year, I was aware of a skillful radio man, a man trained to know the value of sound, and even of the despised "sound effects." I do not mean that the overwhelming effectiveness of Welles's methods derives entirely from his experiences in radio; they are a factor, and the circumstance that he has used his radio experience for stage and screen work proves him far more intelligent than most people in any of the three mediums.

2   My thank-god-not-too-often-too-amiable colleague Mr. Nathan has certainly conveyed to you some sense of the atmosphere in which *Native Son* plays; as I haven't even yet read the book, which the play is said to follow closely, I shan't go over the story again. Actually the production of the play reminded me a little of the American expressionists; they, too, were liberal in outlook, experimental in method; and some of the same characters occur: the rich girl, half tart, half earnest radical; the noble savage, in this case a simple, not intellectual Negro, with a vile temper and a tendency toward crime; the aggressive young man radical; and so on. Occasionally scenes were telescoped, condensed out of all nature, and these "imagist" scenes came between straight realistic passages, which was confusing. But Welles had brought several new technical tricks and a new kind of suspense to the theater. In fact, he used both the old and the new, and the combination makes the suspense of even a Hitchcock picture feel like nothing more than a slightly stretched rubber band.

3   He has used his own suspense in *Citizen Kane,* also, so it is worth examining a little. In *Native Son* you simply wait for something to happen; you wait for the central action to start. You begin with a group of poor Negroes in a one-room tenement, four of them sleeping, getting up, snarling at one another, the big boy furious at his mother's piety, angry at the welfare worker who offers a job. From that time on you wait for an event; and that is Welles's suspense, because you don't know what the event will be. You only feel that it will be violent, maybe tragic. And the dramatization of the story helps, because you are running into a holdup, but you detour, and you get the boy set in a job, still a bit surly, but on the right road; then you see the event beginning to take shape: the employer's idle daughter, the idle white half-patronizing, half-envying the Negro, egging him on to social revolt and sexual conquest. That leads to murder—not a crime of passion, merely the boy's attempt to prevent the girl from betraying his presence to her blind mother; merely that, at first, anyhow.

4   That scene is not suspense, but grim horror; in the pursuit, suspense begins again: the good Hitchcock suspense which depends on the accidental coming together of certain circumstances; the good suspense of the criminal cornered and shot at from all sides; there is even an expressionistic trial at the end, so you have the suspense of not knowing the answer till the end.

5   You can't do that in the theater; experts say you can't. You can't keep people waiting half the night before your main action is even hinted. Well, you can. You can if you can create characters and circumstances which will keep people interested; that's all. I've forgotten Welles's degree of familiarity with the daytime serial of radio; but he has heard of it; he knows that the moment people are concerned with a character they are content to wait; just as they are content to wait for the people they know to do or say something interesting. It is only when characters are not absorbing that we demand action at once.

6   Welles has connected the scenes of *Native Son* with musical bridges; he has invented reasons for bringing on music; you have heard the sounds of the city, full of outcries and motors, or dying down; the locomotives shunting in the railyards, in balance with the searchlights hunting for the hidden criminal. Sound has always been there, creating atmosphere.

7   One other man seems to know about the use of sound to create pictures. It is Robert Edmond Jones, who, in one way or another, gets to know everything about the theater, and most of it exactly right. Jones has written a book on The Dramatic Imagination; he speaks of radio's way of inducing the sense of place by means of "spoken descriptions and so-called 'sound effects.' These devices

have caught the imagination of radio audiences ... It is odd that our playwrights and stage designers have not yet sensed the limitless potentialities of this new enhancement of the spoken word. A magical new medium of scenic evocation is waiting to be pressed into service."

8   Mr. Welles has made a start.

9   In *Citizen Kane* he has gone further. He has created specific psychological effects by use of filters and other devices of the sound engineers. He has given you the effect of space—and of the feeling characters have for one another—by the artificial timbre he has given their voices. He has played the tinkle of a glass, the climax of an orchestra, and the blacking out of a light in a window, in tremendous counterpoint. The whole picture has a web of sound, a pattern traced as surely as it has a pictorial pattern, and an intellectual one.

10   That, by the way, is its supreme virtue: it has sense, in every medium it uses; it has—so emphatically that you can't miss it—a single guiding intelligence, operating right through; the errors of judgment rise from the same intelligence, from a person knowing what he wants, going ahead and getting it—once in every forty minutes or so, that person wanted the wrong thing for about a minute—and you get a dull or a stupid spot. But you have to go back to the days of Griffith, and to the almost forgotten days of one or two Russian and German directors, to catch that feeling of a sure hand *directing* the course of the picture. Our directors generally tell an actor what to do; but the director who makes a picture go in a certain direction is exceedingly rare among us. Welles had it written into his contract that he should write, if he wished, direct, and act in his own pictures; that's the story and with the story came the cackles from Hollywood about this bearded boy who was going to come an awful cropper, because didn't even the great Thalberg put six men merely on writing; didn't Selznick have three directors in succession on this success—or that flop? Thalberg had his reasons, and Selznick, too, for all I know; Thalberg wasn't an effective writer, nor a good director; he was a producer of genius, who could combine the work of others. But not one picture bearing his name has the unity of *Citizen Kane*—the unity inside, which makes everything in it ten thousand times more effective than it would otherwise be—because each item multiplies the effectiveness of all the others.

11   You have heard it said that this is a travesty on the life of Mr. Hearst. Maybe. There are touches of the Thaw legend, touches of even earlier episodes among the rich and unruly. Welles apparently courted scandal when he threw together four or five of the most notable features of one man's life, and added others which

hadn't happened, but easily could have, to the same person. Maybe it will serve Welles right if the newspaper stuff in the picture will prove so dull that people will walk out on it. The struggle between men—not over a woman—may be box office poison. Everything else in the picture is Broadway's gift to Hollywood. From recent reports, I gather Hollywood is grateful. For Welles has shown Hollywood how to make movies.

12   You wonder what good Hollywood directors mean when they say that after seeing *Citizen Kane*, they feel they've never made a real picture in their lives. And when you start looking at *Citizen Kane* you see the camera traveling up, up, up, an enormous fence, with a "no trespass" sign; and presently it's a cage of some obscene monkeys; and gradually a process-shot of a castle on a hillside— and soon you're through the casements and a man lies dying, and the light goes out as the object he holds in his hand falls to the ground; he utters a word . . . and almost at once you are seeing a March-of-Timish newsreel obituary of *Citizen Kane*. What is different? What is so new?

13   The intercutting of sound-and-picture, the beautiful counterpoint of movement and music—that is simply done better than most people do it. The slow suspense of the opening is pictorially better; the angles, here and later, of the camera, are the angles of the German cinematographers, brought to American uses, making sense. (Incidentally, about half of the picture must have been shot with a low camera, making Kane and several other figures loom over you, slightly distorted; a doubtful effect.) The cutting is the Russian montage system brought to American uses, making sense, as it made once for the Russians and was then translated into a trick.

14   You must remember Welles spent some time in Hollywood; the cacklers had their fun when nothing—absolutely not a foot of film—resulted for nearly a year; the flattest and most foolish of actors played practical jokes and told the gossip columnists about them, but Welles was working; he was studying pictures; he knew what he wanted a picture to look like, to sound like, and to feel like. That is the new thing. That is revolutionary. And the second revolution is that he made the picture sound and look and feel just that way. The third revolution, somewhat delayed, is in the public exhibition of the picture. If the scandal doesn't arouse excitement in the backwoods, the tremendous sense of actuality in the picture may offend the lotus eaters. It will be a pity, but only for a little while. Welles can't fail now in making pictures.

15   It's a long picture and the Wellesian suspense keeps Kane out of it for a long time; you see him shrouded in gloom on a deathbed; you catch a glimpse of him in a marvelously faked old-fashioned

newsreel with Teddy Roosevelt, as part of the Time on the March reel; you see him as a bad little boy; but you hear of him for an interminable time before he appears as a young man. (I had by that time become so engrossed in the picture that I didn't even recognize Welles as the actor in the part; it's a good job, but the picture towers over it.)

16   Again, Welles has created your interest in a person by keeping the main action of his life away from you, so that you're almost breathless when he arrives upon the scene.

17   You can say, with justice, that the story he told was obviously derived from the lives of some of the most colorful and exciting characters in America; so he had that to start with. That's true, and his handling of the stories is good, too; so he gets credit. There is a foolishness about "rose-bud"—the dying man's last word and the silly idea, which would never, I hope, occur to an editor of *The March of Time*, that if one knew why he said that word, the meaning of his whole life would be revealed to us. That is the only bit of stale stuff in the picture; and incidentally it's a phony; because we do find out and nothing is any clearer than it was. Apart from that, and the necessity of interviewing half a dozen people, with flashbacks for their stories, the manipulation of the narrative is skillful: if there's too much talk, it's remarkably easy on the ear; the Hollywood clichés have been erased from the script.

18   They have also been erased from the acting. None of the principals are old troupers of Hollywood; many come from Welles's earlier theatrical work. And they hardly ever are allowed to fall into the postures, gestures, grimaces, and tonalities of Hollywood. They are as fresh-seeming as the faces of peasants were when we first glimpsed them in Russian films. They talk and look like human beings; they are.

19   In the past six months I've seen a lot of regular studio pictures which I have liked; and there is always John Ford who, with not one-tenth of Welles's material, can do a great picture. But the Hollywood product has become remarkably slick and smooth and polished; and every studio turns out three pictures about someone who isn't married to the person with whom, for some reason, he or she must share a bedroom. Heaven knows these are wittier jobs than the movies of 1926; they are downright good entertainment; but there isn't any character to them, no stamina, no formative, energetic, pushing intelligence which takes a theme at the beginning, develops it, and brings it to a legitimate end.

20   Orson Welles hasn't shown Hollywood how to get these qualities; he has shown them that you can make a picture by using these qualities. Moreover, the next great picture will not necessarily be another semiscandalous biography—as of Warren Gamaliel

Harding. It may be a romance. Will the next great picture be made by another newcomer, or by an old hand? I don't know. It will be made by someone who forgets a lot—forgets even a lot that Welles has taught—and gets down to the roots of his subject, as Welles has done. For you feel, at times, as if Welles had known everything there is to know of all the techniques of the motion picture, and had used them better than anyone else has used them in a generation; and at other times you feel that he has made such a moving picture as a man of genius would have made if he had never seen a picture before in his life—but was a genius in the monstrously difficult art of writing with images.

21   And just for a bit of mockery, Welles has made exactly the kind of picture that half-a-dozen writers have been describing and predicting for years. Some of the writers went to work in Hollywood, too, and forgot to make their picture. Welles never, to my knowledge, said a word about the movies one way or the other. But he has made the movies young again, by filling them with life.

–Gilbert Seldes

Writing Exercise

State the three types of writing found in the humanities and summarize the characteristics of each.

17 Reading History and the Social Sciences

Active reading in history and the social sciences calls for the exactness of mathematics, the evidence indispensable to experimentation in the natural sciences, and the evaluation necessary to making critical judgments. This chapter will discuss why this is so and how you can use questions, graphic material, and your course outlines to assist you in applying your reading skills to history and the social sciences.

The Nature of the Social Sciences and History

Broadly speaking, the social sciences are those fields that deal with people and how they relate to themselves, to one another, and to their environments. The study of the social sciences is based on an analysis of these relationships from various points of view usually designated as anthropology, the study of the basis for human groupings; archaeology, the study of the life and culture of ancient people; economics, the study of the production, distribution, and consumption of wealth; political science (or government), the study of the principles and organization of government; psychology, the study of mental processes and behavior; and sociology, the study of the ways in which people manage living and working together. These fields are constantly expanding as new areas come under scrutiny and are broken off from their parent areas, as ethnography and demography have from the three fields of political science, economics, and sociology and as psychobiology has from psychology and biology. Some disciplines are more technical than others—for instance, the emphasis on mathematical analysis in economics and archaeology—but all social sciences are alike in that they rest on conclusions based on evidence. With the progress of time, as fresh evidence proves the underlying principles inadequate or wrong, old theories are revised and new ones are introduced.

Because history underlies everything, the study of history is usually included in every field—history of science, economic history, and so on. However, history as a discipline is associated both with the humanities, because of its philosophical base, and with the social sciences, because of its dependence on documentary evidence.

Questioning as You Read

The natural sciences depend on data collected from observing human and natural phenomena; the social sciences depend on data collected from observing human experience. Humans are not nearly as exact nor as predictable as things, so in order to get good answers it is particularly important to follow up on your preview questions with very precise reading questions. The answer to your first question *What is this about?* should be stated carefully. For instance, "It is about the British government" is not as precise as "It is about the development of the British parliamentary system." Your succeeding questions should be equally well focused. Not "What more do I want to know about the British parliamentary system?" but rather such questions as "How did the British parliamentary system develop?" "How does it compare to the U.S. system?" "What is the role of the House of Lords?" will help you to understand and retain what you read.

As you study an article in sociology, your object might be to find out what Smith thinks about Brown's theories. Your questions might be: "What is Smith's statement of Brown's theories?" "Does she agree with any of them?" "Where does she disagree?" "On what does she base her disagreement?" "What is the author's framework?" "How are his conclusions or data new?" Or for an anthropology course you could ask: "What exactly were the O'Malley discoveries?" "Why were they important?" "How did they change our understanding of human evolution?" "What further questions did they raise?" Questions like these are indispensable in guiding you through your reading.

Patterns of organization have particular relevance in history and the social sciences. As you might expect, all the patterns of organization we have referred to can be found here. Authors explain, define, and illustrate; they order material; they compare one finding with another and contrast two or more phenomena to make their points more vivid and thus more easily comprehensible. They show how one thing caused another or how one thing was affected by another. Your ability to recognize the author's use of patterns of organization will help to lead you through the material because you know what question to ask next.

Reading in the social sciences and history requires careful analysis. After previewing and skimming for the topic, key idea, and subtopics, remind yourself constantly about how the key idea relates to the supporting ideas and supporting details by asking the basic reading questions. This will help you to distinguish, locate, and separate the author's principal concept, or generalization, from the supporting material, which defines, describes, amplifies, illustrates, or provides factual backup. Questions like these will be useful in your reading task: "Is the author writing to inform?" "Is the article supposed to be objective?" "Is it objective?" "Is it an explanation of concepts, or is it a series of case histories from which I need to draw conclusions?" "Is it a report on research?" "Is the author writing to convince me?" "Is this a new interpretation?" "Does it present a different point of view?" "What is different about it?" "What supports it?" "What is the author's conclusion?" "On what data is it based?" "How was it collected?" "How is the methodology biased?"

In every case you will search for the author's main points by sectioning the material, noting its structure, and watching for the patterns of organization. As in the other fields, your efficiency and comprehension depend greatly on the skill with which you apply your knowledge of the author's strategies to your reading.

For example, in reading a history text, you will note that the author usually introduces the key concept, then arranges the material chronologically. But if the concept is to have any validity, it must result from careful and skilled questioning and analysis of original sources. As a student of history, you look not only at the content, but at the identity and possible bias of the source; you must be able to defend your conclusion or interpretation by reference to an accumulation of evidence, not from impressions. Such a defense is known as a "reasoned argument" and includes your ability to choose from a range of possibilities to make a logical case.

Example

The following passage from a history of Sierra Leone is a good illustration of the way a historian judges a source:

1   One English writer, Elizabeth Hirst, has tried to show, from oral tradition, that at heart Bai Bureh was a man of peace. According to her and her co-author [Kamara] . . . he had given up fighting for a long time, taking a vow of peace which he broke only when his sense of Lokko [a tribe] patriotism forced him into action when Samori's *sofa* [a leader] menaced the Lokko. While this thesis is apparently supported by some oral Lokko traditions, it conflicts with many Temne [a tribe] traditions which emphasize Bai Bureh's essentially war-like character. Moreover, the archival records reveal that he was almost continuously engaged in war from 1865 until 1898. Indeed, many of the events recorded by Hirst and Kamara . . . do not correspond with what the archives show clearly did happen. Since their book is used in the schools, their portrait of Bai Bureh as a man of peace and a model for Christian school children has gained wide currency in Sierra Leone.

2   It is essential, however, to contradict their thesis . . . both because it is not true, and because it is clear that the major explanation for [Bai Bureh's] success against the British was his experience as a war leader—unparalleled in those parts not only for its length but also for its continuity. . . . The significance of his war with the British was that while many other Africans had the will to resist European penetration, he was one of the few who also had the skill.

—LaRay Denzer and Michael Crowder

On what evidence do Denzer and Crowder base their disagreement with the conclusions of Hirst and Kamara? Why did they consider it important to do so? It is extremely important that you constantly question the basis for statements when reading history and the social sciences. (Conversely, if you are writing a paper in these fields, you must always be aware of the necessity for providing complete data to support your conclusions.)

Readings in economics and archaeology are often technical, because they deal primarily with concepts and their applications are in quantitative terms. As in the sciences, the terms used are exact, and the student needs to know the precise meanings—no guesswork will do here. For instance, *marginal* in common usage means "on the edge," but in the vocabulary of economics it means "additional"; and the word *dig*, normally used as a verb, is used as a noun in archaeology to mean "an archaeological excavation."

To read history and the social sciences efficiently, you must bear in mind the advantages of flexibility. Not everything you read will be dense with many ideas per paragraph. Often, in fact, you will find long passages of explanation or illustration. Dare to read only for the topic, subtopics, key ideas, and supporting ideas if you judge it possible. Eliminate some of the supporting details if you know you understand what the author is saying, why he or she is saying it, and on what evidence the arguments are based. Remember that your objective is to read with understanding, but also to read as efficiently and as quickly as possible.

The Role of Graphics

In the social sciences, like the natural sciences, you can help your understanding of the concepts by drawing diagrams as you read and by learning how to use the tables and figures provided as illustrations of the text. These add another dimension by providing lines, tables, and numbers to clarify the concepts and provide supporting information. Usually,

- diagrams explain or amplify prose,
- tables summarize findings, and
- figures show how two or more variables relate.

It is always important to read the titles, captions, headings, and other material connected with the graphics carefully. They set the stage and usually explain what you are looking at. When looking at graphic material the questions *What is this about?* and *What key idea is the author communicating?* are particularly important, followed closely by *What is being explained? Can I put the summary into words? What relationship or relationships are being illustrated?* Explaining graphics to yourself is an important aid to learning.

Examples

The following three graphs (pages 303–305) all have to do with a reading class in a local college. Figures 1 and 2 both have the same title: "A Comparison of Reading Rates of Classes A, B, and C, September–February." One is a bar graph and the other a line graph; they both show how the rates for the three classes compare. Figure 1 makes the comparisons more obvious, but Figure 2 gives a better sense of the flow of the rate increase. Both make it easier for the instructor to see what has taken place than if the same information was laboriously written out in prose. Now the instructor needs to ask: What made the rates different? Why was one class slower? Were there the same number of students in each class? Might age or sexual composition of the classes make any difference? These questions point the way to the kind of research that needs to be done.

The title of Figure 3 is "Jane Brown's Reading Rate, September–February." Your answers to the first two basic reading questions tell you that the topic is Jane Brown's reading rates and that the key idea is that Jane increased her reading speed. You might then go on to ask: What was Jane's reading rate when she started? What was Jane's reading rate at the end of six months? Did she make smooth progress? Why the dip at the end of December? There seem to be three plateaus. Is that typical of the way reading rates increase?

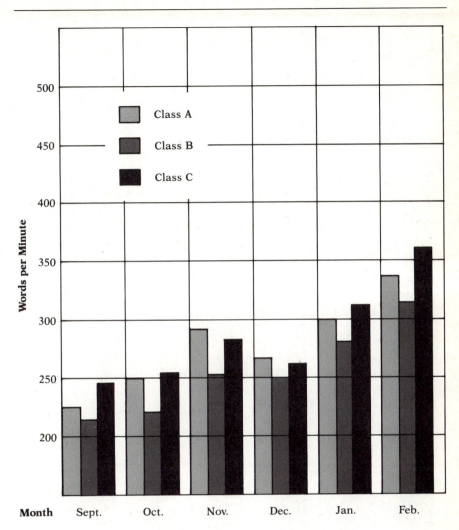

FIGURE 1   **A Comparison of Reading Rates of Classes A, B, and C, September–February**

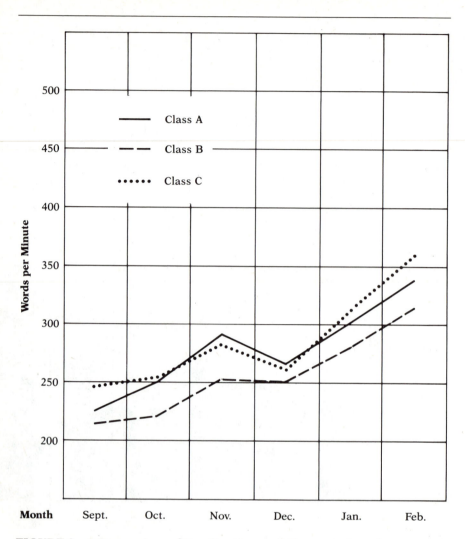

FIGURE 2   A Comparison of Reading Rates of Classes A, B, and C, September–February

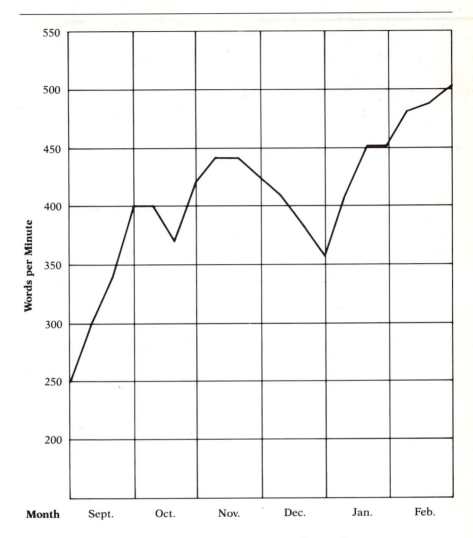

FIGURE 3   **Jane Brown's Reading Rate, September–February**

The Role of the Syllabus

Classroom study of the social sciences, unlike the natural sciences, does not always entail the use of a textbook. Instead, readings often consist of excerpts from books, articles, and—in political science—government documents, like a constitution or parliamentary records. This means that you do not always have texts on which to base your knowledge of the material; you will need to depend on the class. Instead of an introduction and table of contents of a textbook and the syllabus as guides to the course, you only have a syllabus.

The following excerpts from the syllabus of an introductory political science course show how the introduction to the syllabus serves the same function as the introduction to a textbook. Just as you would preview the table of contents to understand the structure of the book, so too you look over your syllabus to see where the course starts, where it ends, and what stages it goes through to get there. This course is based on a comparative study of a variety of political systems, modern and ancient. From the portion of the syllabus on American democracy, you can see that most of the readings consist of chapters from books, articles, or official documents.

Introduction to Politics

Tuesday, Thursday
Fall Semester, 1984

Political Science 101 is an introduction to the study of politics, political ideas, and political systems. The vehicle for our study will be the comparative examination of a variety of contrasting political systems: ancient Athens, Great Britain, the United States, Nazi Germany, and contemporary China. We will examine the philosophical foundations of each of these political systems, their major political institutions, and their characteristic political processes. In particular, we will attempt to understand these different forms of government by emphasizing the similarities and differences in their fundamental conceptions of political leadership, political participation, social and political equality, and liberty.

This course will begin with the study of ancient Greece, the focus of the great political philosophers, Plato and Aristotle. We will examine the classic responses these philosophers gave to the questions of the meaning of political life, the best organization of government, and who should rule and why. We will then compare the liberal democracies of Great Britain and the United States. We will next try to understand why liberal democracy failed in Weimar Germany and how Hitler came to power. Finally we will study Marxism and its distinctive application in contemporary China.

*   *   *   *

Reports in the Social Sciences

Much of the writing in the social sciences is found in the professional journals and consists of research reports based on statistics and on data from case studies and field studies. Although the types of data considered valid and the format for their presentation differ from field to field, the format is always the same within a particular field. Familiarity with the format helps readers to locate the information they need and to anticipate the direction that the writing will take. Some professional organizations issue style guides as an aid to writers in the field. These guides can also prove helpful to the reader. You can check on their existence in your area of study by asking your instructor or a librarian. The report form rests on common sense questions, questions that you would normally bring to your sectioning of the material.

- *What is the author reporting on?* The answer to this question is found in the introduction and provides the background.
- *Why did the author undertake the research?* The answer is the author's hypothesis or statement of what he or she wants to find out.
- *How did the author do the research?* The answer is usually found in the middle of the report, sometimes in a section entitled "Methodology."
- *What did the author discover?* The answer provides the author's findings and is usually located about two-thirds of the way through the report. Sometimes it is labeled "Discussion."
- *What is its importance and relevance?* The answer is found in the conclusion and sometimes in the discussion.

Example

Let's see how this report form works in the following article on hypnosis, "The Partial Reformulation of a Traumatic Memory of a Dental Phobia During Trance: A Case Study." Read it quickly, looking for the answers to the questions listed above.

The Partial Reformulation of a Traumatic Memory of a Dental Phobia During Trance: A Case Study

Abstract: A dental patient undertook hypnosis for the modification of a dental phobia. While she was in trance, the disturbing memory was replaced by a nontraumatic memory. After 2 sessions, the dental phobia was significantly reduced.

1 In the literature of various clinical disciplines, case studies are often published in journals which serve to illustrate the dynamics of the therapeutic process. Case studies often point to new research directions. The present case study is described with these foregoing points in mind.

2 Avoidance reactions to dental therapeutics are often found among adults and children who have acquired fearful traumatic associations within their past experience with dental therapy. It is often difficult to treat such patients for their dental problems when their phobic reactions to dentistry elicit thwarting behavior during the course of therapy. Not only is treatment obstructed, but also phobias prevent people from seeking early treatment for dental problems until their problems fulminate into unmanageable physical symptoms. The fear of treatment increases the perceived pain experienced by the patient, which in turn reinforces the phobic behavior. . . .

3 The present paper is a case-study report which describes how hypnosis was applied in the treatment and subsequent elimination of a long-term dental phobia. It is the intent of this report to support, as other cited researchers

have done, the use of psychological techniques to effect patient adaptation to dental therapy. . . .

4   The case example selected for illustration in the present paper was chosen because the patient presented an intractable dental phobia for 20 years and was unable to come to terms with elements of her phobia.

Case History

5   The subject is a 30-year-old female caucasian, married, and wheelchair bound, who had not been to a dentist in almost 20 years. She was in need of extensive dental restoration, but she reported being very fearful of dental treatment.

6   The initial interview indicated that she could not specify the source of her anxiety, and that she could not go to the dentist until the condition of her mouth became so bad as to make dental restoration imperative. At the point of initial therapy contact, she could not go to a dentist even though she knew it was necessary.

7   Since the patient proved to be exceedingly responsive after rehypnosis, she was given the suggestion to regress to the time when she became frightened of the dentist. She reported at age 9 that she was taken to the hospital for tooth extraction and that she was frightened when she was wheeled into the operating room. She became terrified when the anesthetic mask was placed over her face. She could not recall anyone giving her comfort; she became terror stricken. She began to abreact to her fear with extremely deep breaths and with the beginnings of tears. The therapist decided to stop the abreaction in its initial stage.

8   *Treatment.*   In the place of the abreaction, the therapist told the patient that as she was going into the operating room, the doctor would hold her and stroke her forehead and tell her that she should not be afraid because he would take care of her and that he knew that she was frightened. The therapist repeated this script to her and asked her if she now heard the doctor give her reassurance. She asserted that she heard the doctor and she reported after the reassurance that her fear was diminished as she recalled herself being wheeled into the operating room.

9   One week later she returned for a follow-up session. Trance was rapidly induced and she was again regressed to the age of 9 and to the operation. She recalled that the doctor was telling her not to be afraid, and her degree of abreaction to the event was less. During the regression, she recalled the transplanted memory as an integral part of the scene without altering her reports of the events mentioned during the first regression.

10   While she was in the trance, the therapist repeated the reassurances of the original therapeutic imagery as well as stroking her forehead and hand as he told her that she was protected. After trance was ended, she reported further reduction of her fear of dentistry. Several weeks later she underwent the extraction of two wisdom teeth and she reported no fear of the dentist

or the treatment. Over the last 2 years, she has followed through with cleaning and other forms of tooth restoration.

Discussion

11   The follow-up to this patient indicated that she was able to recall while in
trance the implanted event as an integral part of the memory of the original
event without awareness of the trauma of the original memory. That is, in
recalling the original event at the therapist's request while she was in trance,
she reproduced the original event with the implanted memory fully integrated as though it had always belonged there. The mnemonic prosthesis
seemed to have been fully assimilated into the original trace pattern, thereby
displacing the traumatic event with an event which seemed to elicit a sense
of safety which the recall of the original event could not elicit.

12   The change in behavior which occurred after the implantation of the
mnemonic prosthesis may in reality have been due to the patient's compli-
ance to the implied therapeutic expectations rather than to the quality of the
implanted memory. The improvement might also be a result of our having
helped to desensitize the patient to the troublesome aspects of the remembered event by introducing a calm and reassuring tone to the whole situation. It could also be argued that the authors helped to restructure her memory of the past by encouraging the creation of a warm and pleasant
confabulation involving an attentive and caring doctor. Whatever the true
explanation might be, it is of interest to speculate on the possible usefulness
of this technique. It is clearly more dramatic and likely to exert a greater
influence on the patient than the unembellished suggestion to relax. It is
thus more persuasive and apparently more effective.

13   The procedure just described required only two therapy sessions and two
follow-up inquiries. Hypnosis in situations such as this can be successfully
applied in the dentist's office for many situations which are related to adaptation to dental therapy. Such a strategy as employed with this study can
be applied by a professional dentist with appropriate recognized training in
hypnosis or in partnership with a trained psychotherapist.

14   The present authors recognize that patients with phobic configurations
such as the one discussed in this case report may present an insurmountable
problem to the dentist. The dentist may, as was done in this patient's interest, call upon the professional skills of a licensed psychologist for assistance
with the management of the patient's problem. It may not be an uncommon
experience for such professional liaisons to occur. This case study indicates
the potential interdisciplinary efforts which may occur when there is an en-
lightened approach to the wholistic treatment of the patient.

–Sheldon R. Baker and David Boaz

The title, supplemented by the introduction, gives you the what
and why: This is a case study on the use of hypnosis in dental treat-

ment, and it was undertaken to demonstrate that the use of psychological techniques can help people to feel better about having dentistry done. The section labeled "Case History" deals with the methodology, the how: the reassurance of the patient while in a hypnotic trance. In the discussion you find that the researcher discovered that the patient reacted positively to the experience and that the relevance of the study is the effectiveness of this kind of interdisciplinary treatment.

You will find that, like the natural sciences, most research reports in the social sciences are headed by an abstract, which provides a brief summary of the report.

Several words in this article are peculiar to the areas of science and psychology. It should not be necessary for you to know them to gain an overview of the article. However, to have a complete understanding of the details, you probably would need to learn their meanings. Your personal list of vocabulary words might include "abreaction" and "mnemonic prosthesis."

Critical Reading of History and the Social Sciences

As a critical reader in these fields, you will be judging the author's evidence. Did it prove what the author set out to prove? What assumptions about the reader's knowledge are made? Does the evidence lead to good conclusions based on sound arguments? Is it possible that the sources are biased? Where did the data come from? Does the argument rest on facts or opinion?

You need to know which kind of evidence is generally valid in which discipline. In history it is often the original text, like contemporary letters dealing with the event; in sociology and anthropology, usually interviews or systematic observation; in psychology, experiments and systematic observation; in economics, statistical data; in political science, texts and observed behavior. In each case the value and utility of the writing to the student in the field depend on the author's close observations and accurate reporting.

After your evaluation, your final task is to decide how this information is useful to you. How does it relate to your previous knowledge in this field and in other fields? What future use can you make of it? Does it help to prove a hypothesis of your own? When you put it with other information you have, can you predict what will happen in a certain situation?

Exercises

1. The following table has been taken from an economics textbook. Look at it carefully, read the accompanying text, and answer the following questions.

   What is the topic of this table?
   What is its key idea?
   What kind of income has increased to offset the decline in income from wages, salaries, and other labor?
   What are transfer payments?

Sources of Income

1   The money that households can spend comes mainly from income and from wealth accumulated in the past (savings). Money income is what individual household members earn when they sell services to business firms or governments. Table 5–3 shows the various sources of money income to households in the United States in 1952, 1962, 1972, and 1982. This table shows the percentage distribution of the income that individuals received after employers and governments had made various deductions from paychecks and after corporations had retained some company earnings before paying dividends.

2   The information in Table 5–3 suggests that changes have been taking place in the income sources of Americans. Household income that comes from running one's own business (proprietors'

TABLE 5-3   Personal Income by Source in the United States, 1952, 1962, 1972, 1982 (percentage distribution)

Type of Income	1952	1962	1972	1982
Wages, salaries, and other labor income	70.1	70.1	71.3	66.7
Proprietors' income	16.0	11.3	8.1	4.6
farm	5.6	2.8	2.0	0.7
nonfarm	10.4	8.5	6.1	3.9
Property income	10.4	13.3	13.2	18.4
rent (personal)	3.2	3.6	2.2	1.3
dividends	3.1	3.2	2.5	2.6
interest	4.1	6.5	8.5	14.5
Transfers, net	3.4	5.3	7.4	10.2
total	100.0	100.0	100.0	100.0

Note: Amounts may not add to total because of rounding.
Source: *Economic Report of the President, 1983*, Table B-22.

income) became less important than income from other sources over this period. Dividend and rent income also declined in importance. To earn income from these sources, people must take risks with their rental property or with shares of stock in corporations. The components of household income that grew more important were transfer payments (such as Social Security benefits, unemployment compensation, and welfare) and interest income. These sources about tripled in their relative importance to household money income.

–Martin Bronfenbrenner, Werner Sichel, and Wayland Gardner

2. The figure on page 314 has been taken from the same economics textbook. Look at it carefully, read the accompanying text, and answer the following questions.

   What is the topic of this figure?
   What is its key idea?
   Where does most of the money come from?
   What is the largest source of income for state and local governments?
   What relationship do you see between the state and federal income taxes?

3. The selection on page 315 is from a book on comparative government. Follow the instructions below for previewing, skimming, sectioning, and analyzing the selection. When you are finished, you may find it interesting to discuss your answers with a reading partner.
   a. Preview the whole selection and answer the preview questions below.
      (1) What is the passage about?
      (2) Do the authors state their purpose? If so, where?
      (3) Do you think the authors are writing to inform you, to persuade you, or both? What is the basis for your answer?
      (4) What question are the authors asking, and how do they intend to answer it?
      (5) How have the authors structured the text?
      (6) Make up and write down three questions to ask of the text.
   b. Skim the text, looking for the key idea and as much information as you can get.
   c. Section and title the selection.
   d. Analyze one of your sections, noting the supporting idea(s), supporting details, and pattern(s) of organization in the margin.

FIGURE 6-3   Receipts of National, State, and Local Governments in the United States, 1980 (percentage of total receipts)

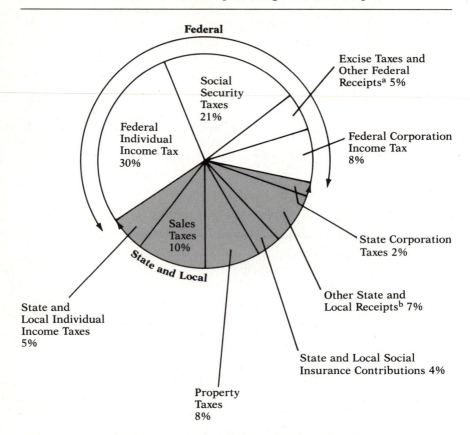

The federal government collects about two-thirds of total government receipts (as shown in the upper part of the circle), and state and local governments collect about one-third (as shown in the lower part). Individual income taxes and Social Security taxes are both assessed on individual earnings and total more than half of total government receipts. Some federal receipts are sent as grants-in-aid to state and local governments. Though they are not specifically shown on this chart, they amount to about 11 percent of total government receipts.

> —*Martin Bronfenbrenner, Werner Sichel, and Wayland Gardner*

a. Other federal receipts include estate and gift taxes, customs duties, and miscellaneous nontax receipts.

b. Other state and local receipts include fees and charges for services and miscellaneous nontax receipts.

Note: Amounts may not add to total because of rounding.

Source: *Survey of Current Business*, July 1982. Tables 3-2 and 3-3.

e. Write an evaluation of what you have read. The following questions will help you get started.
   (1) Did the authors prove what they set out to prove?
   (2) Do you think they have come to good conclusions based on sound arguments?
   (3) What kind of sources did the authors use for their data?
   (4) Where did they get their data? Do any of their sources seem more valid than others?
f. Working with a partner, apply the same exercise to a selection from one of your own history or social science textbooks.

A Politics of Countervailing Trends

1 We can now begin to see the basic paradox of France's political system. Its *political center*, as represented by the party system, is extremely weak. This has produced instability and unpredictable change. Yet the *government center*, as represented by the central administrative bureaucracy and other cohesive French elites, is remarkably strong. It has allowed France to ride out periodic bursts of instability, but it has also blocked reforms that could help France adapt to social and economic change. These countervailing forces, more than any others, are essential to our understanding of French politics. They are probably also decisive for the future of the Fifth Republic.

2 ***Social and Economic Change.*** During the 1950s the French economy began to grow at a faster rate than it had experienced for many years, and this growth continued during the 1960s and early 1970s. Some data for typical products are shown in Table 5.3.

3 The entire time spanned by the data in Table 5.3, 1909–76, [Pages 316–317] can be divided into three periods, corresponding to the political regimes of the Third, Fourth, and Fifth French Republics, respectively; and we can then compute for each period the rough rate of annual growth for the average of five indicators of industrial growth.

4 The results are a little surprising. Our first period, 1909–38, falls under the regime of the Third French Republic (1875–1940), and the rate of industrial growth averages about 7 percent per year. Our second period, 1948–59, falls under the Fourth Republic (1944–58), during which General de Gaulle held political power only briefly, as president from 1944 to 1947, but during which France benefited substantially from United States economic aid under the Marshall Plan and other programs, as well as from the efforts of the French people themselves at material reconstruction.

TABLE 5.3   Approximate Annual Averages of French Industrial Production, 1909–76

	1909–38 (during the Third Republic)			
	A	B	C	D Increase, ca. 1911–36
	1909–13	1925–29	1934–38	100(C − A)/A
Aluminum (thousand tons)	14	29	51	264% 10.6% per annum
Merchant marine (million tons)	2.3	3.3	2.9	26% 1.0% per annum
Automobiles (thousands)	45	254	227	404% 16.2% per annum
Electricity (billion kWh)	—	16	21	$\left(\begin{array}{c}31\%\\3.4\%\text{ per}\\\text{annum}\end{array}\right)$†
Steel (million tons)	5	10	6	20% 0.8% per annum
Average annual increase for the measures of industrial production				7.2%‡

Source: From data in R. C. Macridis, "France," in R. C. Macridis and R. E. Ward, eds., *Modern Political Systems: Europe*, 3rd ed., 1972, and 4th ed., 1978. Adapted by permission of Prentice-Hall, Inc., Englewood Cliffs, N.J.

*Because the time period covered by certain data overlaps the Fourth and Fifth Republics, these data are used for the computation of the percentage increase for both republics.

†Change 1925–29 to 1934–38 only.

‡Aluminum, merchant marine, automobiles, and steel only.

	1948–58 (during the Fourth Republic)			1958–70 (during the Fifth Republic)		1969–76 (Fifth Republic after de Gaulle)	
E	F*	G	H	I		J	K
		Increase, ca. 1950–57		Increase, ca. 1958–69			Increase, ca. 1969–76
1948–52	1955–59	$100(F-E)/E$	1967–70	$100(H-F)/F$		1975–76	$100(J-H)/I^H$
75	218	191% 27.3% per annum	371	70% 6.4% per annum		175	33% 4.6% per annum
2.7	4.5	67% 9.6% per annum	6.0	33% 3.0% per annum		8.5	56% 8.0% per annum
286	1,283	349% 49.9% per annum	2,100	64% 5.8% per annum		3,100	48% 6.9% per annum
41	70	71% 10.1% per annum	132	89% 8.1% per annum		680	83% 11.9% per annum
9	15	67% 9.6% per annum	23	53% 4.8% per annum		27	17% 2.4% per annum
		21.3%		5.6%			6.8%

During this period the average annual rate of increase in our industrial indicators was as high as 21 percent. This period, despite its political and military difficulties, seems to have been the time of the most rapid growth of industry and of basic productive equipment. The third period, 1959–70, after General de Gaulle's return to power, appears to have returned to a slower rate of growth in our industrial indicators, roughly 6 percent per year, but these increases now occurred on a much higher basis—a basis created in large part during the preceding period. This is largely a period under the political regime of the Fifth Republic, and much of it falls under the regime of General de Gaulle, who returned to the presidency for the years 1958–69. During this time President de Gaulle received credit not only for the preservation of national unity, the end of the Algerian War, and the promotion of French independence and prestige in world affairs, but also for the economic progress and modernization that actually were largely the fruits of the economic development that had taken place under his predecessors. After de Gaulle's retirement and death, French industry grew at nearly 7 percent per year, and the Gaullists continued to claim credit for the economic prosperity and growth that had materialized under his administration.

5   No matter who claims credit for the economic changes, they were a visible fact in the 1960s and 1970s. Their scale and their speed were beginning to change the social structure of France at a faster pace than ever before.

6   Each year during the late 1960s, about 1 percent of the French work force shifted out of agriculture and into nonagricultural occupations, and in 1971–75 this shift accelerated to 2 percent per year. By 1975, persons employed in agriculture accounted for only 10 percent of registered voters. A similar shift has been under way from the countryside to the big cities. By 1975, as many as 44 percent of French voters were living in cities of over 100,000 inhabitants, including the Paris agglomeration, where 16 percent of the French people are now concentrated. Another 18 percent of the French now live in cities of between 10,000 and 100,000 inhabitants, and still another 10 percent live in small towns with populations between 2,000 and 10,000—so the French are now altogether a 73 percent urban people. The shift to the cities is continuing, perhaps at a rate of 0.6 percent per year, and small country towns and middle-sized cities are moving toward the next higher classes of population size.[1]

---

[1]From data in "Données sociales: Édition 1978," *Les Collections de INSEE* (Paris: Institut National de la Statistique et des Études Économiques, 1978), p. 8.

7   The increases in the share of the residents of big cities, of persons in nonagricultural occupations, and in the general level of education and exposure to mass media should tend toward increasing the share of change-oriented voters in the electorate. Some other trends, however, may work in the opposite direction. Persons in comfortable white-collar and professional occupations are not generally considered to be oriented toward social and political change. The growing share of white-collar employees and professional people in the French electorate is now 22 percent; together with the 9 percent self-employed *patrons* of nonagricultural enterprises—to whom they are linked through many social conventions, habits, and associations, as well as often through ties of family or neighborhood—they total 32 percent of the electorate, just about equal to the share of workers. In another five or ten years this white-collar and professional share is likely to be larger, easily outweighing any shrinkage that might occur during the same period among the self-employed.

8   Another trend is also at work to reduce the proportion of workers among the French electorate. It is the tendency to employ foreign workers in many occupations requiring heavy, boring, or ill-paid work, both in manufacturing and in the service trades. For these jobs, increasingly unpopular with French workers, foreign workers are imported from Spain, Portugal, and the Arab countries and to some extent from black Africa, so that some factories and some working-class neighborhoods are taking on a new look. There are about 3 million foreigners in France, and perhaps 2 million of these may be working for wages. They are accepted as members by the labor unions, but, being foreigners, they cannot vote. In effect, this might mean that of, say, 12 million workers in France, only 10 million are defined as "French" and have the right to vote—or that about one-sixth of the real industrial work force of the country is in effect disfranchised. Yet even if they cannot vote, they and their next generation can cause trouble. Since no one at present seems to be making any major effort to let these people share in French life, this development may continue to weaken the influence of labor and of parties oriented toward promoting peaceful social change.

9   Other economic trends also cut in different directions. Factors that favored at least a measure of social conservatism were the doubling of real wages from 1955 to 1975 and the rapid diffusion of durable consumer goods and higher living standards. In 1974 as many as 63 percent of French householders owned automobiles, as opposed to only 14 percent a quarter century earlier. Television sets already were in 82 percent of French households, and 88 percent had refrigerators: washing machines were found in 69

percent. Many French families now may feel that they have more to lose than was the case in earlier decades. Yet, having achieved high standards of material growth, more people may become frustrated when that growth is not sustained or proves unsatisfying in terms of the quality of their lives. Both these phenomena occurred during the 1970s.

10   To cope with these social and economic crosscurrents, there are three elements of stability—indeed rigidity—in French politics: a tight set of elites, a powerful bureaucracy, and a constantly fragmented party system. Let us consider each in turn.

11   **A Cohesive Ruling Class.**   The "directing class" (which to a large extent is the ruling class in France)—less than the top 1 percent of the population on a scale of power over the lives of others—has remained remarkably cohesive. Excluding all writers, artists, scholars, and members of the free professions from *Who's Who in France*—that is, all those persons of note who do *not* hold positions of economic, political, administrative, or military power—a team of French sociologists compared large samples of the rest, the power holders in France, for 1954, 1964, and 1974.[2] The power holders are an elite primarily by virtue of the positions they hold and not necessarily by any special talents demonstrated in competition with newcomers from other social groups, for they are themselves a tightly knit social group, closed in on itself. They are recruited from the same social setting, from among the same social class, which almost no outsiders penetrate. Consequently, the children possess the same social characteristics as their parents; in some cases they simply change their professions or their sectors.

12   Within this ruling group there are of course subgroups, such as the "five *great corps of the state*." Similarly, the head of a great industrial enterprise may take a somewhat different view of particular problems than a less profit-oriented top civil servant in the Diplomatic Service. But all such differences are only variations on a larger theme: the underlying social unity and remarkable stability of a single, dominant set of persons at the commanding heights of French political, economic, and social life.[3]

13   Two cartoons sum up the situation. Whereas in earlier times three persons were playing at the poker table—a general, a frock-

[2]Pierre Birnbaum et al., *La Classe dirigeante française* (Paris: Presses Universitaires de France, 1978). All data in this section are from this study.

[3]Ezra N. Suleiman, "Self-Image, Legitimacy and the Stability of Elites: The Case of France," *British Journal of Political Science*, vol. 7, 1977, pp. 191–215.

coated financier, and a dark-suited technocrat—now there is a single person standing before a mirror. Which of his three suits—general's uniform, banker's coat, or technical expert's suit—shall he put on next?

14   It follows that the French state is not simply dominated by big business, nor does it rule business as an impartial arbiter. Rather, the different sectors are held together by the uninterrupted circulation of the directing personnel from one position to another, assuring the cohesion of the whole directing class; and this top class, according to the sociologists' study, has been increasing its social distance from the rest of French society.

15   Within this persistent basic pattern there have been some limited changes. The proportion of *patrons*—that is, owner-managers—has been declining; that of salaried managers, strongly increasing. Many of these managers, however, are sons or daughters of *patrons*, who later succeed to the ownership of the family firm; others remain managers by profession. Still other managers are former *patrons* who have become presidents or directors-general, as well as stockholders, of their enterprises after a juridical and financial merger or reorganization. A growing number of high officials and managers of public enterprises move up during later stages in their careers into high positions in the private sector, as do many of the military. The increasing demand for highly competent and technically skilled managers throughout the private sector continues to foster this mobility of top personnel from the public into the private sector. Altogether, these developments have produced an elite of decision makers who are more favorable to technological innovation, but not necessarily to social, economic, and political reform.

16   ***A Lasting Reality: The Civil Service.***   Death and taxes are inevitable, goes an old saying. And, since the rise of modern tax-collecting states, with the taxes come the officials to collect them and to administer their disbursement. Three figures indicate the importance of the French bureaucracy: about 40 percent of the French gross national product passes through the public sector; about 2.4 million people are employed there; and about 10,000 take part in formulating policy and directing its execution.[4]

17   French administration is organized, like the British, under ministries. The most important of these are the Ministry of the Interior, the Ministry of Finances, and the Ministry of Foreign Affairs. The Ministry of the Interior is in charge of the police and of all

---

[4]Macridis, "Politics of France," p. 128.

general administration throughout the country, including all departmental and local units of government. It appoints, transfers, and can remove by secret decision and at will the key official in charge of the administration of each of the ninety departments: the *prefect*. The *Corps of Prefects* forms one of the five great corps—*les grands corps*—of the French state. In 1978 a group of several hundred provincial *notables*—or prominent citizens—were asked, "Who exercises power in the province?" Almost all of them answered, "The prefect." . . .

18   The mayor—*le maire*—of any of the 36,000 French communes is elected, but then must represent not only that municipality, but also the state. The mayor's decisions regarding the local budget and local taxation must be approved by the prefect; in some other matters the prefect can order the mayor to act in certain ways. If the latter fails to obey, he or she may be suspended or dismissed by an executive order of the prefect. This *tutelage* of the central government over all municipal authorities ensures a high degree of uniformity of administration throughout France. The powers of the elected General Council of each department are much weaker: the centralized and bureaucratic chain of command prevails.[5]

19   The second key ministry, that of finance, has a similar centralizing function. It prepares the budget, draws up estimates, collects taxes, and to some extent controls spending. Working within it, but often reaching beyond its boundaries by its actions, is the *General Inspection of Finances*, another of the great corps of the state. It attracts many of the ablest candidates, as its officials do not merely inspect tax collections and expenditures; they actually take part in drawing up many kinds of legislation. Many of them eventually move on to higher office elsewhere; some are "detached" for service with other governmental agencies without losing their connection with the General Inspection.

20   The third key ministry is that of foreign affairs. The diplomats working under its direction form another of the great corps of the state.

21   Three other bureaucratic agencies are counted among the great corps, the most important of these being the *Council of State*. Since the days of Napoleon, this body, containing its own hierarchy of about two hundred high-level officials and a larger number of lower-ranking ones, has had two functions: first, to advise the head of the state and/or the government on matters of public policy and legislation and, second, to resolve conflicts within the administration. Over time, this second task has made the Council

---

[5]Ibid.

of State a quasi-judicial body, and it has played an important part in offering citizens a recourse against arbitrary bureaucratic acts.

22   Another great body is the *Court of Accounts*. Its members, like judges, cannot be removed from their positions; otherwise, it functions as part of the administrative machinery, not of the judiciary. The fifth great body is the *Diplomatic Service*. And, finally, the *Supreme Administrative Court—la cour de cassation—*is sometimes considered a sixth great body. It has final power to confirm or annul the decisions of administrative agencies.

23   The recruitment of all these high civil servants is remarkably uniform. Most of them, perhaps 90 percent, come from the upper-middle and middle classes. Many are the children of civil servants. Their main channel of entry is through the great schools, chiefly the *École Nationale d'Administration*. Access to these schools requires stiff competitive written examinations; similar skills are indispensable for graduating with the necessary high rank in class; and middle-class children almost exclusively have the educational background for such performance. The result is a proud and competent top-level bureaucracy, open in theory, but largely closed in fact.

24   To a great extent this bureaucracy is permanent. Civil servants generally are secure in their jobs and careers. Ministers come and go, but civil servants remain, unless those of high rank choose the option of *pantouflage,* or the "putting on of bedroom slippers"— that is, lucrative high-level employment in the private sector. Here the permanence of the civil service shades into the remarkable persistence of the larger French managerial and ruling class. The civil service, the army, and the larger ruling elite form a heavy counterweight to the changing contest among the political parties of the *right, left,* and *center* that has been moving France this way and that during nearly two centuries.

25   ***Another Enduring Reality: A Fragmented Party System.*** In the United States and Britain the main constitutional arrangements are older than the parties. In France most of the parties are older than its several constitutions. The fundamental political divisions go back to the Revolution of 1789. Those French people who favored and accepted that revolution and the separation of church and state formed the left of the political spectrum: those whose sympathies lay with the monarchy and the unity of church and state formed the political right. The original terms "left" and "right" derive from the seating order of deputies in a past French legislature—a seating order that later became customary in many European parliaments. In the course of time the terms have acquired other connotations. Parties on the left tend to favor workers

and the poor as well as political and social change—by radical and revolutionary methods if they are far to the left and by more moderate reforms if they are closer to the center. Parties on the right tend to favor tradition, property, and privilege as well as the interests of the well-to-do and of substantial citizens in town and countryside. Parties in the center usually seek compromises between these wings and are often paralyzed by immobilism and attacked by both sides.

26   In France a whole imagery has grown up around the unremitting contest between left and right. "Left is where the heart is," states a French saying: the right is seen as the side closest to the pocketbook. But although these general political tendencies seem perennial in France, issues and problems do change. New policies must be devised to cope with them and new coalitions formed to put these policies to work. In 1946, after World War II, 46 percent of all registered French voters cast their votes for parties of the left, 20 percent for parties of the center, 10 percent for parties of the right, and nearly 24 percent did not vote at all. By the second round of voting in 1978 the left had 48 percent of the vote; the old center had split, one group joining the coalition of the left (2 percent) while most of the rest merged with the government coalition. President Giscard's center-right *Union for Democratic France (UDF)*, which also included most of the former Conservative Independent candidates, won the support of 23 percent of the voters. Further to the right, but still moderate, the newly renamed Gaullist Party (RPR) had risen to collect 26 percent of the electorate. The extreme right declined to 3 percent and the nonvoters to 18 percent. Still another 1.5 percent of the votes cast was provided by scattered minor allies of the government coalition, totaling about 51 percent of the votes cast, enough to win a majority of seats in the Assembly.

27   For a long time the strongest group on the left was the Communist Party. Their main support comes from workers, and, to a lesser extent, from intellectuals, white-collar workers, and even some peasants. From 1920 to 1967 they were stronger than the Socialists. Nowadays they represent nearly a fifth of all eligible French voters and nearly a fourth of those who actually vote. Since 1968 the Socialists have been stronger than the Communists. They have lost much of their former following among manual workers and now get most of their support from public officials, teachers, and other white-collar groups, whose share in the work force is expanding.

28   More moderate than the Communists or Socialists have been a bewildering array of parties that have tried to occupy the political center. They have split, regrouped, renamed themselves, and

sometimes disappeared as they have tried to steer a generally reformist course between antiparliamentary conservatives and revolutionary supporters of republicanism. The oldest of these parties (dating to 1901) are the Radical Socialists. Until recently these centrists have generally allied themselves with the left for electoral purposes and with the right for purposes of parliamentary maneuvering. A small pro-European Christian Democratic Party has taken over from a once-powerful moderate Catholic Party in recent years, while other parties and factions have developed sources of strength at the local level if not nationally. Perhaps the most important point is that by the late 1970s, the distinctions among all these centrist parties at a national electoral level were tending to become obliterated under the overarching political family of Giscard's UDF. In effect, most centrist voters had moved to the moderate right. One new "nonpolitical" center party, the Ecologists, received 3 percent of the votes in the first round of voting in 1978, but lost almost all its voters to the right and left coalitions in the decisive second round.

29   To the right are those French citizens who oppose welfare legislation and nonmilitary public spending. Still further to the right are those who have never fully accepted the Revolution of 1789 and the republics that followed from it. Here one finds some of the remnants of the French nobility, many officers' families, monarchists, and the more tradition-minded Catholics who found the reformist center too liberal. The candidates they vote for are often called Independents. In recent years the Gaullist Party in coalition with the Independents has brought many of these voters back toward the political center and to support of the Fifth Republic, which embodies Gaullist policies. By 1978 most of them had been absorbed into the Gaullist Party (RPR) under Jacques Chirac or, at least, into the progovernment majority. In addition, French individualism has produced a multitude of political splinter groups that often disappear after one or two elections and are usually negligible in size. Sometimes, however, these groups have managed to catch the political mood of the moment sufficiently to disrupt and further fragment the relationship among larger parties. They may do so again in the future.

30   The interaction between change and rigidity suggests that the dynamics of French politics are neither simple nor likely to be found moving in one direction. Political developments in recent years confirm the idea of crosscurrents, with the president in the middle.

–Karl W. Deutsch, Jorge I. Dominguez, and Hugh Heclo

Appendix:
Additional
Readings

This unit contains seventeen readings that are available as supplements to the chapters of *Active Reading*. They allow you to measure your progress in applying the principles of the course and give you practice in reading for comprehension. They can also be used as timed readings to measure your reading rate.

The readings have been chosen from a wide variety of sources. However, they are all the kind of reading you may find or be asked to do in college courses. Each reading is followed by ten comprehension questions. The first five questions for each reading follow in sequence the principles you are learning in the course. Therefore, if you continually miss the question with the same number, you can diagnose where your need for review and practice lies.

You should be aware of a few pitfalls as you practice becoming a more efficient reader.

- Reading too slowly. As a good reader, you adapt your pace to the material. If you read slower than the material warrants, you become bored. Your mind has time to be distracted. You can avoid this pitfall by using questioning and predicting to push yourself on.
- Reading too fast. Check yourself as you read to make sure you are aware of the sections and subtopics of your reading. Also remind yourself about how much detail you need for that particular reading task. Remember, your goal is to read as fast as possible, but with understanding.
- Reading carelessly. An active reader stays on the track by constantly questioning the text. Questioning ties you to the material and ensures that you find the evidence because you are looking for the support that authors provide for their ideas.

- Failing to discriminate the important from the unimportant. An awareness of the distinctions among key ideas, supporting ideas, and supporting details avoids the danger of getting lost in the details and thus missing the relevant connections.
- Substituting your own thoughts for those of the author. It is wise to ask yourself regularly, when you have made a tentative conclusion, where exactly does the author say or imply this? What is the supporting evidence? Otherwise, you may fall into the trap of drawing false conclusions based on what you think the author should have said rather than on what actually is said.

Active Reading is not intended to be a course in speed reading. However, we believe that as you learn how to be a more efficient reader, you will also appreciably increase your reading rate. Taking these tests as you go through the course should prove that this is so. You may find, however, that your improvement in speed and comprehension is somewhat erratic, exhibiting major leaps forward as you apply new principles and then plateaus as you consolidate your new habits.

Part of learning how to read faster is to be very conscious of your desire to read faster. You can benefit from forcing yourself to keep moving ahead. You should dare to read a little faster than you think is comfortable to see how much you take in and understand and then dare to keep pushing yourself a bit more and a bit more, remembering always that you are ultimately the best judge of the speed at which you can or should read. If your comprehension score consistently rides above 80 percent (each of the ten questions represents 10 percent), you can risk reading faster. If, on the other hand, you have trouble getting a comprehension score above 60 percent, try slowing down for a while.

Enjoy the readings. No doubt you have noticed your increased confidence in your approach to reading and the effect that your new skills have had on your course work. You can chart your progress on the graph found on pages 450–451. Graphing your improvement allows you actually to see the progress you are making as you become a more efficient and faster reader.

Don't forget to preview.

1. **The Missing Link**

Loren Eiseley

1   "The greatest prize of all," once confessed the British plant explorer F. Kingdon Ward, "is the skull of primitive man." Ward forgot one thing: there are other clues to primitive men than those confined to skulls. The bones of fossil men are few because the earth tolerated them in scant numbers. We call them missing links on the road to ourselves. A little less tooth here, a little more brain there, and you can see them changing toward ourselves in that long historyless time when the great continental ice sheets ebbed and flowed across the northern continents. Like all the students of that age, I wanted to find a missing link in human history. That is what this record is about, for I stumbled on the track of one.

2   Some men would maintain that a vague thing called atmosphere accounts for such an episode as I am about to relate, that there are houses that demand a murder and wait patiently until the murderer and his victim arrive, that there are great cliffs that draw the potential suicide from afar or mountains of so austere a nature that they write their message on the face of a man who looks up at them. This all may be. I do not deny it. But when I encountered the footprint in the mud of that remote place I think the thing that terrified me most was the fact that I knew to whom it belonged and yet I did not want to know him. He was a stranger to me and remains so to this day. Because of a certain knowledge I had, however, he succeeded in impressing himself upon me in a most insidious manner. I have never been the same since the event took place, and often at night I start up sweating and think uncannily that the creature is there with me in the dark. If the sense of his presence grows, I switch on the light, but I never look in the mirror. This is a matter of old habit with me.

3   First off, though, we must get straight what we mean by a missing link.

4   A missing link is a day in the life of a species that is changing its form and habits, just as, on a smaller scale, one's appearance and behavior at the age of five are a link in one's development to an adult man or woman. The individual person may have changed and grown, but still the boy or girl of many years ago is linked to the present by a long series of steps. And if one is really alive and not already a living fossil, one will go on changing till the end of one's life and perhaps be the better for it. The term "missing link" was coined because some of the physical links in the history of man as a species are lost, and those people who, like myself, are curious about the past look for them.

5   My album is the earth, and the pictures in it are faded and badly torn and have to be pieced together by detective work. If one thinks of oneself at five years of age, one may get a thin wisp of disconnected memory pictures. By contrast, the past of a living species is without memory except as that past has written its physical record in vestigial organs like the appendix or a certain pattern on our molar teeth. To eke out what those physical stigmata tell us, we have to go grubbing about in caves and gravel for the bones of very ancient men. If one can conceive of the trouble an archaeologist might have in locating one's remains a half-million years from now, supposing they still existed, one will get an idea of the difficulties involved in finding traces of man before his bones were crowded together in cities and cemeteries.

6   I was wandering inland along a sunken shore when the thing happened—the thing I had dreamed of so long. In other words, I got a clue to man. The beaches on that coast I had come to visit are treacherous and sandy and the tides are always shifting things about among the mangrove roots. It is not a place to which I would willingly return and you will get no bearings from me. Anyway, what it was I found there could be discovered on any man's coast if he looked sharp for it. I had come to that place with other things in mind, and a notion of being alone. I was tired. I wanted to lie in the sun or clamber about like an animal in the swamps and the forest. To secure such rest from the turmoil of a modern city is the most difficult thing in the world to accomplish and I have only achieved it twice: once in one of the most absolute deserts in the world and again in this tropical marsh.

7   By day and night strange forms of life scuttled and gurgled underfoot or oozed wetly along outthrust branches; luminous tropical insects blundered by in the dark like the lamps of hesitant burglars. Overhead, on higher ground, another life shrieked distantly or was expectantly still in the treetops. Somehow, alone as I was, I got to listening as if all that world were listening, waiting for something to happen. The trees drooped a little lower listening, the tide lurked and hesitated on the beach, and even a tree snake dropped a loop and hung with his face behind a spider web, immobile in the still air.

8   A world like that is not really natural, or (the thought strikes one later) perhaps it really is, only more so. Parts of it are neither land nor sea and so everything is moving from one element to another, wearing uneasily the queer transitional bodies that life adopts in such places. Fish, some of them, come out and breathe air and sit about watching you. Plants take to eating insects, mammals go back to the water and grow elongate like fish, crabs climb trees. Nothing stays put where it began because everything is constantly climbing in, or climbing out, of its unstable environment.

9   Along drowned coasts of this variety you only see, in a sort of

speeded-up way, what is true of the whole world and everything upon it: the Darwinian world of passage, of missing links, of beetles with soldered, flightless wings, of snakes with vestigial feet dragging slowly through the underbrush. Everything is marred and maimed and slightly out of focus—everything in the world. As for man, he is no different from the rest. His back aches, he ruptures easily, his women have difficulties in childbirth—all because he has struggled up upon his hind legs without having achieved a perfect adjustment to his new posture.

10   On this particular afternoon, I came upon a swamp full of huge waterlilies where I had once before ventured. The wind had begun to rise and rain was falling at intervals. As far as I could see, giant green leaves velvetly impervious to water were rolling and twisting in the wind. It was a species of lily in which part of the leaves projected on stalks for a short distance above the water, and as they rolled and tossed the whole swamp flashed and quivered from the innumerable water drops that were rolling around and around like quicksilver in the great cupped leaves. Everything seemed flickering and changing as if in some gigantic illusion, but so soft was the green light and so delicate the brushing of the leaves against each other that the whole effect was quite restful, as though one could be assured that nothing was actually tangible or real and no one in his senses would want it to be, as long as he could sway and nod and roll reflecting water drops about over the surface of his brain.

11   Just as I finally turned away to climb a little ridge I found the first footprint. It was in a patch of damp, exposed mud and was pointed away from the water as though the creature had emerged directly out of the swamp and was heading up the shore toward the interior. I had thought I was alone, and in that place it was wise to know one's neighbors. Worst of all, as I stood studying the footprint, and then another, still heading up the little rise, it struck me that though un-doubtedly human the prints were different in some indefinable way. I will tell you once more that this happened on the coast of another country in a place where form itself is an illusion and no shape of man or beast is totally impossible. I crouched anxiously in the mud while all about the great leaves continued to rotate on their stems and to flash their endlessly rolling jewels.

12   But there were these footprints. They did not disappear. As I fixed the lowermost footprint with every iota of scientific attention I could muster, it became increasingly apparent that I was dealing with some transitional form of man. The arch, as revealed in the soft mud, was low and flat and implied to the skilled eye an inadequate adjust-ment to the upright posture. This, in its turn, suggested certain things about the spine and the nature of the skull. It was only then, I think, that the full import of my discovery came to me.

13   Good Lord, I thought consciously for the first time, the thing is alive. I had spent so many years analyzing the bones of past ages or brooding over lizard tracks turned to stone in remote epochs that I had never contemplated this possibility before. The thing was alive and it was human. I looked uneasily about before settling down into the mud once more. One could make out that the prints were big but what drew my fascinated eye from the first was the nature of the second toe. It was longer than the big toe, and as I crawled excitedly back and forth between the two wet prints in the open mud, I saw that there was a remaining hint of prehensile flexibility about them.

14   Most decidedly, as a means of ground locomotion this foot was transitional and imperfect. Its loose, splayed aspect suggested inadequate protection against sprains. That second toe was unnecessarily long for life on the ground, although the little toe was already approximating the rudimentary condition so characteristic of modern man. Could it be that I was dealing with an unreported living fossil, an archaic ancestral survival? What else could be walking the mangrove jungle with a foot that betrayed clearly the marks of ancient intimacy with the arboreal attic, an intimacy so long continued that now, after hundreds of thousands of years of ground life, the creature had squiggled his unnecessarily long toes about in the mud as though an opportunity to clutch at something had delighted his secret soul.

15   I crouched by the footprint and thought. I remembered that comparisons with the living fauna, whenever available, are good scientific procedure and a great aid to precise taxonomy. I sat down and took off my shoes.

16   I had never had much occasion to look critically at my own feet before. In modern man they are generally encased in shoes—something that still suggests a slight imperfection in our adaptations. After all, we don't normally find it necessary to go about with our hands constantly enclosed in gloves. As I sat contemplating and comparing my feet with the footprints, a faintly disturbing memory floated hazily across my mind. It had involved a swimming party many years before at the home of one of the most distinguished comparative anatomists in the world. As we had sat on the bench alongside his pool, I had glanced up suddenly and caught him staring with what had seemed unnecessary fascination at my feet. I remembered now that he had blushed a deep pink under his white hair and had diverted my inquiring glance deftly to the scenery about us.

17   Why I should have remembered the incident at all was unclear to me. I thought of the possibility of getting plaster casts of a footprint, and I also debated whether I should attempt to trail the creature farther up the slope toward which he appeared to have been headed. It was no moment for hesitation. Still, I did hesitate. The uneasy memory grew stronger, and a thought finally struck me. A little sheepishly and with a glance around to see that I was not observed, I lowered my own muddy foot into the footprint. It fitted.

18   I stood there contemplatively clutching, but this time consciously, the mud in my naked toes. I was the dark being on that island shore whose body carried the marks of its strange passage. I was my own dogging Man Friday, the beast from the past who had come with weapons through the marsh. The wind had died and the great green leaves with their rolling jewels were still. The mistake I had made was the mistake of all of us.

19   The story of man was not all there behind us in the caves of remote epochs. Even our physical bodies gave evidence that the change was not completed. As for our minds, they were still odd compounds of beast and saint. But it was not by turning back toward the marsh out of which we had come that the truly human kingdom was to be possessed and entered—that kingdom dreamed of in many religions and spoken of in many barbarous tongues. A philosopher once said in my presence. "The universe is a series of leaping sparks—everything else is interpretation." But what, I hesitated, was man's interpretation to be?

20   I drew a foot out of the little steaming swamp that sucked at it. The air hung heavily about me. I listened as the first beast might have listened who came from the water up the shore and did not return again to his old element. Everything about me listened in turn and seemed to be waiting for some decision on my part. I swayed a moment on my unstable footing.

21   Then, warily, I stepped higher up the shore and let the water and the silt fill in that footprint to make it, a hundred million years away, a fossil sign of an unknown creature slipping from the shadows of a marsh toward something else that awaited him. I had found the missing link. He walked on misshapen feet. The stones hurt him and his belly sagged. There were dreams like Christmas ornaments in his head, intermingled with an ancient malevolent viciousness. I knew because I was the missing link, but for the first time I sensed where I was going.

22   I have said I never look into the mirror. It is a matter of old habit now. If that other presence grows too oppressive I light the light and read.   *2,563 words*

Comprehension Questions

1. This article might be assigned reading for a course in
   a. archaeology.
   b. philosophy.
   c. critical thinking.
   d. *all of the above*

2. The author would probably argue that
   a. a scientist's first impressions are always true.
   b. the evolution of human beings is complete.
   c. many people mistakenly ignore self-analysis as a source of information.
   d. physical evidence of evolution is irrefutable.
3. _____ is a subtopic.
   a. Missing links
   b. Finding footprints
   c. The marsh
   d. Evolution
4. The phrase "I came upon a swamp full of huge waterlilies where I had once before ventured" (paragraph 10)
   a. helps paint a picture of the scene.
   b. could be easily skipped over.
   c. contains information essential to understanding the rest of the essay.
   d. detracts from the author's main point.
5. The effect of humans' imperfect adjustment to an upright posture is
   a. backaches.
   b. easy ruptures.
   c. childbirth difficulties.
   d. *all of the above*
6. Eiseley's purpose is to
   a. educate the reader about evolution.
   b. describe his vacation.
   c. explore the connection between preconceptions and mistaken conclusions.
   d. explain the significance of footprints.
7. The descriptive details about the animals and plants in the tropical marsh
   a. are crucial facts supporting the author's main idea.
   b. are irrelevant and confusing.
   c. are examples of missing links.
   d. help convey the author's state of mind while in the marsh.
8. "Physical stigmata" (paragraph 5) means
   a. a telltale sign.
   b. an embarrassing defect.
   c. a diseased organ.
   d. *none of the above*
9. When the author refers to the earth as his album and archaeological evidence as faded and torn pictures, he is using the technique of
   a. example.
   b. analogy.

    c. satire.

    d. repetition.

10. Eiseley took off his shoe

    a. to confirm his suspicion that he had made the footprint during his previous visit.

    b. to compare and contrast the known with the unknown.

    c. because it is good scientific procedure to analyze all evidence from a personal point of view.

    d. so he could track the animal through the mud.

2. **The Intimate Machine**

Sherry Turkle

1   It is summer. Robert, seven, is part of a play group at the beach. I have been visiting the group every day. I bring a carton filled with small computer toys and games and a tape recorder to capture the children's reactions as they meet these toys. Robert is playing with Merlin, a computer toy that plays tic-tac-toe. Robert's friend Craig has shown him how to "beat" Merlin. There is a trick: Merlin follows an optimal strategy most of the time, and if neither player makes a bad move, every game will end in a draw. But Merlin is programmed to make a slip every once in a while. Children discover a strategy that will allow them to win, but then when they try it a second time, it usually doesn't work. The machine gives the impression of not being dumb enough to let down its defenses twice. Robert has watched Craig perform the "winning trick" and now he wants to try it himself. He plays his part perfectly but on this round Merlin, too, plays a perfect game, which leads to a draw. Robert accuses the toy of cheating. Children are used to machines being predictable. But this is a machine that surprises.

2   Robert throws Merlin into the sand in anger and frustration. "Cheater. I hope your brains break." He is overheard by Craig and by Greg, aged six and eight, who sense that this may be a good moment to reclaim Merlin for themselves. They salvage the by now very sandy toy and take it upon themselves to set Robert straight.

3   "Merlin doesn't know if it cheats. It doesn't know if you break it, Robert. It's not alive," says Craig.

4   "Someone taught Merlin to play. But he doesn't know if he wins or loses," says Greg.

5   "Yes, he does know if he loses," Robert says. "He makes different noises."

6   "No, stupid. It's smart enough to make the right kinds of noises," Greg says. "But it doesn't really know if it loses. That's how you cheat it. It doesn't know you are cheating."

7   The conversation is over. I found it a striking scene. Children stand in the surf amid their shoreline sandcastles and argue the moral and metaphysical status of a machine on the basis of its psychology: Does the machine know what it is doing? Does it have intentions, consciousness, feelings?

8   What is important is not the yes or no of whether children think computers cheat or even whether computers are alive. What is important is the conversation, both psychological and philosophical, that the object evokes.

9   It was Jean Piaget who discovered the child as a metaphysician. Beginning in the 1920s, Piaget studied children's emerging understandings of causality, life, and consciousness. Why does the stone roll down the slope? "To get to the bottom," says the young child, as if the rock had its own desires. In time the child learns the stone falls because of gravity; intentions have nothing to do with it. And so a dichotomy is constructed: Physical and psychological properties stand opposed to one another in two great systems. The physical is used to understand things, the psychological to understand people and animals. But the computer is a new kind of object, psychological, yet a thing.

10   Marginal objects, objects with no clear place, play important roles. On the line between categories, they draw attention to how we have drawn the lines. Sometimes they incite us to reaffirm the lines, sometimes to call them into question. They are the growing point for new learning, new theory building. Computers, as marginal objects on the boundary between the physical and the psychological, force thinking about matter, life, and mind.

11   Marginal objects are not neutral. Sit silently and watch children pulling the wings off butterflies. They are not simply thoughtless or cruel. They are not playing with butterflies as much as with their evolving ideas, fears, and fantasies about life and death, about what is allowed and not allowed, about what can be controlled and what is beyond control.

12   Laura is six years old. I have interviewed several other six-year-olds from her neighborhood in. . . . Most of them seem streetwise. Laura is an innocent. She watches very little television, some *Sesame Street* and her favorite, *Mr. Rogers' Neighborhood*, which she likes because "there is magic and Mr. Rogers is very kind." She has no mechanical toys, "nothing that winds up or has batteries," she tells me, "just dolls and storybooks."

13   Laura begins her play session calmly. She quickly checks out the toys and forms definite opinions. The toys have "minds," says Laura, but they are not alive because "they don't have a brain." When I ask Laura if her alarm clock "remembers" when to wake her up, she is firm about the answer. "No, you set it. And then it does it. But not by itself."

14   As Laura plays, she becomes less composed. Merlin's "tic-tac-toe mind" turns out to be a formidable opponent. "How does he win so much? It tries to make me lose." Laura is completely engrossed. She doesn't look up. My presence is forgotten. I ask her if she thinks Merlin could lose if it made a mistake. Her "yes" is almost inaudible. She is not sure at all. Laura begins to turn Merlin off between games, a ritual whose intent seems to be to weaken the toy. Her efforts are in

vain; Merlin continues to win. After five minutes of this frustration, she puts Merlin aside and picks up Speak and Spell, a toy that can talk. Laura spells out her name on its keyboard. The toy obediently calls out the letters and displays them on a small screen: L-A-U-R-A. She seems satisfied and relaxes. This is going to be more reassuring than Merlin. Then Laura puts Speak and Spell into "Say it" mode. This is designed for younger children who, like Laura, may not be able to spell much more then their names. In "Say it" mode the machine calls out the phrase "SAY IT" followed by one of the words in its several-hundred-word vocabulary. And the child is given time to repeat the word before being offered another.

15   Speak and Spell is designed so that you can turn it off at will. But the first version of Speak and Spell on the American market has a bug, a programming mistake. You can't turn it off while it is in its "Say it" mode. This mode offers 10 "Say it" commands, and it brooks no interruption until the presentation of the 10 words is finished. You cannot change modes, and you cannot turn the toy off.

16   The uninterruptible cycle takes long enough so that within the first few sessions with Speak and Spell most children try to turn it off while it is in "Say it" mode and discover they cannot. In a small way, they are meeting a situation that is at the heart of almost every science fiction movie ever made about a computer. It is the story of the machine out of control. As far as the child can tell, this machine has developed a mind its own.

17   Halfway through the cycle, Laura wants to turn "Say it" off and get back to spelling her name. She presses the off button. She persists, pressing it again and again, then trying several other buttons. "Why isn't this thing coming off?" She tries four or five buttons in a row, then all of them at once. Now Laura is panicked. She puts one of her hands on as many buttons as it will cover. She tries both of her hands. The machine goes on until it is done. Laura is quite upset.

18   When Paul, seven, discovers the "Say it" bug, he is startled, but he doesn't say anything. His first reaction is to put Speak and Spell on the ground. Then, kneeling above the toy but keeping some distance, he presses "Say it" again. He presses all its buttons in turn and then uses the palms of his hands, trying to press all its buttons at the same time, trying to make it stop. The toy remains unobedient, but when its 10 words have come to an end it stops unexpectedly. Paul puts the Speak and Spell in "Say it" mode again, but this time, just as it is demanding its fourth word, Paul turns it over, opens its back cover, and removes its batteries. Paul has found the way to pull the plug. A group of children gather round and take turns doing Paul's trick. They put the toy in "Say it" mode and then take out the batteries, shrieking their delight about "killing the Speak and Spell." They al-

low the toy its autonomous behavior and then, when it is like a living thing, kill it.

19   Speak and Spell in its "Say it" mode is on the border. It is not alive but seems to act willfully, of its own accord. It can be an occasion for an almost ritual exploration of life and death: pulling out the batteries and putting them back again.

20   When a child explains the descent of a rolling stone by its wish to get to the bottom of the hill, a very primitive psychological category substitutes for a deficient ability in physical thinking. As the child develops, this animism is undermined from two sides: There will be growing sophistication about what domains are appropriately described in psychological terms—the behavior of rocks will not be among these. There will be growing sophistication about how to think about physical causality. Computers, however, don't easily fit into the category of physical objects whose behavior is to be described in physical terms. The world of traditional objects serves as material for a child's construction of the physical; the computer serves as a stimulus to the construction of the psychological.

21   While very young children puzzle over the physical and metaphysical status of the computer, grade school children grow more practical, focusing on mastery of the world around them and how the computer can be made to work for them. When children learn to program, one of their favorite areas of work is computer graphics—programming the machine to place displays on the screen. At a private school I shall call Austen, a school with a long tradition of open classrooms and flexible scheduling, children from preschool through fourth grade learn to program in the Logo computer language, which provides a powerful medium for computer graphics.

22   Thirty-two computational objects called sprites appear on the screen when commanded to do so. Each sprite has a number. When called by its number and given a color and shape, it comes onto the screen: a red truck, a blue ball, a green airplane. Children can manipulate one sprite at a time, several of them, or all of them at once, depending on the effect they want to achieve. The sprites can take predefined shapes, such as trucks and airplanes, or they can be given new shapes designed on a special grid, a sprite "scratchpad." They can be given a speed and a direction and set in motion. The direction is usually specified in terms of a heading from 0 to 360, where 0 would point the sprite due north, 90 would point it due east, 180 south, 270 west, and 360 north again.

23   The teachers think the manipulation of directions, involving the concept of angles, is too complex for second graders, so these children are introduced to the commands for making sprites appear, giving

them shapes and colors, and placing them on the screen, but not for setting them in motion. Motion will be saved for later grades.

24   The curriculum works until one second grader, Gary, catches onto the fact that something exciting is happening on the older children's screens and knows enough to pick up the trick from a proud and talkative third grader. In one sense, the teachers are right: Gary doesn't understand that he is dealing with angles. He doesn't have to. He wants to make the computer do something and he assimilates the concept of angle to something he already knows—secret codes.

25   "The sprites have secret codes, like 10, 100, 55. And if you give them their codes, they go in different directions. I've taught the code to 14 second graders," Gary confides to a visitor. "We're sort of keeping it a secret. The teachers don't know. We haven't figured out all the codes yet, but we're working on it." Two weeks later, Gary and his friends are still cracking the code. "We're still not sure about the big numbers" (sprites interpret 361 as one, one full revolution plus one), but they are feeling very pleased with themselves.

26   Jeff, a fourth grader, has the widest reputation as a computer expert in the school. He is meticulous in his study habits, does superlative work in all subjects. His teachers are not surprised to see him excelling in programming. Jeff approaches the machine with determination and the need to be in control, the way he approaches both his schoolwork and extracurricular activities. He likes to be, and often is, chairman of student committees. He has an idea and he wants to make it work. At the moment, his preoccupation with computers is intense: "They're the biggest thing in my life right now. . . . When I program, I put myself in the place of the sprite. And I make it do things."

27   Jeff is the author of one of the first fourth-grade space shuttle programs. He does it, like he does most other things, by making a plan. There will be a rocket, boosters, a trip through the stars, a landing. He conceives the program globally; then he breaks it up into manageable pieces and programs. "I wrote out the parts on a big piece of cardboard. I saw the whole thing in my mind just in one night, and I couldn't wait to come to school to make it work." Computer scientists will recognize this "top down" strategy as good programming style. And we all recognize in Jeff someone who conforms to our stereotype of a computer person or an engineer—someone who would be good with machines, good at science, someone organized, who approaches the world of things with confidence and sure intent, with the determination to make it work.

28   Kevin is a very different sort of child. Where Jeff is precise in all of his actions, Kevin is dreamy and impressionistic. Where Jeff tends to try to impose his ideas on other children, Kevin's warm, easygoing

nature and interest in others make him popular. Meetings with Kevin are often interrupted by his being called out to rehearse for a school play. He has been given the role of Prince Charming in *Cinderella*. Kevin comes from a military family; his father and grandfather were both in the Air Force. But Kevin has no intention of following in their footsteps. "I don't want to be an Army man. I don't want to be a fighting man. You can get killed." Kevin doesn't like fighting or competition in general.

29   Jeff has been playing with machines all his life—Tinkertoys, motors, bikes—but Kevin has never played with machines. He likes to read, he is proud of knowing the names of a "lot of different trees." He is artistic and introspective. When Jeff is asked questions about his activities, about what he thinks is fun, he answers in terms of how to do them right. He talks about video games by describing his strategy breakthroughs on the new version of Space Invaders: "Much harder, much trickier than the first one." By contrast, Kevin talks about experiences in terms of how they make him feel. Video games make him feel anxious, he says. "The computer is better," he adds. "It's easier. You get more relaxed. You're not being bombarded with stuff all the time."

30   Kevin too is making a space scene. But the way he goes about it is not at all like Jeff's approach. Jeff doesn't care too much about the detail of the form of his rocketship; what is important is getting a complex system to work. But Kevin cares more about the aesthetics of the graphics. He spends a lot of time on the shape of his rocket. He abandons his original idea ("It didn't look right against the stars") but continues to doodle with the scratchpad shape maker. He works without plan, experimenting, throwing different shapes onto the screen. He frequently stands back to inspect his work, finally settling on a white shape with red fire "at the bottom." He spends a long time making the red fireball, finding ways to give it spikes, and adding detail to the ship. New possibilities emerge—insignias, stripes, windows, and Kevin's most enthusiastic project: "It can have a little seat for the astronaut."

31   Kevin has lovingly worked on creating the rocket, the flare, and a background of twinkling stars. Now he wants the stars to stay in place and the rocket and the flare to move through them together. But without a master plan he gets confused about the code numbers he has assigned to the different parts of his program, and the flare doesn't stay with the rocket but flies off with the stars. It takes a lot of time to get the flare and the ship back together.

32   In correcting his error, Kevin explores the system, discovering new special effects as he goes along. He adds a moon, some planets. He

tries out different trajectories for the rocketship, different headings, and different speeds. By the end of the week Kevin too has programmed a space scene.

33   Jeff and Kevin represent cultural extremes. Some children are at home with the manipulation of formal objects, while others develop their ideas more impressionistically, usually with language or visual image, with attention to less formal aspects of the world such as feeling, color, sound, and personal rapport. Scientific and technical fields are usually seen as the natural home for people like Jeff; the arts and humanities seem to belong to Kevin.

34   In a classroom, we often see each type failing at the other's forte. Watching Kevin and Jeff at the same computer shows us two very different children succeeding at the same thing. Each child developed a distinctive style of mastery—styles that can be called hard and soft mastery.

35   Hard mastery is the imposition of will over the machine through the implementation of a plan. A program is the instrument of premeditated control. Getting the program to work is more like getting to "say one's piece" than allowing ideas to emerge in the give and take of conversation. The details of the specific program obviously need to be debugged—there has to be room for change, for some degree of flexibility in order to get it right—but the goal is always getting the program to realize the plan.

36   Soft mastery is more interactive. Kevin is like a painter who stands back between brushstrokes, looks at the canvas, and only from this contemplation decides what to do next. Hard mastery is the mastery of the planner, the engineer. Soft mastery is the mastery of the artist: Try this, wait for a response, try something else, let the overall shape emerge from an interaction with the medium. It is more like a conversation than a monologue.

37   The sprite, the computational object that is there to command on the screen, stands between the world of physical objects and the world of abstract ideas. Ambivalent in its nature, it is taken up differently by the hard and soft masters, the hard masters treating it more like a abstract entity—a Newtonian particle—the soft masters treating it more as a physical object—a dab of paint, a building block, a cardboard cutout.

38   In all of this, the computer acts as a Rorschach [a psychological test in which the subject interprets designs], allowing the expression of what is already there. But it does more than allow the expression of personality. It is a constructive as well as projective medium. It allows "softs" such as Kevin to operate in a domain of machines and formal systems that has been thought to be the exclusive cultural

preserve of the "hards." For the first time Kevin could march into a mathematical world with artistic colors flying full mast.

39   I have used boys as examples in order to detail hard and soft masters without reference to gender. But now it is time to state what might be anticipated by many readers: Girls tend to be soft masters, the hard masters are overwhelmingly male. At Austen, girls are trying to forge relationships with the computer that bypass objectivity altogether. They see computational objects as sensuous and tactile and relate to the computer's formal system not as a set of unforgiving rules but as a language for communicating with, negotiating with, a behaving, psychological entity.

40   In the eyes of a true hard programmer like Jeff, his classmate Anne, also nine, is an enigma. On the one hand she hardly seems serious about the computer. Her projects are frivolous, or at least their goals seem to be. She spends days creating shimmering patterns on the screen and writing "dialogue" programs in which she gets the computer to respond to typed-in messages. Her enthusiasm depends on achieving visual or conversational effects, and she doesn't seem to care whether she gets them with what Jeff would classify as "tricks"—uninteresting from the standpoint of the program code. All the same, this doesn't keep her from getting down to serious programming. She has made some technical inventions, and Jeff and the other male hard masters recognize that if they want to keep abreast of the state of the art at Austen, they must pay attention to what Anne is doing. And Anne knows how to take advantage of her achievements. She was heard explaining to a visitor how much she enjoyed seeing versions of her ideas on half a dozen screens. "They didn't copy me exactly, but I can recognize my idea." Jeff's grudging acknowledgment of what he sees as Anne's not quite serious accomplishments seems almost a microcosm of reactions to competent women in society as a whole. There, as at Austen, there is appreciation, incomprehension, and ambivalence.

41   Anne has become an expert at writing programs to produce visual effects of appearance and disappearance. In one, a flock of birds flies through the sky, disappears at the horizon, and reappears some other place and time. If all the birds are the same color, such as red, then disappearance and appearance could be produced by the commands, "Set color invisible" to get rid of them, and "Set color red" to make them appear. But since Anne wants the birds to have different colors, the problem of the birds reappearing with their original color is more complicated.

42   There is a classical method for getting this done: Get the program to store away each bird's original color before changing that color to "invisible" and then to recall the color when the birds are to reap-

pear. This method calls for an algebraic style of thinking. You have to think about variables and use a variable for each color, for example, letting A equal the color of the first bird, B the color of the second bird, and so on. Anne will use this method when she has to, but she prefers another, a method of her own invention that has a different feel. She lets the bird keep its color, but she makes her program hide it by placing a screen over it. She designs a sprite that will screen the bird when she doesn't want it seen.

43   This way of doing things makes Anne feel in direct contact with her material. She likes to feel that she is there among her birds, manipulating them much in the way she can manipulate physical materials. When you want to hide something on a canvas you paint it out, you cover it with something that looks like the background. This is Anne's solution. She covers the birds with a sky-colored screen to make them disappear.

44   But how does the program "know" where the bird is in order to place the screen on it? Anne attaches the screen to the bird when the bird is created, instead of putting it on later. The screen is on top of the bird at all times and moves with the bird wherever it goes. Thus she has invented a new kind of object, a screened bird. When Anne wants the bird to be seen, the screen is given the "invisible" color, so the bird, whatever its color, shows right through it. The problem of the multiplicity of bird colors is solved. A bird can have any color. But the screens need only two colors, invisible or sky blue. The problem of remembering the color of a particular bird and reassigning it at a particular time has been bypassed.

45   Anne's program is ingenious, but her programming style is characteristic of many of the girls in her class. Most of the boys seem driven by the pleasure of mastering and manipulating a formal system. For them, the programming instructions are what it is all about. For Anne, pleasure comes from being able to put herself in the space of the birds. Her method of manipulating screens and birds allows her to feel that these objects are close, not distant and untouchable things that need designation by variables.

46   Children working with computers are a reflection of the larger world of relations between gender and science. Jeff took the sprite as an object apart from him, an object in a world of its own. When he entered the sprite world, it was to command it better. Kevin used the sprite world to fantasize in. Anne does something more. She moves further in the direction I am calling feminine, further in the direction of seeing the sprite as sensuous rather than abstract. When Anne puts herself into the sprite world, she imagines herself to be part of the system, playing with the birds and the screens as though they were tactile materials.

47 Science is usually defined in terms of the hard masters: It is the place for the abstract, the domain for a clear separation between subject and object. The Austen classroom, with its male hard masters, mirrors the male genderization of science. But what about Anne? What about the other girls like her who are exploring and mastering the computer? At Austen we see not only the male model that characterizes official science, but a model of how females, when given a chance, can find another way to think and talk about the mastery not simply of machines but of formal systems. And here the computer may have a special role. It provides an entry to formal systems that is more accessible to women. It can be negotiated with, responded to, it can be psychologized.

48 Computers affect children's psychological development in many ways. They enter children's perceptions of where they stand in the world of nature and of artifact. In their intimacies and interactions with the machine, children may find new ways to sort out who they are and what they are to become. *4,520 words*

Comprehension Questions

1. This article is about
   a. computers.
   b. children.
   c. control over physical objects.
   d. psychological development.
2. Which of the following best states the author's main point?
   a. Playing with computers frustrates children.
   b. Computers allow development of different approaches to learning.
   c. Computers help girls to work with formal systems.
   d. Children think computers are human.
3. _____ is a subtopic of the article.
   a. Computers
   b. Machines
   c. Children
   d. *none of the above*
4. When young children accuse Merlin of cheating, they are giving it _____ properties.
   a. supernatural
   b. human
   c. machinelike
   d. childlike

5. Physical properties are used to understand
    a. people.
    b. animals.
    c. machines.
    d. things.
6. Psychological properties are used to understand
    a. machines.
    b. things.
    c. computers.
    d. people.
7. Computers force children to think about
    a. machines.
    b. other people.
    c. right and wrong.
    d. "matter," "life," and "mind."
8. The word "intimate" in the title of this article means that computers affect the _____ development of children.
    a. future
    b. psychological
    c. correct
    d. cognitive
9. The author supports her ideas with
    a. examples.
    b. repetition.
    c. scientific research.
    d. statistics.
10. Soft mastery of the computer is more _____ than hard mastery.
    a. fun
    b. interactive
    c. independent
    d. frustrating

taxes, life expectancy, commerce and agriculture, famine or plenty—and here are figures by modern authorities which differ by 100 percent. Chroniclers' figures which seem obviously distorted appear in my text in quotation marks.

3   Discrepancies of supposed fact were often due to mistakes of oral transmission or later misreading of a manuscript source, as when the Dame de Courcy, subject of an international scandal, was mistaken by an otherwise careful 19th century historian for Coucy's second wife, at a cost, for a while, of devastating confusion to the present author. The Comte d'Auxerre in the Battle of Poitiers was variously rendered by English chroniclers as Aunser, Aussure, Soussiere, Usur, Waucerre, and by the *Grandes Chroniques* of France as Sancerre, a different fellow altogether. Enguerrand was written as Ingelram in England. It is not surprising that I took the name Canolles to be a variant of the notorious brigand captain Arnaut de Cervole, only to find, when the circumstances refused to fit, that it was instead a variant of Knowles or Knollys, an equally notorious English captain. Though minor, this sort of difficulty can be unnerving.

4   Isabeau of Bavaria, Queen of France, is described by one historian as a tall blonde and by another as a "dark, lively, little woman." The Turkish Sultan Bajazet, reputed by his contemporaries to be bold, enterprising, and avid for war, and surnamed Thunderbolt for the rapidity of his strikes, is described by a modern Hungarian historian as "effeminate, sensual, irresolute and vacillating."

5   It may be taken as axiomatic that any statement of fact about the Middle Ages may (and probably will) be met by a statement of the opposite or a different version. Women outnumbered men because men were killed off in the wars; men outnumbered women because women died in childbirth. Common people were familiar with the Bible; common people were unfamiliar with the Bible. Nobles were tax exempt; no, they were not tax exempt. French peasants were filthy and foul-smelling and lived on bread and onions; French peasants ate pork, fowl, and game and enjoyed frequent baths in the village bathhouses. The list could be extended indefinitely.

6   Contradictions, however, are part of life, not merely a matter of conflicting evidence. I would ask the reader to expect contradictions, not uniformity. No aspect of society, no habit, custom, movement, development, is without cross-currents. Starving peasants in hovels live alongside prosperous peasants in featherbeds. Children are neglected and children are loved. Knights talk of honor and turn brigand. Amid depopulation and disaster, extravagance and splendor were never more extreme. No age is tidy or made of whole cloth, and none is a more checkered fabric than the Middle Ages.

7   One must also remember that the Middle Ages change color depending on who is looking at them. Historians' prejudices and points

3. **Historical Fact**

Barbara W. Tuchman

1   I come now to the hazards of the [historical] enterprise. First are uncertain and contradictory data with regard to dates, numbers, and hard facts. Dates may seem dull and pedantic to some, but they are fundamental because they establish sequence—what precedes and what follows—thereby leading toward an understanding of cause and effect. Unfortunately, medieval chronology is extremely hard to pin down. The year was considered to begin at Easter and since this could fall any time between March 22 and April 22, a fixed date of March 25 was generally preferred. The change over to New Style took place in the 16th century but was not everywhere accepted until the 18th, which leaves the year to which events of January, February, and March belong in the 14th century a running enigma—further complicated by use of the regnal year (dating from the reigning King's accession) in official English documents of the 14th century and use of the papal year in certain other cases. Moreover, chroniclers did not date an event by the day of the month but by the religious calendar— speaking, for example, of two days before the Nativity of the Virgin, or the Monday after Epiphany, or St. John the Baptist's Day, or the third Sunday in Lent. The result is to confuse not only the historian but the inhabitants of the 14th century themselves, who rarely if ever agree on the same date for any event.

2   Numbers are no less basic because they indicate what proportion of the population is involved in a given situation. The chronic exaggeration of medieval numbers—of armies, for example—when accepted as factual, has led in the past to a misunderstanding of medieval war as analogous to modern war, which it was not, in means, method, or purpose. It should be assumed that medieval figures for military forces, battle casualties, plague deaths, revolutionary hordes, processions, or any groups en masse are generally enlarged by several hundred percent. This is because the chroniclers did not use numbers as data but as a device of literary art to amaze or appall the reader. Use of Roman numerals also made for lack of precision and an affinity for round numbers. The figures were uncritically accepted and repeated by generation after generation of historians. Only since the end of the last century have scholars begun to re-examine the documents and find, for instance, the true strength of an expeditionary force from paymasters' records. Yet still they disagree. J. C. Russell puts the pre-plague population of France at 21 million, Ferdinand Lot at 15 or 16 million, and Edouard Perroy at a lowly 10 to 11 million. Size of population affects studies of everything else—

of view—and thus their selection of material—have changed considerably over a period of 600 years. During the three centuries following the 14th, history was virtually a genealogy of nobility, devoted to tracing dynastic lines and family connections and infused by the idea of the noble as a superior person. These works of enormous antiquarian research teem with information of more than dynastic interest, such as Anselm's item about the Gascon lord who bequeathed a hundred livres for the dowries of poor girls he had deflowered.

8   The French Revolution marks the great reversal, following which historians saw the common man as hero, the poor as *ipso facto* virtuous, nobles and kings as monsters of iniquity. Simeon Luce, in his history of the Jacquerie, is one of these, slanted in his text, yet unique in his research and invaluable for his documents. The giants of the 19th and early 20th centuries who unearthed and published the sources, annotated and edited the chronicles, collected the literary works, read and excerpted masses of sermons, treatises, letters, and other primary material, provided the ground on which we latecomers walk. Their work is now supplemented and balanced by modern medievalists of the post–Marc Bloch era who have taken a more sociological approach and turned up detailed hard facts about daily life— for example, the number of communion wafers sold in a particular diocese, as an indicator of religious observance.   *1,164 words*

Comprehension Questions

  1. A good title for this article is
     a. "Historical Truths."
     b. "The Middle Ages."
     c. "My Life as a Historian."
     d. "The History of France."
  2. The author is primarily concerned with
     a. how to study history.
     b. why history cannot be factual.
     c. France in the Middle Ages.
     d. telling a story.
  3. Which of the following is *not* a subtopic?
     a. inexact dates
     b. careless numbers
     c. many contradictions
     d. noble heroes
  4. Two sources of discrepancies are _____ and _____ .
     a. destruction of records
     b. misuse of numbers
     c. ecclesiastical history
     d. misreadings of manuscripts

5. The use of the religious calendar in the fourteenth century
   a. was obligatory.
   b. confused later dating of events.
   c. was worldwide.
   d. was confined to the monasteries.
6. Which pattern of organization does *not* appear in the article?
   a. cause and effect
   b. compare/contrast
   c. chronological order
   d. process or steps
7. Historians should view contradictions
   a. as a cause of error.
   b. as a fact of life.
   c. as unexpected.
   d. as unusual in accounts of the Middle Ages.
8. French historians have ———— dealt with the common man.
   a. never
   b. always
   c. since the Middle Ages
   d. since the French Revolution
9. This article provides the reader with
   a. a version of fourteenth-century history.
   b. illustrations of the difficulties involved in writing history.
   c. a biography of Isabeau of Bavaria.
   d. factual data.
10. The author implies that all French peasants
    a. did not live on bread and onions.
    b. ate pork, fowl, and game.
    c. were starving.
    d. slept in featherbeds.

4. The Philosopher's Myth

Richard M. Restak, M.D.

> *On the contrary, it is impossible to obtain an adequate version of the laws*
> *for which we are looking unless the physical system is regarded as a whole.*
>
> M. PLANCK, 1931

1   Two former Nobel Prize laureates in physics were recently asked to guess what area of research would win the Nobel Prize for physics in the year 2000. Both of them, without prior consultation and with hardly a hesitation, said brain research. The human brain, they concluded, is our ultimate intellectual challenge in the last quarter of the twentieth century.

2   There is a double irony in the choice of the brain as an area of research worthy of Nobel Prizes in physics. For one thing, physics is one of the "hard sciences," a model of the "objective" view of the world. Brain research, in contrast, has been modeled on biology, a "softer," more fuzzy discipline where disagreement abounds. (Articles are still appearing from time to time attempting to disprove even such well-established biological principles as evolution.)

3   Secondly, brain research is taken up with questions even more fundamental than those which challenge the theoretical physicists: "How do we know what we know?" "What is the *real* world?" "Who am I?" Until very recently such questions were referred to theologians or philosophers, whose speculations provided the foundations for complicated and impressive philosophical systems. But today, philosophy and theology exert a far less compelling influence on our lives. When was the last time you saw a philosopher or theologian on a late-night talk show? And how many of us can get out more than a few mumbled generalizations about the major philosophical thinkers of the last five hundred years?

4   With the collapse of philosophy and theology as major influences on our lives, questions such as "How do we know what we know?" or the ringing "What is truth?" have remained unanswered and, even, largely unasked. In their place, we've focused on questions of a more "practical" nature. Food, energy supplies, pollution, crowding, the breakdown of needed social services—these are some of the areas which have received and continue to receive the most attention. Already some of them are reaching crisis proportions.

5   The world's population, for instance, is expected to double in the next thirty to forty years. In addition, population growth now indicates that each doubling of the population will take place in half the previous time. Instead of thirty to forty years, we move to fifteen to twenty, with our children witnessing a population doubling spaced over one or two decades.

6   Realizations such as this tend to encourage even greater emphasis on the external environment. Birth-control techniques are expanded and, at least in India, sterilization procedures are forced on groups of citizens without their consent. Energy policies are formulated which concentrate on how best to cope with a dwindling supply of oil and energy reserves. Everywhere we are concerned with how we manipulate or manage one crisis after another.

7   In recent years, however, we've experienced a change in the types of crises that immediately threaten us. No one can now board an airplane without a gnawing fear of a hijacking or a bombing. In less than five years, terrorism has become one of the most decisive influences in our lives. It is also one of the most conspicuous examples of an *internal* as well as an external threat to our continued existence.

8   One understandable response to all of this is to turn to the behavioral sciences to provide the answers to the questions that plague us. Although initially appealing, this suggestion overlooks the rather poor track record that the behavioral sciences have shown in the past. Different authorities hold radically different views on why we act the way we do. Things have now become so complicated, in fact, that psychologists trained in one orientation are often unable to agree with other psychologists on such basic concepts as what psychology is about. Those trained in behavioral methods, for instance, operate as if consciousness doesn't exist, while scoffing at their counterparts who value and rely upon subjective experiences.

9   In the last several years, a new field has emerged which may offer us a better means of understanding and controlling some of our internal and external threats. Known as psychobiology, this new discipline is a combination of the behavioral sciences and the brain sciences. It differs from other studies of behavior in some of its initial assumptions. While the working of the brain is often peripheral to most theories of psychology, psychobiology depends primarily on what we have learned about the brain and how it works. The emphasis is on how the brain influences our perceptions of the world, how we know ourselves, the nature of reality—in essence, the questions we mentioned earlier as formerly asked by philosophers and theologians.

10   Basically, psychobiology is concerned with the mind's attempt to know itself through the study of the brain. Today we accept as a truism that the brain is the physical basis of the mind, although this is not quite the same thing as stating that the brain *is* the mind.

11   Throughout history, almost every major part of the body has been credited at one time or another as the seat of the mind or the soul. In civilizations such as the Sumerian and the Assyrian, the liver was

considered the repository of the soul and the physical basis for the personality. To Aristotle, the heart was the central organ, while the brain existed as a sort of cooling mechanism for the blood as it left the heart. This view of the importance of the heart survives today in our popular images of "heartbreak" as a description of the effect of unrequited love, and "bleeding hearts" as a contemptuous term for people who are ruled by sympathy and sentimentalism.

12　Today we look to the brain rather than to the heart for an understanding of the mind. While this is largely an advance over the superstition and ignorance of the past, it presents us immediately with some rather knotty problems. The first of these is an organizational one.

13　The number of neurons in the human brain is almost equal to the number of stars in our Milky Way—over fifteen billion. What are the relationships of the nerve cells to each other? To understand the brain, is it necessary to deal with all possible interactions between nerve cells? or with only some of them? Put another way, What level of organization offers the best hope toward understanding how our brain works?

14　One of the stumbling blocks to understanding the brain can be traced, I believe, to selection of the wrong level of organization. Let me illustrate what I mean.

15　Forget about the fifteen-billion figure I gave you a moment ago, because that is a staggering number to deal with. Instead, let's work with something more manageable: the number of people presently inhabiting the earth. Imagine each person with a telephone capable of calling any other person in the world. In addition, assume that in our model the important information about people's activities and behavior is always discussed over the telephone. Our job will be to keep track of all the calls and to correlate telephone calls with behavior. Some of this may be very easy, as when a person in London calls a friend in New York and invites him to come over for a week. Within a day or two of such a call, the friend in New York can be observed carrying his bags while leaving his apartment on the way to the airport. At such a time we may feel quite confident that our telephone monitoring system is working well and giving us an accurate and useful correlation between person-to-person communication and behavior. As the number of people increases, however, our method will soon break down. Imagine all the telephone calls we would have to monitor to enable us to predict the identity of the passenger list of a jumbo jet leaving for Athens six months from now. Or imagine the number of telephone calls that would be needed to estimate the population of Schenectady, New York. . . .

16　Perhaps you think such a task could be handled very well by computers. To see why this is impossible, let's simplify the situation a bit by reducing the number of variables from fifteen billion to a mere thirty-two. Thirty-two just happens to be the maximum number of pieces we can play on a chessboard at any one time. At a typical point in the game, thirty permissible moves are open to each player. If it's white's turn to play, for instance, each of his thirty moves can be countered by thirty moves on the part of black, which leads to about one thousand variations at the end of one round of play.

17   With white's next move and black's response, everything is computed again, yielding one million positions. By the third move we're at one billion, and so on. In a very short time the number of possible calculations becomes, for all practical purposes, infinite.

18   In the case of our telephone system we are helped by the fact that every person isn't likely to call everyone in the world. Barriers of language, common interest, and acquaintance limit somewhat the number of possible calls. In chess a similar situation exists, since not every move is equally good and some are downright disastrous, leading to a quick checkmate. In the brain, however, we have no rules that would enable us to know beforehand with absolute certainty whether one brain cell is influencing the activity of another one. This gets us back to the stars-in-the-galaxy-neurons-in-the-brain situation, which represents a level of complexity no human mind or computer can ever be prepared to deal with. In short, if we focus our attention on the neurons and their interconnections, we're selecting a level of organization that can never satisfy our efforts at understanding.

19   On the other hand, if the level chosen is too sweeping, we come out with generalizations that are useless. "The brain works as an information-processing system" is intended to be informative, but it really doesn't tell us anything at all. The key is to focus on the correct level of organization.

20   Another related problem in our attempts to understand brain functioning is a more philosophical one. We live in a world of *things*. Our perceptions are geared to encountering objects and people who change very little from day to day. "A rose is a rose is a rose," according to Gertrude Stein, and she might have selected, with equal validity, any one of the tens of thousands of objects and people we encounter every day.

21   The alternative view, never a popular one, holds that the world consists of *processes* and that what we perceive around us are only frames in a movie. The Greek philosopher Heraclitus said you never step into the same river twice, since the water continues to flow and tomorrow you will encounter different water than today. Things are always in a process of change, like a flame converting combustible substances into heat, light, and hot gases. A fire is not a thing but a process of combustion.

22   Modern physics is very much a *process* science and poses the great-

est challenge to our *things* view of the universe. Quarks, black holes, and particles of antimatter are neither accessible to our direct experience nor can they be considered fixed entities. Despite this, each of these strange-sounding words has already become part of our everyday vocabulary. With the discovery of the atom and the subsequent exploration of the inner world of subatomic physics, the mechanistic *things* view of the universe began to crumble. Even before that, nineteenth-century scientists demonstrated that the movement of a magnet near a coil of copper created electrical energy described by the experimenters as a "disturbance" or a "condition" rather than a thing. By the third decade of this century the mechanistic *things* view of space and time yielded to the concept of a space-time continuum. All measurements involving space and time thus lost any absolute significance.

23   Today, physics is the study of interactive processes rather than discrete particles. In such a model the atom is not solid but a tiny universe of energy, with the nucleus and its orbiting charges separated by vast space. If the actual mass of our brain were condensed minus that energy space, it would occupy an area smaller than the head of a pin.

24   My purpose in introducing physics at this point is to contrast it with our approach to the study of the brain. While physics has become very much a *process* science, our ways of thinking about the brain have been locked into looking at the brain as a thing. This creates some immediate, and occasionally subtle, difficulties.

25   Is the brain the mind? This question at first seems sensible and capable of verification. It has in fact stimulated the imaginations of scientists and philosophers for centuries. Some now feel that the answer is obvious: The mind is nothing but the action of the brain and is a meaningless concept without reference to a brain. As a neurologist, I felt for the longest time that this view was correct. But the question is actually a trick, of the "Have you stopped beating your wife?" type, where either a yes or no carries with it undesirable implications. In both instances, the proper response is to focus on the question itself and show how the form of the question results in a "loaded dice" situation.

26   The philosopher Gilbert Ryle once described the mind-brain dilemma as a "philosopher's myth" based on what he called a "category mistake."

27   Imagine an eight-year-old boy taking his first trip to Washington, D.C. He's been told in school that Washington is the seat of the nation's government. On the first day, the boy visits Congress. On day two, he takes a tour of the White House. On the third day, he's shown the Supreme Court building. At this point the boy seems puzzled and asks: "But where is the government? I've seen Congress, the White

House, and the Supreme Court, but I still haven't seen the government." Ryle would explain our young man's puzzlement as resulting from a category mistake. Congress, the White House, and the Supreme Court are things—at least each of them can be physically located in space and time. The government, in contrast, is quite another category altogether. It is, in fact, a supercategory which describes the interactions of the other three.

28   In a similar manner the brain can be dissected, electrically stimulated, or even placed in a blender and homogenized to a few ounces of froth. The mind, however, remains as elusive as the "government" our eight-year-old was trying to find in Washington.

29   When we're trying to relate the brain to the mind, we're dealing with a category mistake, since the brain is best conceived as a process rather than a three-pound lump of protoplasm. Think of the problems that resulted from our telephone model of human communication, and that model involved only the population of the earth instead of the fifteen-billion interactions that are possible within our heads! Understanding ultimately depends on our ability to concentrate on the process. Once a process is understood, the actual mechanisms of how it is carried out are of less importance. To correlate brain with mind, or vice versa, is a category mistake that insists on equating two different processes. The trick is to exercise care in distinguishing a prerequisite from a cause.

30   On any given morning, the Los Angeles Freeway is a prerequisite for thousands of commuters getting to work. It is hardly a causative explanation, however, of how a particular commuter, say a stockbroker, can be found at nine o'clock propping his feet on his desk while perusing a list of client telephone numbers.

31   The question "Is the brain a sufficient explanation for the mind?" was anticipated by the biologist Sir Julian Huxley: "The brain alone is not responsible for mind, even though it is a necessary organ for its manifestation. Indeed, an isolated brain is a piece of biological nonsense as meaningless as an isolated individual."

32   For the sake of argument, however, let's assume that we've reached a point where every mental event, every product of "mind," can be correlated with something going on within our brain. This is yielding a lot, incidentally, since we're not anywhere near the point of making such correlations. But for the moment, let's imagine it's possible that we can. Since we think of the world as being governed by physical laws, the explanation for such a correlation seems obvious: The brain events are the cause of the mental phenomenon of thinking, perception, whatever. In essence, the mind is dependent on the brain. But logically, isn't just the opposite explanation—The brain is dependent on the mind—equally likely? From a strictly logical point of view,

this is an equally valid stance to take, given the postulated parallel between mental events and brain processes.

33   Despite the seeming logic of all this, most people have a terribly strong hunch that such a view ultimately doesn't make sense. The mind created the brain? I don't believe it for an instant, and I hope you don't. I am only bringing it up to show why the mind-brain controversy may never be resolved. Category mistakes result from our equating the brain and mind as *things* when they are actually *processes*. This confusion immediately leads to mistakes in the way we think about behavior. Naturally, if we start from wrong premises, we are going to end up with theories that are useless and don't work.

2,840 words

Comprehension Questions

 1. "The Philosopher's Myth" deals with
     a. the new science of psychobiology.
     b. the study of the mind.
     c. brain research.
     d. the behavioral sciences.
 2. The brain should be considered
     a. a thing.
     b. a cooling mechanism for the blood.
     c. another word for the mind.
     d. a process.
 3. The author believes that answers to the eternal questions may be provided by
     a. theologians.
     b. philosophers.
     c. physicists.
     d. psychobiologists.
 4. The study of mind and brain has concentrated on
     a. which came first.
     b. which influences the other.
     c. wrong premises.
     d. the fact that they are the same thing.
 5. The author has some expertise because he is
     a. a biologist.
     b. a physicist.
     c. a neurologist.
     d. a psychologist.
 6. Modern brain research is
     a. the mind's attempt to know itself through the study of the brain.
     b. carried out mainly by physicists.

    c. an effort to answer moral questions.
    d. well organized.
7. Which of the following is not a category mistake?
    a. equating mind and brain
    b. equating Congress with the government
    c. equating grapes with cherries
    d. equating a desk with the office
8. The first six paragraphs of this article
    a. contain a summary of the article.
    b. serve as an introduction.
    c. set out the author's views.
    d. tell us how to deal with crises.
9. Level of organization and _____ are two problems connected with the mind versus brain dilemma.
    a. process science
    b. our perceptions
    c. large numbers
    d. trick questions
10. There are _____ stars in the Milky Way.
    a. over 50 million
    b. over 20 trillion
    c. over 15 billion
    d. over 15 million

5. 'You Must Go and See for Yourself'

Florence Ladd

1   To go or not to go?

2   How can a black American morally justify a trip to South Africa— even in the interest of a good cause? Since it is a very good cause, how can one refuse to go? My job as a consultant in international education was to meet educators in South Africa who prepare students for US universities.

3   Advised by black South Africans, and Americans, black and white, who had traveled there, I listed their travel tips or, more accurately, travel warnings:

1. Dress like, look like, act like an American. (To be mistaken for a South African woman in a situation that is restricted could have unhappy consequences.)
2. Have your passport ready to present "on demand."
3. Avoid traveling alone; witnesses are important.
4. If an accident occurs, do not call the police. (If you have been injured, their treatment will aggravate the injury.)

4   With the warnings and well wishes of friends, I boarded a flight that would take me from New York to Johannesburg. I settled into a snug coach seat next to an attractive, young Afrikaner woman. Director of a modeling agency, she was returning to "Jo'burg" from a business trip to Las Vegas and New York. In flight, we sometimes meet people whom we never would meet on the ground.

5   She briefed me on getting around in Johannesburg. "Visit the Market Theater complex and the Carlton Center," she advised. "Go to the railway station early in the morning and at the end of the day and observe the separate streams of blacks and whites entering and leaving Jo'burg. Ask someone to take you to Soweto so you can see how the blacks live. Visit Lenasia where the Indians live; and try to get to one of the Colored townships." (Coloreds, in South Africa, are persons of mixed race.) She added: "Walk through the commercial section of Hillbrow on a Saturday afternoon. Hillbrow is very multiracial." With a chilling insensitivity, she had described the social geography of apartheid.

6   She turned to the operation of her modeling agency, assuring me that there is an easy, egalitarian exchange among the models she employs: several white models, one Colored and two who are black. Moving closer to home, she spoke of her husband, their daughter and

their "girl." Their "girl" is an African woman, a Zulu, who lives with them, serving as maid and baby sitter, cook and valet, gardener and handy woman. "She can do anything, everything," the model agent marveled. "Her daughter is the age of ours—6 years old. You should see them together when her daughter visits. You should see them lying side by side in our lounge watching television. They eat together in our kitchen. Her daughter eats what our daughter eats when she visits. It is beautiful!" she quietly exclaimed. She was totally unaware of how much she had told me of her maid-and-madame relationship, unaware of the social and political messages in her "beautiful" anecdote.

7   I related what I had heard over the years about black-white relations in South Africa, cited the evidence I had gleaned from the Amnesty International publications I dared not bring, and confessed my apprehension about traveling in her country. "The impressions you have are unfair to us," she insisted. "You cannot understand the way we—blacks and whites—depend on each other, the affection we feel for each other."

8   When I related the accounts I had read of the Soweto "riots" and the death of Steve Biko, she frowned and said, "You must go and see for yourself." "Go and see for yourself," was the refrain that followed each statement I offered.

9   As the plane landed at Jan Smuts Airport, my companion for 16 hours gave me her business card on which she had penciled her home address and telephone number. She urged me to phone her and visit their home during my South African sojourn. I did not call her. Her voice and her refrain, "Go and see for yourself," accompanied me throughout the visit, however.

10   The reception desk of the Holiday Inn was staffed with African, Colored, Indian and white personnel, reflecting the population categories of the apartheid system. There were greetings in English and Afrikaans: WELCOME/WELKOLM.

11   "Are you here on holiday?" inquired a skeptical porter, an elderly black man, who lifted my luggage onto a dolly. It was the first of several such questions posed by curious black and white South Africans I encountered in my travels. This time I answered simply, "No, I am here on business." Eventually, I began to reply: "I am here on business. I would not come to South Africa for a holiday." This reply was received with strained silence, a change of subject or an understanding nod of recognition of the stress and ambivalence a black American woman would experience in South Africa.

12   Guided by my Johannesburg hosts, black educators, I made my way from one appointment to the next; I visited university offices,

private schools, educational agencies and corporations in a climate that ranged from cordiality to indifference. (I had been warned that I would be accorded the status of "honorary white." Nowhere was the term stamped in my passport: yet I experienced the immunity accorded a foreigner on a benign mission.) When asked, "How were you treated?" I must answer, "No better or worse than I have been treated in the US." With the guidance of my hosts, however, it was unlikely that I would have been exposed—personally—to insult or injury.

13   The fast-paced processions of thousands of blacks in downtown Johannesburg on weekdays, however, brought me face-to-face with faces and eyes that presented evidence of generations of insults and injuries. Their faces expressed their anguish and their despair, their courage and determination. They were pumped into Johannesburg every morning, the source of human energy that runs the machinery of a strange and alienating city. They arrived in the morning in the fatigued state to which one is reduced by a long, overcrowded commute. They departed looking even more tired, exhausted—I imagined—by the chores, the inconveniences, the insults, the injuries that were part of an ordinary workday.

14   I sharpened my sense of social conditions by eliciting personal accounts from blacks I met. Informal interviews with taxi drivers, newspaper vendors, women domestics waiting for buses, shop clerks and hotel personnel enlarged my view of conditions that surround the everyday lives of blacks. They lived in fear, fear of irrational acts of invasion and harassment perpetrated by the police. Several recounted episodes of police invasions of their homes or offices or the police's abduction of a relative or acquaintance charged with subversive activity for charitable acts of improving the lot of blacks.

15   I began to wonder what my life would be like if I lived in Johannesburg. ("Go and see for yourself.") I had learned that only black domestic servants were permitted under the Group Areas Act to live within what once must have been the city limits. A visit to Soweto (the acronym for the South West Township) informed me of where and how I would live. Residents of Soweto told me that they lived in Johannesburg; yet the township, Soweto, lies approximately 15 miles southwest of central Johannesburg.

16   Soweto is a very dense development of cinder block, brick and stucco cottages and bungalows and hostels (dormitories for men only, men whose families are not permitted to accompany them to urban areas where they may seek employment) where 2 million blacks live in varying degrees of inconvenience and discomfort. Water faucets and toilet facilities were in yards behind dwellings. Roads had not been paved. Recreational facilities were extremely scarce. There were

a few "take away" food services (e.g., Kentucky Fried); but there was no restaurant where one might sit and dine. Parks and attractive open spaces did not exist in Soweto.

17   On one visit to Soweto, I was accompanied by Dr. B. Our point of entry into Soweto was in the vicinity of Baragwanath Hospital. "I want to show you the Hospital," Dr. B. offered. I was overwhelmed by the high density of the ward. Beds, each one occupied, lined the walls; and between each bed on the floor were pallets, each occupied by a patient. Some were in hospital gowns; some wore the clothing they must have been wearing when admitted to the hospital. . . . I was reminded of depictions of hospital settings in the Crimean War. I prayed that I would not need to be hospitalized in South Africa!

18   We resumed our journey to Dr. B.'s home. Most of the dwellings we passed were small structures that stood cheek by jowl to each other on small house lots, like matchboxes on chess boards. Most were two-bedroom dwellings, I was told. Regardless of family size, two-bedroom houses were built by the government. As we approached his house, Dr. B. prepared me for the dimly lit interior. "We have not had electricity in this area for 3 weeks. Nor have they paved the streets," he said as we stepped around a mud puddle.

19   Over a candlelit cold supper, Dr. B. and his family listened politely to my litany of violent and nonviolent anti-apartheid strategies. Then, carefully, they explained to me why none of the strategies that I had proposed would work. They, their relatives, colleagues and friends for several decades had considered proposals for the destruction of apartheid, considered them and dismissed them as lacking in some respect. "The gears of the apartheid machine are well oiled and tightly meshed," lamented Dr. B. They seemed resigned to the prospect of a protracted evolutionary process that eventually would overcome the inhumanity of apartheid.

20   Dr. B. offered to drive me back to the Holiday Inn in Johannesburg. (Buses did not run into the city in the evening; and it seemed highly unlikely that a Johannesburg taxi would fetch me.) On an unlit highway on the outskirts of Soweto, several cars and vans were stopped. I exclaimed: "There's been an accident?" "No," said Dr. B., "it is a roadblock, a police check." We, too, were signaled to pull over to the side of the road. A black motorcycle policeman in riot attire approached, demanded Dr. B.'s documents, and scanned the interior of the car with a large beamed flashlight. Dr. B. turned on the ceiling light in the car and handed over his papers, which the policeman examined. He returned Dr. B.'s documents and peered inside the car, focusing on my Mexican dress. He then declared, "You may continue." Giddy with relief, Dr. B. said as we drove off, "I turned on the light so that he would see that you are a foreigner. He saw your for-

eign dress." Being in the company of a foreigner afforded some protection, I realized. The police appeared to be searching the other vehicles thoroughly; passengers were stepping out of vans and cars. Lines of passengers who stood on the edge of the road were being frisked.

21   The next day I was again in a line at Jan Smuts Airport with other would-be passengers en route to Durban. We would be passengers if the computer would be "up" before flight time and if the baggage conveyor belt could be reactivated. Crisp, blond South African Airlines agents pretended that they were running a First World operation that unexpectedly had failed. The Third World human infrastructure upon which their contrived society rests was resisting, refusing to function that day. My immediate would-be fellow travelers, an elderly woman with an English accent in front of me and a 30-ish Afrikaner in a business suit behind me, simultaneously asked (to pass the time and feed their curious appetites): "Are you here on holiday?" *1,191 words*

Comprehension Questions

1. The topic of this article is
   a. South Africa.
   b. blacks in South Africa.
   c. a holiday in South Africa.
   d. a black American's impressions of South Africa.
2. The best statement of the key idea is that
   a. the author saw the conditions in South Africa for herself.
   b. the author enjoyed her visit to South Africa.
   c. the author was surprised by how well blacks were treated in South Africa.
   d. more people should visit South Africa.
3. Life in Soweto is a(n)
   a. example.
   b. subtopic.
   c. unimportant observation.
   d. reason for writing the article.
4. A supporting idea is that
   a. blacks and whites have different lives.
   b. whites and blacks have similar lives.
   c. visitors are treated very well.
   d. it is better if people don't know you are a visitor.
5. _____ is a supporting detail.
   a. Only whites work in the hotels
   b. Many whites commute to Johannesburg

    c. Black and white children play together
    d. The description of Soweto

6. The article was written to
    a. warn black Americans against visiting South Africa.
    b. raise money for South African relief.
    c. urge people to "see for themselves."
    d. raise consciousness about conditions in South Africa.

7. The author makes her points by
    a. quoting authorities.
    b. using historical documents.
    c. telling a fictional story.
    d. recounting her personal experiences.

8. _____ is the best description of how the author felt about the woman she met on the plane.
    a. Admiration
    b. Astonishment at her insensitivity
    c. Gratitude for her information
    d. Warm friendship

9. The fact that the author was a foreigner
    a. subjected her to harassment by the police.
    b. meant that no black person in South Africa would speak to her.
    c. is unimportant to the account.
    d. gave her special immunity.

10. This article implies that
    a. conditions for blacks are improving in South Africa.
    b. the reality is worse than the author anticipated.
    c. there is a lot of social interaction between blacks and whites in South Africa.
    d. everything in South Africa depends on the black worker.

6. **Depression**

Ernest Keen

1   Depression is not like other symptoms. Since patients can become depressed when they deprive themselves of their symptoms, we may think that depression has merely been substituted as a different symptom. But depression happens at a different level of our being. In fact, depression is in many ways the paramount nonsymptom. *Symptoms* are ways of coping; *depression* neither tries to cope, nor succeeds. *Symptoms* grant us some substitute gratification, however autistic; *depression* eschews gratification. *Symptoms* offer illusions; *depression* is the final disillusionment. *Symptoms* are life, struggling, however maladaptively, to survive; *depression* is a ceasing of the struggle and the beginning of death. In its purest form, depression is giving up.

2   Depression is experienced as the stoppage of time, the emptiness of space, and the reification of others. Time stops; development of myself, of situations, and of relationships all grind to a halt. Everything appears static, dead, with no change except a progressive deterioration like rusting or rotting. Most of all, the future ceases being really future, really new, unknown, fruitful. Rather, the future seems to promise only a dreary repetition of the past. Space is empty. There are things, but they have lost their importance. My house, once a haven and a home, is a mere building, drained of its echoes of vitality and love. My clothes, once full of interest for me, now hang gaping stupidly in my closet. My books are dead, my tennis racquet a mere thing. And other people—their development in time, like my own, gave the future its hope and cast meaning into spaces and places—now are mere things, walking and talking like manikins, mechanically echoing scripts written long ago.

3   Depression runs counter not only to rationality, as symptoms do, and it violates not only the rules of reality, as symptoms do. It also runs counter to and violates the *elan* of life itself, that vital force that lies so deep in our being that we never notice it—until it is absent, as in death, or blocked and negated, as in depression.

4   The giving up of depression is saying, simply, "I can't"—a feeling of hopelessness and helplessness. Adjacent to "I can't" are "I won't," which is angry, and "I shouldn't," which is guilty. All these yield paralysis, but the anger and the guilt are agitated; they have not yet given up. Agitated depression is, if you will, less depressed than the hopelessness of pure depression.

5   In addition to pure depression and agitated depression, there is a kind of pseudodepression, which imitates depression. That imitation

is a way of coping, a way of gaining some substitute gratifications by forcing others to feel sorry for me or to take care of me. In pseudo-depression, I have not really given up, but I am playing *at* it and playing with it. I am threatening to give up if I don't get something I desperately need. I am still struggling, so my condition is not yet hopeless to me, but I am not necessarily kidding. Continued frustration in the struggle can eventually lead to genuine depression, to that giving up that walks death's gait on life's path.

6   Finally, I need to distinguish a fourth kind of depression, a subclinical depression, in which I am depressed and don't know it. It is possible for me to give up or lose touch with life's force and yet keep myself from knowing. I perform this magnificent ruse by indulging myself in a thousand distractions that life makes available to me—mass media, tranquilizing drugs, alcohol, or an all-consuming work role. Each of these has elaborate ideological meanings that convince me that I am fine when I am really desperate. I become dependent on such distractions because their loss confronts me with what I am escaping—my emptiness. At some level I may know of my desperation, but in general I am depressed and don't know it; my depression is subclinical.

7   Emerging from depression, from agitated depression, from pseudodepression, and from subclinical depression are not alike, but each form of emergence has in common the necessity of facing and surviving that utmost of human horrors—death in life, being alive and conscious without a script, myth, or story line that provides meaning, life without life's reason, death without death's sleep.

8   Kierkegaard, over a hundred years ago, said,

> Despair is never ultimately over the external object but always over ourselves. A girl loses her sweetheart and she despairs. It is not over the sweetheart, but over herself-without-the-sweetheart. And so it is with all cases of loss, whether it be money, power, or social rank. The unbearable loss is not really in itself unbearable. What we cannot bear is being stripped of the external object. We stand denuded and see the intolerable abyss of ourselves.

9   "The intolerable abyss of ourselves": To Kierkegaard, oneself was an abyss because of man's alienation from God, his source and his destiny. Freud, three-quarters of a century later, also spoke of loss, its role in depression, and the struggles with the self that follow. Oneself becomes an intolerable abyss for Freud when mourning fails, when, in the absence of the lost object, our love and our hatred turn back to ourselves in a convoluted orgy of guilt, oneself becoming intolerable and abysmal.

10   Modern phenomenologists don't construe the universe as either Kierkegaard or Freud did, but we nevertheless are indebted to their

insights. In depression it is oneself that is the issue, as Kierkegaard said, and mourning a loss is a crucial part of emerging from depression, as Freud suggested. We might put it this way: The work of mourning is the work of becoming someone new after a loss, of creating a new way of being myself, now in the absence of an anchor in the world that formerly tied me to a definition of myself in space and time. Parents, lovers, automobiles, jobs—the losses that make us depressed—all define us when they're here and leave us undefined when they abandon us. We rebel against the loss, but more importantly, we rebel against being someone else, against being some other way. Emerging from depression, then, is essentially a matter of reinventing ourselves.

11   Depression in its pure form is death-like because we have ceased being who we were before the loss, and we have not become someone again. We have lost who we are, our being. In pure depression, we *are* not. In pseudodepression, we *are*, but we are playing at not being and playing *with* not being. In subclinical depression, we are playing *at* being by clinging desperately to irrelevant and trivial story lines embedded in life's distractions.

12   One more feature of becoming depressed must be taken into account before we can speak of emerging from depression, and that is the self-deception that attempts to protect us from sadness.

13   Sadness, the feeling, can be lived through and survived. The *escape* from sadness, especially the fantasies that would pretend the loss has not happened, cannot be lived through. Once embraced, these fantasies begin to live us, to control us and prevent us from accepting the truth that something is lost, that I am no longer who I used to be, and that I must work out a new way to be myself.

14   Now I know, of course, when my parent dies, that that loss is real and I must accept it. Nothing so vividly testifies to the existence of the unconscious as the discovery that even though "I know" I have lost my parent, at the same time I do not know it—or I expect my lost parent to return. This expectation is an unconscious fantasy—unconscious because, after all, "I know" the parent is lost, and a fantasy because it magically transforms reality from what it is to what I would wish it to be. I have access to this fantasy only at the edges of my consciousness, when I catch myself looking at the clock or glancing out the window at the time of my parent's customary return, or when I think I see him on the street, or when I make a mental note to tell him such and such. Beneath these signs lies an unconscious fantasy that I have *not* lost my parent. This fantasy rebels against the reality of the loss as "I know" it and tries to cling to the being I was before the loss occurred.

15   As long as this fantasy is active and important, every waking realization that my parent is lost is the occasion of anger. But since "I

know" better, the anger too remains beyond the edge of my consciousness, visible only in my lack of patience with the key that sticks
in the lock or the shoestring that breaks. Little and ordinary things
become contemptible. Whence this contempt? I locate its origin in
the things themselves. The visible world now becomes dreary, repet-
itive, grey, and uninteresting. I do not recognize that I am angry, and
I do not recognize that my anger is at the loss of my parent, because
I do not know that I still expect him to be there. The sadness led to
the fantasy, that led to the contradiction by what "I know" is true,
that led to the anger, that led to the discoloration of the world. I am
becoming depressed, not in the healthy sense of mourning and working through the sadness of the loss toward accepting its truth and
toward reinventing myself. Rather, I am caught in a web of self-
deceptions and denials, the only outcome of which is a regeneration
of the anger and rebellion in a perpetual circle of misery that we have
called pseudodepression. The playing *at* and playing *with* the giving
up of true depression, like a symptom, struggles on behalf of life. But
genuine giving up and pure depression become, in the frustrations of
my vicious circle of self-deception, a real possibility.

16   To summarize so far: Depression is a profound negation of life
while one is still alive, a phenomenon so paradoxical that it puzzles
us much more than symptoms, which struggle, however vainly, on
behalf of life. Pseudodepression, however, uses depressive themes and
styles to try to perpetuate illusions or achieve gratifications. The unconscious fantasies that deny loss are key symptoms of pseudodepression. The fantasies are condemned to frustration. Continuing frustration can inspire the angry "I won't" or the guilty "I shouldn't" of
agitated depression, or even the hopeless "I can't" of true depression.
Subclinical depression is being derailed from the vital force of life
without knowing it. Covering up the emptiness in subclinical depression is an addiction to such distractions as tranquilizers, alcohol,
mass media, or an all-consuming work role.

Emerging from Depression

17   Emerging from depression of all four types involves not the disappearance of a symptom but the reappearance, reinvention, or redis-
covery of a self with a past and a future. My present life, which leads
from the past into the future, matters when it is part of a historical
unfolding within which I can place myself in an integral part. Having
a job, being a parent, engaging in crafts, for example, *can* supply such
a story. In depression, these ordinary aspects of life have been neu-
tralized—rendered meaningless—by the death themes of depression:
the stoppage of time, the emptiness of space, and the reification of
people. The reestablishment of a future, the refurnishing of space

with significance and vitality, and the repersonification of others are all implicated in reinventing myself and emerging from depression.

18   To rebuild a temporal flow so I can throw in some effort of my own to affect a future whose shape matters to me—what kind of rebuilding is that? To rebuild the significance of places, home, my place, your place, public places, so that getting from one to another matters to me—what kind of rebuilding is that? To repersonify others so that their otherness is a center of vitality that touches me and moves me, and can be moved by me—what kind of rebuilding is that?

19   It has to begin with a memory of life, but the memory is not enough. In addition, it takes something like a faith that one can come alive again. I do not know what inspires that faith. I know you cannot create it for me if I don't somehow want to have it, to live. If I've really given up, only a new decision by me can initiate the faith necessary to begin to rebuild.

20   But rebuilding is tedious; it seems nearly hopeless; it is full of storms, rages, guilts, disgust, and self-contempt. Every beginning seems artificial, and frail, so weak in the face of the overwhelming influences of my having given up. Building laboriously on an artificial starting point leads to collapse, and to giving up once again in hopelessness, despairing a starting point that feels reliable.

21   If I should find the faith to overcome hopelessness, I must now deal with the anger and the guilt of agitated depression. If you want to help me now, you will have to sustain a relationship that can survive this anger and guilt. I need to be able to trust you, to know you will not leave me abandoned on the desert once again. I need to find I can't destroy you, for destroy you I will try, convinced as I am that I don't deserve this foothold in life. I need to contribute something to the relationship, so it is partly my creation, not a mere gift. But I am dead; I have nothing to contribute. I need to vent carloads of anger, directed alternately at you, then at myself, making the theme of the relationship one of hatred, guilt, disdain, and despair. Amidst all that pain, I must somehow believe that it's all worth it, and I have to believe that you believe it is too. I have to come to trust that you'll be there even as I disappear beneath the waves of remorse that seem like oceans, washing me mindlessly out to sea where memories matter no more. As if all that is not enough, I need a relationship that does two opposite things at once; it must give me what I may want— another chance at life—and it must punish me as I deserve by leaving me the speechless despair of a death in life. If it fails to give me the chance at a starting point of life, it is useless to me. If it succeeds, it is a gift I do not deserve, is artificial, and hence must be rejected. What relationship can do both—can be both A and not A at the same time?

22   If I decide to have the faith to try life again, if you can survive my anger and guilt, if I can find in you a relationship that can be as paradoxical as my own life—if all of these happen, I am now faced with the task of rebuilding. That building must reengage the struggles of self-deception and pseudodepression, it must deal with the rebellion and the frustration of the vicious circle that eventuated in my having given up in the first place. The self-deceptive fantasies denied a loss and protected me from the sadness of enduring that loss, of mourning and letting go, of finding what of myself remains, and marshalling the energy to continue as someone else, someone with memories. The self-deceptive fantasies must be confronted and destroyed, and their protection must vanish so I am vulnerable to the sadness and the emptiness of life, now lived in the salient presence of an absence.

23   You cannot protect me from this pain. My protecting myself has resulted in a vicious circle; my only way out is to submit to the loss and let its force tear at the fabric of my being in the world. At some point we shall see what, if anything, is left. Before, I spiralled into a circle of anger and frustration that had no resolution. I imitated giving up in order to wrest from you and from the environment some substitutes for what was lost and some filling for my inner emptiness. I must do it differently this time; I must mourn and I must rebuild a world and I must reinvent who I am.

24   From having given up, I somehow venture a faith. From this faith I somehow trust a relationship. From this relationship, I somehow confront my self-deceptions, and somehow I find the courage to undergo the sadness so desperately escaped.

25   I come now to the final stage of emerging from depression, and that is to resist the temptations of the easy solutions offered by psychoactive drugs, alcohol, the amusements of popular culture, or all-consuming work roles. None of these temptations is simply evil, but each leaves us addicted, protected from the sadness of my life—not in the self-defeating vicious circle of unconscious fantasies, but now in very pleasant distractions.

26   The final truth seems to be that emerging from depression is never really complete. The work of remembering, and feeling the sadness, must be renewed a little every day. The flight into distractions avoids that sadness and makes us more cheerful, perhaps. But it is the superficial good cheer of the game show host, or the empty pride of the dedicated professional achiever. Addiction to happiness is no less an addiction than the vilest narcotic. Withdrawal provokes panic. Flexibility is gone; dependency is complete.

27   The sadness of memories is far preferable to the happiness of subclinical depression, for it throws into relief the really good things in life, and makes them shine forth. In this way, ecstasy and tragedy are

two sides of the same coin. Depression can be devastating, but having emerged, I find that depression is enriching and enlivening as I live the reinvented self, born in the struggle of emergence.

28   By referring to depression as a human possibility, and a structured one, I am claiming to describe an ontological characteristic of human being. This puts depression into a finite list of human possibilities. Its place in that list seems to me to be at a border, or boundary of human experience. Giving up is a possibility rarely actualized. It is an extreme reaction to an extreme of human travail. Yet its presence as a possibility is not limited to the extreme. It is possible to be "a little bit depressed," not in the sense that what one is has not come to a limit, but in the sense that most of us come to that limit simultaneously with other, still struggling projects.   *3,483 words*

Comprehension Questions

1. The topic of the article is
    a. depression.
    b. emerging from depression.
    c. helping someone emerge from depression.
    d. the results of depression.
2. In its purest form depression
    a. is giving up.
    b. is a symptom.
    c. grants substitute gratification.
    d. is struggling.
3. The author discusses ———— type(s) of depression.
    a. one
    b. two
    c. three
    d. four
4. A depressed person uses ———— to attempt to protect himself from sadness.
    a. self-deception
    b. selfishness
    c. humor
    d. illness
5. For many people depression results from
    a. biological imbalance.
    b. not having enough money.
    c. not dealing adequately with grief.
    d. working too hard.
6. Emerging from depression involves the
    a. rediscovery of a self with a past and a future.
    b. disappearance of a symptom.

    c. giving up.
    d. protection from pain.
7. The author uses _____ to support his ideas.
    a. personal experience
    b. scientific experiments
    c. surveys
    d. facts
8. In depression it is _____ that is the issue.
    a. oneself
    b. loss
    c. guilt
    d. another person
9. The purpose of the article is to
    a. inform the reader about depression.
    b. persuade the reader not to be depressed.
    c. compare and contrast depression and its symptoms.
    d. list types of depression.
10. According to the article, one can infer that helping a depressed person is
    a. difficult.
    b. impossible.
    c. artificial.
    d. protective.

7. Nursing as Metaphor

Claire Fagin, Ph.D., R.N. and
Donna Diers, M.S.N., R.N.

1   For some time now we have been curious about the reactions of people we meet socially to being told, "I am a nurse." First reactions to this statement include the comment, "I never met a nurse socially before": stories about the person's latest hospitalization, surgery, or childbearing experiences; the question "How can you bear handling bedpans (vomit, blood)?" or the remark, "I think I need another drink." We believe the statements reflect the fact that nursing evokes disturbing and discomforting images that many educated, middle-class, upwardly mobile Americans find difficult to handle in a social situation. As nurses, we are educated to give comfort, so it is something of a paradox when we make ourselves and others uncomfortable socially.

2   It is easy to say that some reactions are based on an underlying attitude toward nurses that we tend to think of as a stereotype. But labeling the attitude does not help us explain it or escape it. Perhaps we can deal with the social perception by examining the metaphors that underlie the concept of "nurse"—metaphors that influence not only language but also thought and action. An exploration of the metaphorical underpinnings of nursing must start with the etymology of the word "nurse," which is derived from the Latin for "nourish."

3   Nursing is a metaphor for mothering. Nursing has links with nurturing, caring, comforting, the laying on of hands, and other maternal types of behavior, all of which are seen in our society as essentially mundane and hardly worth noticing. Even the thought of the vertical nurse over the horizontal patient evokes regressed feelings in a woman or man who is told, "I am a nurse." Adults do not like to be reminded, especially in an adult, socially competitive setting, of the child who remains inside all of us.

4   Nursing is a metaphor for class struggle. Not only does nursing represent women's struggles for equality, but its position in the health world is that of the classic underdog, struggling to be heard, approved, and recognized. Nurses constitute the largest occupational group in the health-care system (1.6 million). They work predominantly in settings that are dominated by physicians and in which physicians represent the upper and controlling class. Dominant groups yield ground reluctantly, especially to those who are regarded as having simply settled for a job instead of choosing a more prestigious profession.

5   Nursing is a metaphor for equality. Little social distance separates the nurse from the patient or the patient from other patients in the nursing-care setting, no matter what the social class of each. Nurses themselves make little distinction in rank among persons with widely varying amounts of education. Nurses are perceived as members of the working class, and although this perception is valuable to the patient when he or she is ill and wants to be comforted, it may be awkward to encounter one's nurses at a black-tie reception, where working-class people do not belong.

6   Among physicians, nursing may be a metaphor for conscience. Nurses see all that happens in the name of health care—the neglect as well as the cures, the reasons for failure as well as those for success. The anxiety, not to mention the guilt, engendered by what nurses may know can be considerable. Nurses recognize that many of the physician's attempts to conquer death do not work. They are an uncomfortable reminder of fallibility.

7   Nursing is a metaphor for intimacy. Nurses are involved in the most private aspects of people's lives, and they cannot hide behind technology or a veil of omniscience as other practitioners or technicians in hospitals may do. Nurses do for others publicly what healthy persons do for themselves behind closed doors. Nurses, as trusted peers, are there to hear secrets, especially the ones born of vulnerability. Nurses are treasured when these interchanges are successful, but most often people do not wish to remember their vulnerability or loss of control, and nurses are indelibly identified with those terribly personal times.

8   Thanks to the worst of this kind of thinking, nursing is a metaphor for sex. Having seen and touched the bodies of strangers, nurses are perceived as willing and able sexual partners. Knowing and experienced, they unlike prostitutes, are thought, to be safe—a quality suggested by the cleanliness of their white uniforms and their professional aplomb.

9   Something like the sum of these images makes up the psychological milieu in which nurses live and work. Little wonder, then, that some of us have been badgered (at least in our earlier days) about our choice of career. Little wonder, then, that nurses have had to develop a resilience required of few other professionals. Little wonder, too, that it is so difficult for us to reply to our detractors. One may wonder why any self-respecting, reasonably intellectual man or woman chooses nursing as a lifelong career. Our students at Pennsylvania and Yale are regularly asked questions like this by family, friends, and acquaintances: "Why on earth are you becoming a nurse? You have the brains to be a (doctor, lawyer, other)." All of them, long before entering schools such as ours, must answer this question for themselves and their questioners in a way that permits them to begin and to continue nursing. Their responses and ours frequently focus

on the role of the nurse, the variety and mobility possible in a nursing career, or the changing nature of the profession. That kind of answer doesn't get to the heart of the problem in the mind of the questioner. Although it may elicit an "Oh, I didn't realize that," it doesn't make any permanent points for anyone. The right answer has to address the metaphors, since these are the reasons for the concern. The answer must convey the feeling of satisfaction derived from the caring role: indifference to power for its own sake; the recognition that one is a doer who enjoys doing for and with others; but most of all, the pleasure associated with helping others from the position of a peer rather than from the assumed superordinate position of some other professions.

10   The metaphors, if we turn them around, can easily work to explain our position. Intimacy—why shrink from the word, even while we educate our listeners about its finer meaning—equality, conscience, and the many qualities of motherhood (another word that can usefully be separated from its stereotype) are exactly what draw people into nursing and keep them there.

11   If we could manage to be wistfully amused by the reactions we evoke at social events rather than defensive, life would be easier. Educated, middle-class, upwardly mobile—we are indeed the peers of others at these social gatherings. We are peers informed about disease prevention, the promotion of health, and rehabilitation. We are not disinterested experts but advocates, even for those who misinterpret us. Others may be only dimly aware of our role, but it is rooted deep in our history and exemplified by the great nursing leaders who have moved society forward: Lavinia Dock, so active in pursuing women's rights; Lillian Wald (a nurse whom society has preferred to disguise as a social worker), who developed the Henry Street Settlement and educated all of us in understanding and approaching health and social problems; Margaret Sanger, who faced disdain, ignominy, and imprisonment in her struggle to educate the public about birth control; and Sister Kenny, who was once the only hope for polio victims.

12   So much for the metaphors of others. For ourselves? We think of ourselves as Florence Nightingale—tough, canny, powerful, autonomous, and heroic.   *1,194 words*

Comprehension Questions

1. This article
   a. explains why people go into nursing.
   b. explains why people use metaphors.
   c. ridicules people who go into nursing.
   d. talks mainly about women.

2. The key idea of this article is
   a. that nurses need a better public image.
   b. that metaphors can help to explain the qualities of the nursing profession.
   c. that nursing is primarily a metaphor for more important issues.
   d. that metaphors create misconceptions about nurses.
3. The authors support their key idea with
   a. illustrations.
   b. case histories.
   c. metaphors.
   d. arguments.
4. The authors claim that nurses are
   a. reticent.
   b. egalitarian.
   c. boorish.
   d. belligerent.
5. Of the four actual nurses cited as examples, _____ are praised on purely medical grounds.
   a. one
   b. two
   c. all
   d. none
6. Students of nursing sometimes are asked questions that imply that nursing is
   a. dangerous.
   b. prestigious.
   c. challenging.
   d. easy.
7. When meeting nurses socially, people are usually
   a. full of admiration.
   b. fearful.
   c. disgusted.
   d. uncomfortable.
8. The authors suggest _____ possible metaphorical interpretations of nursing.
   a. two
   b. three
   c. five
   d. four
9. The majority of the metaphors show a connection between nursing and
   a. doctors.
   b. women.

    c. hospitals.

    d. wisdom.

10. Which of the following best states the authors' view about nursing?

    a. Nurses should be second-class citizens.

    b. The nursing profession is well understood.

    c. Nurses should be admired.

    d. Most nurses wish they were doing something else.

8. The Detective as Scientist

Irving M. Copi

1   . . . A perennial favorite in this connection is the detective, whose problem is not quite the same as that of the pure scientist, but whose approach and technique illustrate the method of science very clearly. The classical example of the astute detective who can solve even the most baffling mystery is A. Conan Doyle's immortal creation, Sherlock Holmes. Holmes, his stature undiminished by the passage of time, will be our hero in the following account:

2   **1. The Problem.**   Some of our most vivid pictures of Holmes are those in which he is busy with magnifying glass and tape measure, searching out and finding essential clues which had escaped the attention of those stupid bunglers, the "experts" of Scotland Yard. Or those of us who are by temperament less vigorous may think back more fondly on Holmes the thinker, ". . . who, when he had an unsolved problem upon his mind, would go for days, and even for a week, without rest, turning it over, rearranging his facts, looking at it from every point of view until he had either fathomed it or convinced himself that his data were insufficient."[1] At one such time, according to Dr. Watson:

> He took off his coat and waistcoat, put on a large blue dressing-gown, and then wandered about the room collecting pillows from his bed and cushions from the sofa and armchairs. With these he constructed a sort of Eastern divan, upon which he perched himself cross-legged, with an ounce of shag tobacco and a box of matches laid out in front of him. In the dim light of the lamp I saw him sitting there, an old briar pipe between his lips, his eyes fixed vacantly upon the corner of the ceiling, the blue smoke curling up from him, silent, motionless, with the light shining upon his strong-set aquiline features. So he sat as I dropped off to sleep, and so he sat when a sudden ejaculation caused me to wake up, and I found the summer sun shining into the apartment. The pipe was still between his lips, the smoke still curled upward, and the room was full of a dense tobacco haze, but nothing remained of the heap of shag which I had seen upon the previous night.[2]

3   But such memories are incomplete. Holmes was not always searching for clues or pondering over solutions. We all remember

---

[1]"The Man with the Twisted Lip."
[2]Ibid.

those dark periods—especially in the earlier stories—when, much to the good Watson's annoyance, Holmes would drug himself with morphine or cocaine. That would happen, of course, between cases. For when there is no mystery to be unraveled, no man in his right mind would go out to look for clues. Clues, after all, must be clues for something. Nor could Holmes, or anyone else, for that matter, engage in profound thought unless he had something to think about. Sherlock Holmes was a genius at solving problems, but even a genius must have a problem before he can solve it. All reflective thinking, and this term includes criminal investigation as well as scientific research, is a problem-solving activity, as John Dewey and other pragmatists have rightly insisted. There must be a problem felt before either the detective or the scientist can go to work.

4   Of course the active mind sees problems where the dullard sees only familiar objects. One Christmas season Dr. Watson visited Holmes to find that the latter had been using a lens and forceps to examine "... a very seedy and disreputable hard-felt hat, much the worse for wear, and cracked in several places."[3] After they had greeted each other, Holmes said of it to Watson, "I beg that you will look upon it not as a battered billycock but as an intellectual problem."[4] It so happened that the hat led them into one of their most interesting adventures, but it could not have done so had Holmes not seen a problem in it from the start. A problem may be characterized as a fact or group of facts for which we have no acceptable explanation, which seem unusual, or which fail to fit in with our expectations or preconceptions. It should be obvious that *some* prior beliefs are required if anything is to appear problematic. If there are no expectations, there can be no surprises.

5   Sometimes, of course, problems came to Holmes already labeled. The very first adventure recounted by Dr. Watson began with the following message from Gregson of Scotland Yard:

> My Dear Mr. Sherlock Holmes:
>   There has been a bad business during the night at 3, Lauriston Gardens, off the Brixton Road. Our man on the beat saw a light there about two in the morning, and as the house was an empty one, suspected that something was amiss. He found the door open, and in the front room, which is bare of furniture, discovered the body of a gentleman, well dressed, and having cards in his pocket bearing the name of 'Enoch J. Drebber, Cleveland, Ohio, U.S.A.' There had been no robbery, nor is there any evidence as to how the man met his death. There are marks of blood in the room, but there is no wound upon his person. We are at a loss as to how he came

---

[3]"The Adventure of the Blue Carbuncle."
[4]Ibid.

into the empty house; indeed, the whole affair is a puzzler. If you can come round to the house any time before twelve, you will find me there. I have left everything in statu quo until I hear from you. If you are unable to come, I shall give you fuller details, and would esteem it a great kindness if you would favour me with your opinion.

Yours faithfully
TOBIAS GREGSON[5]

Here was a problem indeed. A few minutes after receiving the message, Sherlock Holmes and Dr. Watson "were both in a hansom, driving furiously for the Brixton Road."

6   **2. Preliminary Hypotheses.**   On their ride out Brixton way, Holmes "prattled away about Cremona fiddles and the difference between a Stradivarius and an Amati." Dr. Watson chided Holmes for not giving much thought to the matter at hand, and Holmes replied: "No data yet. . . . It is a capital mistake to theorize before you have all the evidence. It biases the judgment."[6] This point of view was expressed by Holmes again and again. On one occasion he admonished a younger detective that "The temptation to form premature theories upon insufficient data is the bane of our profession."[7] Yet for all of his confidence about the matter, on this one issue Holmes was completely mistaken. Of course one should not reach a *final judgment* until a great deal of evidence has been considered, but this procedure is quite different from *not theorizing*. As a matter of fact, it is strictly impossible to make any serious attempt to collect evidence unless one *has* theorized beforehand. As Charles Darwin, the great biologist and author of the modern theory of evolution, observed: ". . . all observation must be for or against some view, if it is to be of any service." The point is that there are too many particular facts, too many data in the world, for anyone to try to become acquainted with them all. Everyone, even the most patient and thorough investigator, must pick and choose, deciding which facts to study and which to pass over. He must have some working hypothesis for or against which to collect relevant data. It need not be a *complete* theory, but at least the rough outline must be there. Otherwise how could one decide what facts to select for consideration out of the totality of all facts, which is too vast even to begin to sift?

7   Holmes' actions were wiser than his words in this connection. After all, the words were spoken in a hansom speeding towards the

---

[5]*A Study in Scarlet.*
[6]Ibid.
[7]*The Valley of Fear.*

scene of the crime. If Holmes really had no theory about the matter, why go to Brixton Road? If facts and data were all that he wanted, any old facts and any old data, with no hypotheses to guide him in their selection, why should he have left Baker Street at all? There were plenty of facts in the rooms at 221-B, Baker Street. Holmes might just as well have spent his time counting all the words on the pages of all the books there, or perhaps making very accurate measurements of the distances between each separate pair of articles of furniture in the house. He could have gathered data to his heart's content and saved himself cab fare into the bargain!

8   It may be objected that the facts to be gathered at Baker Street have nothing to do with the case, whereas those which awaited Holmes at the scene of the crime were valuable clues for solving the problem. It was, of course, just this consideration which led Holmes to ignore the "data" at Baker Street and hurry away to collect those off Brixton Road. It must be insisted, however, that the greater relevance of the latter could not be *known* beforehand but only conjectured on the basis of previous experience with crimes and clues. It was in fact a *hypothesis* which led Holmes to look in one place rather than another for his facts, the hypothesis that there was a murder, that the crime was committed at the place where the body was found, and the murderer had left some trace or clue which could lead to his discovery. Some such hypothesis is always required to guide the investigator in his search for relevant data, for in the absence of any preliminary hypothesis, there are simply too many facts in this world to examine. The preliminary hypothesis ought to be highly tentative, and it must be based on previous knowledge. But a preliminary hypothesis is as necessary as the existence of a problem for any serious inquiry to begin.

9   It must be emphasized that a preliminary hypothesis, as here conceived, need not be a complete solution to the problem. The hypothesis that the man was murdered by someone who had left some clues to his identity on or near the body of his victim was what led Holmes to Brixton Road. This hypothesis is clearly incomplete: it does not say who committed the crime, or how it was done, or why. Such a preliminary hypothesis may be very different from the final solution to the problem. It will never be complete: it may be a tentative explanation of only part of the problem. But however partial and however tentative, a preliminary hypothesis is required for any investigation to proceed.

10   **3. Collecting Additional Facts.**   Every serious investigation begins with some fact or group of facts which strike the investigator as problematic and which initiate the whole process of inquiry. The initial facts which constitute the problem are usually too meagre to suggest

a wholly satisfactory explanation for themselves, but they will suggest—to the competent investigator—some preliminary hypotheses which lead him to search out additional facts. These additional facts, it is hoped, will serve as clues to the final solution. The inexperienced or bungling investigator will overlook or ignore all but the most obvious of them; but the careful worker will aim at completeness in his examination of the additional facts to which his preliminary hypotheses lead him. Holmes, of course, was the most careful and painstaking of investigators.

11   Holmes insisted on dismounting from the hansom a hundred yards or so from their destination and approached the house on foot, looking carefully at its surroundings and especially at the pathway leading up to it. When Holmes and Watson entered the house, they were shown the body by the Scotland Yard operatives, Gregson and Lestrade. ("There is no clue," said Gregson. "None at all," chimed in Lestrade.) But Holmes had already started his own search for additional facts, looking first at the body:

> . . . his nimble fingers were flying here, there, and everywhere, feeling, pressing, unbuttoning, examining. . . . So swiftly was examination made, that one would hardly have guessed the minuteness with which it was conducted. Finally, he sniffed the dead man's lips, and then glanced at the soles of his patent leather boots.[8]

Then turning his attention to the room itself,

> . . . he whipped a tape measure and a large round magnifying glass from his pocket. With these two implements he trotted noiselessly about the room, sometimes stopping, occasionally kneeling, and once lying flat upon his face. So engrossed was he with his occupation that he appeared to have forgotten our presence, for he chattered away to himself under his breath the whole time, keeping up a running fire of exclamations, groans, whistles, and little cries suggestive of encouragement and of hope. As I watched him I was irresistibly reminded of a pure-blooded, well-trained foxhound as it dashes backward and forward through the covert, whining in its eagerness, until it comes across the lost scent. For twenty minutes or more he continued his researches, measuring with the most exact care the distance between marks which were entirely invisible to me, and occasionally applying his tape to the walls in an equally incomprehensible manner. In one place he gathered up very carefully a little pile of gray dust from the floor and packed it away in an envelope. Finally, he examined with his glass the word upon the wall, going over every letter of it with the most minute exactness. This done, he appeared to be satisfied, for he replaced his tape and his glass in his pocket.

---

[8]*A Study in Scarlet.*

> "They say that genius is an infinite capacity for taking pains," he re-
> marked with a smile. "It's a very bad definition, but it does apply to de-
> tective work."[9]

12   One matter deserves to be emphasized very strongly. Steps 2 and
3 are not completely separable but are usually very intimately connected and interdependent. True enough, we require a preliminary
hypothesis to begin any intelligent examination of facts, but the additional facts may themselves suggest new hypotheses, which may
lead to new facts, which suggest still other hypotheses, which lead to
still other additional facts, and so on. Thus having made his careful
examination of the facts available in the house off Brixton Road,
Holmes was led to formulate a further hypothesis which required the
taking of testimony from the constable who found the body. The man
was off duty at the moment, and Lestrade gave Holmes the constable's name and address.

> Holmes took a note of the address.
> "Come along, Doctor," he said: "we shall go and look him up. I'll tell
> you one thing which may help you in the case," he continued, turning to
> the two detectives. "There has been murder done, and the murderer was
> a man. He was more than six feet high, was in the prime of life, had small
> feet for his height, wore coarse, square-toed boots and smoked a Trichin-
> opoly cigar. He came here with his victim in a four-wheel cab, which was
> drawn by a horse with three old shoes and one new one on his off fore-leg.
> In all probability the murderer had a florid face, and the fingernails of his
> right hand were remarkably long. These are only a few indications, but
> they may assist you."
> Lestrade and Gregson glanced at each other with an incredulous smile.
> "If this man was murdered, how was it done?" asked the former.
> "Poison," said Sherlock Holmes curtly, and strode off.[10]

13   **4. Formulating the Hypothesis.**   At some stage or other of his investigation, any man—whether detective, scientist, or ordinary mortal—
will get the feeling that he has all the facts needed for his solution.
He has his "2 and 2," so to speak, but the task still remains of "putting
them together." At such a time Sherlock Holmes might sit up all
night, consuming pipe after pipe of tobacco, trying to think things
through. The result or end product of such thinking, if it is successful,
is a hypothesis which accounts for all the data, both the original set
of facts which constituted the problem, and the additional facts to

[9]Ibid.
[10]Ibid.

which the preliminary hypotheses pointed. The actual discovery of such an explanatory hypothesis is a process of creation, in which imagination as well as knowledge is involved. Holmes, who was a genius at inventing hypotheses, described the process as reasoning "backward." As he put it,

> Most people if you describe a train of events to them, will tell you what the result would be. They can put those events together in their minds, and argue from them that something will come to pass. There are few people, however, who, if you told them a result, would be able to evolve from their own inner consciousness what the steps were which led up to that result.[11]

Here is Holmes' description of the process of formulating an explanatory hypothesis. . . . Granted its relevance and testability, and its compatibility with other well-attested beliefs, the ultimate criterion for evaluating a hypothesis is its predictive power.

14   **5. Deducing Further Consequences.**   A really fruitful hypothesis will not only explain the facts which originally inspired it, but will explain many others in addition. A good hypothesis will point beyond the initial facts in the direction of new ones whose existence might otherwise not have been suspected. And of course the verification of those further consequences will tend to confirm the hypothesis which led to them. Holmes' hypothesis that the murdered man had been poisoned was soon put to such a test. A few days later the murdered man's secretary and traveling companion was also found murdered. Holmes asked Lestrade, who had discovered the second body, whether he had found anything in the room which could furnish a clue to the murderer. Lestrade answered, "Nothing," and went on to mention a few quite ordinary effects. Holmes was not satisfied and pressed him, asking, "And was there nothing else?" Lestrade answered "Nothing of any importance," and named a few more details, the last of which was "a small chip ointment box containing a couple of pills." At this information,

> Sherlock Holmes sprang from his chair with an exclamation of delight. "The last links," he cried, exultantly. "My case is complete."
> The two detectives stared at him in amazement.
> "I have now in my hands," my companion said, confidently, "all the threads which have formed such a tangle. . . . I will give you a proof of my knowledge. Could you lay your hands upon those pills?"
> "I have them," said Lestrade, producing a small white box. . . .[12]

---

[11]Ibid.
[12]Ibid.

15   On the basis of his hypothesis about the original crime, Holmes was able to predict that the pills found at the scene of the second crime must contain poison. Here deduction has an essential role in the process of any scientific or inductive inquiry. The ultimate value of any hypothesis lies in its predictive or explanatory power, which means that additional facts must be deducible from an adequate hypothesis. From his theory that the first man was poisoned and that the second victim met his death at the hands of the same murderer, Holmes inferred that the pills found by Lestrade must be poison. His theory, however sure he may have felt about it, was only a theory and needed further confirmation. He obtained that confirmation by testing the consequences deduced from the hypothesis and finding them to be true. Having used deduction to make a prediction, his next step was to test it.

16   **6. Testing the Consequences.**   The consequences of a hypothesis, that is, the predictions made on the basis of that hypothesis, may require various means for their testing. Some require only observation. In some cases, Holmes needed only to watch and wait—for the bank robbers to break into the vault, in the "Adventure of the Red-headed League," or for Dr. Roylott to slip a venomous snake through a dummy ventilator, in the "Adventure of the Speckled Band." In the present case, however, an experiment had to be performed.

17   Holmes asked Dr. Watson to fetch the landlady's old and ailing terrier, which she had asked to have put out of its misery the day before. Holmes then cut one of the pills in two, dissolved it in a wineglass of water, added some milk, and

> . . . turned the contents of the wineglass into a saucer and placed it in front of the terrier, who speedily licked it dry. Sherlock Holmes's earnest demeanour had so far convinced us that we all sat in silence, watching the animal intently, and expecting some startling effect. None such appeared, however. The dog continued to lie stretched upon the cushion, breathing in a laboured way, but apparently neither the better nor the worse for its draught.
>
>   Holmes had taken out his watch, and as minute followed minute without result, an expression of the utmost chagrin and disappointment appeared upon his features. He gnawed his lip, drummed his fingers upon the table, and showed every other symptom of acute impatience. So great was his emotion that I felt sincerely sorry for him, while the two detectives smiled derisively, by no means displeased at this check which he had met.
>
>   "It can't be a coincidence," he cried, at last springing from his chair and pacing wildly up and down the room: "it is impossible that it should be a mere coincidence. The very pills which I suspected in the case of Drebber are actually found after the death of Stangerson. And yet they are inert. What can it mean? Surely my whole chain of reasoning cannot have been false. It is impossible! And yet this wretched dog is none the worse.

Ah, I have it! I have it!" With a perfect shriek of delight he rushed to the box, cut the other pill in two, dissolved it, added milk, and presented it to the terrier. The unfortunate creature's tongue seemed hardly to have been moistened in it before it gave a convulsive shiver in every limb, and lay as rigid and lifeless as if it had been struck by lightning.

Sherlock Holmes drew a long breath, and wiped the perspiration from his forehead.[13]

By the favorable outcome of his experiment, Holmes' hypothesis had received dramatic and convincing confirmation.

18   **7. Application.**   The detective's concern, after all, is a practical one. Given a crime to solve, he has not merely to explain the facts but to apprehend and arrest the criminal. The latter involves making application of his theory, using it to predict where the criminal can be found and how he may be caught. He must deduce still further consequences from the hypothesis, not for the sake of additional confirmation but for practical use. From his general hypothesis Holmes was able to infer that the murderer was acting the role of a cabman. We have already seen that Holmes had formed a pretty clear description of the man's appearance. He sent out his army of "Baker Street Irregulars," street urchins of the neighborhood, to search out and summon the cab driven by just that man. The successful "application" of this hypothesis can be described again in Dr. Watson's words. A few minutes after the terrier's death,

> . . . there was a tap at the door, and the spokesman of the street Arabs, young Wiggins, introduced his insignificant and unsavoury person.
>
> "Please, sir," he said touching his forelock, "I have the cab downstairs."
>
> "Good boy," said Holmes, blandly. "Why don't you introduce this pattern at Scotland Yard?" he continued, taking a pair of steel handcuffs from a drawer. "See how beautifully the spring works. They fasten in an instant."
>
> "The old pattern is good enough," remarked Lestrade, "if we can only find the man to put them on."
>
> "Very good, very good," said Holmes, smiling. "The cabman may as well help me with my boxes. Just ask him to step in, Wiggins."
>
> I was surprised to find my companion speaking as though he were about to set out on a journey, since he had not said anything to me about it. There was a small portmanteau in the room, and this he pulled out and began to strap. He has busily engaged at it when the cabman entered the room.
>
> "Just give me a help with this buckle, cabman," he said, kneeling over his task, and never turning his head.
>
> The fellow came forward with a somewhat sullen, defiant air, and put

---

[13]Ibid.

down his hands to assist. At that instant there was a sharp click, the jangling of metal, and Sherlock Holmes sprang to his feet again.

"Gentlemen," he cried, with flashing eyes, "let me introduce you to Mr. Jefferson Hope, the murderer of Enoch Drebber and of Joseph Stangerson."[14]

19   Here we have a picture of the detective as scientist, reasoning from observed facts to a testable hypothesis which not only explains the facts but permits of practical application.   *3,903 words*

_____

[14]Ibid.

Comprehension Questions

1. A good statement of the topic is
   a. Sherlock Holmes.
   b. problem solving.
   c. detectives and scientists.
   d. the nature of science.
2. The author is primarily concerned with
   a. showing how good a detective Sherlock Holmes is.
   b. demonstrating the scientific method.
   c. crime and punishment.
   d. teaching the reader how to think.
3. "Collecting additional facts" is a
   a. key idea.
   b. supporting detail.
   c. metaphor.
   d. subtopic.
4. A testable hypothesis
   a. allows practical application.
   b. does not explain the facts.
   c. is unnecessary in crime detection.
   d. was Sherlock Holmes's trademark.
5. According to this article, a scientist or detective can go to work only when there is a
   a. problem.
   b. case.
   c. crime.
   d. need.
6. Which of the following is *not* included in the seven steps a scientist takes in applying the scientific method?
   a. formulating a preliminary hypothesis
   b. collecting additional facts
   c. testing the consequences
   d. discounting evidence that is hard to understand

7. Which of the following patterns of organization does the author use in this article?
   a. cause and effect
   b. compare/contrast
   c. order
   d. *all of the above*
8. A hypothesis is a prediction based on
   a. guesses.
   b. experience.
   c. experiment.
   d. facts.
9. Once a problem is identified, a person should proceed with
   a. no preconceived notions.
   b. a firm plan of attack.
   c. some preliminary theories based on prior factual knowledge.
   d. great haste.
10. Theories _____ facts.
    a. exclude
    b. lead to
    c. are
    d. confuse

9. Sugar: How Sweet It Is — And Isn't

*Chris W. Lecos**

1   Sugar, "that honey from reeds," as one author described it more than 2,000 years ago, has been a part of mankind's diet for as long as anyone cares to remember.

2   Cave drawings tell us of prehistoric man's taste for honey, figs, and dates. The beekeeping practices of Egyptians are depicted in the artwork in tombs dating around 2600 B.C.

3   The Bible tells us that the "promised land" flowed with milk and honey. It turned into a flood once sugarcane was discovered.

4   In the writings of an obscure officer in Alexander's army during its invasion of India, one finds the first written mention of sugarcane. That was around 325 B.C.

5   Yet, despite this long history, the use of sugar in the diet has become a controversial issue in recent years that has involved doctors, scientists, nutritionists, private citizens, the Government, and the industry itself.

6   Why all the fuss?

   • Because there is a growing body of expert opinion that believes Americans would be healthier if they ate less sugar, not because it's bad for you, but because its only real contribution is taste and Calories.

   • Because sugar has become the leading ingredient added to foods in the United States today. That is, most of the sugar consumed is added before it gets to the consumer.

   • Because most people don't know how much sugar they eat, and many want to know. This is a principal reason the Food and Drug Administration wants the total amount of all sugars identified on more foods. The total would include both naturally occurring and added sugar.

   • Because sugar, though blamed wrongly for many ills, is one of a number of contributors to dental caries. Americans are spending $10 billion a year for dental care.

7   To most people, sugar is what you find on the kitchen table, put into coffee, or mix in a cake. This, of course, is the sugar refined from cane and beets.

---

*Chris Lecos is a member of FDA's public affairs staff.

8   Actually, there are more than a hundred substances that are sweet and which chemists can correctly describe as sugars. Sucrose, or table sugar, is just the most common and abundant of them all.

9   Industry literature describes sugar as a cheap source of food energy, a major contributor to food processing and general nutrition, and a substance that makes many foods with other nutrients taste better.

10   "Good nutrition," says a brochure from the Sugar Association, "begins with eating."

11   Its point, of course, is that if food is sweetened, people will eat the foods with the nutrients they need. However, many nutritionists and others concerned with American eating habits dispute sugar's value.

12   In a 1976 evaluation of the health aspects of sucrose as a food ingredient, the Federation of American Societies for Experimental Biology (FASEB) stated in a report to FDA: "Unlike most other foods, sucrose furnishes virtually only energy."

13   Many nutritionists concur and describe sugar as an "empty Calorie." If sugar is to be part of the diet, they say, it is preferable to get it from fruits, vegetables, and other items where it's a natural part of the product.

14   As it does with most other carbohydrates, the body converts sugar into glucose, the primary fuel of the body. During digestion it is broken down into equal parts of two simple sugars: glucose (dextrose) and fructose (levulose).

15   These components enter the bloodstream through the walls of the small intestine, and the blood carries the sugars to the tissues and the liver. There it is used or converted into glycogen and stored until the body needs it. The hormone insulin makes it possible for glucose, or blood sugar, to enter nearly all the cells of the body, where it is used as an energy source.

16   When more energy is needed, the liver converts glycogen into glucose, which is then delivered by the bloodstream to other organs or muscle tissue. Glucose not needed by the cells is metabolized in the liver into fatty substances called triglycerides. The body can call upon this stored energy during dieting and fasting.

17   Because of these energy reserves, nutritionists discount the argument that sugar is useful for quick energy needs before physical activity.

18   Americans get about 24 percent of their Calories from sugar—of which 3 percent comes in natural form from fruits and vegetables, 3 percent from dairy products, and the balance from sugar added to foods.

19   If sugar provides about 20 percent of a person's Calories, he must get the other 80 percent by selecting foods that supply the other nu-

trients his body needs—which is not easy to do, say some nutritionists, if one is trying to lose weight.

20   For many Americans, weight is a problem. A study released in 1978
by the National Center for Health Statistics indicated that one-third
of the population was overweight.

21   In a study of 13,600 people whose weights between 1971 and 1974
were compared with adults of equivalent height a decade earlier, the
Center found that men and women under 45 were, on the average,
3.8 and 4.7 pounds heavier, respectively. Those over 45 had gained an
average of 4.8 pounds.

22   There is no accurate measurement of how much sugar the average
American eats. The best available barometer of sugar use is the per
capita consumption figures of the U.S. Department of Agriculture
(USDA).

23   Although the per capita figures do not tell how much a person actually eats, they do show the amount of sugar that "disappears" into
the marketplace—that is, the amount shipped by sugar producers for
industrial, home, and other uses.

24   Citing USDA figures, sugar industry spokesmen maintain that
sugar consumption in the United States has been relatively stable for
more than 50 years now, at around 100 pounds a year per person.

25   However, that figure refers only to the consumption of refined cane
and beet sugar. It does not reflect the growing impact of a variety of
corn sweeteners now in use. The term "corn sweeteners" includes
various corn sirups (high fructose corn sirup, glucose) plus other Caloric sweeteners, such as dextrose, that are derived from corn.

26   Refined sugar, corn sirup, and corn sugar account for the bulk of
the sweeteners consumed in this country. Among the remainder are
honey, maple, and other edible sirups.

27   All of these are Caloric, and when all are taken into account, USDA
figures show a rise in per capita consumption from 122 pounds in
1970 to 128 pounds in 1978.

28   Per capita consumption of just refined sugar hovered around the
100 pounds per year level between 1960 and 1974. Since then, the
trend generally has been downward, falling below 93 pounds in 1978,
according to USDA. Fred Gray, an agriculture economist for USDA,
predicted a further drop of several pounds for 1979.

29   The decline in refined sugar consumption has been more than offset by the steady rise in corn sweetener usage—from a per capita rate
of 19 pounds in 1970 to almost 34 pounds in 1978.

30   Norris Bollenback, scientific director for the Sugar Association,
said the primary impetus for the increase has come from the growing industrial use of high fructose corn sirups, especially by soft
drink producers.

31   The use of high fructose corn sirups was negligible—less than a pound per capita, on the average—in the early 1970's. The industry was in its infancy then, and food and beverage manufacturers relied almost entirely on cane and beet sugar for their products because those sugars were cheap and plentiful, selling for about 11 or 12 cents a pound wholesale.

32   The rapid escalation of sugar prices in 1974—up to around 33 cents a pound wholesale—compelled the food and beverage industries to turn to other sweeteners, and the most attractive of them all was the high fructose corn sirups.

33   By the end of 1975, USDA figures show that per capita consumption of these corn sirups had risen to 5 pounds and 3 years later up to 11 pounds. Gray predicted that high fructose corn sirup usage would reach 15 pounds in 1979 and 18 pounds by the end of 1980.

34   Bollenback cited figures that showed that high fructose corn sirup producers have maintained their product's price consistently below that of refined sugar—roughly from 3 to 10 cents a pound less at the wholesale level. Last year, the wholesale price of high fructose corn sirup was around 13 cents a pounds compared to 20 cents for refined sugar.

35   "If (refined) sugar proponents think things will be back the way they were, they are being unrealistic," Bollenback noted.

36   Things also aren't the way they used to be in how sugar gets to our stomachs. Fifty years ago, two-thirds of the sugar produced went directly into the home, which meant control was directly in the hands of the housewife or individual who bought it. The balance was used mostly by industry.

37   Now, the reverse is true. Sixty-five percent of the refined sugar produced today is being consumed by the food and beverage industries and only 24 percent is going for home use.

38   The beverage industry—comprised of soft drink bottlers and beer and wine producers—is the leading industrial user of refined sugar and of high fructose corn sirups. It used 26 percent of the 9.8 million tons of refined sugar shipped in 1978 and about 40 percent of the high fructose corn sirups.

39   Although there has been a considerable amount of public controversy over the amount of sugar in cereals, the bakery and cereal industries combined used only 13.4 percent of all the sugar produced for food purposes in 1978. USDA figures did not separate the two.

40   Producers of confectionery products had the next highest usage at 9.2 percent, followed by 7 percent for the processed food and canning industries, and 5.6 percent for dairy products.

41   The consumer today is confronted by a wide variety of sugars and other nutritive sweeteners, and there is no significant difference in the amount of Calories each provides.   *1,532 words*

Comprehension Questions

1. The topic of this article is
   a. sugar.
   b. artificial sweeteners.
   c. fructose.
   d. the Food and Drug Administration.
2. The key idea of this article is that
   a. sugar use is rising.
   b. sugar is bad for your health.
   c. sugar is an essential part of many foods.
   d. the use of sugar in the diet has raised many controversial issues.
3. _____ is a subtopic.
   a. High fructose corn sirup
   b. Sugar prices
   c. Beet sugar
   d. Overweight Americans
4. Which of the following is a supporting idea?
   a. Sugar use is rising.
   b. The use of corn sweeteners is increasing.
   c. Consumers have less control over their daily intake of sugar than in the past.
   d. *all of the above*
5. The statistics cited in the article
   a. are important because the precise data is crucial information.
   b. show that the author is scholarly.
   c. indicate trends supporting the author's arguments.
   d. are unimportant and distracting.
6. An "empty calorie" is
   a. energy without nutritive value.
   b. a doughnut hole.
   c. a starchy food.
   d. an artificial sweetener.
7. That the author works for the Food and Drug Administration leads the reader to assume that
   a. he is favorably disposed to the sugar industry.
   b. he is concerned about the health of the American people.
   c. he knows very little about the topic.
   d. he wrote the article to help him get promoted to full professor.
8. The author's purpose for writing this article is to
   a. discourage the use of sugar.
   b. promote the use of natural sugars.
   c. educate the consumer about the prevalence of sugar in the American diet.
   d. criticize Americans for being overweight.

9. The author would probably support
   a. a ban on all sugar in cereals.
   b. a requirement that the sugar content of all products be stated on the label.
   c. research regarding noncaloric sweeteners.
   d. a trade embargo of all sugar-producing nations.
10. The switch to corn sirups after the escalation of sugar prices is an example of
   a. a cause-and-effect relationship.
   b. compare/contrast.
   c. chronological sequencing.
   d. *none of the above*

10. **Power Skills in Use**

Rosabeth Moss Kanter

1   What it takes to get the innovating organization up and running is essentially the same two things all vehicles need: a person in the driver's seat and a source of power.

2   The acts of myriad individuals drive the innovating organization. There would be no innovation without someone, somewhere, deciding to shape and push an idea until it takes usable form as a new product or management system or work method. And that process of pushing and shaping requires power sources and skills.

3   Thus, the first step in change mastery is understanding how individuals can exert leverage in an organization—the skills, strategies, power tools, and power tactics successful corporate entrepreneurs use to turn ideas into innovations. Getting a promising new idea through the system—or pushing others to do it—is the way in which corporate citizens with an entrepreneurial spirit make a difference for their organizations.

The Quiet Entrepreneurs

4   "Corporate entrepreneurs" are the people who test the limits and create new possibilities for organizational action by pushing and directing the innovation process. They may exercise their power skills in a number of realms—not only those which are defined as "responsible for innovation" like product development or design engineering.

5   Thus, the quiet, sometimes local innovations that corporate entrepreneurs recount are not always by themselves "big changes" or "big events." Only in retrospect can a company point to a particular decision or specific event as one that brought it into a new state, and by the time this happens, large numbers of other people will have to have been involved.

6   But if these innovators are not alone or individually the architects of sweeping reconstructions of a company, they are cumulatively a major force for change. The hundreds of small improvements, subtle readjustments, and visibly successful new techniques they initiate can, in the aggregate, gradually move or improve a company.

7   It would be appealing to say that corporate entrepreneurs are idealists captivated by the idea itself and eager to show its value; but they are human like the rest of us and driven by the same mixes of "pure" and "impure" human emotions and needs. But once they begin on the route toward innovation, the logic of the process takes over, and individual differences fade.

8   Though innovators are diverse people in diverse circumstance,

they share an integrative mode of operating which produces innovation: seeing problems not within limited categories but in terms larger than received wisdom; they make new connections, both intellectual and organizational; and they work across boundaries, reaching beyond the limits of their own jobs-as-given.

9   They are not rugged individualists—as in the classic stereotype of an entrepreneur—but good builders and users of teams, as even classic business creators have to be. And so they are aided in their quest for innovation by an integrative environment, in which ideas flow freely, resources are attainable rather than locked in budgetary boxes, and support and teamwork across areas are the norm.

10   However differently they start, corporate entrepreneurs soon find that they have something in common: the need to exercise skills in obtaining and using power in order to accomplish innovation.

Power and Innovation

11   Innovative accomplishments stretch beyond the established definition of a "job" to bring new learning or capacity to the organization. They involve *change*, a disruption of existing activities, a redirection of organizational energies that may result in new strategies, products, market opportunities, work methods, technical processes, or structures.

12   And change, no matter how desired or desirable, requires that new agreements be negotiated and tools for action be found beyond what it takes to do the routine job, to maintain already established strategies and processes.

13   To initiate and implement an innovation, people need that extra bit of power to move the system off the course in which it was heading automatically, like the extra muscle thrust to turn a boat or the extra engine power to turn an airplane. As long as people are merely the custodians of already determined routines and directions, they too can operate automatically, staying within their segment, working within the resources or information handed down to them. But innovation, in contrast, requires that the innovators get enough power to mobilize people and resources to get something *nonroutine* done.

14   Innovative accomplishments differ from merely doing one's basic job—even if the person does it well—not only in scope and long-run impact but also in what it takes to carry them out. And this is why power is so important.

15   Power, as I define it, is intimately connected with the ability to produce; it is the capacity to mobilize people and resources to get things done. But people who are "just doing their jobs" do not need to "mobilize."

16   Thus, nonentrepreneurs, when they do achieve, tend to produce only a narrow range of accomplishments: those clearly identified

with the specific mandate in their job, such as incremental improvements in individual or unit performance, or importing and implementing a well-known practice. They stay within their identified segment and define problems segmentally—as small, isolated, bounded pieces.

17   They are likely already to possess nearly everything they need to carry out the related activities. And so they tend to act alone. Their ability to act unilaterally is, of course, a function of these two features, which make the accomplishments low-risk as well as, generally, low-gain.

18   But innovations are not safe, bounded, or easy; nor can innovators generally just "command" their subordinates or ignore their critics. Innovative accomplishments, when compared directly with basic non-entrepreneurial ones, are perceived by those involved as riskier, and they are more controversial—they generate stronger feelings around the organization both pro and con.

The Politics of Change

19   Only in retrospect does a successful innovation look "inevitable," like the right thing to do all along. Up to that point, just about all innovating has a "political" dimension—even though the use of the term "political" is unpopular, and managers like to act as if there were not a "political" side to innovation.

20   But I am not using "political" in the negative sense of backroom deal making but in the positive sense that innovation requires campaigning, lobbying, bargaining, negotiating, caucusing, collaborating, and winning votes. That is, an idea must be sold, resources must be acquired or rearranged, and some variable numbers of other people must agree to change in their own areas—for innovations generally cut across existing areas and have wider organizational ripples, like dropping pebbles into a pond.

21   The enterprise required of innovating managers and professionals, then, is not the creative spark of genius that invents a new idea, but rather the skill with which they move outside the formal bounds of their job, maneuvering through and around the organization in sometimes risky, unique, and novel ways.

22   This is what the corporate entrepreneur has in common with the classic definition of an entrepreneur. Organizational genius is 10 percent inspiration and 90 percent acquisition—acquisition of power to move beyond a formal job charter and to influence others.

23   Here is where the environment—the organization's structure and culture—enters the picture. All the enterprise, initiative, and bright ideas of a creative potential innovator may go nowhere if he or she cannot get the power to turn ideas into action.

Sources of Power

24   Organizational power derives from supplies of three "basic commodities" that can be invested in action: *information* (data, technical knowledge, political intelligence, expertise); *resources* (funds, materials, space, staff, time); and *support* (endorsement, backing, approval).

25   Even though corporate entrepreneurs can find some portion of these power tools already attached to their positions, especially in the more empowering companies, it is more typical that innovations require a search for additional supplies, for additional "capital," elsewhere in the organization. Thus, a great deal of the innovation process consists of a search for power.

26   Despite the differences in the innovations themselves (how creative, how technical), the composition of an innovation seems to follow a common logic, one in which the finding and investing of power tools figures as a dominant motif. The acquisition of power tools can be the longest and most difficult theme in an innovative accomplishment, and innovation thus depends on how easy the organization makes it to tap sources of power.   *1,300 words*

Comprehension Questions
1. What is this article about?
   a. power
   b. innovations
   c. innovation and power
   d. management
2. What is the author's most important idea?
   a. Innovation is inevitable.
   b. Successful innovators need power and resources.
   c. Corporate entrepreneurs test limits and create new possibilities.
   d. Innovations involve change.
3. Which of the following is not a subtopic?
   a. entrepreneurs
   b. politics
   c. resources
   d. nonentrepreneurs
4. _____ is a supporting idea.
   a. Change is easy to bring about
   b. Change is difficult to bring about
   c. Innovators can bring about change by themselves
   d. Innovation is doing one's job well

5. Why do innovators need power?
   a. to get something nonroutine done
   b. to impress their bosses
   c. to maintain established strategies
   d. to get more information
6. From the text you would guess that "unilaterally" means
   a. one-sided.
   b. acting alone.
   c. working with units.
   d. moving to the side.
7. According to the author, to be a successful innovator you do not need
   a. to make connections.
   b. to be an idealist.
   c. a creative spark.
   d. a sympathetic environment.
8. This article was written to
   a. instruct.
   b. convince.
   c. inform.
   d. describe.
9. The article implies that
   a. a good innovator will be rewarded.
   b. a good innovator will be resented.
   c. innovations involve only one segment of the organization.
   d. bringing about innovation is easy if you know how.
10. Organizational power comes from
    a. resources, information, and support.
    b. skills, resources, and support.
    c. information, skills, and support.
    d. resources, skills, and information.

11. Benjamin Franklin as a Psychotherapist

Z. J. Lipowski

1   The life and works of Benjamin Franklin (1706–1790), a scientist, politician, and writer, have been studied with so much zeal that hardly any fragment of them seems to have escaped the curiosity of his numerous biographers. Moreover, his own autobiographical writings are an ample source of information about his life, work, and relationships [1]. Hence, it is surprising that the episode to be reported here is unknown to the American students of Franklin's life (W. B. Willcox, personal communication, January 10, 1983). This is probably so because its account has been buried in an unpublished manuscript of the memoirs of a Polish princess and, to the best of my knowledge, been quoted only by Polish scholars [2, 3]. Yet this episode offers a fascinating glimpse of the man's charisma and empathy. Moreover, in this brief vignette Franklin not only plays the part of a shrewd if amateur psychotherapist but also brings out in high relief some of the key ingredients of effective brief psychotherapy.

Franklin Meets the Princess

2   I have translated this piece from its original quotation in Polish which appeared in a monograph published almost a century ago [2]. According to the author of that work, the cited fragment was taken from a handwritten manuscript of the memoirs of Princess Izabella Czartoryska (1746–1835), the wife of a Polish aristocrat and a man who came close to becoming a king of Poland, Prince Adam Czartoryski. The princess was surely one of the more colorful women of the late eighteenth century. Wealthy, pampered, bright, and cultivated, she was perennially pursued by powerful men and moved from one stormy love affair to another. At least three of her six children are believed to have been illegitimate, including a daughter fathered by the last king of Poland [3]. Two years prior to the episode recounted here, the princess had given birth to a son whose alleged father was her current lover, a Russian prince, Nikolai Repnin [3]. Her husband, whom she had married when she was only 15 years old and at first did not love, ignored her and her infidelity [3]. In the spring of 1772, the princess and Repnin journeyed to London, and she was later joined by her husband. During her lengthy stay there she apparently suffered from a serious depression, and her husband sought to cheer her up by introducing her to the famous American. As Franklin wrote in August of that year, "Learned and ingenious foreigners that come

to England almost all make a point of visiting me; for my reputation is still higher abroad than here" [1, p. 279]. The Czartoryskis fitted that description well. When they met, the princess was 26 years old, Franklin 66. The following is my literal translation from Polish of her personal account of their unusual encounter:

> I was ill, in a state of melancholia, and writing my testament and farewell letters. Wishing to distract me, my husband took me to Franklin. On the way my husband explained to me who Franklin was and to what he owed his fame, since I barely knew then that a second hemisphere existed. Franklin had a noble face with an expression of engaging kindness. Surprised by my immobility, he took my hands and gazed at me saying: *pauvre jeune femme.* He then opened a harmonium, sat down and played long. The music made a strong impression on me and tears began flowing from my eyes. Then Franklin sat by my side and looking with compassion said, "Madam, you are cured." Indeed, that moment was a reaction in my state of melancholia. Franklin offered to teach me how to play the harmonium—I accepted without hesitation, hence he gave me twelve lessons. I have retained memory of him for my whole life. [2, p. 97]

Follow-up

3   That effective music therapy most likely involved not a harmonium but a harmonica, or "armonica" as Franklin called it, a musical instrument which he invented around 1761 by adapting the principle of musical glasses and of which he wrote: "The advantages of this instrument are that its tones are incomparably sweet beyond those of any other" [1, p. 134]. The princess seemed to agree. Despite her dramatic response to Franklin's ministration, however, the stability of her "cure" appeared short-lived. One would say today that it was a transference cure in response to a sensitive approach by a charismatic and empathetic older man. One notes that at the end of December 1772, the Duke de Lauzun, a future lover of the princess, met her at a party in London and found her to be charming, gay, and coquettish [4, p. 121], hardly a picture of melancholic immobility. Yet only the next year the princess, apparently torn by conflict between her new love for the dashing young duke and her ties to both her husband and to Repnin, developed frequent and violent "attacks of nerves" and fainting spells, symptoms which prompted the duke to consult secretly the famous Dutch physician Gaubius [4]. In November 1773, following a passionate and tearful love scene with the duke, the princess attempted suicide by drinking poison [4]. That torrid romance with the duke continued for a few years and resulted in the birth of an illegitimate son [3, 4]. More love affairs followed, as well as tragedy, when her newly born daughter died, and, almost at the same time, her oldest daughter burned to death. The princess reacted by becoming temporarily paralyzed, a condition which reportedly

yielded to an electric therapy [3]. All this suggests that the princess was a neurotic and restless woman, one prone to both melancholia and hysterical symptoms. Today she might get a diagnostic label of the borderline personality disorder. In this she was not unlike many other prominent women of her time [5]. It is noteworthy, however, that, despite her stormy and chaotic younger years, Princess Izabella displayed remarkable creativity, courage, loyalty, sense of humor, and serenity in the second half of her life, and had remained intellectually alert until her death at 89 years [3]. She clearly had a good deal more ego strength and resilience than her earlier erratic behavior and symptoms may have suggested. Her professed remembrance of Franklin indicates that he had made a deep and lasting impression on her.

Franklin and Women

4   Franklin's unusual appeal for women was likely to have played a part in this story. As one of his biographers summed it up, "Women, young and old, loved him because he took a keen interest in them, not merely as objects of desire, but as people with a different outlook, with their own contribution to make. He listened to them, he was not afraid of them . . ." [5, p. 20]. It is of some interest that about 5 years after the episode related here, at the age of 71, Franklin developed an intimate friendship with a young woman, Madame Brillon, who seems to have shared certain characteristics with the princess. Like the latter, she was intelligent and sophisticated as well as unhappily married, restless, and self-centered [5]. Also like the princess, Mme. Brillon was a music lover and suffered from episodes of depression and various somatic symptoms. Curiously, however, when at one time she complained to Franklin about her deep melancholia and anguish, he tried to ascribe her complaints to physical causes, asked whether bloodletting had relieved her, and urged her to exercise by going up and down steps every day [5, p. 75]. While that forerunner of jogging seems to have had no appeal for Mme. Brillon, Franklin had little else to offer, as he himself was in the midst of a severe and protracted flare-up of his gout. Evidently, empathy and even keen therapeutic skills may become weakened when the therapist is not only personally too involved with the patient but also infirm.

Comment

5   It may seem exaggerated to speak of Benjamin Franklin as a precursor of brief psychotherapy on the basis of a single anecdote. Yet one cannot fail to be impressed by his remarkable display of these elements of such therapy which are essential to its success. Empathy and sensitivity, genuine and focused interest, a confident attitude and a touch of suggestion ("Madam, you are cured"), and reinforcement

(12 sessions or "lessons"), are all key ingredients. To what extent the addition of the "dynamic" comments by the therapist enhances the worthwhile, if rather limited, success of such therapy remains an open question. Reflecting on the above episode, one may wonder if music could be just as effective.

6   The importance of suggestion in therapy has been stressed by some psychoanalytic writers. Zetzel [6] observed that "Increasing emphasis on the part played by the analyst's personality in determining the course of the individual transference implies recognition of unavoidable suggestion tendencies in the therapeutic process." Suggestion may be particularly important in the treatment of a patient with what Arieti [7] called "claiming depression," in which the patient's symptoms are a cry for help and which represents a reaction to the failure by the *dominant other* person, often the spouse, to give as much as the patient expects. Such an individual clamors, verbally or not, to be accepted and valued, and the therapist should meet this need. "When this immediate craving for being given acceptance is somewhat satisfied," writes Arieti, "the depression will considerably diminish, but will not disappear." This therapeutic approach suggests to the patient that he or she can be redeemed, that there is hope. Franklin seemed to follow these precepts intuitively and successfully in his effort to help Princess Izabella break out of her melancholia. Not only was his general attitude accepting and contained an explicit element of encouraging suggestion, but he also offered her a precious gift of sharing with her his beloved musical instrument and his time. And during his London stay he was a busy man indeed, one intensely involved in political and social activities [1].

7   ***The Role of Music.***   Last but not least, music played a major part in this remarkable therapeutic encounter. As a medical historian points out, music has been used as a therapy for the sick since antiquity [8]. Mesmer, whom Franklin met in Paris in 1784 and whose "animal magnetism" was a treatment method which foreran hypnotherapy, that "historical godfather of psychoanalysis" [9], employed Franklin's harmonica to provide background music for his therapeutic sessions [5]. Today, musicotherapy is a recognized and valued adjunct to psychotherapy and has been found to be especially effective in improving hospitalized patients' self-image and behavior [10]. Kohut [11] has put forth some interesting hypotheses about the psychological and therapeutic effects of music. He proposed that musical activity affects the whole personality—the ego, the id, and the super-ego—and can be viewed as play, as catharsis, and as an aesthetic mastery. It enables nonverbal discharge of emotions and id-derived tensions, and expiation "in the area of sounds," one outside the realm of concepts, people, and conflicts.

8   Princess Izabella's flood of tears suggests a catharsis and expiation. Her biography confirms that she suffered from bouts of guilt feelings related to her liaisons and that on at least one occasion she confessed them to her husband [3]. Her suicidal attempt was clearly triggered by conflict and sense of guilt and shame [4]. With Franklin, and through music, she could discharge her pent-up emotions in a controlled manner, expiate "in the area of sounds," and have a share in a famous man's mastery. Thus, her readiness for a transference cure was enhanced, and her will to live was rekindled. Could a professional therapist have achieved a better result? It is true that she apparently suffered relapses of symptoms, but it is equally notable that later in life she managed to face numerous adversities with surprising fortitude, was loyal to her family and country, and displayed considerable creativity as a writer and founder of a formidable art collection [3]. The latter included a portrait of Franklin, about whom she wrote in the collection's catalog that he "tore off the thunder from the sky and the scepter from a tyrant's hand" [3]. Positive transference clearly endured beyond the brief London encounter. Is it too much to suggest that it may have played a part in Princess Izabella's growth as a person?

1,992 words

References

1. Van Doren, C. (ed.). *Benjamin Franklin's Autobiographical Writings.* New York: Viking, 1945.
2. Debicki, L. *Pulawy (1762–1830),* vol. 1. Lwow: Gubrynowicz & Schmidt, 1887.
3. Pauszer-Klonowska, G. *Pani na Pulawach.* Warszawa: Czytelnik, 1980.
4. Lacour, L. (ed.). *Mémoires du duc de Lauzun.* Paris: Poulet-Malassis & de Broise, 1858.
5. Lopez, C. A. *Mon Cher Papa. Franklin and the Ladies of Paris.* New Haven, Conn.: Yale Univ. Press, 1966.
6. Zetzel, E. R. The concept of transference. *Int. J. Psychoanal.* 37:369–376, 1956.
7. Arieti, S. The psychotherapeutic approach to depression. *Am. J. Psychotherapy* 16:397–406, 1962.
8. Sigerist, H. E. *Civilization and Disease.* Ithaca, N.Y.: Cornell Univ. Press, 1943.
9. Alexander, F. G., and Selesnick, S. T. *The History of Psychiatry.* New York: Harper & Row, 1966.
10. Linn, L. Occupational therapy and other therapeutic activities. In *Comprehensive Textbook of Psychiatry,* 3d ed., edited by H. I. Kaplan, A. M. Freedman, and B. J. Sadock. Baltimore: Williams & Wilkins, 1980.
11. Kohut, H. Some psychological effects of music and their relation to music therapy. *Music Ther.* 5:17–20, 1955.

Comprehension Questions

1. This article is about
   a. the usefulness of psychotherapy.
   b. the history of psychotherapy.
   c. the techniques of psychotherapy.
   d. Benjamin Franklin.
2. The point of the article is that
   a. Franklin was an amateur psychotherapist.
   b. Franklin acted like a psychotherapist.
   c. psychotherapy aided the princess to retrieve her health.
   d. the princess needed psychotherapy.
3. Which of the following is *not* a subtopic?
   a. music
   b. women
   c. brief psychotherapy
   d. infidelity
4. The author says Franklin failed to "treat" Mme. Brillon because
   a. he was not interested in her.
   b. he did not use music in the treatment.
   c. he was untrained.
   d. he was too close to her.
5. The author reports that the princess's husband
   a. disliked her.
   b. loved her.
   c. did not ignore her affair.
   d. tried to cheer her up.
6. The author makes greatest use of _____ to prove his point.
   a. primary sources
   b. secondary sources
   c. metaphors
   d. questions
7. The author does *not* say that the princess could be described as
   a. suicidal.
   b. neurotic.
   c. having a borderline personality disorder.
   d. unique.
8. "Claiming depression" results mainly from
   a. the patient's inability to get as much as she expects.
   b. a chemical imbalance in the brain.
   c. feelings of being dominated by someone else.
   d. rejection by a loved one.
9. One source claims that music is useful in therapy because
   a. it affects everyone the same way.
   b. it is calming.

    c. it is nonverbal.

    d. it provides a distraction from the patient's problems.

10. One can conclude from the article that a "transference cure"

    a. is permanent.

    b. "transfers" the patient's depression to those around her.

    c. is closely connected to the patient-therapist relationship.

    d. is a desirable outcome of therapy.

12. **Flu/Cold—Never The Strain Shall Meet**

*Tim Larkin**

1   According to ancient legend, the Greek goddess Thetis heard a prophecy that her son, Achilles, would die in battle. To protect him, she attempted what might be called the first inoculation by dipping him head first into the magical River Styx. This made him invulnerable—except for the part of his body that Thetis held onto, his heel. Thus, we get the colorful phrase "Achilles heel" for a weak point in an otherwise strong person. In terms of an invasion route for many bacteria and viruses, our Achilles heel is located at the other end of the anatomy, the respiratory tract: the nose, throat, windpipe, bronchial tubes and lungs.

2   Every day, as we inhale some 500 cubic feet of air, equivalent to a large walk-in closet, all kinds of unwanted visitors tag along: dust particles and the mites that often accompany them, pollen, a variety of airborne debris, and numerous bacteria and viruses. The body has various defenses protecting its respiratory tract. Strong, rough hairs in the nostrils stop the largest of these unwelcome guests. Smaller invaders then encounter the equivalent of flypaper, a sticky film of mucus that traps bacteria and particles. These are then pushed by the continual beating of legions of tiny whiplike hairs, the cilia, back to the gullet where they descend into the digestive tract and are consumed. Bacteria that make it past these obstacles encounter a variety of other defense mechanisms which together prevent the many organisms we inhale every day from causing disease.

3   Despite these formidable barriers, occasional harmful bacteria or viruses do manage to gain a foothold. Among these can be any of 200 viruses in eight groups or families that produce the common cold. There are also three types of influenza virus: type A, the most frequently encountered and often the most severe; B, which commonly causes localized outbreaks and occasionally severe epidemics; and C, which occurs rarely. Among the influenza A viruses, there are numerous subtypes that exist in the animal kingdom, three of which are known to be capable of infecting man.

4   The spread of influenza viruses from person to person depends on whether an infected individual comes in contact with someone who is susceptible. It is thought that infection with one influenza virus leaves a person resistant indefinitely to infection with the exact same

---

*Tim Larkin is a freelance writer.

virus. When a strain of influenza virus appears in a population for the first time, outbreaks that occur are likely to be limited in size. Outbreaks that affect large numbers of individuals over a wide geographic area are referred to as epidemics, and worldwide epidemics affecting all age groups are called pandemics.

5   The capacity of influenza viruses to produce significant outbreaks year after year is the result of their diversity. Pandemics occur when viruses of an influenza A subtype emerge that have not been present for many years. Such pandemics occurred with the emergence of "Spanish flu" in 1918, "Asian flu" in 1957, and "Hong Kong flu" in 1968. The viruses that caused these pandemics were each representatives of different subtypes of influenza A.

6   In addition to the differences in types of variation seen in influenza and cold viruses, there are important differences in the types of disease they cause. The common cold is well-known as a self-limited illness that is usually no more than a nuisance for two or three days. By comparison, influenza is a major killer worldwide. The Spanish flu pandemic of 1918 was the worst pestilence that ever afflicted mankind. It has been estimated that a half million people died in the United States, and 20 to 40 million died worldwide. In 1957, more than 50 thousand people died in the United States from Asian flu. Even in years between pandemics there are usually thousands of deaths in this country, mostly in elderly persons or those with chronic illnesses such as cystic fibrosis, asthma or heart disease.

7   It is this capacity to produce sudden, widespread epidemics of varying severity that once made influenza appear to be a mysterious affliction. Many theories were proposed to account for the speed and intensity of a flu epidemic. In 1657, the English physician Thomas Willis, remarking on the sudden way so many were afflicted with chills, aches and fever, attributed it to the malign influence of the stars—in Italian, *influentia coeli*, from which we get the word influenza. The word *grippe*, sometimes also *la grippe*, was once often used as a synonym for influenza. While this may seem like a precise French word for the harsh grip of the disease on the body, it actually comes from the Russian word *krip*, or hoarseness.

8   Those caught in influenza's grip are far from caring how the disease was christened but are more concerned with how to get rid of it.

9   During the 1918 pandemic, the question of whether the early signs of respiratory distress signaled only another common cold or the dreaded onset of Spanish flu and a brush with death was of sharp and immediate concern. *The Denver Post* of Oct. 11, 1918, seeking to conserve the energies of that city's physicians, who were exhausted from dealing with so many desperately ill persons, tried to tell its readers the difference between a cold and the flu. The beginning of a cold, the paper said, was not as sudden, its aches not as severe, its fever not as high. And, the *Post* added, a cold is distinguished by

"chilliness rather than definite chills." In terms of diagnosis outside a laboratory, the truth is we haven't really progressed much past the vague advice in that 1918 newspaper. What is possible now that wasn't possible in 1918 is a sure way of knowing whether a person has flu by laboratory testing for presence of the specific antibody associated with the flu virus. It's also possible to provide a precise list of symptoms that distinguish flu from a cold. But the list deals with generalities and averages.

10   One reason it's so difficult to tell definitely from symptoms alone that a person has the flu or a cold is that humans differ widely in how they react to these respiratory infections. Some may become quite ill from a cold; others may exhibit only mild distress from the flu. In fact, there is no single symptom that distinguishes flu from the common cold—or even from the early stages of bronchitis or strep throat. From controlled experiments with volunteers, the best that can be said is the following:

- Regarding fever: colds rarely are accompanied by fever, except in children; flu usually begins with fever.
- Regarding onset: flu is swift and severe; colds tend to build more slowly.
- Regarding location: colds show localized symptoms such as sneezing, runny nose, etc.; flu has general symptoms such as weakness, muscular pain, chills, headache.
- Regarding other symptoms: 90 percent of flu victims have a dry, hacking cough; 60 percent have sore eyes; 50 percent have a flushed face and hot, moist skin. Such symptoms appear less often in cold sufferers.

11   The point to note is that there is no absolute way to tell by symptoms alone which infection a person is suffering from. The best that can be said is that if a patient is suddenly stricken with fever, chills, general weakness, headache and muscular pains, accompanied by a severe cough, sore eyes and flushed face, *and if there is a flu outbreak in the area*, then he or she *probably* has influenza. But since children and older persons differ in the severity of symptoms, and since symptoms are further clouded by differences between individuals—such as prior history of exposure to influenza, genetic endowment, stress or personal health—it is simply impossible to state on the basis of symptoms alone that a respiratory infection is or is not the flu.

12   Unfortunately, even if we could tell from symptoms whether a person has influenza, there is no medicine now known to cure it, although some drugs are being studied. Penicillin and other antibiotics have no effect on flu or other viruses, although they may help fight certain complicating infections, such as bronchitis and some types of pneumonia. A physician is the best judge of when to use antibiotics.

13   Nevertheless, while influenza cannot yet be cured, it can be pre-

vented by vaccination. However, because flu virus often drifts or shifts into a form new to the body's immune defenses, inoculation against one flu strain does not necessarily protect against the next epidemic. Such protection requires inoculation with a vaccine specific for the strain or strains currently circulating.

14   If flu can be only prevented, not cured, how can it be treated, once caught? In the 1918 pandemic, nurses were in greater demand than physicians, since the main need for flu victims was tender loving care. That's still the best treatment. The patient should drink lots of water and fruit juice, keep warm and comfortable, and remain in bed until temperature returns to normal. To ease discomfort from muscle pains or headaches, aspirin or a substitute may be taken by an adult. An aspirin substitute (or aspirin, if directed by a physician) may be taken by children. It's important that the patient be closely observed to detect signs of complications. This includes just about every infectious respiratory tract disease, such as acute bronchitis, pharyngitis, tonsillitis, laryngitis, croup, sinusitis and pneumonia. Ordinarily such complications don't involve the digestive or intestinal system. Therefore, influenza virus is seldom if ever responsible for what is erroneously called "intestinal flu" or "stomach flu."

15   Finally, how serious is the flu? Obviously, as the Spanish flu pandemic of 1918 shows, flu can be a life-threatening disease. This is why, when a flu strain appeared in 1976 (the "swine flu") that seemed to resemble the 1918 flu virus, the government geared up for inoculation of every American. This proved to be a false alarm. But new flu strains that are far less virulent than that which caused the 1918 pandemic can still exact a huge toll in losses of life and in illness. For example, the Asian flu pandemic of 1957 caused 45 million cases of influenza in the United States alone.

16   In the absence of such potent influenza strains, the kinds of influenza we usually encounter tend to produce moderately severe illnesses but are not serious health threats to most healthy individuals. Complete recovery can be expected within a week. For certain high-risk groups—old people, children, the chronically ill, and pregnant women—any form of flu can be a serious problem since the disease or its complications may be life threatening. The mortality curve of influenza—the death rate for each age group—usually takes a U-shaped form on a graph, evidence of flu's special danger to the very young and the very old. (The single exception was the Spanish flu, which showed a W-shaped form, attesting that millions in the prime and healthiest years of life died either from the flu or its complications.) There is also some evidence that pregnant women may have more severe influenza than healthy, non-pregnant women. Any pregnant woman who catches influenza should report it promptly to her physician.

17   Special precautions are necessary with children who contract influenza. It can strike with far more severity than in an adult, and include fever above 104 degrees Fahrenheit, along with such complications as convulsions, croup or pneumonia. With both types of flu (as well as with chickenpox) there is danger for children from infancy to the late teen years of a life-threatening illness called Reye syndrome (pronounced "rye"). Reye syndrome usually takes the following course: The child is recovering from a mild viral illness such as influenza. Suddenly, in rapid succession, the child has vomiting, violent headaches, listlessness, irritability (even combativeness), delirium, disturbed breathing, stiffness of arms and legs, and then coma. A parent should not wait until there is a full progression of these symptoms or enough of them to substantiate fear that the child has Reye syndrome. Immediate action is called for. The family physician should be called right away. If a physician cannot be reached, the child should be taken to a hospital emergency room. A Reye syndrome attack moves so fast, and the penalty for failure to respond with equal speed is so severe, that not a second should be lost.

18   The word "syndrome" is applied when medicine recognizes a fixed pattern of symptoms but doesn't fully understand their cause (or causes). Thus, no one yet knows what causes Reye syndrome. However, there are studies indicating that the appearance of Reye syndrome in children may be associated with (not the same as "caused by") aspirin and other drugs that contain salicylates (the chemical basis of aspirin). Therefore, the U.S. surgeon general has advised against giving aspirin and other salicylate-containing products to children with flu or chickenpox unless directed by the child's physician. This is why the Food and Drug Administration announced that it is considering a regulation which would require the labels on aspirin and other salicylate-containing products to warn against giving such products to children under 16 with flu or chickenpox without consulting a physician.

19   Medicine has come a long way from the time when influenza was blamed on an evil star. The only certainty is that even the mildest illness must be treated with respect, and the patient not only cared for but observed carefully.   *2,295 words*

Comprehension Questions

   1. The title of the article implies that the topic is
      a. the differences between flus and colds.
      b. the similarities of flus and colds.
      c. the dangers of getting ill.
      d. medical advances in the treatment of children.

2. The wealth of information about flu
   a. is irrelevant to the topic of the article.
   b. is simply supporting detail for the point that flus and colds are different.
   c. is the essence of the article, and the comparison of colds and flus is of secondary importance.
   d. is interesting background material.
3. The discussion of Reye syndrome
   a. is a distraction, since it is not a result of a flu or a cold.
   b. provides supporting details of the subtopic, the care of children who contract influenza.
   c. is the main topic of the article.
   d. is an unsupported attack on aspirin manufacturers.
4. The author's purpose in describing the symptoms of flus is to
   a. allow readers to self-diagnose and treat their illness.
   b. reinforce the notion that it is difficult to identify a flu or cold from symptoms alone.
   c. demonstrate the extent of the research he conducted when preparing this article.
   d. scare people into seeking medical attention.
5. The term influenza is derived from
   a. English.
   b. Italian.
   c. Russian.
   d. French.
6. The author uses the technique of _____ when discussing flus and colds.
   a. analogy
   b. example
   c. compare/contrast
   d. metaphor
7. Flu epidemics
   a. are generally life-threatening.
   b. affect women more than men.
   c. pose special risks for the young and old.
   d. are no longer a concern, given modern medicines.
8. That the author is identified as a freelance writer
   a. creates the expectation that the article will be well written.
   b. means he has no special expertise in the area.
   c. supports an inference that he has no vested interest or preconceived position to defend.
   d. *all of the above*
9. The article can best be described as
   a. persuasive.
   b. controversial.

    c. informational.

    d. historical.

10. "Syndrome" refers to

    a. the reaction of a hypochondriac.

    b. a fixed pattern of symptoms.

    c. an inexplicable death.

    d. a fixed pattern of symptoms, the cause of which is not understood.

13. Atropine Poisoning in Hawthorne's *The Scarlet Letter*

Jemshed A. Khan, M.D.

1   This article presents evidence that surreptitious atropine poisoning accounts for the bizarre behavior and ultimate demise of the Reverend Arthur Dimmesdale in Nathaniel Hawthorne's classic work, *The Scarlet Letter*.[1] This poisoning of a major character in a widely read novel, written by a celebrated author, has escaped forensic detection for more than a century. This should be of interest to the medical community, because the poisoning was accomplished through the agency of a physician.

2   As an aid to the reader, a summary of the plot of *The Scarlet Letter* is provided. The plot centers on three major characters: an adulteress, an adulterer, and a cuckolded husband. Hester Prynne, the adulteress, conceives and bears a child during the prolonged absence of her husband. As penance for her sin of adultery she is condemned to display a scarlet letter "A" on her clothing. The adulterer, the Reverend Arthur Dimmesdale, attempts to conceal his involvement with Hester Prynne and suffers from the torment of a guilty conscience and the vengeance of the cuckolded husband. The husband, Dr. Roger Chillingworth, discerns that Dimmesdale has fathered the illegitimate child, and is preoccupied with revenge. This article is concerned with the methods and effects of Chillingworth's revenge.

3   Historically, critics have ascribed Dimmesdale's bizarre behavior and ultimate demise to a powerful guilt neurosis, which was secretly and deliberately nurtured by his vengeful physician and companion, Dr. Roger Chillingworth. Critics have maintained and perpetuated the narrow view that Chillingworth's methods of revenge were of a purely psychological nature, unwittingly ignoring[2-5] or even denying[6] the possibility of poisoning. Trollope wrote of Chillingworth, "He simply lives with his enemy ... attacking not the man's body,—to which indeed he acts as a wise physician,—but his conscience." A computer-generated literature search failed to produce any references to atropine in connection with *The Scarlet Letter*.[7]

4   However, there is sufficiently explicit evidence in *The Scarlet Letter* to warrant the view that Dr. Chillingworth may have concocted an atropine-based poison and administered it to Dimmesdale. I have researched and developed four major arguments in support of the atropine-poisoning theory. First of all, Chillingworth certainly had the motive, circumstances, and knowledge necessary for the preparation and administration of a poison intended for Dimmesdale. Secondly, certain plants mentioned in the novel are commonly known to be poisonous. Such plants, if administered, would result in characteristic atropine poisoning. Thirdly, at the time *The Scarlet Letter* was written, atropine and its effects were probably well known to Hawthorne. Finally, a review of Dimmesdale's symptoms and behavior suggests a pattern that is remarkably consistent with atropine poisoning.

Motive—A Dark Purpose

5   There is little doubt that Chillingworth's motive was revenge against Dimmesdale, the man who had impregnated Chillingworth's wife. Hawthorne describes this desire for revenge as "a new purpose . . . dark enough to engage the full strength of his [Chillingworth's] faculties" (p. 87). Later in the story Chillingworth "had grown to exist only by perpetual poison of the direst revenge!" (p. 124), but Hawthorne leaves it to the reader to discern "the hidden practices of his revenge" (p. 141).

Circumstance—Physician of the Young Minister Whose Health Had Suffered of Late

6   Dimmesdale's symptoms developed over a prolonged period, indicating that they were probably the result of chronic poisoning. This would suggest that the victim was repeatedly subjected to small doses of poison. In order to avoid suspicion, Chillingworth would have had to administer the poison surreptitiously either with meals or in the guise of a medicine. The more plausible possibility is that Dimmesdale was poisoned by his physician's concoctions.

7   Chillingworth, being "extensively acquainted with the medical science of the day . . ." (p. 87), presented himself as a physician. Indeed, "it was understood that this learned man was the physician as well as friend of the young minister . . ." (p. 80). As physician to Dimmesdale, Chillingworth had ample opportunity to poison his patient. It was "at a hint from Roger Chillingworth [that] . . . the two were lodged in the same house" (p. 91). Dimmesdale certainly did not improve under the watchful eye of Chillingworth. In fact, the pastor's "health had suffered as of late . . ." (p. 80), and Chillingworth was "anxious to attempt the cure . . ." (p. 89). It was observed that Chillingworth often gathered herbs and plants, "even in the graveyard" (p. 95), and "arranged his study and laboratory with distilling apparatus, and the means of compounding drugs and chemicals, which the practised alchemist knew well how to turn to purpose . . ." (p. 92).

8   Chillingworth did not accomplish these actions without arousing suspicion. Hester Prynne, adulteress and estranged wife of Chillingworth, suspected "the continual presence of Roger Chillingworth,— the secret malignity, infecting all the air about him . . ." (p. 139), and

she questioned "his authorized interference, as a physician, with the minister's physical and spiritual infirmities . . ." (p. 139). Even Dimmesdale questioned the benefit derived from Chillingworth's "kindly care of this weak frame of mine" (p. 97).

Knowledge—The Practiced Alchemist

9   Not only was Chillingworth "extensively acquainted with the medical science of the day . . .," but in his travels among the Indians "he had gained much knowledge of the properties of native herbs and roots . . ." (p. 87). He even boasted about his knowledge of "recipes that were as old as Paracelsus" (p. 55). Chillingworth's sophistication in alchemy was manifested in his distilling apparatus, and Dimmesdale would sometimes stand idly by, "watching the processes by which weeds were converted into drugs of potency . . ." (p. 95). Hawthorne even implies that the doctor had previously been associated with the then-infamous Dr. Forman, who was involved in the murder-by-poison plot against Sir Thomas Overbury (p. 93).

Toxic Plants—All Manner of Vegetable Wickedness

10   Traditionally, references to various plant species in *The Scarlet Letter* have been interpreted either in purely symbolic terms or as an extension of New England folklore.[8,9] However, the mention of identifiably poisonous plants raises the possibility of their use as poisonous agents. There are two passages with specific references to poisonous plants. Hawthorne plants the first poisonous seedling of suspicion early in the novel, with a reference on the first page to apple of Peru (*Nicandra physalodes*), which may contain cardioactive solanine glycoalkaloids.[10,11]

11   Although the suspicion is carefully nurtured through vague and frequent references to poisons, plots, clysters, and the like, it is not until late in the novel that the second specific reference to poisonous plants appears. The seedling reaches full and venomous bloom in the mind of Hester Prynne, who imagines Chillingworth sinking into a barren blasted spot of earth "where, in due course of time, would be seen deadly nightshade, dogwood, henbane . . ." (pp. 126–127). It is telling that Hawthorne should select these particular plants. Deadly nightshade (*Atropa belladonna*) contains atropine, as well as the related poisons scopolamine and hyoscyamine.[10] Henbane (*Hyoscyamus niger*) contains hyoscyamine, scopolamine, and atropine.[10] The so-called dogwood (*Rhus vernix*), known in Massachusetts as poison dogwood, causes a cutaneous reaction similar to that of the closely related poison ivy (*Rhus toxicodendron*).[12,13]

Hawthorne's Sources

12   The alkaloids derived from the solanaceous plants have been known as poisons since the Egyptian and Hindu civilizations; mention is made of them as antispasmodics in the Ebers Papyrus (1550 B.C.). They were a favorite agent of the professional poisoners of the Middle Ages, and their mydriatic effects were known to Galen. Linnaeus (1707 to 1778) recognized the deadly effects of the plant nightshade and gave it the name Atropos, after the oldest of the three Fates, who cut the delicate thread of life.[14]

13   Records compiled from the Salem Athenaeum during Hawthorne's "solitary years," 1825 to 1837, indicate that the writer was "deeply engaged in reading everything he could lay his hands on. It was said in those days that he read every book in the Athenaeum. . . ."[15] A perusal of Hawthorne's reading list reveals several books of a botanical nature, one of which sheds light on the references to atropine-containing plants in *The Scarlet Letter*.[16] Deadly nightshade and henbane appear close to each other in Sowerby's *English Botany*.[17] It seems unlikely that references to the same toxic plants in *The Scarlet Letter* are merely coincidental. This connection between a description of toxic plants in a book that Hawthorne was known to have borrowed from the Athenaeum and the subsequent mention of the plants in his novel, along with characteristic symptoms of poisoning from these plants, indicates the probable source of Hawthorne's information about poisonous plant forms.

The Symptoms—A Nervous Despondency in His Air

14   Intoxication with atropine, a tertiary amine, results in both central and peripheral nervous-system manifestations.[18] The early symptoms are visual disturbances, xerostomia [dryness of mouth], mydriasis [dilated pupils], and photophobia [extreme sensitivity to light]. Dysphagia [difficulty in swallowing] and speech disturbances may also be present. The skin becomes dry and hot, and a diffuse nonpunctate erythematous [red] rash may appear, especially over the face, neck, and chest. Confusion, incoordination, auditory and visual hallucinations, psychotic behavior, and convulsions may also occur. The pulse is weak and rapid, and in severe cases, the patient may progress to stupor, then coma, and finally stertorous respiration [a heavy snoring sound in breathing] and cyanosis [bluish discoloration of the skin].[10] Sedation, fatigue, dizziness, and postural hypotension [a feeling of dizziness when standing or sitting up] have also been described as symptoms of atropine poisoning.[18] To a remarkable degree, many of these symptoms are described in *The Scarlet Letter*.

Cardiovascular Symptoms—
Gripping Hard at His Breast

15   A rapid weak pulse and flushing are the most prominent cardiovascular symptoms of atropine poisoning. There are two descriptions of Dimmesdale with a flushed appearance. One is in conjunction with chest pain: "he was often observed, on any slight alarm, to put his hand over his heart, with first a flush and then a paleness, indicative of pain" (p. 88). It is tempting to postulate that Dimmesdale suffered from angina [chest pain] exacerbated by atropine-induced tachycardia [excessively fast heartbeat]. Hawthorne certainly emphasizes the presence of disease in Dimmesdale's heart, with descriptions of him gripping his chest "as if inflicted with an importunate throb of pain" (p. 96). At other times, Hawthorne refers to "the disease . . . in his [Dimmesdale's] heart . . ." (p. 113) and the appearance of what "had now become a constant habit, rather than a casual gesture, to press his hand over his heart" (p. 88). Even Dimmesdale became aware "that the poison of one morbid spot was infecting his entire heart's substance . . ." (p. 102).

Gait Disturbances, Tremors, and
Convulsions—Tremulously Put Forth

16   Muscular incoordination and convulsions occur under the influence of atropine. Hawthorne is particularly keen in his description of these afflictions. Initially, there was only a nervous "despondency in his [Dimmesdale's] air . . ." (p. 135). However, Dimmesdale's condition deteriorated, and there was the appearance of "a listlessness of his gait" (p. 137). Close to death, the minister had a "Deathlike hue" and "tottered on his path so nervously" that his "passage resembled the wavering effort of an infant . . ." (p. 177). He tore off his shirt with a "convulsive motion" (p. 180) and died soon thereafter.

Visual Disturbances and Hallucinations—
He Indistinctly Beheld

17   The classic symptom of atropine ingestion is mydriasis. "Belladonna," the name of the atropine-containing plant deadly nightshade, is derived from an Italian root word meaning "fair lady." This derivation stems from the atropine-induced pupillary dilatation that gave an appearance of large and supposedly desirable eyes in women who used the plant. *Atropa belladonna* is a member of the genus solanum, a word derived from the root "solar," reflecting the plant's stupefying power, similar to that of the sun. In one reference to mydriasis, and possibly also to photophobia, it is noted that Dimmesdale's "large dark eyes had a world of pain in their troubled and melancholy depth" (p. 83).

18   Even defenders of Hawthorne's elegantly symbolic prose have conceded that the writer transcended the boundaries of credibility in one particular scene.[3] The scene in question involves Dimmesdale's viewing of a scarlet letter in the heavens above the Puritan town (p. 113). In view of the fact that atropine may induce visual disturbances and hallucinations, it is reasonable to postulate that the scene is a realistic portrayal of a visual hallucination. Indeed, on reviewing this scene, it seems that such an interpretation is implicit in the text: "We impute it, therefore, solely to the disease in his own eye and heart that the minister, looking upward toward the zenith, beheld there the appearance of an immense letter—the letter A—marked out in lines of dull red light" (p. 113).

Dysphagia and Speech Disorders— His Voice Had a Prophecy of Decay in It

19   Speech difficulties and dysphagia in atropine poisoning result from suppression of salivation.[10] Hawthorne notes changes in the character of Dimmesdale's voice: it "had a certain melancholy prophecy of decay in it . . ." (p. 88) and was "more tremulous than before . . ." (p. 89).

20   Although there are no direct references to dysphagia, Hawthorne notes several times that Dimmesdale's "form grew emaciated . . ." (p. 88); "his cheek was paler and thinner . . ." (p. 89). Close to death, "he looked haggard and feeble . . ." (p. 135).

The Scarlet Letter—A Rash Conclusion?

21   On his deathbed, Dimmesdale tore the garments from his chest, as if to reveal and expiate his guilt. Thus, before "the gaze of the horror-stricken multitude . . ." (p. 180), he revealed the red stigmata of guilt that festered on his chest. It is my conclusion that "this burning torture . . ." (p. 181) on Dimmesdale's chest was a diffuse nonpunctate erythematous rash.

22   The rash, that is, of atropine poisoning.   *2,370 words*

References

1. Bradley S, Beatty R, Long E, eds. Nathaniel Hawthorne: *The Scarlet Letter.* New York: WW Norton, 1962.
2. Brownell WC. American prose masters. New York: Scribner, 1909.
3. Gorman H. Hawthorne, a study in solitude. New York: George H. Doran, 1927.
4. Michaud R. The American novel today: a social and psychological study. Boston: Little Brown, 1928:32–45.
5. Spiller RE. The mind and art of Nathaniel Hawthorne. Outlook 1928; 149:650–2, 676, 678.

6. Trollope A. The genius of Nathaniel Hawthorne. North Am Rev 1870:129(September):203–22.
7. Modern Language Association International Bibliography—1967–1980.
8. Waggoner HH. Hawthorne: a critical study. Cambridge, Mass.: Belknap Press of Harvard University Press, 1955.
9. Wellborn GP. Plant lore and *The Scarlet Letter*. Southern Folklore Q 1963; 27:160–7.
10. Lampe KF, Fagerstrom R. Plant toxicity and dermatitis. Baltimore: Williams and Wilkins, 1968:118–41.
11. Hardin JW, Arena JM. Human poisoning from native and cultivated plants. Durham, N.C.: Duke University Press, 1978.
12. Bailey WW. Our poisonous plants. Am Naturalist 1873; 7:4–13.
13. Foster FP. Some poisonous plants. Galaxy 1870; 10:704–8.
14. Duke-Elder S. Pharmacological agents II: systemic effectors. In: Duke-Elder S, ed. System of ophthalmology. Vol. 7. St. Louis: CV Mosby, 1962:541–50.
15. Fields JT. Yesterdays with authors. Boston: Houghton Mifflin. 1900:47.
16. Kesselring ML. Hawthorne's reading 1828–1850. New York: New York Public Library, 1975.
17. Sowerby J. English botany; or, coloured figures of British plants, with their essential characters, synonyms, and places of growth. To which will be added, occasional remarks. Volume 9. London: James Sowerby, 1799.
18. Meyers F, Jawetz E, Goldfien A. Review of medical pharmacology. Los Altos, Calif.: Lange, Medical Publications, 1978:70–8.

Comprehension Questions

1. This article could be entitled
   a. "Hawthorne's *Scarlet Letter*."
   b. "The Consequences of Adultery in *The Scarlet Letter*."
   c. "A Case of Murder in Hawthorne's *Scarlet Letter*."
   d. "The Medical Background of Hawthorne's *Scarlet Letter*."
2. It is the author's thesis that *The Scarlet Letter*
   a. is about a poisoning.
   b. is Hawthorne's best book.
   c. is mainly about Hester Prynne.
   d. portrays a man dying from guilt.
3. The author supports his thesis with
   a. evidence from other doctors.
   b. the opinions of literary critics.
   c. evidence from the book itself.
   d. Hawthorne's diaries.
4. The evidence for the theory of poisoning rests on
   a. motive, knowledge, and symptoms.
   b. observation, motive, and knowledge.
   c. written diaries, symptoms, and motive.
   d. reports of neighbors, knowledge, and observations.

5. Which of the following is *not* named as a poison?
   a. deadly nightshade
   b. henbane
   c. lye
   d. dogwood
6. The author should know what he is talking about because he is
   a. a close student of Hawthorne's work.
   b. a doctor of botany.
   c. a doctor of history.
   d. a medical doctor.
7. _____ is the pattern of organization most used in this article.
   a. Compare/contrast
   b. Cause and effect
   c. List
   d. Chronology
8. From the context you might guess that the Salem Athenaeum is
   a. a library.
   b. a museum.
   c. a store.
   d. a theater.
9. The author believes that Dimmesdale
   a. was a victim of hallucination.
   b. was not an adulterer.
   c. knew Chillingworth was poisoning him.
   d. suffered from heart attacks.
10. The article states that doctors in the period of *The Scarlet Letter*
   a. made their own drugs from available plants.
   b. got all their drugs from the Indians.
   c. knew a lot about drugs.
   d. had no laboratories.

14. **Third World in the Global Future**

Peter H. Raven

1   The problems associated with the Third World affect us all. If we are wise enough or lucky enough to avoid nuclear war, how we deal with those problems will largely determine our future, and that of our children and grandchildren.

2   What was already, in 1950, a record human population tripled during the course of a single human lifetime. This represents an extraordinary and unprecedented situation. The challenge presented to the productivity capacity of the earth by this increase is neither "normal" nor a circumstance that we can expect to deal with by applying the standard behaviors of the past.

3   The worldwide distribution pattern of this population growth ought also to be a major cause of concern. During the past 34 years, well over two billion people have been added in the less developed countries alone. This number equals the entire world population as recently as 1932. During the same period "only" 300 million people were added in the developed countries, including those of the Near East and Korea which are not tropical. About 90 percent of such countries do lie wholly or partly in the tropics, a relationship that is important to understand.

4   During our single hypothetical lifetime, from 1950 to 2020, the proportion of people living in developed countries will fall from about a third of the total world population to about a sixth. Over the same period, the population of the mainly tropical, less developed countries will grow from approximately 45 percent of the total to more than 64 percent. In sum, the plurality of people live in the tropics, and their percentage of the world population is rapidly increasing, while ours is rapidly falling. Small wonder that we hear more and more about El Salvador, Nicaragua, the Philippines, Africa and other tropical regions and that we are steadily becoming more and more concerned with the development of appropriate policies to pursue in these hitherto unfamiliar parts of the world.

5   The worldwide rate of economic growth has fallen substantially from the 4 percent characteristic of the third quarter of the twentieth century. For the next two decades, many estimate that it may be no higher than 2 percent, as it has been for the past several years. This sort of economic environment, in the context of the much-discussed debts of countries like Brazil, Mexico, Nigeria and Kenya, makes it difficult to imagine how these countries will be able to meet the or-

dinary needs of their people, much less be able to improve conditions in the future.

6   The developed countries, with less than a quarter of the people in the world and an average per capita income of more than $9,000, control some 80 percent of the global economy. In stark contrast, the less developed countries, with an average per capita income of less than $1,000, control only about 17.6 percent of that economy. Further, the developed countries consume about 80 percent of the total world supply of energy, the less developed countries about 12 percent. And, as a final index to the disproportionate distribution of wealth, the consumption of iron, copper and aluminum by developed countries ranges from 86 to 92 percent, by the less developed countries, even including China, from 8 to 14 percent.

7   A quarter of the world's population (a proportion that is rapidly dropping) controls more than four-fifths of the world's goods, while a majority of the population (rapidly increasing in size) have access to no more than a sixth of any commodity involved in the world's productivity. Can this relationship be sustained as the disproportionate distribution of people becomes ever more extreme? The consequences of population growth in Kenya today are absolutely different from those in Europe or the United States of a century ago, and a direct comparison between the two situations is invalid.

8   An associated global problem is that of the rapid destruction of the forests and other potentially renewable tropical resources. In 1981, the Tropical Forest Resources Assessment Project of the U.N. Food and Agriculture Organization (FAO) estimated that 44 percent of the tropical rainforests had already been disturbed. The study estimated that about 1.1 percent of the remainder was being logged each year at that time. The total area of the remaining forest amounted to approximately the size of the United States west of the Mississippi River, with an additional area about half the size of Iowa being logged each year. If the clearing were to continue at this rate, all of the tropical rainforests would be gone in 90 years—a minimum estimate of the time necessary for their disappearance.

9   This estimate only begins to suggest the gravity of the problem. First, clearcutting is merely the most extreme form of forest conversion. Norman Myers, in his outstanding book *The Primary Source* (Norton, 1984), estimates the overall rate to be two to three times as great as that suggested by the FAO figures, or more than 2 percent per year. At that rate, even with no acceleration, the forests will all have been converted in less than 50 years. And other kinds of forest conversion are also threatening the extinction of species.

10   In the next 36 years alone, the population of the tropical countries will approximately double from its present level to about five billion. The governments of these countries are already faced with staggering

debts, a sluggish world economy and the rapid loss of the productive capacity of their lands. For these governments to be able to expand their economies rapidly enough to continue to care for the needs of their people at 1984 levels clearly would be an unprecedented economic miracle. But even if they were able to do so, the numbers of their people living in absolute poverty would continue to increase as rapidly as their populations as a whole. Poor people would obviously continue to destroy their forests more and more rapidly with each passing year.

11   The rate of destruction and deterioration of tropical forests is by no means uniform. Three large forest blocks—in the western Brazilian Amazon, in the interior of the Guyanas and in the Congo Basin—are larger, less densely populated, and therefore being exploited more slowly than the remainder. Some of the forests in these three regions might actually persist in a relatively undisturbed condition for another 40 years or so, until the surging populations of their respective countries finally exhaust them. But all of the remaining forests in other parts of the tropics will surely be gone, or at least profoundly altered in nature and composition, much earlier. For the most part, these forests will not remain undisturbed beyond the end of the present century. This process of destruction is apparently irreversible, and it is accelerating rapidly. The tropical forests certainly will never recover from this onslaught.

12   The uneven distribution of wealth is one major factor in the destruction of tropical forests. The World Bank estimates that, of the 2.5 billion people now living in the tropics, one billion exist in absolute poverty. This term describes a condition in which a person is unable to count on being able to provide food, shelter and clothing for himself and his family from one day to the next. According to the World Health Organization, between 500 and 700 million people, approximately one out of every four living in the tropics, are malnourished. UNICEF has estimated that more than 10 million children in tropical countries starve to death unnecessarily each year. Worse, many millions more exist in a state of lethargy, their mental capacities often permanently impaired by lack of access to adequate amounts of food.

13   Shifting cultivation and other forms of agriculture generally fail quickly in most tropical regions. The reason lies in some of the characteristics of the soils and plant communities that occur in these areas. Although tropical soils are extremely varied, many are highly infertile. They are able to support lush forests, in spite of their infertility, because most of the meagre amounts of nutrients present actually are held within the trees and other vegetation. The roots of these trees spread only through the top inch or two of soil. Quickly

and efficiently, the roots recover nutrients from the leaves that fall to the ground, transferring them directly back into the plants from which they have fallen.

14   Once the trees have been cut, they decay or are burned, releasing relatively large amounts of nutrients into the soil. It is then possible to grow crops on this land successfully for a few years, until the available nutrients are used up. If the cut-over areas are then left to recover for many years, and if there is undisturbed forest nearby, the original plant communities may eventually be restored. This process normally takes decades, even centuries, depending upon the type of forest involved. But rarely will it be allowed to reach completion anywhere in the world in the future. There are simply too many people and consequently too little time. The relentless search for firewood, the most important source of energy in many parts of the tropics, is one reason that the forests usually cannot recover.

15   Shifting cultivation, particularly under circumstances where the time of rotation must be short, virtually guarantees continued poverty for the people who practice it. Agricultural development in the tropics without proper management of the soil is not successful. Cultivation can be sustained on the better tropical soils under ideal conditions, involving fertilization, but such conditions lack meaning for the roughly 40 percent of the people who make up the rural poor—those who actually are destroying most of the forests. Trees generally make more productive crops in the humid tropics than do other kinds of plants; and agroforestry, the combination of annual crops and pastures with trees, is probably the most suitable form of agriculture for many of these regions. Unfortunately, very little research is being done in this area, and the practical options are few.

16   The FAO estimates that a 60 percent increase in world food production will be needed by the year 2000 if the world's population is to be fed. It does not appear that current efforts will lead to our even beginning to approach this goal, although some optimistic estimates have suggested that we might achieve half of it. In *World Indices of Agricultural and Food Production,* issued last year, the U.S. Department of Agriculture calculated that there has been little progress since 1973 in raising food consumption per capita for the world as a whole. Only greatly expanded efforts might offer the hope of improving this record significantly in the near future.

17   In Sub-Saharan Africa, the problem is worse than elsewhere. There, per capita food production has declined every year since at least 1961; the Department of Agriculture estimated that in 1982 it was 11 percent less than in 1970. Currently, food production in this region is growing at about 1.3 percent per year, the population at about 3 per-

cent. Even worse, food production *per acre* has been declining in recent years, despite some $8 billion of international aid spent annually in Africa.

18   For tropical countries, only sustainable local agricultural productivity—not food exports—will lead to stability. There are indications that other regions, including northeastern Brazil, the Andean countries, Central America and the Indian subcontinent, may soon face the same difficulties in food production that Africa does now, if their rapid population growth, soil erosion and underinvestment in agriculture continue unchecked. Only about 8 percent of the food eaten in tropical countries is imported, and it is highly improbable that this total could be increased significantly, especially in the face of these nations' staggering debts and their rapid population increases.

19   Unless we recognize and address these problems, we can expect the instability now characteristic of so many tropical countries to spread and to become increasingly serious. About two-thirds of the people in these countries are farmers, and this number includes most of the truly poor, many with very little land, or none at all. Only if we can find better ways to use tropical land productivity for human benefit, concentrating on the areas that will be most productive and on the rural poor, shall we be making a genuine contribution to peace and harmony for those who come after us.

20   The population of Central America is about 23 million. In concentrating on that area, we are concerning ourselves with only one percent of all the people in the tropics—and their total number is projected to double in the next 30 years or so! To attain our political and economic goals throughout the world, we must find some way to help to alleviate the plight of the billion people in the tropics who are at the edge of starvation. If we cannot collectively find the means to eliminate rural poverty in these regions, as many experienced observers have concluded, these poor people will soon topple any government, be it friendly or unfriendly to us.

21   Yet despite these realities, the authors of the Kissinger Report on Central America pay very limited attention to the ecological problems that underlie the complex difficulties confronting that region. Although the Report explicitly recognizes the contribution of widespread poverty and population pressures to the difficulties of that area, it fails to connect them with their underlying ecological causes. Only by coping with all these factors can true regional stability be attained, and we can begin to secure U.S. interests there.

22   It is no coincidence that El Salvador is ecologically the most devastated of all the countries of Central America. For well over a decade, the relationship between its degraded environment, the lot of its people and its persistent internal conflicts has been stressed by

virtually everyone concerned with that country's future. Throughout Central America and the other tropical regions, the best land is held by relatively few people; half of the farmland in El Salvador is owned by 2 percent of the population, for example. In practice, such a pattern tends to force the peasants to shifting cultivation in, and consequent permanent destruction of, the productivity of marginal lands.

23   Today, about a sixth of all American manufactured exports go to tropical countries, exports which support over 600,000 jobs in the United States alone. We also send nearly half of our agricultural exports to these areas and obtain many of our most important commodities from them. Such commerce will not be possible in the kind of world that is rapidly developing. The instability spreading throughout the tropics, including the constant threat of war, arises in many cases because of the prevalent extreme poverty and resource depletion. This poverty has brought about massive emigration. The U.S. Immigration and Naturalization Service in 1982–1983 apprehended over a million illegal immigrants at the Mexican border alone and estimates that 30 to 40 million more Latin Americans may enter the country illegally by the end of the century, in addition to the number who enter legally. Such a pattern occurs precisely because after 40 years of sustained economic growth, fully half of the population of Mexico still lives in poverty.

24   Beyond the social and political consequences of the exhaustion of tropical resources, however, is a still more fundamental problem. It is the extinction of a major fraction of the plants, animals and microorganisms during the lifetime of a majority of people on earth today.

25   Approximately 1.5 million kinds of organisms have been named and classified, but these include only about 500,000 from the tropics. The total number of species of organisms in temperate regions is estimated to be approximately 1.5 million, but in relatively well-known groups of organisms—birds, mammals and plants—there are about twice as many species in the tropics as in the temperate regions. It may therefore be estimated that at least three million species exist in the tropics. Of these, we have named, and therefore registered, no more than one in six.

26   Many tropical organisms are very narrow in their geographical ranges and are highly specific in their ecological and related requirements. Thus, tropical organisms are unusually vulnerable to extinction through disturbance of their habitats. More than half of the species of tropical organisms are confined to the lowland forests. In most areas, these forests will be substantially altered or gone within the next 20 years.

27   Nearly 20 percent of all the kinds of organisms in the world occur in the forests of Latin America outside the Amazon Basin; another 20

percent occur in the forests of Asia and Africa outside the Congo Basin. All of the forests in which these organisms occur will have been destroyed by early in the next century. What would be a reasonable estimate of the loss of species that will accompany such destruction?

28   The loss of half of the species in these forests would amount to at least 750,000 species, about most of which we know nothing. This amounts to more than 50 species a day—fewer in the immediate future, more in the early part of the next century. And, because of the subsequent destruction of the remaining large forest blocks, there will be a continuing acceleration in the rate of extinction. The ultimate possibility is that of reaching stability after the human population does so, but only after many additional organisms have become extinct.

29   What we have in the tropics, therefore, is a record and explosively growing human population, already well over twice as large as it was in 1950 and projected to double again in size in the next 30 years or so. More than one out of every four of these people are malnourished, many of them actually living at the edge of starvation. These people are dealing with the natural resources of their countries largely without regard to their sustainability, since no other options are available to them.

30   A human population with these characteristics will certainly exterminate a major proportion of the living species of plants, animals and microorganisms on earth before it begins to approach stability. For those unfamiliar with ecology and tropical biology to ignore or attempt to minimize the importance of events of this magnitude is to court disaster for themselves and for all the rest of us.

31   The extinction event projected within our lifetimes and those of our children may be about as extensive as that which occurred at the end of the Cretaceous Period 65 million years ago. For that time, David Raup, professor of geology at the University of Chicago, has estimated very approximately that about 20 to 30 percent of the total number of species may have disappeared permanently. There has been no comparable event since.

32   With the loss of organisms, we give up not only the opportunity to study and enjoy them, but also the chance to utilize them to better the human condition, both in the tropics and elsewhere. The economic importance of wild species, a tiny proportion of which we actually use, has been well documented elsewhere. Suffice it to say that the entire basis of our civilization rests on a few hundred species out of the millions that might have been selected, and we have just begun to explore the properties of most of the remaining ones.

33   The process of extinction cannot be reversed or completely halted. Its effects can, however, be moderated by finding the most appro-

priate methods of utilizing the potentially sustainable resources of tropical countries for human benefit. The explicit relationship between conservation and development was well outlined in the World Conservation Strategy, issued jointly in 1980 by the International Union for the Conservation of Nature and Natural Resources, the World Wildlife Fund and the United Nations Environmental Program.

34 Beyond the extinction of species, we are participating passively in the promotion of unstable world conditions in which it will no longer be possible to enjoy the benefits of civilization as we know them. It may seem comforting, temporarily, to use unwarranted scepticism and inadequate understanding of ecology as a basis for offering false reassurance to our leaders. To do so, however, is to offer them exceedingly bad advice at an extraordinarily dangerous time.

3,562 words

Comprehension Questions

1. The topic of the article is
   a. overpopulation.
   b. global economics.
   c. the Third World.
   d. resource depletion.
2. The author's key idea is that
   a. overpopulation causes destruction of tropical forests.
   b. the extinction of species affects us all.
   c. the problems of underdeveloped countries have global implications.
   d. military intervention will not preserve world peace.
3. This article was probably published in the *Bulletin of the Atomic Scientists* because
   a. plants are made up of atoms.
   b. the journal needed to fill up space.
   c. it deals with issues affecting world stability and peace.
   d. *all of the above*
4. Overpopulation and uneven distribution of wealth are _____ the destruction of tropical forests.
   a. causes of
   b. effects of
   c. irrelevant to
   d. *none of the above*
5. That half the best farmland in El Salvador is owned by 2 percent of the population is
   a. a conclusion.
   b. an inference.

    c. a supporting detail.

    d. a key idea.

6. The author's purpose is to

    a. outline solutions to the problem of world hunger.

    b. educate the reader about a complex topic.

    c. hold up the developed countries to ridicule.

    d. scare the reader.

7. The author primarily uses the _____ pattern of organization to educate the reader about the differences between the developed and underdeveloped countries.

    a. cause-and-effect

    b. order

    c. list

    d. compare/contrast

8. That the author is a botanist

    a. is irrelevant to the subject matter of the article.

    b. adds credibility to his statements about tropical organisms.

    c. undermines his statements about the effects of overpopulation.

    d. is an interesting bit of trivia.

9. News reports about famine in Ethiopia and Sudan

    a. help the reader understand the author's analysis.

    b. add credibility to the author's arguments.

    c. heighten the reader's interest in the topic.

    d. *all of the above*

10. A reader could infer that the author would

    a. support an increase in the United States' defense budget.

    b. support the shift of manufacturing facilities from developed to underdeveloped countries.

    c. support research in agroforestry.

    d. support obligatory sterilization of Third World women who already have two children.

15. **Once upon a Time There Was a Volcano in Boston . . . and This Is How They Know**

Margaret Thompson

1   In the geological course of things, hills are leveled and seas become dry land. Boston's landscape is no stranger to such changes, even during the time of man. Buried remnants of Indian fish weirs uncovered when the Boylston Street subway was excavated in 1913 testify that sea level was lower in these parts about four thousand years ago than it is now. With the advent of white settlers and the need for more land, English and American inhabitants of the burgeoning town worked to push back the encroaching shoreline. Their efforts altered the natural skyline as well. Today's Beacon Hill is a ghost of the picturesque Trimountain whose other two summits were hauled by the cartload between 1799 and 1824 to fill a shallow cove of the sea near the present site of North Station. The Beacon Hill Monument, a sixty-foot column, now rising at the rear of the State House, is an unwitting yardstick for this remarkable Yankee enterprise. The monument, designed in commemoration of the American Revolution by Boston's renowned architect Charles Bulfinch, stood on considerably higher ground until 1811 when, with the land beneath it, it fell victim to the filling operation. The eagle on the pinnacle of today's reproduction erected in 1899 marks the height of the hilltop before it was cut down to its present level.

2   Even more ambitious earth-moving projects in the mid-nineteenth century added commercial land along the waterfront and converted the marshy Back Bay into a gracious residential district.

3   There is a certain irony in all these man-made alterations to Boston's landscape. While centuries of human labor have outwardly cloaked the city in civilization, its rocky foundation contains the primordial record of a barren and untamed place. To find out what Boston looked like in this ancient time requires a journey into prehistory, the realm of geology.

4   Commuters may escape Boston's city limits at the end of each day, but their homes in Brookline, Newton, Needham and Wellesley still lie within the geological province known as the Boston Basin. The Basin is a wedge-shaped lowland nestled between Milton's Blue Hills on the south and Medford's Pine Hill on the north. It narrows toward the west until it finally pinches out in the neighborhood of Natick. The edge of the basin, especially on its north side, is often marked by

steep cliffs of pink Dedham granite. Travelers on Interstate 93 or Route 2 speed by some of these as they enter the city from the north or west. Other fine examples are visible along the Boston and Maine Railroad tracks between Wellesley and Wellesley Hills. Those who approach the city haltingly through the traffic lights on Route 9 or the Green Line's subway stations at Newton Center or Chestnut Hill may notice low, rounded masses of a decidedly lumpy-looking rock mottled in shades of gray, purple or rusty brown. This is the Roxbury Conglomerate that makes up much of the Basin's floor. It is the conglomerate and other kinds of rock sometimes found with it that hold the key to seeing the ancient scenery of Boston.

5   As its name implies, the Roxbury Conglomerate is composed of a tightly cemented mass of smoothly rounded boulders and pebbles. Popularly and perhaps more suggestively, it is called "puddingstone." The nineteenth century poet-philosopher Oliver Wendell Holmes described it with affection as "a thing to look at, to think about, to study over, to dream upon, to go crazy with, to beat one's brains out against." His final assessment was not intended in a scientific sense, but it could have been.

6   In spite of its immediately distinctive appearance, this rock, like the plum pudding it conjures up, contains much that is hidden. Its age confounded geologists for a century and its mode of origin continues to be debated. The questions are perhaps as intriguing as the recent progress in answering them. How *do* earth scientists approach such problems?

7   In sedimentary rocks, that is rocks originating as layers of mud, sand and gravel on beaches, river beds or the sea floor, fossils are the basis for age determinations. Although sedimentary, the Roxbury Conglomerate has seemed stubbornly without fossils. By happenstance and good fortune, the puzzle has recently been solved. The missing pieces, understandably overlooked as it turns out, were found in the new subway tunnel north of Harvard Square in Cambridge. Far from the shelled creatures, plants and even dinosaur footprints of sedimentary rocks elsewhere in New England, the fossils of the Boston Basin are dark spherical blebs—bubbles—of algae that can only be seen with a microscope, and only then by someone looking carefully.

8   U.S. Geological Survey Geologist Clifford Kay discovered them several years ago while looking for something else! This new evidence indicates an age of approximately 600 million years for the sedimentary rocks of the Boston Basin, three times older than previously thought. So old is the Basin, in fact, that more commonly found fossilized forms had yet to evolve. Whatever the details of Boston's land surface in this so-called Late Precambrian period of geologic time, it was bare of plant and animal life.

9   The Roxbury Conglomerate also contains other clues to the Late Precambrian landscape of Boston. Finding these, many non-geologists are surprised to learn, involves no digging. The process consists instead of criss-crossing the area repeatedly in search of all localities where bedrock emerges above the usual mantle of soil and glacial deposits.

10   A "field" geologist in Boston incongruously spends a great deal of time inspecting cliffs and ledges along highways, in cemeteries and golf courses, and in the parking lot of the Chestnut Hill Shopping Mall. Each of these outcroppings is recorded on a map and note is taken of the color of the conglomerate and the size and composition of the pebbles it contains. Compiling a regional picture of the distribution and variability of the conglomerate enables comparison with presently accumulating gravels in such disparate settings as river beds, beaches and zones of glacial melting. Matching the characteristics of the ancient Roxbury deposits with those of modern conglomerate-in-the-making is the only way to infer which environment existed in the Boston Basin 600 million years ago.

11   My work, . . . and that of students under my supervision, has in the last three years included examination of thousands of pebbles in the Roxbury Conglomerate. Most of them are bigger than plums, though none remotely approaches the proportions alleged in Holmes's whimsical verses about the Dorchester Giant who fed his offspring "a pudding stuffed with plums as big as the State House dome."

12   Typical pebble diameters range from an inch or two to a foot or two. More important than individual pebble size, however, is our finding that pebbles of different sizes are not randomly distributed, but show a distinctive arrangement. To someone flying over the area 600 million years ago, the pattern is that of a fully unfolded lady's fan, with the largest pebbles (visible on Hammond Street in Brookline) centered on the hinge and increasingly smaller ones radiating systematically outward along the ribs. Sedimentary deposits with this form are laid down by rivers or streams and are called alluvial fans.

13   Modern alluvial fans festoon the edges of Death Valley in California and are commonplace throughout Nevada's Basin and Range country. They form where swiftly flowing streams from steep mountain slopes enter flat valleys below. Stones carried in that current drop out as it slows down. The largest ones fall nearest the valley wall while smaller ones travel farther onto the valley floor. Oddly enough, it is the searing aridity of the southwest that sustains it alluvial fans. Rainfall, though infrequent, comes in torrents and scours freely as flash floods across the plantless hills. Late Precambrian Boston may have exceeded Death Valley in precipitation, but its utter lack of vegetation suited it equally well for alluvial fan formation. The Roxbury

Conglomerate, in short, records a rugged frontier setting that contrasts starkly with our modern "hub" of cultural refinement.

14   The wildness of Boston's geological past is underscored by the message to be found in other rocks of the Boston Basin, principally the Dedham Granite and its affiliate, the Mattapan Volcanics. These rocks are formed by the activity of molten rock, or magma. When magma secretes itself within the earth, it cools and solidifies quietly to form granite. With equal frequency, it may burst to the surface in a spectacle like the recent one at Mount St. Helens. The deposits of ash, mud and lava produced by such an eruption of magma are collectively termed volcanics. Geologists interpret ancient volcanics as they do sedimentary rocks by comparing them to recently formed examples. In the case of the Mattapan Volcanics, an extremely instructive lesson comes from the Indonesian island volcano Krakatau which came to life a century ago last August in probably the most famous eruption of historic times.

15   While Krakatau is remembered in the western world for the spectacular sunsets produced by its ash circulating high in the atmosphere, the scene in the neighborhood of the volcano was far less romantic. More than thirty-thousand souls perished in the hundred-foot waves that inundated coastal Java and Sumatra. The few survivors endured skies blackened by ash and artillery-like detonations (one of which was heard thousands of miles away in the Indian Ocean). For all the power of this outward explosion, however, scientists have shown that the real climax of the eruption was actually a downward collapse of the volcanic cone into the partially drained reservoir of magma below it. Where Krakatau formerly rose some two-thousand feet above sea level, there now exists a depression in the sea floor measuring miles across and hundreds of feet deep.

16   No one, of course, saw the downward collapse of Krakatau, for the major events took place deep beneath the sea floor. In the Boston Basin, however, hundreds of millions of years of erosion have created windows into the roots of a volcano like Krakatau. Here the collapse is recorded in a jumble of Dedham Granite and Mattapan Volcanic rocks found in the Stonybrook Reservation, a large woodland park straddling Washington Street and Hyde Park Avenue in Boston's Hyde Park section. The deposit consists of chunks of various older volcanic rocks (some of these do approach the size of the State House dome) embedded in a greenish-gray scaly looking rock that proves microscopically to be rich in pumice. Pumice (sold commercially as buffing stone) is produced when gas-charged magma erupts explosively as it did at Krakatau. Its chaotic cargo of other rocks is plausibly explained as the result of the landsliding of steep cliffs into the actively erupting crater. With continued eruption, the whole volcanic

mixture foundered into the magma remaining in the chamber below. This magma finally solidified to form Dedham Granite.

17   Climbers, gardeners and builders are probably most aware of the rocky foundation of greater Boston. Even among these however, ledges of Roxbury Conglomerate, Mattapan Volcanics and Dedham Granite may represent no more than static backdrops to busy human purpose. Yet the 600-million year old landscapes evoked by these rocks were scenes of momentous activity and relentless change. The torrential rivers that deposited the alluvial fans in the Roxbury Conglomerate plucked their loads from the slopes of once explosive Mattapan volcanoes. Millions of years later when the volcanoes were gone, continued erosion laid bare the granites below. The entire panorama is accessible to an inquiring eye.   *1,913 words*

Comprehension Questions

1. The purpose of this article is to
    a. tell the reader how geologic history is determined.
    b. persuade the reader to act to preserve the environment.
    c. compare modern times with ancient times.
    d. show how volcanoes come into existence.
2. Which of the following is the best statement of the central idea of the article?
    a. Geologists have discovered that where Boston now is was once a volcano.
    b. Rocks that are plainly visible can tell us about the ancient environment.
    c. People have improved Boston's landscape.
    d. You have to dig to discover the geologic past.
3. The significance of the Roxbury Conglomerate is that
    a. it holds the key to the ancient scenery of Boston.
    b. it is composed of smoothly rounded boulders and pebbles.
    c. it is called "puddingstone."
    d. its age confounds geologists.
4. You can learn a lot about Boston by studying the volcano named
    a. Mt. Etna.
    b. Mt. Saint Helens.
    c. Vesuvius.
    d. Krakatau.
5. _____ is a type of rock not found in the Boston area.
    a. Dedham Granite
    b. Mattapan Volcanics
    c. Fitzwilliam Granite
    d. Puddingstone

6. In the context of this article the word *arid* means
   a. flat and cold.
   b. bare and dry.
   c. hilly and moist.
   d. verdant and tropical.
7. Geologists learn about the past by
   a. digging deep underground.
   b. studying volcanoes.
   c. matching ancient characteristics with modern formations.
   d. examining individual rocks.
8. The Precambrian period was about _____ years ago.
   a. 100 million
   b. 600 million
   c. 1 million
   d. 500,000
9. One can usually tell the age of sedimentary rocks by
   a. studying fossils.
   b. comparing them to nonsedimentary rocks.
   c. identifying blebs of algae in them.
   d. compiling a map of their regional distribution.
10. Granite is solidified
    a. sand and clay.
    b. conglomerate.
    c. magma.
    d. lava.

16. **The Chicanos**

Tino Villanueva

1　The Mexican-American War (1846–1848) caught Mexico in complete prostration. She lost the war; and as a consequence of the Treaty of Guadalupe Hidalgo of February 2, 1848 received the sum of $15,000,000, but had to cede half her territory, the area which today makes up the five southwestern states—Texas, New Mexico, Colorado, Arizona and California, as well as Nevada and Utah.

2　February 2, 1848 constitutes, therefore, a turning point in Chicano history. From one day to the next Mexican citizens became American citizens. The Treaty carried provisions for a measure of protection for those Mexican citizens who wished to remain north of the Rio Grande (Article VIII: "Mexicans now established in territories previously belonging to Mexico . . . shall be free to continue where they now reside . . . retaining the property which they possess in the said territories . . . property of every kind, now established there, shall be inviolably respected"; Article IX: "Mexicans, in the territories aforesaid . . . shall . . . be admitted at the proper time . . . to the enjoyment of all the rights of citizens of the United States"; Article X, later deleted by President Polk and the Department of State: "All the land grants made by the Mexican government or by the competent authorities which pertained to Mexico in the past and which will remain in the future within the boundaries of the United States, will be respected as valid"). In reality these *de facto* American citizens ended up a defeated and colonized community. They were, as the renowned phrase goes, strangers in their own land. Many were cheated out of or were run off their legally-owned land under the threat of violence by Anglo settlers; the unskilled laborers in most cases became no more than virtual serfs for the new-landed Anglo Americans. When they were not *vaqueros* (cowboys) on cattle ranches and trails, sheep herders and shearers, copperminers, or livery-stable hands, Mexican Americans turned to being servants, laundresses, gardeners, cooks and seamstresses. In a large sense the Mexican American way of life paralleled the Black-American way of life, although for the former there was no Emancipation Proclamation.

3　In the cities, and afterwards in the emerging towns, these new Americans became craftsmen in adobe-making, stonemasonery, furniture repair, plumbing, silversmithing, tinsmithing and blacksmithing. Others found employment as *arrieros* (mule and ox drivers) involved in the freight business, or as street vendors of consumable products (vegetables, goat meat, sun-dried beef, cakes, confectionery, Mexican food, arts and crafts and needlework). A significant though less numerous class included sheriffs, postmasters, policemen, newspaper editors, teachers, medical doctors, lawyers, druggists, and even clerks at the municipal and federal government administration level. Only a small class of property-owners and urban entrepreneurs were able to retain some semblance of their preconquest status. They were proprietors not only of farm land, livestock and real estate, but of retail stores, bakeries, restaurants, saloons, hotels, drug stores, barbershops and printshops as well.

4   Those who were not employed relied on seasonal migrant work (all the more so in the twentieth century), travelling around the Southwest, to the Midwest and East Coast as field hands and pickers, or as railroad construction workers, section hands and maintenance employees, occupations sometimes involving the whole family. Although many left for the cities when industry started up in this century (thus the beginnings of Mexican American communities in the Midwest, especially), agricultural work remained a source of employment for many, particularly for the new, unskilled immigrants from Mexico who began to flow across the border from the period of the Mexican Revolution (1910) to the present. Many chose to stay and become citizens; in this fashion they changed the demographics of Chicano communities throughout the United States.

5   As Anglo Americans settled the southwestern United States, the more contact Americans of Mexican descent had with the new socio-economic, political and cultural order, with its particular brand of educational system and, most importantly, with the English language. Unskilled, uneducated, illiterate for the most part, and, at the outset, untutored in English, the Mexican American of the late nineteenth century became the easy target of discrimination for the Anglo American. The tradition of racial superiority and dominance also figured prominently in the patterns of prejudice against these new citizens, their language and Catholic religion, patterns which, to some extent, still survive albeit to a lesser degree. Assimilation into the mainstream society (always with limitations) does not begin to occur until the 1940s, after World War II, when Mexican American servicemen returned home with newly-acquired skills and with the sense that through education (and a solid foundation in the English language) they could improve themselves and the lot of their brethren, and, moreover, pursue their version of the American Dream, all of which signaled the emergence of a significant middle class.

6   In 1928 LULAC (League of United Latin American Citizens) became the first Mexican American organization to form itself to answer the needs of citizens of Mexican heritage, whereas before, only voluntary associations of the mutual benefit type had existed, among them *La Alianza Hispano Americana* (1894) and *La Sociedad Mutualista Mexicana* (1918). Organizing activity did not thrive until the

post-World War II period. In 1947 the CSO (Community Service Organization) was established in California around civic issues as a conscious attempt at "Americanization" and "assimilation." But it was the G. I. Forum (1948) in Texas which began to make significant social reforms and political gains, challenging and, in some cases, striking down segregation policies against Mexican Americans in the public schools and successfully running candidates for local public office. In the 1950s other coalitions were formed, such as MAPA (Mexican American Political Association, 1958), while PASSO (Political Association of Spanish-Speaking Organizations) was formed in 1960.

7   Not until the mid-1960s, on the heels of the Black Civil Rights Movement, did Mexican Americans gain national and international attention, media coverage and a not insignificant measure of potential for political power. The series of farmworker strikes and lettuce and grape boycotts (begun in 1965) in California against long-standing unfair labor practices and general worker exploitation solidified into the United Farmworkers Union under the leadership of César Chávez. So significant were these developments that some referred to them as the second *Grito de Dolores*.

8   The labor movement, together with the land-grant movement in New Mexico headed by Reies López Tijerina (which exposed the violation of the 1848 Treaty of Guadalupe Hidalgo and demanded the restitution of stolen lands), urban mass demonstrations in the streets and electoral action, protests against the Vietnam War and similar activism by university students demanding more recruitment of Chicanos to the college ranks, financial aid, tutoring and support services and the establishment of Chicano Studies Departments, proved once and for all that a neglected people had come of age, that it could assert itself in the interest of self-determination. Many organizations were formed by a new generation of grassroots and university-based activists, such as the Crusade for Justice (urban civil rights and cultural movement), La Raza Unida Political Party, MAYO (Mexican American Youth Organization) and MECHA (Movimiento Estudiantil Chicano de Aztlán). Community leaders and educators urged school boards to institute bilingual programs as a needed pedagogic tool to accelerate the learning capacity of students whose primary home-language had been Spanish, and to minimize the incidence of student frustration at the seemingly disdainful attitude of some teachers toward the Spanish language and Mexican culture, an attitude believed by some to be responsible for a disproportionately high dropout rate among Mexican Americans.

9   Concomitant with the Chicano Movement—known to some as *La Causa* (The Cause)—an attendant movement of arts and letters and intellectual activity flourished. Many painters (including muralists), writers of all genres and social scientists who made up the *Chicano*

Renaissance, as it is known in academic circles, registered their psycho-social reality with penetrating testimonies and analyses about existence in America, acknowledged their pre-Columbian past and Indo-Hispanic (*mestizo*) history. In that process they prophesied the eventual liberation of Chicanos from the psychological bondage common to conquered and annexed people, subjugated in the aftermath of reconstruction. In their search for Chicano history, university students, artists and intellectuals were drawn to their pre-Hispanic past. In so doing, they no longer referred to the Southwest as such, but rather as Aztlán (Náhuatl for "land to the north," presumably the Southwest), that mythical ancestral home of the Aztecs before migrating south, where, in 1325 they settled on Lake Texcoco, the site of present-day Mexico City. The fundamental concept of Aztlán provided a geographical center, a political rallying point and the notion of a territorial base to be defended. This sense of belonging gave rise to ethno-cultural identity (something not felt toward mainstream Anglo America), inspired a new awareness of self and purpose, and became the source of much creative thinking.

10   Alongside the traditional, universal themes which were also evident in literature, these compelling self-reflections and life-concerns found a ready audience gathered around the many *barrio* and university tabloids, newspapers and literary and social science journals that suddenly sprang up, publications which writers, literary critics, sociologists and political scientists (not a few of them graduate students) greatly needed to display and convey their art and remarkable flurry of ideas. While some of these publications have seen their demise in the past fifteen years, others have taken their place, among them, *Imagine*, which in no small measure owes its belletristic spirit to the decades of the 1960s and 70s and traces its historical, ideological and emotional roots to the Southwest, even though its intellectual formation has occurred on the East Coast. What started out as localized interest in arts and letters has now national and international ramifications, reflecting the editorial staff's own aesthetic and personal journey from the Southwest (California, Texas) to eastern universities, eventual residency in New England and travel abroad.

11   The currency of the term *Chicano* itself grew out of and took hold in the mid-1960s on the University of California campuses and extended itself eastward to Texas. For all practical purposes it supplanted *Mexican American* (except among the older generations), and others which had preceded it, such as *Mexican, Latin American* and *Latin. Spanish American* and *Hispano*, terms peculiar to the Spanish-surnamed people of New Mexico and southern Colorado, more often than not held their own, except among some community members and college-age youth.

12   As an ethnic designation, *Chicano*, according to one commentator,

has been around since the eighteenth century in the southwest and northern Mexico to refer to any invading foreigner from the south. As far as can be verified, the first time *Chicano* was recorded is on July 27, 1911 in a Laredo, Texas, newspaper to signify an (unskilled) Mexican national recently arrived in the United States, and therefore, naïve about American customs or those of "Americanized Mexicans." Early twentieth century generations of Mexican Americans had a special aversion toward the label, as it connoted different nuances of "low-class." Teenagers in the 1950s, nonetheless, appropriated it as an in-group, positive self-designation to distinguish themselves from their elders' reference to their generation as *mexicanos*, which had the double application to a Mexican national or to an American of Mexican lineage.

13   When *Chicano* was brought into broader use in the 1960s by the more activist students, it came to mean, as it still does today, first, an act of defiance, then self-determination, ethnic pride and political consciousness. As such, the concept expressed by the word *Chicano* is not merely ethnic or racial, but also an historical position, and must be equated in spirit and substance with *Black*, which a few years earlier had replaced *Negro* as a consequence of Black consciousness grown out of similar socio-economic conditions of Americans of African descent.

14   There exist theories too numerous to be discussed here regarding the origin of the word *Chicano*. The most convincing traces the term back to Náhuatl (the language of the Aztecs). At the time of the conquest (1519–1521) the natives referred to themselves as "Mexica" (pronounced Meh-SHEE-kah). The Spaniards, as a result, called them "Meshicanos." In the speech sounds of sixteenth century Spanish the unvoiced palatal fricative *sh* [š] was represented by the letter *x*, hence, "México." As the Spanish language evolved, the ancient sound value of *sh* became the contemporary Spanish sound of the letter *j*, a voiceless velar fricative, approximated in English by the *h* of *hue*, but which is harsher and raspier (has more friction) in Spanish. After "Mexicano" (pronounced Meh-shee-KAH-noh) was replaced by "Mejicano" (pronounced Meh-hee-KAH-noh), palatalization of the *j*, which became [č] (spelled *ch*), and apheresis occurs. The latter linguistic phenomenon, the omission of the unstressed initial syllable *Me-*, constitutes the final step in the history of the word: [mexikano > mecikano > cikano], that is, *Chicano* (pronounced Chee-KAH-noh).

15   The gains that Chicanos have made during the post–World War II period might be considered impressive, understanding that many more must be made before full equality with mainstream American society is achieved. In the area of politics alone eight Americans of Mexican ancestry are currently serving in the House of Representatives in Washington; about eighty senators and representatives can

be found in state legislatures. More Chicanos serve on city councils and school boards than ever before. At this writing two major southwestern cities have voted into office mayors of Mexican descent: Denver (Federico Peña) and San Antonio (Henry Cisneros). Although only a few Chicanos are now judges, many hold federal positions. In the recent past, ambassadorships have been assigned to Raúl H. Castro (El Salvador) of Arizona, later to be governor of the state; Benigno C. Hernández (Paraguay) of New Mexico. Currently, the governor of New Mexico is Toney Anaya, while in the 1970s Jerry Apodaca held the same position for one term. There are more Chicano teachers, professors, engineers, scientists, designers, draftsmen, auditors, accountants, technicians, businessmen and women, musicians, doctors, lawyers, social workers, artists, writers, film producers and Hollywood actors and actresses than there were a quarter of a century ago.

16   Finally, to return again to the elemental question of language: since 1848, Chicanos finding themselves within the borders of a newly expanded United States have experienced the superimposition of an alien language and culture. During these decades, the survival of Spanish amongst Mexican Americans is evidenced in varying degrees. Some families retained the sole usage of Spanish, while others adopted, either unwittingly or not, an ambience of bilingualism, the level of proficiency in either language having always depended upon the individual's generation, education, socio-economic standing and, latterly, on ethnic pride and consciousness of the importance of bilingualism in the public schools and in public life, affirmations born of the 1960s. It is an irrefutable fact that adequate knowledge of and clear proficiency in the English language have, during the past decades, figured preeminently in the singlemost recognized area of success for Mexican Americans, i.e., the achievement of upward social mobility, gauged traditionally by educational and economic accomplishment.

17   Until recently then, the historical situation of the Chicano has served as a metaphor for victimization by conquest and colonialism, but since the decade of the 1960s serves more appropriately as a metaphor, at the least, for survival and at most, for growth and an increasing recognition of accomplishment and contribution.

2,476 words

Comprehension Questions
1. This article is about
   a. Hispanics.
   b. Latin Americans.

    c. Mexican Americans.

    d. Anglo-Americans.

2. The best statement of the key idea is that

    a. Chicanos are second-class citizens.

    b. Chicanos are politically active.

    c. Chicanos have their own culture.

    d. Chicanos are survivors and accomplishers.

3. Political and _____ activities are two subtopics.

    a. linguistic

    b. intellectual

    c. social

    d. military

4. That Chicanos have achieved some of their goals is due mainly to

    a. the fact that they learned English.

    b. *La Causa.*

    c. the Treaty of Guadalupe Hidalgo.

    d. their skill as craftspeople.

5. Which of the following is not seen as evidence of Chicano self-determination?

    a. labor activism

    b. student activism

    c. the land grant movement

    d. armed conflict

6. The term Chicano was used first in the

    a. 1950s.

    b. 1960s.

    c. early 1900s.

    d. early 1500s.

7. _____ is Aztlán.

    a. The mythical Mexican home of the Aztecs

    b. A name given to California

    c. A name given to the Southwest of the United States

    d. Another name for Mexico City

8. When the Mexicans became Americans, they

    a. prospered.

    b. were treated as slaves.

    c. retained their preconquest status.

    d. were taught English.

9. Bilingual programs were instituted at the urging of

    a. the U.S. government.

    b. César Chávez.

    c. community leaders.

    d. schoolchildren.

10. Although Chicanos have made impressive gains, at the time of the writing of this article no Chicano had been
    a. elected mayor.
    b. appointed ambassador.
    c. elected governor.
    d. elected U.S. senator.

17. Signs and Symbols in Language and Thought

Susanne K. Langer

1   A symbol is not the same thing as a sign; that is a fact that psychologists and philosophers often overlook. All intelligent animals use signs; so do we. To them as well as to us sounds and smells and motions are signs of food, danger, the presence of other beings, or of rain or storm. Furthermore, some animals not only attend to signs but produce them for the benefit of others. Dogs bark at the door to be let in; rabbits thump to call each other; the cooing of doves and the growl of a wolf defending his kill are unequivocal signs of feelings and intentions to be reckoned with by other creatures.

2   We use signs just as animals do, though with considerably more elaboration. We stop at red lights and go on green; we answer calls and bells, watch the sky for coming storms, read trouble or promise or anger in each other's eyes. That is animal intelligence raised to the human level. Those of us who are dog lovers can probably all tell wonderful stories of how high our dogs have sometimes risen in the scale of clever sign interpretation and sign using.

3   A sign is anything that announces the existence or the imminence of some event, the presence of a thing or a person, or a change in a state of affairs. There are signs of the weather, signs of danger, signs of future good or evil, signs of what the past has been. In every case a sign is closely bound up with something to be noted or expected in experience. It is always a part of the situation to which it refers, though the reference may be remote in space and time. In so far as we are led to note or expect the signified event we are making correct use of a sign. This is the essence of rational behavior, which animals show in varying degrees. It is entirely realistic, being closely bound up with the actual objective course of history—learned by experience, and cashed in or voided by further experience.

4   If man had kept to the straight and narrow path of sign using, he would be like the other animals, though perhaps a little brighter. He would not talk, but grunt and gesticulate and point. He would make his wishes known, give warnings, perhaps develop a social system like that of bees and ants, with such a wonderful efficiency of communal enterprise that all men would have plenty to eat, warm apartments—all exactly alike and perfectly convenient—to live in, and everybody could and would sit in the sun or by the fire, as the climate demanded, not talking but just basking, with every want satisfied, most of his life. The young would romp and make love, the old would

sleep, the middle-aged would do the routine work almost unconsciously and eat a great deal. But that would be the life of a social,
superintelligent, purely sign-using animal.

5   To us who are human, it does not sound very glorious. We want to
go places and do things, own all sorts of gadgets that we do not absolutely need, and when we sit down to take it easy we want to talk.
Rights and property, social position, special talents and virtues, and
above all our ideas, are what we live for. We have gone off on a tan-
gent that takes us far away from the mere biological cycle that animal generations accomplish; and that is because we can use not only
signs but symbols.

6   A symbol differs from a sign in that it does not announce the presence of the object, the being, condition, or whatnot, which is meaning, but merely brings this thing to mind. It is not a mere "substitute
sign" to which we react as though it were the object itself. The fact
is that our reaction to hearing a person's name is quite different from
our reaction to the person himself. . . .

7   If I say: "Napoleon," you do not bow to the conqueror of Europe as
though I had introduced him, but merely think of him. If I mention a
Mr. Smith of our common acquaintance, you may be led to tell me
something about him "behind his back," which is just what you
would *not* do in his presence. Thus the symbol for Mr. Smith—his
name—may very well initiate an act appropriate peculiarly to his
absence. Raised eyebrows and a look at the door, interpreted as a *sign*
that he is coming, would stop you in the midst of your narrative; *that*
action would be directed toward Mr. Smith in person.

8   Symbols are not proxy for their objects, but are *vehicles* for *the
conception of objects*. To conceive a thing or a situation is not the
same thing as to "react toward it" overtly, or to be aware of its presence. In talking *about* things we have conceptions of them, not the
things themselves; and *it is the conceptions, not the things, that symbols directly "mean."* Behavior toward conceptions is what words normally evoke; this is the typical process of thinking.

9   Of course a word may be used as a sign, but that is not its primary
role. Its significant character has to be indicated by some special
modification—by a tone of voice, a gesture (such as pointing or staring), or the location of a placard bearing the word. In itself it is a
symbol, associated with a conception,[1] not directly with a public object or event. The fundamental difference between signs and symbols

---

[1]Note that I have called the terms of our thinking conceptions, not concepts. Concepts are abstract forms embodied in conceptions; their bare presentation may be
approximated by so-called "abstract thought," but in ordinary mental life they no
more figure as naked factors than skeletons are seen walking the street. Concepts,
like decent living skeletons, are always embodied—sometimes rather too much.

is this difference of association, and consequently of their *use* by the third party to the meaning function, the subject; signs *announce* their objects to him, whereas symbols *lead him to conceive* their objects. The fact that the same item—say, the little mouthy noise we call a "word"—may serve in either capacity, does not obliterate the cardinal distinction between the two functions it may assume.

10   The simplest kind of symbolistic meaning is probably that which belongs to proper names. A personal name evokes a conception of something given as a unit in the subject's experience, something concrete and therefore easy to recall in imagination. Because the name belongs to a notion so obviously and unequivocally derived from an individual object, it is often supposed to "mean" that object as a sign would "mean" it. This belief is reinforced by the fact that a name borne by a living person always is at once a symbol by which we think of the person, and a call-name by which we signal him. Through a confusion of these two functions, the proper name is often deemed the bridge from animal semantic, or sign-using, to human language, which is symbol-using. Dogs, we are told, understand names—not only their own, but their masters'. So they do, indeed; but they understand them *only in the capacity of call-names*. If you say "James" to a dog whose master bears that name, the dog will interpret the sound as a sign, and *look for* James. Say it to a person who knows someone called thus, and he will ask: "What about James?" That simple question is forever beyond the dog; signification is the only meaning a name can have for him—a meaning which the master's name shares with the master's smell, with his footfall, and his characteristic ring of the door-bell. In a human being, however, the name evokes the *conception* of a certain man so called, and prepares the mind for further conceptions in which the notion of that man figures; therefore the human being naturally asks: "What about James?"

11   There is a famous passage in the autobiography of Helen Keller, in which this remarkable woman describes the dawn of Language upon her mind. Of course she had used signs before, formed associations, learned to expect things and identify people or places; but there was a great day when all sign-meaning was eclipsed and dwarfed by the discovery that a certain datum in her limited sense-world had a *denotation*, that a particular act of her fingers constituted a *word*. This event had required a long preparation; the child had learned many finger acts, but they were as yet a meaningless play. Then, one day, her teacher took her out to walk—and there the great advent of Language occurred.

12   "She brought me my hat," the memoir reads, "and I knew I was going out into the warm sunshine. This thought, if a wordless sensation may be called a thought, made me hop and skip with pleasure.

13   "We walked down the path to the well-house, attracted by the fragrance of the honeysuckle with which it was covered. Some one was drawing water and my teacher placed my hand under the spout. As the cool stream gushed over my hand she spelled into the other the word *water,* first slowly, then rapidly. I stood still, my whole attention fixed upon the motion of her fingers. Suddenly I felt a misty consciousness as of something forgotten—a thrill of returning thought; and somehow the mystery of language was revealed to me. I knew then that w-a-t-e-r meant the wonderful cool something that was flowing over my hand. That living word awakened my soul, gave it light, hope, joy, set it free! There were barriers still, it is true, but barriers that in time could be swept away.

14   "I left the well-house eager to learn. Everything had a name, and each name gave birth to a new thought. As we returned to the house every object which I touched seemed to quiver with life. That was because I saw everything with the strange, new sight that had come to me."[2]

15   This passage is the best affidavit we could hope to find for the genuine difference between sign and symbol. The sign is something to act upon, or a means to command action; the symbol is an instrument of thought. Note how Miss Keller qualifies the mental process just preceding her discovery of words—"This thought, *if a wordless sensation may be called a thought.*" Real thinking is possible only in the light of genuine language, no matter how limited, how primitive; in her case, it became possible with the discovery that "w-a-t-e-r" was not necessarily a sign that water was wanted or expected, but was the *name* of this substance, by which it could be mentioned, conceived, remembered.

1,790 words

---

[2]Helen Keller, *The Story of My Life* (1936; 1st ed. 1902), pp. 23–24.

Comprehension Questions

1. A good title for this article is
   a. "Putting Thoughts into Words."
   b. "The Use of Symbols."
   c. "The Difference Between Signs and Symbols."
   d. "Sign Language."
2. The best statement of the key idea is that
   a. people use signs and symbols interchangeably.
   b. people are different from animals because they use symbols.
   c. words convey signs and symbols.
   d. a sign is something to act upon; a symbol is an instrument of thought.

3. The story about Helen Keller is
   a. why the article was written.
   b. unnecessary.
   c. an example.
   d. a metaphor.
4. Which of the following does a sign *not* indicate?
   a. a concept or idea
   b. the presence of a person or thing
   c. that something has happened
   d. a direction
5. A proper name is
   a. only a sign.
   b. only a symbol.
   c. a bridge joining a sign and a symbol.
   d. not concrete.
6. The principal pattern of organization used by the author is
   a. compare/contrast.
   b. cause and effect.
   c. chronological order.
   d. list.
7. Animals use
   a. signs and symbols.
   b. only signs.
   c. only symbols.
   d. neither signs nor symbols.
8. According to this article, language makes _____ possible.
   a. symbols
   b. ideas
   c. communication
   d. speech
9. The article was written to
   a. inform.
   b. persuade.
   c. amuse.
   d. tell a story.
10. One of the greatest events in Helen Keller's life was the discovery that
    a. water flowed.
    b. words conveyed thoughts.
    c. she could enjoy being outdoors.
    d. she used signs.

Rate and Comprehension Progress Chart, Additional Readings

Reading No.:	1	2	3	4	5	6	7	8	9	
Rate (WPM)										
Comprehension Score *(Number Correct)*										Compre-hension Questions

Rate (WPM) Words Per Minute	Comprehension Questions
1000	10 correct
975	
950	
925	
900	9 correct
875	
850	
825	
800	8 correct
775	
750	
725	
700	7 correct
675	
650	
625	
600	6 correct
575	
550	
525	
500	5 correct
475	
450	
425	
400	4 correct
375	
350	
325	
300	3 correct
275	
250	
225	
200	2 correct
175	
150	
125	
100	1 correct

How to Chart Your Progress

1. Using the Rate Chart, figure out your reading rate (WPM) and record it with your comprehension score below the numbered reading at the top of this chart.
2. Using the Rate (WPM) column on the left, find your rate and place an "x" at that point

450

Rate and Comprehension Progress Chart, Additional Readings

Reading No.:	10	11	12	13	14	15	16	17	
Rate (WPM)									
Comprehension Score *(Number Correct)*									Comprehension Questions

Rate (WPM) Words Per Minute		Comprehension Questions
1000		10 correct
975		
950		
925		
900		9 correct
875		
850		
825		
800		8 correct
775		
750		
725		
700		7 correct
675		
650		
625		
600		6 correct
575		
550		
525		
500		5 correct
475		
450		
425		
400		4 correct
375		
350		
325		
300		3 correct
275		
250		
225		
200		2 correct
175		
150		
125		
100		1 correct

below the numbered reading. Using the right-hand column, find your comprehension score and place an "o" at that point below the numbered reading.

3. Connect each of the "o's" with one line and the "x's" with another so that you can chart your progress for both rate and comprehension.

Rate Charts for Additional Readings

To find your reading rate (WPM), first look along the top of the chart to locate the time it took you to read the numbered reading. Then look down that column until you come to the line for the reading in question. Where the two lines cross, you will find a number indicating how many words per minute (WPM) you have read. If you read Reading number 1 in 9 minutes your reading rate is 285 words per minute. Once you've found your score, enter it on the Progress Chart.

Reading Time (Min:Sec)

Reading Number:	1:00	1:30	2:00	2:30	3:00	3:30	4:00	4:30	5:00	5:30	6:00	6:30	7:00
1	2,563	1,709	1,282	1,025	854	732	641	570	513	466	427	394	366
2	4,520	3,013	2,260	1,809	1,507	1,291	1,130	1,104	904	822	753	695	646
3	1,164	776	582	466	388	333	291	259	233	212	194	179	166
4	2,840	1,893	1,420	1,136	947	811	710	631	568	516	473	437	406
5	1,191	794	596	476	397	340	298	265	238	217	199	183	170
6	3,483	2,322	1,742	1,393	1,161	995	871	774	697	633	581	536	498
7	1,194	796	597	478	398	341	299	265	239	217	199	184	171
8	3,903	2,602	1,952	1,561	1,301	1,115	976	867	781	710	651	600	558
9	1,532	1,021	766	613	511	438	383	340	306	279	255	236	219
10	1,300	867	650	520	433	371	325	289	260	236	217	200	186
11	1,992	1,328	996	797	664	569	498	443	398	362	332	306	285
12	2,295	1,530	1,148	918	765	656	574	510	459	417	383	353	328
13	2,370	1,580	1,185	948	790	677	593	527	474	431	395	365	339
14	3,562	2,375	1,781	1,425	1,187	1,018	891	792	712	648	594	548	509
15	1,913	1,275	957	765	638	547	478	425	383	348	319	294	273
16	2,476	1,651	1,238	990	825	707	619	550	495	450	413	381	354
17	1,790	1,193	895	716	664	511	448	398	358	325	298	275	256

Reading Time (Min:Sec)

Reading Number:	7:30	8:00	8:30	9:00	9:30	10:00	10:30	11:00	11:30	12:00	12:30	13:00	13:30
1	342	320	302	285	270	256	244	233	223	214	205	197	190
2	603	565	532	502	476	452	430	411	393	377	362	348	335
3	155	146	137	129	123	117	111	106	101	97	93	90	86
4	379	355	334	316	299	284	270	258	247	237	227	218	210
5	159	149	140	132	125	119	113	108	104	99	95	92	88
6	464	435	410	387	367	348	332	317	303	290	279	268	258
7	159	149	140	133	126	119	114	109	104	100	96	92	88
8	520	489	459	434	411	390	372	355	339	325	312	300	289
9	204	192	180	170	161	153	146	139	133	128	123	118	113
10	173	163	153	144	137	130	124	118	113	108	104	100	96
11	266	249	234	221	210	199	190	181	173	166	159	153	148
12	306	287	270	255	242	230	219	209	200	191	184	177	170
13	316	296	279	263	249	237	226	215	206	198	190	182	176
14	475	445	419	396	375	356	339	324	310	297	285	274	264
15	255	239	225	213	201	191	182	174	166	159	153	147	142
16	330	310	291	275	261	248	236	225	215	206	198	190	183
17	239	224	211	199	188	179	170	163	156	149	143	138	133

Reading Time (Min:Sec)

Reading Number:	14:00	14:30	15:00	15:30	16:00	16:30	17:00	17:30	18:00	18:30	19:00	19:30	20:00
1	183	177	171	165	160	155	151	146	142	139	135	131	128
2	323	312	301	292	283	274	266	258	251	244	238	232	226
3	83	80	78	75	73	71	68	67	65	63	61	60	58
4	203	196	189	183	178	172	167	162	158	154	149	146	142
5	85	82	79	77	74	72	70	68	66	64	63	61	60
6	249	240	232	225	218	211	205	199	194	188	183	179	174
7	85	82	80	77	75	72	70	68	66	65	63	61	60
8	279	269	260	252	244	237	230	223	217	211	205	200	195
9	109	106	102	99	96	93	90	88	85	83	81	79	77
10	93	90	87	84	81	79	76	74	72	70	68	67	65
11	142	137	133	129	125	121	117	114	111	108	105	102	100
12	164	158	153	148	143	139	135	131	128	124	121	118	115
13	169	163	158	153	148	144	139	135	132	128	125	122	119
14	254	246	237	230	223	216	210	204	198	193	187	183	178
15	137	132	128	123	120	116	113	109	106	103	101	98	96
16	177	171	165	160	155	150	146	141	138	134	130	127	124
17	128	123	119	115	112	108	105	102	99	97	94	92	90

Reading Time (Min:Sec)

Reading Number:	20:30	21:00	21:30	22:00	22:30	23:00	23:30	24:00	24:30	25:00			
1	125	122	119	117	114	111	109	107	105	103			
2	220	215	210	205	201	197	192	188	184	181			
3	57	55	54	53	52	51	50	49	48	47			
4	139	135	132	129	126	123	121	118	116	114			
5	58	57	55	54	53	52	51	50	49	48			
6	170	166	162	158	155	151	148	145	142	139			
7	58	57	56	54	53	52	51	50	49	48			
8	190	186	182	177	173	170	166	163	159	156			
9	75	73	71	70	68	67	65	64	63	61			
10	63	62	60	59	58	57	55	54	53	52			
11	97	95	93	91	89	87	85	83	81	80			
12	112	109	107	104	102	100	98	96	94	92			
13	116	113	110	108	105	103	101	99	97	95			
14	174	170	166	162	158	155	152	148	145	142			
15	93	91	89	87	85	83	81	80	78	77			
16	121	118	115	113	110	108	105	103	101	99			
17	87	85	83	81	80	78	76	75	73	72			

*An Active Reader's Glossary**

abstract *(adj)* Considered apart from concrete existence: *an abstract concept.* Conceived in general or theoretical terms.

    (n) A statement summarizing the important points of a given text.

abstracting *(n)* The process of moving from particular details to a generalization stating the unifying principle of the whole.

analogy *(n)* Similarity in some respects between things otherwise dissimilar. *Example:* "Laws are like cobwebs, which may catch small flies, but let wasps and hornets break through." (Jonathan Swift)

analysis *(n)* The breaking down of a whole into its parts for individual study.

analyze *(v)* To separate into parts so as to determine the nature of the whole; to examine methodically.

appendix *(n)* A collection of supplementary material, usually at the end of a book.

application *(n)* The act of putting something to a particular use or purpose: *an application of a new method.*

association *(n)* (1) A connection or relation between thoughts, feelings, ideas, or sensations. (2) The result of connecting or joining things together.

classification *(n)* An arrangement according to class or category. *Example:* Birds is the classification for robins, sparrows, and blue jays.

close read or study *(v)* To apply one's mind purposefully to the acquisition of knowledge or understanding.

concept *(n)* (1) A general idea or understanding, especially one derived from specific instances or occurrences. *Example:* justice. (2) A thought or notion.

conclusion *(n)* The final part of a reading selection, which pulls together the ideas presented in the introduction and the development. A conclusion may be a summary of or a commentary on the selection.

connection *(n)* (1) An association or relationship. (2) Anything that joins, relates, or connects; a link or bond. (3) The relationship of a word or idea to the surrounding text.

connotation *(n)* A suggested or implied meaning a word has in addition to its literal, or dictionary, meaning. *Example:* Some people use the word "politician" to suggest dishonesty or corruption but use the word "statesman" to refer to an honest politician.

context *(n)* The larger part of a statement that controls the meaning of a word or phrase within it, which if taken separately could be differently understood.

critical thinking *(n)* Actively using intelligence, knowledge, and reading skills to analyze and evaluate.

---

*This glossary is derived in part from definitions from *The American Heritage Dictionary,* Second College Edition, Copyright © 1982 by Houghton Mifflin Company. Used by permission from Houghton Mifflin Company.

criticize *(v)* To judge the merits and faults of something; to analyze and evaluate.

deduction *(n)* (1) The act of making a conclusion by using reasoning. (2) The act of making a conclusion from specific facts or premises.

deductive reasoning *(n)* (1) A process of reasoning in which a conclusion necessarily follows from a stated premise. *Example:* All humans are mortal. Socrates is human. Therefore Socrates is mortal. (2) A process of reasoning from a general statement or idea to a specific instance.

denotation *(n)* The explicit or dictionary meaning of a word. *Example:* A politician is someone who holds or seeks a political office.

describe *(v)* To give a verbal account; to tell about in detail.

development *(n)* The body of a reading selection, which includes the key idea, supporting ideas, and supporting details.

discourse *(n)* A formal and often lengthy discussion of a subject, either written or spoken.

discuss *(v)* To examine in speech or writing.

enumerate *(v)* To count off or name one by one; to list.

essay *(n)* A short literary composition on a single subject that usually presents the personal view of the author.

evaluate *(v)* To examine and judge carefully; to determine the value of something.

explain *(v)* To make plain or comprehensible; to offer reasons for or a cause of; to justify.

explicit *(adj)* Expressed with clarity and precision; clearly defined; specific.

exposition *(n)* Writing or speaking that explains.

fact *(n)* Something that has been objectively verified.

figurative language *(n)* An expression in which words are used not in their literal sense but pictorially to create a more forceful or dramatic image. *Example:* the eye of a storm

generalization *(n)* (1) An act or instance of generalizing. (2) A principle, statement, or idea having general application.

generalize *(v)* To infer a single meaning from many particulars; to draw an inference or a general conclusion from specific data.

glossary *(n)* A list of difficult or specialized words with their definitions, often placed at the back of a book.

hypothesis *(n)* (1) An assertion or claim subject to verification or proof; a proposition stated as a basis for argument or reasoning; a premise from which a conclusion is drawn. (2) An explanation that accounts for a set of facts and can be tested by further investigation; a theory.

illustrate *(v)* To clarify by use of examples or comparisons.

implication *(n)* Something suggested or understood, though not stated.

implicit *(adj)* Implied or understood rather than directly expressed.

imply *(v)* To say or express indirectly; to hint or suggest.

index *(n)* An alphabetized listing that gives page numbers of names, places, and subjects included in a printed work.

induction *(n)* The process of deriving general principles from particular facts or instances.

inductive reasoning *(n)* The process of using specific facts or individual cases to form a general conclusion. *Example:* Since the number of deaths from automobile accidents has decreased in the states that have seat belt laws, all states should have seat belt laws.

infer *(v)* To conclude from evidence or premises; to find a meaning not directly stated by the author.

inference *(n)* The process of drawing a conclusion from facts or premises; the process of finding an unstated meaning.

informational writing *(n)* Writing that presents data in a straightforward and objective way.

interpret *(v)* To explain the meaning of something; to offer an explanation.

introduction *(n)* The beginning of a reading selection, which usually includes the key idea of the selection and sometimes contains the subtopics. It presents a plan of the material, provides background information, or explains the importance of the key idea.

irony *(n)* The use of words to convey a meaning different from or opposite to their literal meaning. *Example:* To say "that certainly explains it" when in fact the explanation obscures rather than clarifies.

key idea *(n)* The central thought or principal idea that the author wants to communicate to the reader; the main idea of a reading selection. The answer to the question: *What is the most important thing the author is saying about the topic?*

key words *(n)* The strong words in a sentence, usually nouns and verbs, that convey most of the author's meaning.

literate *(adj)* Able to read and write; educated.

logic *(n)* The study of the principles of reasoning.

logical *(adj)* Showing consistency of reasoning.

main idea *(n)* The key idea of a reading selection.

metaphor *(n)* An implied comparison in which a word or phrase usually used for one thing is applied to another. *Example:* The ocean liner plowed the waves.

objective *(adj)* (1) Not influenced by emotion, guess, or personal prejudice. (2) Based on observable phenomena; presented factually.

opinion *(n)* A belief or conclusion held with confidence, but not substantiated by adequate knowledge or convincing proof.

organize *(v)* To put together into an orderly, functional, structured whole.

organization *(n)* The structure of a reading selection.

outline *(n)* A summary of a written work or speech, usually arranged by headings and subheadings.

pattern of organization *(n)* A specific method authors use to present their ideas to clarify the topics, subtopics, and key ideas and to show the relationship between the key ideas and the supporting ideas and supporting details. Patterns of organization include *list, order, compare/contrast,* and *cause and effect.*

paragraph *(n)* A distinct division of a written work or composition that expresses a thought or point relevant to the whole but is complete in itself. It may consist of a single sentence but usually has several.

perceive *(v)* To become aware of directly through any of the senses; to take notice of; to observe.

perspective *(n)* Point of view.

persuasive writing *(n)* Information presented to convince the reader to do or believe something.

phrase *(n)* A group of words—usually part of a sentence—read or spoken as a unit.

predict *(v)* To state or make an educated guess about the contents of a reading selection in advance, especially to do so by reading actively (previewing, and so forth).

preface *(n)* A statement or essay, usually by the author, that introduces a book and explains its scope, intention, or background.

prefix *(n)* A letter or group of letters attached to the beginning of a word to change or modify its meaning, such as "dis-" in disbelief, or "pre-" in preheat.

premise *(n)* A proposition upon which an argument is based or from which a conclusion is drawn.

preview *(v)* To survey a reading selection in advance by asking *What is this about? What is the author's most important idea about it? Why am I reading this? What do I already know about it? Why did the author write it?*

principal *(adj)* First or highest in importance, rank, or worth.

principle *(n)* A basic truth, law, or assumption: *the principles of democracy.*

prove *(v)* To establish the truth or validity of something by presenting evidence.

read *(v)* To examine and grasp the meaning of written or printed characters, words, or sentences.

reading rate *(n)* The speed at which one reads, measured in words per minute.

reason *(n)* The basis or motive for an action, decision, or conviction. The capacity for rational thought, inference, or discrimination.

reasoning *(n)* The use of reason, especially to reach conclusions, inferences, or judgments.

refer *(v)* To direct to a source for help or additional information.

reference *(n)* A note in a publication referring the reader to another passage or source.

relation *(n)* A logical or natural association between two or more things.

sectioning *(n)* A strategy of dividing reading selections into component parts to see how authors develop and support their ideas. A section is a unit of one or several paragraphs that can be grouped under one title because they have the same subtopic.

sentence *(n)* A grammatical unit usually containing a subject and a verb that states, asks, commands, or otherwise expresses a thought.

sequence *(n)* The following of one thing after another; a related or continuous series.

signal words *(n)* Words that authors use to connect ideas and to help readers follow the direction of the authors' thoughts. *Examples:* also, besides, although, but, finally

simile *(n)* A figure of speech in which two essentially unlike things are compared, usually in a phrase introduced by "like" or "as." *Example:* "He was as strong as a bull."

skim *(v)* To read or glance through quickly or superficially.

subjective *(adj)* Particular to a given individual; personal.

suffix *(n)* A letter or group of letters attached to the end of a word to form a new word, such as "-ness" in gentleness, or "-ing" in walking.

summarize *(v)* To make a summary of; to restate briefly.

summary *(n)* A condensation of a larger work; an abstract or abridgment.

supporting detail *(n)* Illustrations, examples, verifying statistics, reasons, or descriptions that back up the supporting ideas by answering the questions *how? who? why? where? when? what? which?* and *what kind?*

supporting idea *(n)* The key idea of a section of a reading. The supporting idea elaborates on and develops the key idea of the entire passage and answers the questions *how? who? what? where? when? which? what kind?* and *why?*

synopsis *(n)* A brief statement or outline of a subject; an abstract.

synthesis *(n)* (1) The unification of separate elements into a coherent whole. (2) The whole formed by such a process.

synthesize *(v)* (1) To combine separate elements to form a new, complex whole. (2) To produce by combining separate elements.

terminology *(n)* The vocabulary of technical terms and usages appropriate to a particular field or subject.

thesis *(n)* A proposition that is supported by argument or other evidence.

topic *(n)* A subject treated in a speech, essay, thesis, or portion of discourse.

verify *(v)* (1) An attempt to prove the truth of something by presenting evidence or testimony: *Two neighbors verified his story.* (2) To determine or test the truth or accuracy of something.

Acknowledgments

Sheldon R. Baker and David Boaz   Selection from "The Partial Reformulation of a Traumatic Memory of a Dental Phobia during Trance: A Case Study" from *International Journal of Clinical and Experimental Hypnosis*, 1983, Vol. XXXL, No. 1, reprinted by permission of Sheldon R. Baker.

Carol Ruth Berkin and Mary Beth Norton   Selection from *Women of America: A History* copyright © 1979 by Houghton Mifflin Company. Reprinted by permission of the publisher.

Anthony Bower   "Citizen Kane" from *The Nation*, April 26, 1941, reprinted by permission of The Nation/Nation Institute.

Bronfenbrenner, et al.   From Martin Bronfenbrenner, Werner Sichel, and Wayland Gardner, *Economics*, copyright © 1984 by Houghton Mifflin Company. Reprinted by permission of the publisher.

Gloria Blum Byron   Excerpt from "The Go-Between" from *Health*, January, 1985, reprinted by permission of Family Media.

T. Stephen Cheston   Reprinted from *The Phenomenon of Change* © 1984, Cooper-Hewitt Museum, The Smithsonian Institution's National Museum of Design.

Dale Cohen   Excerpts from "Can a Rat Count to Four?" reprinted by permission of the author.

Irving M. Copi   Reprinted with permission of Macmillan Publishing Company from *Introduction to Logic*, 6th ed., by Irving M. Copi. Copyright © 1982 by Irving M. Copi.

D. Dempsey and P. G. Zimbardo   From *Psychology and You* by D. Dempsey and P. G. Zimbardo. Copyright © 1978 by Scott, Foresman and Company. Reprinted by permission.

LaRay Denzer and Michael Crowder   Reprinted by permission of Oxford University Press from Robert I. Rotberg and Ali A. Mazrui, *Protest and Power in Black Africa*, 1970.

Karl W. Deutsch, et al.   From Karl W. Deutsch, Jorge I. Dominguez, and Hugh Heclo, *Comparative Government: Politics of Industrialized and Developing Nations*, copyright © 1981 by Houghton Mifflin Company. Reprinted by permission of the publisher.

Frederick J. Duncan, Jr., M.D. and Barbara A. Rockett, M.D.   "Malpractice Costs Hurt All" reprinted by permission of the authors.

Loren Eisley   Excerpted from "The Creature from the Marsh" from *The Night Country*. Copyright © 1971 Loren Eiseley. Reprinted with the permission of Charles Scribner's Sons.

Claire Fagin and Donna Diers   Reprinted by permission of *The New England Journal of Medicine*. Vol. 309, pp. 116–117, 1983.

Roger Fisher   Reprinted with permission of the *ABA Journal*, The Lawyer's Magazine.

Garis, et al.   Jeff W. Garis, H. Richard Hess, and Deborah J. Marron, "For Liberal Arts Students Seeking Business Careers, Curriculum Counts." *Journal of College Placement*, Winter 1985. Reprinted by permission of the College Placement Council, Inc.

Dharam P. Ghai   Excerpt from "The Bugandan Trade Boycott" from Robert I. Rotberg and Ali A. Mazrui, *Protest and Power in Black Africa*, 1970, reprinted by permission of Oxford University Press.

Richard D. Heffner   From *A Documentary History of the United States* by Richard D. Heffner. Copyright © 1952, 1965, 1976, 1985 by Richard D. Heffner. Reprinted by arrangement with New American Library, New York, New York.

Houghton Mifflin   Excerpt from *A Guide for Authors* reprinted by permission of Houghton Mifflin. Copyright © 1974 by Houghton Mifflin Company.

Darlene V. Howard   Reprinted with permission of Macmillan Publishing Company from *Cognitive Psychology: Memory, Language and Thought* by Darlene V. Howard. Copyright © 1983 by Darlene V. Howard.

David Hume   Reprinted with permission of Macmillan Publishing Company from David Hume, *An Inquiry Concerning the Principles of Morals with a Supplement: A Dialogue* edited by Charles W. Hendel. Copyright © 1957 by Macmillan Publishing Company.

Morton Hunt   Copyright © 1982 by Morton Hunt. Reprinted by permission of Simon & Schuster, Inc.

Mark Irvings   "Excerpt from Arbitration Decision" and "Dispute Resolution" reprinted by permission of the author.

H. W. Janson   Reprinted from *History of Art*, 2nd Ed., 1977, by H. W. Janson. Published by Harry N. Abrams, Inc., New York. All rights reserved.

Rosabeth Moss Kanter   Copyright © 1983 by Rosabeth Moss Kanter. Reprinted by permission of Simon & Schuster, Inc.

Ernest Keen   "Emerging from Depression," *American Behavioral Scientist*, Vol. 27, No. 6 (July/August 1984), pp. 803–812. Copyright © 1984 by Sage Publications, Inc. Reprinted by permission of Sage Publications, Inc.

Jemshed A. Khan   Reprinted by permission of *The New England Journal of Medicine*. Vol. 311, pp. 414–416, 1984. Copyright 1984 Massachusetts Medical Society.

Florence Ladd   Reprinted by permission of the author.

Susanne K. Langer   "The Lord of Creation" reprinted from *Fortune*, January 1944. © 1944 Time Inc. All rights reserved. Excerpt reprinted by permission of the publishers from *Philosophy in a New Key: A Study of the Symbolism of Reason, Rite, and Art*, 3rd ed., by Susanne K. Langer, Cambridge, Mass: Harvard University Press, Copyright 1942, 1951, 1957 by the President and Fellows of Harvard College; renewed 1970 by Susanne K. Langer; 1985 by Leonard C. R. Langer.

Oscar Lewis   Excerpt from *Life in a Mexican Village: Tepoztlán Restudied* by Oscar Lewis. Copyright 1951 by the Board of Trustees of the University of Illinois. Reprinted by permission of the publisher and the author.

Z. J. Lipowski   "Benjamin Franklin as a Psychotherapist: A Forerunner of Brief Psychotherapy," by Z. J. Lipowski from *Perspectives in Biology and Medicine*, 27, no. 3, Spring 1984, pp. 361–366. © 1984 by The University of Chicago. All rights reserved. Reprinted by permission of the author and the University of Chicago Press.

Roy C. Macridis   Roy C. Macridis "Politics of France" in *Modern Political Systems: Europe*, Macridis ed., © 1978, pp. 99, 105. Adapted by permission of Prentice-Hall, Englewood Cliffs, New Jersey.

Everett Dean Martin   Reprinted from THE MEANING OF A LIBERAL EDUCATION by Everett Dean Martin by permission of W. W. Norton & Company, Inc. Copyright © 1926 by W. W. Norton & Company, Inc. Copyright renewed 1954 by Daphne Mason.

Thomas S. Mautner   Abridged version of "Dyslexia—My Invisible Handicap" reprinted from the *Annals of Dyslexia*, Vol. 34, 1984, by permission of the Orton Dyslexia Society.

Francisco M. Nicosia　Excerpts from the Preface to *Advertising, Management, and Society: A Business Point of View* 1974 by Francisco M. Nicosia reprinted by permission of McGraw-Hill Book Company.

Judith Oringer　Excerpt from *Passion for the Piano* by Judith Oringer. Copyright © 1983 by Judith Oringer. Reprinted by permission of Jeremy P. Tarcher, Inc.

James H. Otto and A. Towle　Extract from *Modern Biology*, Otto and Towle, page 554. Copyright © 1973 by Holt, Rinehart and Winston, Publishers. Reproduced by permission. All rights reserved.

Peter H. Raven　Reprinted by permission of the *Bulletin of the Atomic Scientists*, a magazine of science and world affairs. Copyright © 1984 by the Educational Foundation for Nuclear Science, Chicago, IL 60637.

Richard M. Restak　"The Philosopher's Myth" from *The Brain: The Last Frontier* by Richard M. Restak, M.D. Copyright © 1979 by Richard M. Restak. Reprinted by permission of Doubleday & Company, Inc.

John Storm Roberts　From *Black Music of Two Worlds* by John Storm Roberts. Copyright © 1972 by Praeger Publishers, Inc. Reprinted by permission of CBS College Publishing.

Marvin Rosen　Selection from *Introduction to Photography*, 1982, copyright © 1982 by Houghton Mifflin Company. Reprinted by permission of the publisher.

David J. Sargent　"Blame Negligent Doctors, not Insurance" reprinted by permission of the author.

Gilbert Seldes　Reprinted with permission from *Esquire* (August 1941). Copyright © 1941, 1969 by Esquire Associates.

Alan Sherman et al.　From Alan Sherman, Sharon Sherman, and Leonard Russikoff, *Basic Concepts of Chemistry*, copyright © 1984 by Houghton Mifflin Company. Reprinted by permission of the publisher.

Liu Heung Shing　From *China After Mao: 'Seek Truth From Facts'* by Liu Heung Shing (Penguin Books, 1983), p. 114, copyright © Liu Heung Shing, 1983. Reproduced by permission of Penguin Books Ltd.

Ralph D. Shipp, Jr.　From Ralph D. Shipp, Jr., *Retail Merchandising: Principles and Applications*, copyright © 1985 by Houghton Mifflin Company. Reprinted by permission of the publisher.

Sam Singer and Henry R. Hilgard　From *The Biology of People* by Sam Singer and Henry R. Hilgard. W. H. Freeman and Company. Copyright © 1978. Reprinted by permission of the publisher.

Sol Steinmetz　"DeSexing the English Language" by Sol Steinmetz, *The New York Times Magazine*, August 1, 1982. Copyright © 1982 by The New York Times Company. Reprinted by permission.

Dawn Stover　"Reinventing the Wheel" by Dawn Stover. First appeared in *Science Digest*, Vol. 93, No. 6 (June 1985). © 1985 by The Hearst Corporation.

Margaret Thompson　"Once Upon a Time There Was a Volcano in Boston . . . and This Is How They Know" by Margaret Thompson. *Wellesley* alumnae magazine, Spring 1984. Reprinted by permission of the Wellesley College Alumnae Association and the author.

Sheila Tobias　Reprinted from OVERCOMING MATH ANXIETY by Sheila Tobias, by permission of W. W. Norton & Company, Inc. Copyright © 1978 by Sheila Tobias.

Barbara W. Tuchman　From *A Distant Mirror: The Calamitous 14th Century*, by Barbara W. Tuchman. Copyright © 1978 by Barbara W. Tuchman. Reprinted by permission of Alfred A. Knopf, Inc.

Sherry Turkle   From *The Second Self* by Sherry Turkle. Copyright © 1984 by Sherry Turkle. Reprinted by permission of Simon & Schuster, Inc.

Tino Villanueva   Excerpted from the "Introduction" to *Imagine: International Chicano Poetry Journal*, Vol. I, No. 1 (Summer 1984) by Tino Villanueva. Copyright © 1984 by Tina Villanueva. Reprinted by permission.

Michele Wallace   Excerpt from *Black Macho and the Myth of the Superwoman* by Michele Wallace. Copyright © 1978, 1979 by Michele Wallace. Reprinted by permission of Doubleday & Company, Inc., and John Calder.

David Wallechinsky and Irving Wallace   Excerpts from *The People's Almanac* by David Wallechinsky and Irving Wallace. Copyright © 1975 by David Wallace and Irving Wallace. Reprinted by permission of Doubleday & Company, Inc.

Washington Post   Excerpts from *The Editorial Page* © 1977, Washington Post Writers Group, reprinted with permission.

Lois Wasserspring   Syllabus for Political Science 101, courtesy of Lois Wasserspring and the Political Science Department, Wellesley College.

Joseph Weisberg   From Joseph S. Weisberg, *Meteorology*, copyright © 1981 by Houghton Mifflin Company. Reprinted by permission of the publisher.

Paul R. Wendt   "The Language of Pictures" by Paul R. Wendt, from *The Use and Misuse of Language* by S. I. Hayakawa (New York: Fawcett, 1970). Reprinted by permission of S. I. Hayakawa.

Heinrich Zimmer   From Heinrich Zimmer, *The King and the Corpse*, ed. Joseph Campbell, Bollingen Series XI. Copyright 1948, © 1957, 1975 renewed by Princeton University Press.

Index

To the Student:

We hope that you will take a few minutes to fill out this question-naire. The comments you make will help us plan future editions of *Active Reading*. After you have completed the following questions, please mail this sheet to:

College Marketing
Houghton Mifflin Company
One Beacon Street
Boston, MA 02108

1. Name of college or university _____

2. How would you rate *Active Reading*?

   ☐ excellent   ☐ good   ☐ average   ☐ poor

3. Which chapters did you find especially helpful? Why? _____

   _____

   _____

4. Which chapters did you find least helpful? Why? _____

   _____

   _____

5. Did you find most of the reading selections interesting? _____

   Which did you enjoy most? _____

   _____

   Which did you enjoy least? _____

   _____

6. Can you suggest other topics you would be interested in reading

   about? _____

   _____

7. Did you find the exercises useful? _____

   _____

8. Were the rate and comprehension charts useful? _____

   _____

9. Did you find that your reading improved after using this text?

   _____

   _____

10. What did you learn from this book that was most helpful to you

    in your other courses? _____

    _____

    _____

    _____

11. Please make any additional comments that you think might be

    useful. _____

    _____

    _____

    _____

Reading Notes

Reading Notes

Reading Notes

Reading Notes

Reading Notes